T0345163

The Usage and Impact of ICTs during the COVID-19 Pandemic

This book takes a holistic view of the role of information and communication technologies (ICTs) during the pandemic through the lens of social informatics, as it is critical to our understanding of the relations between society and technology. Specific attention is given to various stakeholders and social contexts, with analysis at the individual, group, community, and society levels.

Pushing the boundaries of information science research with timely and critical research questions, this edited volume showcases information science research in the context of COVID-19, by specifically accentuating sociotechnical practices, activities, and ICT interventions during the pandemic. Its social informatics focus appeals to a broad audience, and its global and international orientation provides a timely, innovative, and much-needed perspective to information science. This book is unique in its interdisciplinary nature as it consists of research studies on the intersections between ICTs and health, culture, social interaction, civic engagement, information dissemination, work, and education. Chapters apply a range of research methods, including questionnaire surveys, content analyses, and case studies from countries in Asia, Europe, and America, as well as global and international comparisons.

The book's primary target audience includes scholars and students in information and library science, particularly those interested in the social aspect of the information society. It may be of interest to information professionals, library practitioners, educators, and information policymakers, as well as scholars and students in science and technology studies, cultural studies, political science, public administration, sociology, and communication studies.

Shengnan Yang is a PhD candidate in the Luddy School of Informatics, Computing, and Engineering at Indiana University in Bloomington. Her main areas of research focus on social informatics, information policy, and digital inequality.

Xiaohua (Awa) Zhu is an Associate Professor at the School of Information Sciences at the University of Tennessee, Knoxville. Her research focuses on digital rights, information policy, social informatics, and academic libraries.

Pnina Fichman is a Professor of Information Science at the Luddy School of Informatics Computing and Engineering, and the Director of the Rob Kling Center for Social Informatics at Indiana University, Bloomington. She has published five co-authored/edited books and over a hundred peer-reviewed journal articles, conference papers, and book chapters about social informatics, trolling, information mediation, and communities of practice.

Routledge Studies in Library and Information Science

The following list includes only the most-recent titles to publish within the series.

A list of the full catalogue of titles is available at: https://www.routledge.com/Routledge-Studies-in-Library-and-Information-Science/book-series/RSLIS

The Usage and Impact of ICTs during the COVID-19 Pandemic

Edited by Shengnan Yang, Xiaohua Zhu, and Pnina Fichman

Routledge
Taylor & Francis Group

LONDON AND NEW YORK

First published 2023
by Routledge
4 Park Square, Milton Park, Abingdon, Oxon OX14 4RN

and by Routledge
605 Third Avenue, New York, NY 10158

Routledge is an imprint of the Taylor & Francis Group, an informa business

British Library Cataloguing-in-Publication Data
A catalogue record for this book is available from the British Library

ISBN: 978-1-032-13974-6 (hbk)
ISBN: 978-1-032-13975-3 (pbk)
ISBN: 978-1-003-23176-9 (ebk)

DOI: 10.4324/9781003231769

Typeset in Times New Roman
by MPS Limited, Dehradun

An electronic version of this book is freely available, thanks to the support of libraries working with Knowledge Unlatched (KU). KU is a collaborative initiative designed to make high quality books Open Access for the public good. The Open Access ISBN for this book is 9781003231769. More information about the initiative and links to the Open Access version can be found at www.knowledgeunlatched.org.

Contents

Figures

Tables

Contributors

Katriina Byström is a Professor in Library and Information Science at the Oslo Metropolitan University, Norway. Her research focuses on information flows in the workplace, with particular attention paid to relationships between work tasks and information activities. Her interests in workplace information range from the impact of task complexity on information activities to the effects of digitalization on information practices at work. Some years ago, she framed her research on information activities in a wordplay between officeless people and peopleless offices; the former referring to remote workers and the latter to a futuristic organizational change that was unexpectedly realized on a broad front in 2020.

Xiaolong Chen is a Postgraduate Student at the Department of Information Management, Peking University. His primary research area is information behaviors.

Meredith Dedema is a PhD student from Department of Information and Library Science, Luddy School of Informatics, Computing, and Engineering, Indiana University Bloomington. She received her Bachelor in Information Management and Information System from Peking University, China. She is a student fellow of the Rob Kling Center for Social Informatics and the Center of Computer Mediated Communication. Her research interests include Human-Computer Interaction, Computer-Supported Collaborative Work, and Social Informatics. She is currently working on multiple research projects and completing her coursework at IU.

Aaron J. Elkins is an Associate Professor at Texas Woman's University in Denton, Texas. A former National Board Certified school librarian, he received his PhD in Library and Information Studies at Florida State University. Dr. Elkins' current research streams are focused on unpacking social information culture and improving diversity, equity, inclusion, and justice in the LIS field and academy and enhancing 21st-century literacies through gaming.

Pnina Fichman is a Professor of Information Science at the Luddy School of Informatics Computing and Engineering, and the Director of the Rob Kling Center for Social Informatics at Indiana University, Bloomington. She is the director of the Doctoral Program in Information Science and the Doctoral Minor in Social Informatics. Her Ph.D. is from the University of North Carolina, Chapel Hill. She has published five co-authored/edited books and over a hundred peer-reviewed journal articles, conference papers, and book chapters about social informatics, trolling, information mediation, and communities of practice.

Noriko Hara is a Professor and Department Chair in the Department of Information & Library Science in the Luddy School of Informatics, Computing, and Engineering at Indiana University. Her research in Social Informatics focuses on public engagement with science, knowledge sharing, communities of practice, and collective behaviors in mediated environments. She is currently investigating social media use for two-way communication between scientists and the public. Her research has been funded by several grants including the National Science Foundation. She received a Ph.D. in Instructional Systems Technology at Indiana University and was a postdoctoral research fellow in the NSF Science and Technology Center at University of North Carolina, Chapel Hill.

Xinmei Hu is an Undergraduate Student at the Department of Information Management, Peking University. She is interested in information-behavior-related research.

Shijuan Li is an Associate Professor at the Department of Information Management, Peking University. She holds a Ph.D. in Health Informatics from the University of Salford, UK. Her research areas are in health informatics, digital reading promotion, and library information services. She is particularly interested in how innovative ICTs influence people's activity and behavior, and assist them in making informed decisions. Hui Lin and Xinmei Hu are undergraduate students in the Department of Information Management, Peking University.

Hui Lin is an Undergraduate Student at the Department of Information Management, Peking University. She is interested in research on information behavior.

Chang Liu is a Doctoral Candidate in Informatics at the University of Illinois at Urbana-Champaign. He uses interdisciplinary approaches to study sociotechnical issues concerning labor and the digital economy, with a focus on social justice. He defended his dissertation in June 2022, which explores the gap between technological imagination and the reality of production work, sociotechnical systems that enroll marginalized laborers to fuel economic growth, and consequences for the local community and economy, based on an ethnography of Chinese furniture manufacturing and technology-driven economic reform. He holds a B.Eng. in Architecture and an M.Eng. in Systems Innovation from the University of Tokyo.

Howard Rosenbaum is a Professor of Information Science in the Department of Information and Library Science in the Luddy School of Informatics and Computing at Indiana University. He is Director of Graduate Programs, Director of the Masters of Information Science program, and Co-director of the Graduate Certificate in Information Architecture program. He has been at Indiana University since 1993 and is currently interested in social informatics and critical data studies. He has published in a variety of information science journals and has presented at ASIS&T, iConferences, and elsewhere. He has been involved in social informatics since 1997 and works with collaborators to raise the profile of SI in information science.

Madelyn Rose Sanfilippo is an Assistant Professor in the School of Information Sciences at the University of Illinois at Urbana-Champaign (UIUC). Her research empirically explores governance of sociotechnical systems, as well as outcomes, inequality, and consequences within these systems. Using mixed-methods, including computational social science approaches and institutional analysis, she addresses research questions about: participation in and legitimacy of sociotechnical governance; social justice issues associated with sociotechnical governance; privacy in sociotechnical systems; and differences between policies or regulations and sociotechnical practice. Her work practically supports decision-making in, management of, and participation in a diverse public sphere. She is the Principal Investigator in the Governance Lab on Sociotechnical Systems (GLOSS) and a Faculty Affiliate at the Center for Global Studies and the Informatics Institute at UIUC, as well as co-director of the interuniversity Workshop on Governing Knowledge Commons.

Rachel (Rea) N. Simons is an Assistant Professor at Old Dominion University in Norfolk, Virginia, United States. Their work is driven by asking how the field of Library and Information Studies (LIS) can better support communities—including communities of both learning and practice—in designing and/or using information and communication technologies (ICTs) to foster equitable and inclusive spaces. Their research agenda combines the frameworks of social and community informatics with critical race and gender theory to investigate equity and inclusion within the design and use of ICTs. While much of their work has focused on using research to inform the education of information professionals, they have recently turned their attention to examining and sharing best practices for addressing diversity, equity, inclusion, and justice (DEIJ) across LIS curricula.

Honglei Lia Sun is currently an Assistant Researcher of the School of Information Management, Nanjing University, China. She graduated with her PhD in library and information science from Nanjing University. Her research interests have focused on social informatics, library science, and public cultural service.

Shengnan Yang is a PhD candidate in the Luddy School of Informatics, Computing, and Engineering at Indiana University in Bloomington. Her main areas of research focus on social informatics, information policy, and digital inequality. Focusing on the role of technology in the nonprofit sector, her dissertation studies the effects of digital tools on the social world by examining nonprofit organizations. She employs a mixed-methods approach to conduct research, including qualitative interviews, quantitative surveys, and big data analysis. Before pursuing an academic career, she worked as an IT consultant in Accenture Greater China.

Xiaohua (Awa) Zhu is an Associate Professor at the School of Information Sciences at the University of Tennessee, Knoxville. She received her Ph.D. in Library and Information Studies from the University of Wisconsin-Madison. Her primary research areas include information policy, social informatics, and academic libraries. Her work focuses on three themes at the intersection of those areas: Rights related to digital intellectual properties, especially access rights and ownership rights; government information use and access, especially open government data; digital transformation and their impact on libraries, especially academic libraries. Her work combines qualitative and quantitative methods, and often draws on social theories and historical perspectives.

Acknowledgments

We'd like to express our thanks to Dr. Kitty McClanahan for editing and proofreading the entire manuscript, and to Dr. John Pavlik for his help in the reviewing process.

Introduction: Social Informatics in the Context of the COVID-19 Pandemic

Shengnan Yang, Xiaohua Zhu, and Pnina Fichman

The Pandemic and ICTs

At the very beginning of the outbreak of coronavirus disease in China in early 2020, while rumors disseminated on social media platforms turned out to be the truth, a set of digital solutions were initiated in China to cope with the strict lockdown policy. The use of information and communication technologies (ICTs) piqued our scholarly curiosity, in the context of this epidemic. From casual chats to formulating research ideas, we started to work on a panel proposal for the 2020 Annual Meeting of the Association for Information Science and Technology (ASIS&T), entitled "The Use of ICT during COVID-19". This conference panel captured the attention of a publisher, which led to the publication of this book. Soon after our initial discussion, the epidemic developed into the COVID-19 pandemic, spreading throughout the world. The pandemic triggered countless innovative designs and inspired new ways of ICT use across different environments worldwide. Thus, ICTs' role has extended beyond identifying, tracing, understanding, managing, treating, and perceiving pandemics, by enabling people's interconnectedness across diverse cultures, traditions, histories, and political systems (Wilson & Jumbert, 2018).

The pandemic was a "great accelerator" of digital transformation (Armano, 2020), in which all sectors of society and communities across the globe significantly increased their reliance on ICT for various reasons (Hakmeh et al., 2021; Meiller, 2020; Tosheva, 2020). Since the beginning of the COVID-19 outbreak in early 2020, many people, businesses, organizations, and governments have experienced unprecedented ICT adoption and use, willingly or not. Social media platforms, mobile-based applications, and artificial intelligence have enabled faster responses and continuous connectivity, by supporting information dissemination, large-scale user participation, and mass collaborations across national boundaries. This reliance on ICTs, paired with other societal changes such as quarantine, isolation, and political tensions, stimulated unparalleled individual and social deliberation about ICT-related issues. Although scholars explained ICTs' profound roles and consequences in the information society (Castells, 2000;

DOI: 10.4324/9781003231769-1

Webster, 2014), the pandemic stirred discussion everywhere. Arguably, never before have ICTs been a topic of such frequent mention by the media—on radio, TV, and magazines—and in daily conversations, leading to intense scrutiny of ICT use by both academics and the public. The current public discourse reveals a sophisticated understanding of the intended and unexpected consequences of ICTs—control versus resistance, gratitude versus criticism, development versus inequality, and the public interest versus individual rights and privacy—making the research in our book particularly timely and relevant.

The backdrop of the COVID-19 pandemic provides a unique opportunity for us to reflect on and reexamine our relationships with ICTs, as we envision the postpandemic era. It is imperative that we investigate the complexities and consequences of ICT use, implementation, and regulation during this crisis, to shed light on practices that maximize the benefits and minimize the harm to society. The fact that ICTs were interjected into the daily lives of so many individuals is another reason why the pandemic constitutes an ideal setting for deepening our understanding of ICTs. In the past few decades, researchers in informatics, science and technology studies, and communication studies have refuted technological determinism, and instead largely adopted the approach of co-construction and mutual shaping of technology and society (Gillespie et al., 2014; Lievrouw, 2014; Meyer, 2014). However, when technology use is pressed upon people and society rather than merely offered as an option—such as using ICTs during lockdowns for work and education—deterministic approaches to understanding technology dominate much of the discourse. Claims like "[t]he rapid rise of digital technologies is transforming economic and social activities around the world" (UNGIS, 2021) are common. Moreover, as Boczkowski and Lievrouw (2008) suggested, it was not sufficient merely to acknowledge the complexity of the sociotechnical system, and the "tension between determination and contingency" (p. 996); ICT research should tackle the specific contexts and conditions that may alter the subtle balance between determination or contingency. The pandemic context offers us a valuable opportunity to examine these tensions, and the specific sociotechnical configurations of ICTs, using case studies and comparative analyses.

Social Informatics

Readers who are new to social informatics may benefit from making an acquaintance with this field. We see social informatics as the study of the interdependencies among people, digital technologies, and their contexts of use (Sawyer & Jarrahi, 2014). Building upon the widely used concept of sociotechnical systems, ranging from the early iconic works of Rob Kling (Kling & Jewett, 1994; Kling et al., 2005) to more recent anthologies and monographs such as *Social Informatics: Past, Present and Future* (Fichman & Rosenbaum, 2014), *Social Informatics Evolving* (Fichman et al., 2015), and the recent special *JASIST* issue "The Social Informatics of Knowledge" (Meyer et al., 2019), social informatics scholars have stressed the importance of the context—historical, cultural, geographical, and beyond—in studying ICTs. Through this lens, scholars can understand a wide variety of topics linked by the recognition of the integration of ICTs into organizations and people's social lives (Fichman & Rosenbaum, 2014). Informed by this line of work, we see the COVID-19 pandemic as a valuable context for social informatics research because of the scale of ICT adoption and use, the increase in public awareness, and the noticeable impact of ICT on society. Each of the chapters in this book report on research that was primarily conducted during the first two years of the pandemic, in 2020–2021, a period of time that serves as a significant historical moment to capture and reflect upon.

The concept of "social informatics" in this book is used in two ways. First, it serves as an underlying theoretical perceptive across all the chapters. It is used to evaluate, examine, and analyze the interaction among human agencies (individuals, groups, and institutional actors), technologies (social media, online communities, and algorithms), technology-related activities (policymaking, information behavior, collaboration, and communication), and related contexts (types of regimes, public health crisis, culture, working environments, and so on). All chapters either explicitly or implicitly examine the mutually shaping process between human agencies and nonhuman ones, unpack the unintended consequences of the process, and emphasize the importance of context. For instance, Fichman and Dedema (Chapter 3) examine the relationships between technology and society by illustrating how the dystopian context of COVID-19 quarantine and the utopian imagination of ICTs converged to create a complex and even paradoxical contextual setting for ICT use by boundary maintenance and boundary-crossing processes. Sun and Fichman's study of online depression self-help communities (Chapter 6) discusses contextual factors related to topic shift, in addition to socio-psychological aspects. Hara and Dedema (Chapter 7) unbox the use of Twitter by scientists and medical professionals, pseudo-experts, and government health organizations, using a lens of social informatics by considering online public engagement with science as a sociotechnical system.

Second, social informatics serves as a theoretical foundation for developing new theories in context because of its flexibility. For example, Simons and Elkins (Chapter 4) extend the term "information culture" from the traditional organizational model to a sociotechnical context related to misinformation spreading. They leverage the frameworks of social informatics, cultural competency, and psychosocial understandings of information behavior, to propose a "social information cultural competency" framework for designing contextualized information literacy efforts. Zhu and Yang (Chapter 1) incorporate social informatics into policy design studies and propose a comprehensive framework for analyzing misinformation-related policies across different regimes. Rosenbaum (Chapter 9) provides a sketch of a conceptual framework using the concepts from phenomenology, postphenomenology, and critical data studies to explain how algorithmic assemblages shape the lifeworld and the natural attitude. Building upon the social informatics conceptualization of assemblage, Sanfilippo and Liu (Chapter 2) propose an applied conceptualization of governance assemblages to address how design and management, infrastructure and use, and practice and regulation intersect to impact privacy as experienced in three arenas: education, healthcare, and labor.

This book is unique also because it provides an international and comparative perspective on the use of ICTs during the COVID-19 pandemic, enhancing our understanding of ICT's role across international environments during the various stages of the pandemic. Chapters in the book demonstrate that, even though people have been confronting the same health crisis around the globe, the intentions and consequences of ICT use vary by region, nation, and community. A set of comparative and international studies, such as Zhu and Yang's work in Chapter 1 and Fichman and Dedema's work in Chapter 3, are included. In the end, the geographical coverage of this book includes empirical evidence from different regions and cultures—Europe (Chapters 3 and 8), North America (Chapters 1 and 3), and Asia (Chapters 1, 5, and 6).

Organization of the Book

This book is organized into four sections: 1) governance, 2) information behavior, 3) community, and 4) everyday life. These sections echo major concerns around ICT use and consequences during the pandemic.

The **Governance** section in our book covers the interventions and regulatory strategies implemented by governmental agencies, digital platforms, and related stakeholders. This health crisis nested in the infosphere has triggered a consequential information crisis (Xie et al., 2020), especially when we confront the challenges of misinformation, attitude polarization, and the dilemma between protecting privacy and ensuring public safety. Effective interventions and governance are required but often lag. The first two chapters in this book focus on the formal regulation and governance related to information and digital platforms. Zhu and Yang (Chapter 1) propose a comprehensive framework combining basic components of policy design studies and sociotechnical dimensions to understand information policies for misinformation regulation. Their framework emphasizes the sociotechnical nature of misinformation and its regulatory practices. The empirical findings of their study also demonstrate how governments vary in their regulatory reactions to misinformation, and the uniqueness of local contexts related to information policies. Sanfilippo and Liu (Chapter 2) focus on privacy issues on digital platforms when the context of ICT use was blurred during the pandemic. Built upon the analysis of the privacy governance of ICTs, using a three-layer institutional hierarchy, they further develop creative and holistic governance assemblages for responding to emergency circumstances.

The second section of the book, **Community**, presents two chapters focusing on online user interactions for social support on social media platforms. Social media are the channels mediating individuals' communication, but they also forge the emergence and evolution of online communities, as Chapters 3 and 4 demonstrate. Both studies draw on the concept of communities of practice. Simons and Elkins (Chapter 4) focus on specific sociotechnical communities mediated by social media and examine how they are related to the dissemination of COVID-19 misinformation. This study pushes our understanding of misinformation-sharing behavior beyond psychological factors at the individual level. Instead, they emphasize that people's connections to others form a unique "social information culture" that influences their misinformation-sharing behavior. Fichman and Dedema (Chapter 3) examine the relationships between technology and society by illustrating how the dystopian context of the COVID-19 quarantine and the utopian imagination of ICTs converged to create a complex and even paradoxical contextual setting for ICT use through communities of practice's boundary maintenance and boundary-crossing processes.

Chapters in the third section, **Information Behavior**, analyze people's information behaviors to fulfill their needs in coping with this global crisis. The pandemic triggers diverse information needs, particularly about health-related issues. Li and her colleagues (Chapter 5) trace the middle-aged user group and their information-seeking behaviors in multiple regions in China. They explore the interaction between information behavior and emotional change, and its influencing factors in the Public Health Emergency of International Concern (PHEIC). Dedema, Hara, and Knox (Chapter 7) focus on online public health communication, examining what and how scientists, medical professionals, and public health organizations communicated with the public on social media during and about the COVID-19 pandemic in the United States. Sun and Fichman (Chapter 6) showcase an online communicative pattern by investigating the discussion topics and analyzing the language features in online depression communities before, during, and after the COVID-19 lockdown in China, using data from two online depression self-help groups on Chinese social media.

The fourth section zooms in on individuals' **Everyday Life**. The last two chapters in this book take a critical perspective, either explicitly or implicitly, to highlight ICT use in everyday life or work routines. Incorporating technical, material, and social aspects of algorithm systems, Rosenbaum (Chapter 9) introduces *algorithmic assemblages* that are embedded in our everyday routines and practice. The pandemic provides important examples, demonstrating how algorithmic assemblages are shaping the lifeworld and the natural attitude. This chapter sheds light on the critical study of the power and information asymmetries inherent in sociotechnical systems. Byström (Chapter 8) focuses on the everyday working-from-home (WFH) impact in a Scandinavian university, examining how regular work practices and office routines were sustained and altered by ICT use. However, contextual and personal relationships at work were poorly supported by ICTs during the lockdown period. Whereas the results point to an overall positive attitude toward ICT tools, her work showcases the challenges and difficulties related to the social facets of remote working, such as insufficient support in the all-digital work environment, the need for work community, and potential conflicts between groups and individuals.

The Pandemic, and ICTs' Role, Goes on

In today's global network society, social structure and organizational arrangements are largely supported by information networks powered by ICTs (Castells, 2000). Constant connectivity allows us to head into an age of digital interdependence (Leonardi & Treem, 2020; United Nations, 2019). But never before have ICTs been at the center of society's response to a global health crisis like the COVID-19 pandemic, which may have a far-reaching fallout (World Health Organization, 2020).

We take a holistic view of the role of ICTs during this global pandemic, through the lens of social informatics, as it is critical to our understanding of the relations between society and technology. Our book advances the concepts, methods, and theories that are informed by and support the social informatics perspective. The various chapters emphasize the mutual interactions among people, technologies, and their particular contexts of use. This book provides evidence in multiple contexts to highlight that ICTs do not simply bring change to society, organizations, groups, and people's lives; ICTs are also bound by the power dynamics of stakeholders and are embedded in specific contexts. Our emphasis on the intersection between ICTs and health, culture, art, social interaction, governance, information dissemination, and work will hopefully be of interest to readers from various disciplines and will stimulate interdisciplinary conversations around these exciting topics.

When we developed the book proposal, we assumed the pandemic would have ended by the time the book was finished. We envisioned then, at least partly, that this book would capture the complex relationships between ICTs and society during an unusual and temporary context, the COVID-19 pandemic, and thereby contribute to the empirical and theoretical development of social informatics. However, as we write this introduction in August 2022, we are still living with an ongoing pandemic. A consensus has formed that human beings will have a greater reliance on digital technology for good and ill, as we embrace the new normal of a "tele-everything" world (Anderson et al., 2021). It might be too early to make final conclusions about the role of ICTs in the pandemic. However, the studies in this book can shed light on the importance of ICTs, and help to unpack the complexity of technology-related practices during a global crisis. We hope to intrigue more researchers to trace the emerging social change and evolving digital tools in a still-unfolding pandemic era.

References

Anderson, J., Rainie, L., & Vogels, E.A. (2021, February 18). Experts say the 'new normal' in 2025 will be far more tech-driven, presenting more big challenges. *Pew Research Center: Internet, Science & Tech.* https://www.pewresearch.org/internet/2021/02/18/experts-say-the-new-normal-in-2025-will-be-far-more-tech-driven-presenting-more-big-challenges/

Armano, D. (2020, September 9). COVID-19 will be remembered as the 'great accelerator' of digital transformation. *Forbes.* https://www.forbes.com/sites/davidarmano/2020/09/09/covid-19-will-be-remembered-as-the-great-accelerator-of-digital-transformation/?sh=799147e33cb2

Boczkowski, P., & Lievrouw, L.A. (2008). Bridging STS and communication studies: Scholarship on media and information technologies. In E.J. Hackett, O. Amsterdamska, M. Lynch, & J. Wajcman, (Eds.). *The handbook of science and technology studies*, 3rd ed. (pp. 949–977). The MIT Press.

Castells, M. (2000). Toward the sociology of the network society. *Contemporary Sociology, 29*(5), 693–699. 10.2307/2655234

Fichman, P., & Rosenbaum, H. (Eds.). (2014). *Social informatics: Past, present and future.* Cambridge Scholars Publishing.

Fichman, P., Sanfilippo, M., & Rosenbaum, H. (2015). *Social informatics evolving.* Morgan & Claypool Publishers.

Gillespie, T., Boczkowski, P.J., & Foot, K.A. (2014). Introduction. In T. Gillespie, P.J. Boczkowski, & K.A. Foot (Eds.), *Media technologies: Essays on communication, materiality, and society* (pp. 1–17). The MIT Press.

Hakmeh, J. (2021, February 16). The COVID-19 pandemic and trends in technology. *Chatham House – International Affairs Think Tank.* https://www.chathamhouse.org/2021/02/covid-19-pandemic-and-trends-technology

Kling, R., & Jewett, T. (1994). The social design of worklife with computers and networks: A natural systems perspective. *Advances in Computers, 39,* 239–293.

Kling, R., Rosenbaum, H., & Sawyer, S. (2005). *Understanding and communicating social informatics: A framework for studying and teaching the human contexts of information and communication technologies.* Information Today.

Leonardi, P.M., & Treem, J.W. (2020). Behavioral visibility: A new paradigm for organization studies in the age of digitization, digitalization, and datafication. *Organization Studies, 41*(12), 1601–1625. 10.1177/0170840620970728

Lievrouw, L.A. (2014). Materiality and media in communication and technology studies: An unfinished project. In T. Gillespie, P.J. Boczkowski, & K.A. Foot (Eds.), *Media technologies: Essays on communication, materiality, and society* (pp. 21–51). The MIT Press.

Meiller, Y. (2020). Digital transformation, COVID-19 crisis, digital transformation. In P. Bunkanwanicha, R. Coeurderoy, & S.B. Slimane (Eds.), *Managing a post-COVID19 Era: ESCP Impact Papers* (pp. 171–178). ESCP Research Institute of Management. https://escp.eu/faculty-research/erim/Impact-Papers/managing-a-post-Covid-era

Meyer, E.T. (2014). Examining the hyphen: The value of social informatics for research and teaching. In P. Fichman & H. Rosenbaum (Eds.), *Social informatics: Past, present and future* (pp. 57–74). Cambridge Scholarly Publishers.

Meyer, E.T., Shankar, K., Willis, M., Sharma, S., & Sawyer, S. (2019). The social informatics of knowledge. *Journal of the Association for Information Science and Technology, 70*(4), 307–312.

Sawyer, S., & Jarrahi, M.H. (2014). Sociotechnical approaches to the study of information systems. In H. Topi & A. Tucker (Eds.) *Computing handbook, 3rd ed: Information systems and information technology.* CRC Press.

Tosheva, E. (2020). COVID-19 crisis as an accelerator of digital. In G. Ilik & A. Stanojoska (Eds.), *Proceedings of International Scientific Conference "Towards a Better Future: Human Rights, Organized Crime and Digital Society"* (Vol. II, pp. 179–187). St. Kliment Ohridski University, Faculty of law. http://eprints.uklo. edu.mk/6215/1/Conference-Proceedings-vol.2.pdf

United Nations. (2019). *The age of digital interdependence: Report of the UN Secretary-General's High-level Panel on Digital Cooperation.* https://www.un.org/ en/pdfs/DigitalCooperation-report-for%20web.pdf

United Nations Group on the Information Society (UNGIS). (2021). *UNGIS contribution to the 2021 high-level political forum on sustainable development.* United Nations Sustainable Development Knowledge Platform. https://sustainabledevelop ment.un.org/index.php?page=view&type=30022&nr=2733&menu=3170

Webster, F. (2014). *Theories of the information society,* 4th ed. Routledge.

Wilson, C., & Jumbert, M.G. (2018). The new informatics of pandemic response: Humanitarian technology, efficiency, and the subtle retreat of national agency. *Journal of International Humanitarian Action, 3*(8). 10.1186/s41018-018-0036-5

World Health Organization. (2020, September 23). *Managing the COVID-19 infodemic: Promoting healthy behaviours and mitigating the harm from misinformation and disinformation.* https://www.who.int/news/item/23-09-2020-managing-the-covid-19-infodemic-promoting-healthy-behaviours-and-mitigating-the-harm-from-misinformation-and-disinformation

Xie, B., He, D., Mercer, T., Wang, Y., Wu, D., Fleischmann, K.R., Zhang, Y., Yoder, L.H., Stephens, K.K., Mackert, M., & Lee, M.K. (2020). Global health crises are also information crises: A call to action. *Journal of the Association for Information Science and Technology, 71*(12), 1419–1423. 10.1002/asi.24357

Part I
Governance

1 Toward a Sociotechnical Framework for Misinformation Policy Analysis

Xiaohua Zhu and Shengnan Yang

Introduction

At the beginning of 2020, fake news, rumors, myths, misinformation, disinformation, malign/subversive information, false information, conspiracy theories, and even hate speech began to spread more rapidly and widely than ever before. As United Nations Secretary-General António Guterres said in a video message, a "global 'misinfo-demic' is spreading", which travels faster than the virus itself ("Hatred going viral", 2020). Using social media and other Information and communications technology (ICT) to disseminate misinformation is certainly not a new phenomenon—scholars already claim we now live in a post-truth era (Wimberly, 2021). However, the pandemic exacerbated the existing problem to such an extent that the world is becoming aware of the damage misinformation can generate. Recent events in 2022, such as Elon Musk's alleged plan to privatize Twitter (Associated Press, 2022) and the "World's First Tiktok War" (Chayka, 2022) accompanying the Russia-Ukraine war, raised more concerns and debates over the definitions of truth, free speech, democracy, and many other social values and norms in the social media environment.

Before the pandemic, many governmental organizations, as critical actors in the sociotechnical system of communications and information, had begun to make laws or investigate means against misinformation, as exemplified by the European Union's *Code of Practice on Disinformation* (EU, 2018), and more recently by the *Digital Services Act* (EU, 2022). Several countries, including Singapore and China, adopted stricter criminal laws to punish misinformation creators and distributors. It is not surprising that much of this legislation targets ICT, mainly social media platforms, as the platforms have been the primary means of misinformation dissemination. For the same reason, however, passing such legislation in many other countries has been challenging. For example, the United States has traditionally relied on corporations to regulate themselves in many information-related issues such as privacy (Jaeger & Taylor, 2019, p. 3), and social media platforms, as business entities, have a great degree of autonomy (Gillespie, 2010, 2018).

DOI: 10.4324/9781003231769-3

During the pandemic, governmental organizations at all levels around the world responded immediately to the misinformation problem by publishing fake news debunkers and providing accurate, scientific information about the coronavirus and its treatment, to protect their citizenry. Meanwhile, policymaking regarding misinformation and its dissemination via social media platforms has become an urgent issue for many governments. Given the different circumstances and value systems, it is only natural that different countries utilize different policy tools; however, in modern society, policy-making is often not isolated to each government, but rather is influenced by other political entities (Schmitt, 2012). As misinformation policies are being developed around the world, a systematic examination of policies on misinformation in different countries is warranted; policymakers and experts need a deep understanding of the various misinformation policies adopted by different governments and the development of misinformation policies at different stages. Existing comparative research on the regulation of mis-information is often descriptive in nature (e.g., de Gregorio & Radu, 2019; Radu, 2020; Rodrigues & Xu, 2020; Pielemeier, 2020), and there is a need for suitable analytical tools for systematic and comparative policy studies.

Social informatics provides valuable perspectives in developing analytical tools for such analysis. As Kling et al. (2005) argued in their landmark social informatics monograph, *Understanding and Communicating Social Informatics,* social informatics perspectives can help us mitigate the un-certainty in ICT policymaking and improve the policymaking process (p. 52). Conversely, the sociopolitical landscape surveyed in such policy studies provides a window for social informatics scholars to examine and gain perspectives on the complexity of the sociotechnical networks of ICT, and a particular aspect of the network—the government regulation of ICT applications. Using the sociotechnical lens, we also hope to bridge the artificial gap between social informatics research and information policy research in the field of information science.

Taking a social informatics perspective, we focused on the actors and their actions, as well as the contexts of such actions, to develop an analytical framework for comparative misinformation policy analysis. This framework includes context, agents, targets, issues, channels, and actions as the main analytical dimensions, for each of which we identified a list of elements. We tested the framework in two different contexts/situations, the United States and China. For the empirical comparisons and analyses of the two cases, we used a content analysis method, aiming to answer the following guiding question: How did the governments of the United States and China react to the infodemic during the COVID-19 pandemic (2020–2021)? The findings of this study reveal multiple threads of social and political narratives em-bedded in the text of policy documents. The differences and similarities in the policy documents demonstrate the complexity of misinformation reg-ulations that sometimes contradict to popular beliefs and often simplified political reasoning.

Definitions of key terms

In this study, *misinformation* is used as an umbrella term to cover related concepts, including fake news, disinformation, false information, rumors, conspiracy theories, malignant information, inaccurate information, and more. In the literature and policy documents, these terms often have specific (and varying) definitions and unique usages. For example, in the EU context, disinformation (désinformation in French and desinformation in German) is used almost exclusively; in China, rumor (谣言 in Chinese) and false information (虚假信息 in Chinese) are used more often. But in the public discourses, they are often used interchangeably and ambiguously, with misinformation as arguably the most widely used one, especially in the US context.

Drawing from Dye's (1976) classic, broad definition of public policy, "whatever governments choose to do or not to do" (p. 1), and Jaeger and Taylor's (2019) comprehensive definition of information policy (p. 3), we define *misinformation policy* in this study as what governments choose to do, via lawmaking and other activities, regarding various aspects of misinformation. Comparative policy analysis often looks at similarities and differences in public policies and policymaking processes in different jurisdictions (Schmitt, 2012). This study examines not only the content of *policy documents* that serve as governments' decisional output (laws, regulations, executive orders, etc.) but also those created in the government misinformation policymaking process, including bills, proposed rules, reports, strategies and plans, announcements, and other informational items documenting the governmental behaviors and intentions.

Terms like digital platforms, social media platforms, and online platforms are often used interchangeably, and often cause confusion because of different perspectives and understandings. In this study, a digital platform or online platform is broadly defined as a website or mobile application that provides a public-facing forum for content distribution and/or user interactions and the entity that owns/runs the website or application. It can be state-owned or commercial in nature. Social media platforms constitute a subset of digital platforms. A social media platform is defined as a commercial website or mobile application that provides a public-facing forum for users to interact with other users, and the company/business that owns and runs it.

Case selection and background

We analyzed and compared the policy documents generated by the US federal government and the Chinese central government for several reasons. First, the two countries' distinct characteristics regarding political systems, authoritarian and democratic regimes respectively, make their government forms, policymaking processes, and social norms and values notably different from each other. They can serve as two extreme cases of policy analysis and offer a wide range of variations for a deep understanding of misinformation policies. Second, as two leading technologically advanced countries in the world, both of them started to regulate the internet, including fighting misinformation mediated by digital technology, prior to the pandemic, reflecting different backgrounds and various approaches. Third, both countries suffered greatly from misinformation during the pandemic, including health-related misinformation, political misinformation, and conspiracy theories. This section outlines the backgrounds of both countries, particularly related to their existing (mis)information regulatory frameworks and practices.

General background of misinformation regulation in the United States

Before the pandemic, the US's focus on combatting misinformation included "[p]olitical ads, foreign disinformation, general misinformation, media literacy and deepfake videos" (Funke & Flamini, n.d.). What they lacked, however, was a top-down, national policy response or large-scale collaborative initiatives. During the 2016 presidential campaign, many incidents of hacking, social media account manipulation, and foreign interference were reported and investigated (CNN Editorial Research, 2016). The US Senate announced a bill in October 2017 to regulate political ads on the internet, called the *Honest Ads Act*, aiming to bring rules similar to those used for traditional media to social media platforms (Honest Ads Act, 2018). The effort to regulate platforms regarding political advertisements was unsuccessful, and social media platforms remained largely self-regulated. Facebook, Twitter, and Google admitted to the Senate that Russia manipulated their platforms, but they were confident in their own measures to monitor fake accounts and ad buyers (The Guardian, 2017). Faced with the spread of fake news, some state governments introduced bills trying to monitor misinformation on social media, but these failed too (CBS Sacramento, 2018). The only successful policy action was enacting several state laws that mandated improving media literacy through civic or public education (Funke & Flamini, n.d.).

General background of misinformation regulation in China

China had sophisticated internet control under direct regulation by the government (Yang, 2012) with a focus on cyberspace security, socialist spiritual civilization, and social stability. China started to set up its direct regulation mechanism in the early 2000s. At that time, the internet and online media were mainly treated as an extension of traditional propaganda tools and were regulated accordingly. Enhanced centralized control of the online sphere began in the early 2010s. A thorough restructuring of China's internet governance landscape was launched in 2014, when President Xi made the announcement about building China into a "strong Internet power" (网络强国 in Chinese) and treated the internet as "the most unpredictable variable" (Xi, 2014). Internet governance was reconstructed with a set of organizations, priorities, and regulations (Creemers, 2017). High-level regulatory institutions were established in 2014. In particular, the Cyberspace Administration of China (CAC) was founded under the new Central Leading Group for Cybersecurity and Informatization, with responsibilities of regulating online content and promulgating new rules on subjects ranging from malicious software in mobile app stores to the use of social media accounts. Fighting "fake news", which was primarily referred to as "rumors", has been prioritized as a crucial regulatory action. Correspondingly, regulatory tactics were enacted, including creating government agencies as regulators, enacting laws and policies to regulate information creators and providers, criminalizing misinformation, and building centralized channels for fact-checking, official information spreading, and rumor-reporting. Moreover, the misinformation regulations in China were placed under a set of formalized policies at the national level, including amending the *National Security Law* in 2016 and the *Criminal Law Amendment Act* in 2015. The control of misinformation became stricter when China added "fabricating and disseminating misinformation that seriously disturbs public order" as a crime to its criminal laws, and publicly deployed cyber police to patrol the internet for illegal and harmful information (Magnier, 2015).

Literature Review

In the past few years, scholars shifted the focus of online misinformation (broadly defined) research from the narrow category of "political advertisements", to the broader scope of "paid for" content (Shattock, 2021). Meanwhile, the research has become more profound, evolving from summarizing "what happened", to analyzing "why it happens and how to prevent it". During the COVID-19 pandemic, much research on misinformation has emerged, mainly on three aspects of the misinformation challenge. The first thread uses a technological perspective, with the purpose of misinformation identification and detection (e.g., Abdali, 2022; Alam et al., 2021; Hossain et al., 2020; Kolluri & Murthy, 2021; Zhou & Zafarani, 2020). The second thread emphasizes the social aspect of and individuals' beliefs or behaviors related to misinformation, oftentimes under the discussion of conspiracy theory. This thread of research focuses on who engages with misinformation and what their motivations are, how people are exposed to and affected by misinformation, and how this may vary across subpopulations and personal networks (e.g., Cassese et al., 2020; Imhoff & Lamberty, 2020; Miller, 2020; Pummerer et al., 2022). Research in these two threads usually concentrates on specific misinformation and examines the conditions and consequences of its spread.

The third thread is macro-level political research. It examines a variety of misinformation regulatory practices in different regions and the roles of related stakeholders, particularly digital platforms. The governance models and the difficulty of regulation are the main topics within this thread, identifying and analyzing regulation models and the underlying relations between governments and social media platforms (Gillespie, 2018; Rochefort, 2020; Tenove, 2020; Van Dijck, 2020). These models operate along a spectrum of increasing governmental control, from little oversight to intense regulation (Durach et al., 2020; Rochefort, 2020; Gorwa, 2019). At one end of the spectrum is the regulation that emphasizes the role of governments in moderating content on platforms, in which governments directly regulate platforms via legislation. At the other end of the spectrum, called self-regulation, is the regulation that focuses on the social media platforms themselves, with limited, if any, governmental oversight. In the middle of the spectrum is the co-governance approach that combines platforms and governments together. In practice, more and more countries have been adopting the co-governance model. The COVID-19 pandemic has motivated many governments around the world to prioritize COVID-19-related actions, such as providing guidance to social media platforms about taking down false content, establishing special agents to fight against misinformation, and criminalizing malicious falsehoods related to the pandemic (Radu, 2020). One of the results is the increased complexity of regulatory practices and the misalignment between the practices and the models identified by researchers. For instance, Zhu et al. (2022) examined anti-misinformation policies in five countries, ranging from authoritarian countries to democratic ones, and noted a trend of combining different regulation strategies in practice, which blurred the boundaries of existing models.

Meanwhile, the difficulty of misinformation regulation has sparked much discussion not only about different regulatory models and legislative strategies but also about the pandemic context specifically. According to Shattock (2021), the intrinsic limitation of self-regulation is that its voluntary nature does not promote concrete "structured cooperation between platforms" (European Commission, 2020). Platforms do not face material sanctions for implementation failures. Moreover, the constant debate between the need to update misinformation regulations, versus its potential threat to freedom of expression, also reflects the difficulty of regulating misinformation (Baade, 2018; Pielemeier, 2020). In addition, the ambiguous definition of misinformation and its unique characteristics, compared with other types of prohibited content, raise concerns about legislation strategies. As Pielemeier (2020) argued, one regulatory regime to rule all forms of online content might not fit the merits of misinformation. In the context of the pandemic, the difficulty of misinformation regulation is rooted both in the tension between the state's control versus individual freedom and the broader sociopolitical environment, such as "the public diplomacy campaigns of competition by geopolitical actors" (Vériter et al., 2020, p. 569).

Among the discussions of regulatory practices and models, digital technologies, particularly social media platforms and algorithms, are regarded as the essential factors affecting the dissemination of misinformation. Social media have become the leading news outlets, as the primary information source for many users, despite lacking quality control (Humprecht, 2019). The unique technological features of social media, such as likes, shares, and comments, have contributed to the spread of misinformation. Social media help connect and inform people, while rewarding online engagement rather than accuracy and allowing emotionally charged misinformation to spread more easily than fact-based or emotionally neutral content (Vosoughi et al., 2018). During the COVID-19 pandemic, social media have been both the culprit of and antidote to misinformation. Countering disinformation online became as important as providing much-needed medical equipment and supplies for health workers, in the first month of the pandemic (Radu, 2020). In such a context, social media platforms are frequently being reformed, either through self-initiatives or under the regulation and oversight of government.

The existing studies provide insight into misinformation governance with a few salient limitations. First, the existing literature is dominated by the context of political elections. Originating from the narrow category of "political advertisements", prior discussions were often framed by a dichotomy in the international political context, democracy versus autocracy, stating that democratic countries were affected by the misinformation campaigns (or foreign propaganda) from nondemocratic countries. This predefined ideological assumption, amid limited context, ignored the complexity of the misinformation-related phenomenon. Even though there is a shift of focus to a broader scope, in which paid-for content and economic concerns have become essential in some policies, discussions beyond political concerns are still insufficient in the existing literature. Second, studies at the macro level lack a systematic review of the legal, legislative, and police practices. Specific practices in a single country or regime remain the focus of most studies. As mentioned, there is a misalignment between evolving regulatory practices and scholarly models. More diversified regulatory approaches are merging, such as various co-governance-related practices, with multiple regulatory strategies in different countries. Thus, a comprehensive analytical tool is needed to understand these complexities.

Methodology

Data collection

With the goal of creating a comprehensive review of misinformation policies, we started with an exhaustive search of policy documents issued by the US federal government and the Chinese central government, between January 1, 2020 and December 31, 2021, a two-year period during the pandemic.

To collect the US data, we relied on two major sources: govinfo.gov, a central depository of US federal government documents, and the government websites of the US Supreme Court, all of the cabinet-level departments, the White House, and a few specialized government agencies (e.g., the Cyberspace Solarium Commission, the Global Engagement Center, and the Cybersecurity and Infrastructure Security Agency) whose responsibilities cover misinformation-related issues. We used the advanced search options on govinfo.gov to search for legislative information (proposed or passed bills); congressional hearings, reports, and other documents; executive orders and other presidential information; and proposed and passed regulations. The search functions of government agency websites did not always generate accurate and complete results; therefore, we used Google's "site search" function to conduct an exhaustive search on each government agency's website. The keywords we used for both sources included "fake news", "misinformation", "disinformation", and "conspiracy theories".

After the exhaustive search and data collection, we manually filtered, deduplicated, and sorted nearly 2,000 documents into four categories: highly relevant, somewhat relevant, informational items, and irrelevant.[1] Only 92 highly relevant documents that were mainly about or directly addressed misinformation issues were included in the final analysis, including 20 proposed bills, 4 congressional resolutions, 1 adopted regulation, 7 congressional hearings and reports, 8 executive orders and other presidential documents (remarks, proclamations, and notices), 3 Supreme Court decisions, and 49 web documents from cabinet-level executive departments and special agencies. It is worth mentioning that many of the policy documents do not reflect what the government actually did or will do, as they were proposals, bills, or other discussion items, but they still fit our definition of misinformation policy, in revealing the various policymakers' viewpoints in the sociopolitical "action situation" (Ostrom, 2005).

In China, policy documents were collected mainly from two sources: official government-document databases, including the State Council's Policy Database (国务院政策文件库 in Chinese), the Administrative Regulations Database (行政法规数据库 in Chinese), and Legislative and Regulatory Databases (法律规章数据库 in Chinese); and the government websites of all of the 26 constituent departments of the State Council, and 16 internal divisions of the Central Committee of the Chinese Communist Party, including the specialized government agency, the Cyberspace Administration of China (CAC), whose responsibilities cover misinformation-related issues. Similar to the searching and browsing process of the US data collection, we used the searching functions on each database and website, as well as Google's site search, to find relevant documents. In the Chinese context, misinformation is often referred to as "rumor", "false and unhealthy information", "fabrication", and "fake news". Through keyword searching, we collected 127 relevant government documents that included cogent policies and regulatory practices. The irrelevant and informational items were filtered out in the search process. We then excluded documents that were either not highly relevant or repetitive, such as newsletters reporting the enforcement of specific regulatory policy by local governmental agencies, summary reports publicizing the achievement of anti-misinformation activities, and those documents only roughly mentioning the principle of prohibiting misinformation but without detailed guidance of the implementation. As a result, only 47 highly relevant governmental documents, mainly about or directly addressed misinformation issues, were included in the final analysis, including 6 laws and regulations enacted by the central government, 3 presidential speeches, 10 departmental rules released by CAC, and 28 special action plans and regulatory practices initiated by CAC and other government agencies.

We developed a web crawling tool using Python to batch download relevant policy documents and convert them into PDF format, before importing them into NVivo R1 for qualitative coding. In the data collection process, we noticed that the Chinese government published more formal policies and policy implementation outcomes, compared to the United States, which had more discussion/proposal documents related to debunking misinformation. There are two possible reasons for this difference. First, cyberspace regulation in China was in the stage of implementation and evaluation, while the United States was at the policy-designing stage. Second, the opacity of the decision-making process in China caused difficulty in retrieving documents related to their policy design (Williamson & Magaloni, 2020).

Content analysis method

This policy analysis study is a content analysis. According to Neuendorf (2002), content analysis is the "systematic, objective, quantitative analysis of message characteristics" (p.1). This kind of content analysis, according to Altheide (1987, 1996), is a conventional quantitative content analysis with certain limitations. Altheide suggested applying "several aspects of an ethnographic research approach ... to produce *ethnographic content analysis*" (1996, p.14). Instead of placing data into predefined categories, the ethnographic content analysis uses protocols more flexibly, allowing for the emergence of new concepts, categories, and variables. It emphasizes constant discovery and constant comparison of meanings, both of which are suggested by grounded theorists (Glaser & Strauss, 1967; Glaser, 1978).

Another categorization of content analysis was suggested by Gerbic and Stacey (2005) based on the method of developing the analysis framework. In the "clean slate approach" (p. 50), researchers adopt an existing theory or model as their content analysis framework. In the "grounded theory approach" (p. 50), the framework for analysis is not developed at first, but instead emerges from the data analysis. This approach is advantageous when the phenomenon under study is relatively new, and little is known about it.

In this study, we initially conducted some pilot analysis based on a set of heuristics/dimensions of policy design and analysis, including policy goals, instruments, targets, agents, sources, and content (Schneider & Ingram, 1990; Howlett, 2011). However, we soon found them insufficient in supporting detailed and granular analysis. This insufficiency is partly because of the complexity of the misinformation-related issues, and partly because of the nature of the policy documents we collected—not all of them are officially approved/enacted, actionable policies. Instead, they contain a wide range of issues, actions, and stakeholders with different standpoints. A deductive approach, with a set of predefined, general policy elements, could not cover those specifics for a detailed and meaningful analysis. In addition, we aimed to discover and compare the patterns of misinformation policies over a period of two years in the pandemic context, rather than testing existing theories or hypotheses. Therefore, we followed the ethnographic content analysis approach introduced by Altheide (1996), and the grounded theory approach suggested by Gerbic 2005), to generate the framework from the data itself through constant comparison and modification.

Developing the analytical framework

Employing a social informatics perspective, the initial open coding of all policy documents enabled us to recognize the sociotechnical nature of misinformation. This trait is often ignored by the policy-focused literature that underlines the sociopolitical aspect, and the library and information science literature that highlights the technological aspect. We argue that misinformation is a complicated and multidimensional phenomenon, and misinformation policymaking can be best understood as a sociotechnical network consisting of various "tangible and intangible components", including people, hardware, software, techniques, support resources, information structures, etc. (Kling et al., 2005, pp. 54–55). While Kling and his colleagues (2005) used sociotechnical networks to conceptualize ICTs themselves, and expected this model to facilitate ICT policy analysis, it is logical to extend the model for the examination of a broader ICT phenomenon such as misinformation.

Through the combination of a deductive approach (with initial heuristics and dimensions based on the literature) and an inductive approach (using open coding of all policy documents and constant comparisons and discussions between researchers), as well as the inspiration of the sociotechnical network model, we developed an analytical framework to facilitate the examination of governments' countermeasures to misinformation, from a policy analysis angle. The framework includes six major analytical dimensions, for each of which we identified multiple specific elements. The definitions of major dimensions and the specific elements are presented in Table 1.1. Elements in the actions and targets dimensions include subelements, which are specified in the *Findings* section (Tables 1.6–1.7).

Table 1.1 Misinformation policy analytical dimensions

Analytical Dimension	Definition and Elements Identified in this Study
Contexts	The broad or specific background of (and mentioned in) the policy document.
	Business and economy, COVID-19, domestic politics, education and capacity building, human rights and development, international relations, internet integrity, legislation, public administration, security and defense, societal discourse, and cyber ecology.
Agents	The government agencies and other organizations/individuals that are charged with certain roles in dealing with misinformation by this policy, or the government agencies and other organizations/ individuals that took certain actions against misinformation according to the policy document.
	Education institutions, interagencies, intergovernmental actors, local government agencies, special government agencies, health organizations, journalists and news organizations, nonprofit organizations, private sectors, researchers, scientists, and experts, digital platforms, and the public
Issues	Different types of misinformation or misinformation-related matters regulated or discussed by policymakers.
	Conspiracy theory, economy-related misinformation, general misinformation, health-related misinformation, ideology-related misinformation, news and media, and political misinformation
Channels	Carriers or channels of misinformation creation, distribution, and consumption, in particular, the ICT-based ones.
	Algorithms, social media, applications other than social media, data and online traffic, hardware, and infrastructure
Targets	Misinformation stakeholders (e.g., consumers, creators, and distributors) that the policy document aims to act on. For example, a policy may include direct actions to help, regulate, or punish certain groups; these groups are the policy targets. They are passive actors in the policy.
	Misinformation consumers, misinformation creators, and misinformation distributors
Actions	Actions that the policy document serves/creates (e.g., condemning certain behaviors), mandates (in the case of bills or regulations), reports (in the case of many government website news and announcements), or suggests (in the case of congressional hearings and various government reports).
	Direct actions, expenditure-based actions, information-based actions, and policymaking

The dimension of *contexts* (which also can be called action situations) was inspired by the influential institutional analysis and development (IAD) framework developed by Elinor Ostrom (2005). The action arena, a key component of IAD, consists of participants and action situations. An action situation is a social space where sociopolitical actors (i.e., participants) interact with other actors and direct resource allocation to achieve favorable outcomes. This concept is essential for us to compare policies from different governments.

Actors are an essential component of any institutional or policy analysis. In this study, we followed two types of actors, agents and targets. In a simple sense, agents are the regulators, and targets are those being regulated by policies. Because we focused on policy analysis, government agencies, as the policymakers, are the main agents examined in this study. However, other agents are often involved, because governments may require or mobilize other stakeholders, such as digital platforms, to fight misinformation. In addition, governments often act through partnerships with nonprofit organizations or private firms to achieve policy goals (Girard et al., 2009).

With the evolvement of ICT, the research on detecting misinformation has expanded the focus from a single modality to multimodal (Abdali, 2022), from human-generated ones to social bots (Shao et al., 2018), even powered by algorithms and AI (Adams, 2017). The expansion of misinformation also drives policymakers to design more detailed laws and rules. The creation and dissemination of misinformation rely on technology carriers and channels, including but not limited to hardware as the foundations, code and algorithms for developers' design, applications for users to utilize, and data as the representation of information. We grouped and named these elements in our framework "*channels*", as a unique dimension to capture the technologies associated with misinformation creation and distribution.

In policy design and analysis, the term *targets* means actors and populations whose behavior is linked to the achievement of policy goals, such as individuals, households, groups, and business firms (Schneider & Ingram, 1990). In our analysis, however, targets' behaviors are not simply "linked to" but are in effect regulated/changed in certain ways by the policies. This narrower definition helped us distinguish agents and targets in the analysis as these two groups overlap. For example, a digital platform can be an agent in fighting misinformation, as well as a target whose business model is questioned. It is critical to differentiate the active agents versus the passive ones in misinformation policy analysis.

Actions are the tools that governments use to achieve policy objectives. For instance, financial instruments are deployed to encourage desirable behaviors by providing economic incentives, according to Pal's classification of policy instruments (Pal, 2014 p. 134). We identified various actions from the policy documents; but it is important to note that, in this chapter, only governments' actions are included, as government agencies are the main actors we followed in this study. Each actor's actions are worth examining in future research.

Among the six analytical dimensions, three are worth special attention. They are the essence of what we call the misinformation phenomenon—people, ICT, and information. Governments' misinformation countermeasures are often developed to regulate human *targets* (i.e., various social groups involved in the creation, distribution, and consumption of misinformation), ICT carriers or channels of misinformation (regarding *how* misinformation was created, called *"channels"* in this study), and the specific types, topics, issues, and manifestations of misinformation (we call them *"issues"*). In short, targets, channels, and issues are the three significant aspects of misinformation that government policies tend to tackle. Emphasizing the sociotechnical nature of the misinformation phenomenon and breaking down the policy subjects into the three dimensions helped us examine and compare policy documents in a more granular manner, and therefore gain more insight into policy content and goals.

Data analysis

After developing the codebook with dimensions, elements, definitions, and coding notes, the two authors conducted a final round of data analysis, based on the proposed framework, using NVivo R1. The method used in developing the framework and the comprehensiveness of the codebook, prevented, to a great degree, the disagreements between the two coders. When discrepancies appeared, they were immediately solved by discussion, and decisions made during discussions were incorporated into the codebook.

The coding was on the paragraph and sentence level, but the general analysis and reporting in this chapter use the document as the unit of analysis, for convenience and clarity. The next section presents the findings using both quantitative and qualitative means. The quantitative analysis focuses on the number of occurrences of each analytical element, that is, the number of documents that contain the element. Percentages are used to compare and contrast the policy documents in the two countries. It should be noted that the numbers alone cannot provide an accurate picture of the policy arena, especially regarding the comparisons between the two governments.

Findings

Contexts

We started the research assuming that the COVID-19 pandemic was a critical factor in misinformation policy development in various countries. Indeed, in both the United States and China, COVID-19 was often mentioned in the policy document as the background, context, and rationale for government policymaking and other actions. But other contextual factors also stood out in the analysis, and the two countries exhibited different emphases. For example, in the United States, politics was the most cited context. "International relations" appeared in over 40% of the policy documents, and about 20% contained "domestic politics". Along the same line, "security and defense" was frequently mentioned. In contrast, China's

Table 1.2 Frequency and percentage of contexts elements in policy documents from the United States and China

Contexts	United States		China	
	Occurrence	Percentage	Occurrence	Percentage
Business and economy	7	7.6	10	22.2
COVID-19	38	41.3	13	28.9
Domestic politics	18	19.6	2	4.3
Education and capacity building	11	12.0	4	8.9
Human rights and development	7	7.6	3	6.7
International relations	38	41.3	4	8.9
Internet integrity	0	0.0	3	6.7
Legislation	21	22.8	7	15.6
Public administration	13	14.1	6	13.3
Security and defense	35	38.0	10	21.3
Societal discourse	38	41.3	16	34.0
Cyber ecology	10	10.9	24	51.1

policies seldom mentioned political issues, and "cyber ecology" (网络生态 in Chinese), which often involves the overall internet content construction and regulation, for the purpose of cleaner cyberspace and more positivity, appeared in more than half the documents (Table 1.2).

In our analysis, "international relations" was used to refer to any policies related to foreign affairs or the relationship between multiple countries or regions. "Domestic politics" was coded when the policy document focused on political issues, particularly related to elections, public engagement, and political participation in the country, and did not include foreign influences on domestic politics. As is presented in other sections ("*issues*" and "*targets*"), the US government's reactions to misinformation had a strong focus on foreign actors (Russia, China, Iran, etc.) and influences of these actors on the US election and other political matters, which was a continuation of the US government's political trend since at least the 2016 election. Even during the pandemic, politics was the top concern of the US government.

In China, the contexts had a domestic focus. Since the central government enacted a policy titled *Wǎngluò xìnxī nèiróng shēngtài zhìlǐ guiding* (translated into English as *Provisions on Ecological Governance of Cyber Content*) (2020), with the purpose of creating clean cyberspace and a sound network ecosystem, "cyber ecology" has served as the overarching guidance of online information regulations. The government imposed two top-down tactics for misinformation prevention—directing online content construction and establishing a comprehensive online network governance system. On the one hand, this policy emphasizes the activities of "promoting positive energy and the socialist core values" and "disposing of illegal and harmful information conducted by the government, enterprises, society, Internet users, and other parties". On the other hand, the policy establishes the governance mechanism—online platforms must implement their internal procedures to moderate real-time online content and handle online rumors.

Society discourse was an essential backdrop of misinformation policies in both countries. Many policy documents mentioned broad social aspects of misinformation, such as influencing people's perceptions, as one of the reasons for regulating misinformation-related issues. However, a scrutinization of the societal discourse revealed different patterns. In the United States, the society discourse covered in policy documents tended to be either general (such as "a rise of misinformation that impacts the daily lives of people in the United States, including misinformation about the virus, public health, our democracy, and the government's response" [COVID-19 Misinformation and Disinformation Task Force Act, 2020]) or politics-oriented (such as "domestic extremist groups such as white supremacists and anti-government extremists have made use of online platforms to spread their messages and connect with like-minded individuals" [National Commission on Online Platforms and Homeland Security Act, 2020]). In China, the content of societal discourse was more specific, including creating and disseminating "good-quality online content (优质内容 in Chinese)" to the public and "cultivating positive online culture (培育积极健康、向上向善的网络文化 in Chinese)" (CAC, 2020a) for them.

It is worth mentioning that business and economy often served as a background in China's misinformation policies, as opposed to the US's political focus. Some policies state that their purposes are to maintain the order of the market economy and protect individuals' economic rights. As discussed in later sections, business and economy were not simply a background, but rather were part of the holistic approach to regulating cyberspace.

Issues

Our analysis revealed a range of specific issues/topics related to the misinformation phenomenon being considered by policymakers in the two governments. As Table 1.3 shows, the issues emphasized by governments through policies were different in almost all aspects.

In both counties, the misinformation phenomenon encompassed a wide range of issues. The only similarity was the health-related misinformation, although it was discussed more in the United States than in China. For example, the US Congress received bills such as the *Health Misinformation Act* (2021) and the *COVID-19 Disinformation Research and Reporting Act* (2021), and the US Surgeon General issued an advisory to warn the public against health misinformation (OSG, 2021). In China, combatting COVID-19-related misinformation was presented in the *White Paper: Fighting COVID-19: China in Action* (State Council Information Office of China, 2020). In the third meeting of the Central Committee for the Comprehensive Rule of Law, President Xi emphasized the importance of

Table 1.3 Frequency and percentage of issues elements in policy documents from the United States and China

Issues	United States		China	
	Occurrence	Percentage	Occurrence	Percentage
Conspiracy theory	4	4.3	0	0.0
Economy-related misinformation	1	1.1	13	27.7
General misinformation	6	6.5	17	36.2
Health-related misinformation	30	32.6	8	17.0
Ideology-related information	42	45.7	4	8.5
News and media	1	1.1	9	19.1
Other misinformation	2	2.2	3	6.4
Political misinformation	31	33.7	7	14.9

fighting against COVID-19 rumors as one critical aspect of pandemic prevention ruled by law (Xi, 2020).

The most noticeable difference is that the topics covered in Chinese policies were relatively evenly distributed, while in the United States, there was a clear emphasis on ideology-related information (especially the foreign influences on American elections) and general political misinformation.

As mentioned in the previous section, the US misinformation policy had a strong political focus and national defense emphasis. US government agencies had prioritized combatting foreign disinformation since the 2016 presidential election, which continued into the pandemic period. In September 2018, former US President Donald Trump declared a national emergency to deal with the threat of "foreign interference in a United States election" (Executive Order No. 13848, 2018). Several agencies, particularly the Department of State, issued multiple reports from 2017 to 2021 that examined various aspects of foreign state-sponsored disinformation and the strategies of the federal government agencies, especially the diplomatic measures (DOJ & DHS, 2021; GEC, 2020; NIC, 2021; Park Advisors, 2019; Powers & Kounalakis, 2017; Walker & Walsh, 2020). Related bills were introduced in the US Congress in 2020 and 2021, including *Protecting Democracy from Disinformation Act* (2020), *Protect Against Public Safety Disinformation Act* (2020), *Anti-CCP Espionage via Social Media Act* (2021), *No Social Media Accounts for Terrorist and State Sponsors of Terrorism Act* (2021), etc. These bills were still under discussion while the chapter was being written.

Although foreign interference was especially emphasized by the Trump administration, the shift in administrations in 2021 did not seem to have altered the trajectory of misinformation policymaking—current US president Joseph Biden, in September 2021, announced to continue "the National Emergency with Respect to Foreign Interference in or Undermining Public Confidence in United States Elections" (Notice, 2021), with almost identical content to Trump's earlier notices on the same matter (Notice, 2019; Notice, 2020). More recently, the Global Engagement Center, arguably the most important special agency against foreign disinformation,[2] issued a new report on Russia's disinformation activities (GEC, 2022). Furthermore, because of the role of election misinformation in the January 6 Capitol riot of 2021, domestic political misinformation issues, including domestic terrorism and conspiracy theories, began to gain more attention. For example, the *Security Clearance Act* (2021) was introduced to Congress to strengthen the national security clearance by requiring more information about individuals' involvement in spreading conspiracy theories.

In contrast to the US's political and ideological focuses, Chinese policies, besides regulating misinformation in general, concentrated on misinformation harmful to the domestic economy. For example, the government made several rules to regulate online economic activities, including advertisements mediated by live streaming services, online public/official accounts[3] for information spreading and branding, and algorithm-based digital services for automatic recommendations.

One of the prominent subcategories under the business and economic issue was related to the fan economy in the entertainment industry, which largely relied on online traffic to attract fans' and general users' attention. Several specific policies were implemented to battle against the spread of inflated data and misleading content, such as faked fan accounts and botnets that manipulated online comments and purposefully misled the public. Financial issues were also quite notable. CAC, in collaboration with the Development and Reform Commission, the Ministry of Finance, and the People's Bank of China, initiated a "special action" to regulate noncompliant financial news on commercial websites, and self-media/we-media social media by punishing problematic websites and platforms following laws and regulations (CAC, 2020b). Another salient aspect of misinformation regulation in China is news and media. Nine documents mentioned battling fake and fabricated online news mediated by social media platforms and digital applications (such as pop-ups and push notifications on mobile applications), to avoid misleading audiences and to "purify" cyberspace (for example, CAC (2020a), CAC (2021c)). These regulations mainly focused on the legitimacy of the news creators and the authority of their data sources.

Channels

Different from topics/issues of misinformation, the channels dimension is specially designed to capture the policy elements about the technological carriers and channels that facilitated the creation and distribution of misinformation. In recent scholarly discourse, misinformation is frequently associated with social media. It may appear that social media is a dominant issue within misinformation regulation; however, treating it as a channel can

Table 1.4 Frequency and percentage of channels elements in policy documents from the United States and China

Channels	United States		China	
	Occurrence	Percentage	Occurrence	Percentage
Algorithms	13 [less]	14.1	8	17.0
Social media	18	19.6	14	29.8
Applications other than social media	3	3.3	15	31.9
Data and online traffic	0	0.0	11	23.4
Hardware and infrastructure	4	4.3	2	4.3
Other channels	3	3.3	0	0.0

provide more insight. It is not surprising that both governments tried to regulate social media through their misinformation policies. For example, several US bills were related to social media regulation, including the *Social Media Fraud Mitigation Act* (2021). In China, CAC released *Hùliánwǎng yònghù gōngzhòng hào xìnxī fúwù guǎnlǐ guīdìng* (translated into English as the *Provisions on the Administration of Public Account Information Services of Internet Users*) (2021b), primarily for regulating social media.

However, our policy analysis revealed additional technological aspects being discussed or governed in misinformation policies, and we observed quite meaningful differences between the two governments in terms of algorithms, applications other than social media, and data and online traffic (Table 1.4).

Both governments paid attention to algorithms. In China, two general policies—*Wǎngluò xìnxī nèiróng shēngtài zhìlǐ guiding* (translated into English as *Provisions on Ecological Governance of Network Information Content*) (2020a) and *Guānyú jìnyībù yā shí wǎngzhàn píngtái xìnxī nèiróng guǎnlǐ zhǔtǐ zérèn de yìjiàn* (translated into English as *Opinions of the Cyberspace Administration of China on Further Pushing Websites and Platforms to Fulfill Their Primary Responsibility for Information Content Management*) (2021a)—forbid misusing algorithms to fabricate information. In late 2021, one more specified policy was released, the *Provisions on the Management of Algorithmic Recommendations for Internet Information Services* (2021e), to prevent the abuse and misuse of technologies in internet information services. This policy made China one of the first countries to tackle the regulations of algorithmic recommendations and deep synthesis directly. Digital service platforms were required to optimize the algorithm recommendation by prioritizing good-quality content and preventing the spread of false and harmful information. The US Congress received several bills on regulating algorithms, including the *Deep Fakes Accountability Act* (2020) and the *Algorithmic Justice and Online Platform Transparency Act* (2021). Compared to the Chinese regulations, these bills have a narrower political focus. In addition, all other policies that mentioned algorithms are very vague regarding the specific measures.

China has very specific policies regarding applications and online traffic besides social media and algorithms. A recent example is the *Wǎngluò zhíbò yíngxiāo guǎnlǐ bànfǎ (shìxíng)* (*translated into English as Measures for the Administration of Live Streaming Marketing [for Trial Implementation]*) (2021d). The CAC issued this domain-specific policy and clarified a set of forbidden behaviors, including but not limited to transaction fabrication, traffic fraud, and false information spreading, as entities or individuals using live streaming applications to participate in online commercial activities.

Agents

In this study, agents are defined as individuals, groups, or organizations that are or should be carrying certain active roles in fighting misinformation, according to government policies. This definition is broad, and we coded it with special attention because we intended to identify all of the actors whom governments considered or planned to utilize or mobilize as agents in fighting misinformation. Since we only analyzed government policy documents in this study, it is not surprising that government agencies appeared in all documents as initiators, regulators, or announcers. To capture more characteristics of government actors in dealing with misinformation, we focused on a few types and patterns of government organizations—interagencies (when multiple government agencies were involved in policymaking or actual intervention), intergovernmental actors (when government agencies in different countries were involved), local government agencies (when they were named in the policy), and special government agencies (special agencies established or primarily used to fight misinformation) (Table 1.5).

Table 1.5 Frequency and percentage of agents elements in policy documents from the United States and China

Agents	United States		China	
	Occurrence	Percentage	Occurrence	Percentage
Education institutions	8	8.70	3	6.4
Interagencies	48	52	10	21.3
Intergovernmental actors	6	6.52	0	0.0
Local government agencies	8	8.70	5	10.6
Special government agencies	10	10.87	28	59.6
Health organizations	7	7.61	1	2.1
Journalists and news organizations	9	9.78	4	8.5
Nonprofit organizations	14	15.22	9	19.1
Other agents	5	5.43	0	0.0
Private sector	9	9.78	11	23.4
Researchers, scientists and experts	10	10.87	3	6.4
Digital platforms	11	11.96	16	34.0
The public	9	9.78	7	14.9

Both governments had established or utilized special agencies in their counteractions for the prevention of misinformation. In the United States, special agencies, such as Cyberspace Solarium Commission (CSC), Global Engagement Center (GEC), Cybersecurity and Infrastructure Security Agency (CISA), National Telecommunications and Information Administration (NTIA), and the US Agency for Global Media were the notable agencies that were often involved in misinformation countermeasures, especially against foreign misinformation and related issues. The "*issues*" section cites a few reports published by GEC. However, in the policymaking arena, as seen from our data collection, the US special agencies have not been playing as critical a role as a particular Chinese government agency, the CAC, has. As the centralized Internet regulator assigned by the central government, CAC is responsible for coordinating and supervising online content regulation. More than half of the Chinese policies were issued by CAC. It also directed the implementation of policies by initiating special actions to battle misinformation behaviors.

There were other major differences between the two governments regarding the "agents" dimension. The United States appeared to have a more collaborative approach emphasizing partnership, and China's approach was more centralized. The United States stresses the collaboration of various government organizations; over half of the policy documents involved multiple agencies. The government established or suggested setting up interagency task forces and commissions, such as the National Commission on Online Platforms and the Homeland Security and Task Force on Algorithmic Processes on Online Platforms. Many bills called on multiple government agencies in different branches to take responsibility. The Chinese government policies also showed a certain degree of collaboration, such as the party-state collaboration, a few joint actions initiated by multiple agencies, and policies requiring multiple agencies to implement. However, CAC has been the predominant government agency leading the relevant policymaking.

In addition, the US policies had more actors involved than China's policies. Higher and secondary education institutions, health organizations, journalists and news organizations, researchers, scientists and experts, and community leaders were often called upon to serve in different roles for fighting misinformation—research, education, public engagement, and more. The United States emphasized public and private partnerships prominently in some of its policy documents. In addition, other countries and US allies, coded as intergovernmental actors in the analysis, were also mentioned as partners in fighting misinformation, again often in the context of foreign propaganda. In contrast, the Chinese government highly stressed the roles and responsibilities of social media platforms and various digital service providers concerning the governance and moderation of online information. They were required to develop and implement online information content ecology regulatory mechanisms to monitor unhealthy information, promote socialist core values, and cultivate a positive, healthy and optimistic online culture. For one instance, platforms were required to "regulate the set-up of topics, strictly prevent acts of malicious transmission such as stirring up hot topics, faking originality, coarseness and vulgarity, creating or spreading rumors, or aggregating negative information" (CAC, 2021a). For another example, platforms were required to monitor and assess public accounts and prevent them from fabricating subscription numbers, followers, click rates, or the number of forwards and comments (CAC, 2021b). They were also required to establish complete mechanisms for the early warning, discovery, tracing back, screening, dispelling, and elimination of online rumors and other misinformation.

Targets

The "targets" dimension in the analytical framework captures the social actors, including individuals, groups, businesses, and populations, whose behaviors the policy aims to change in certain ways. As with agents, misinformation targets also involved various stakeholders, ranging from one or a few individuals to the general public (populations in and outside of a country). Different from agents who have played or are expected to play certain roles in fighting against misinformation though, targets are treated in the policy documents as passive actors being regulated, educated, protected, punished, or treated in some other ways. Some actors, such as social media platforms, are sometimes considered both agents and targets, even in the same document.

We put the wide range of misinformation targets into three categories for easier identification—targets who are or potentially can be involved in misinformation consumption, targets who are participants in misinformation creation, and targets who may be involved in misinformation distribution. Like most other elements in this framework, these targets are not mutually exclusive; within one policy document, there can be many different targets.

In terms of consumption, both countries had multiple policies that aimed to protect different populations from the influence of misinformation or to prevent them from consuming misinformation in the future. Over half of the United States' policies mentioned the general population as current or potential misinformation consumers. The specific populations mentioned (usually briefly) in the US policies include veterans, women, racial and ethnic communities, vulnerable populations, and children. In China, there was more emphasis on specific populations, particularly those relatively vulnerable groups—children and youth, women, the elderly, low-income, and the disabled. The US policies often did not spell out what exactly should be done for the specific groups, while Chinese policies were usually more specific and targeted, and typically presented as protective and educative

Table 1.6 Frequency and percentage of targets elements in policy documents from the United States and China

Targets	United States		China	
	Occurrence	Percentage	Occurrence	Percentage
Misinformation Consumers	56	60.9	17	40.5
Content consumers	11	12.0	5	10.6
General population	49	53.3	11	23.4
Specific population(s)	11	12.0	9	19.1
Misinformation Creators	54	58.7	24	51.1
Advertisers	3	3.3	8	17.0
Foreign government(s)	33	35.9	4	8.5
Foreign individuals and organizations	24	26.1	1	2.1
Digital service users	0	0.0	5	10.6
General content creators	21	22.8	15	31.9
Misinformation Distributors	27	29.3	24	51.1
Digital platforms	26	28.3	21	44.7
Traditional media or press	3	3.3	3	6.4
Other actors being regulated	10	10.9	1	2.1

programs with the goal of empowering adults by increasing the awareness of misinformation and preventing children from accessing false and unhealthy information.

Regarding misinformation creation, both countries touched on a similar set of targets, but their weights were markedly different. Not surprisingly, the United States' policies stressed foreign actors, including foreign governments—Russia, China, Iran, etc.—and foreign individuals/organizations, who oftentimes appeared together in the same documents. In contrast, China had far fewer references to foreign actors, and when they did, the United States was often the target. The two countries' policies on advertisers and general content creators were also unlike each other. Again, the US's policies did not always spell out the specific actions of the misinformation creators, with a few exceptions. In China, a set of prescribed actions targeted various digital service users who might misuse specific digital channels or platforms for misinformation creation. The prohibited behaviors included using social live-streaming services to manipulate online traffic for click fraud, using digital synthesis services to spread false information, utilizing the internet information service for fraudulent traffic, voting, comments, and transactions, and using public accounts to fabricate untruthful information.

The two governments showed some similarities in regulating misinformation distribution. In particular, both highlighted the regulation of digital platforms. In the United States, for example, several bills mentioned regulating social media accounts for security reasons. In China, nearly half of the policies mentioned digital platforms as the main targets related to the distribution of misinformation. Compared to the United States, which primarily focused on social media platforms, Chinese policies covered a larger range of digital platforms, including both content-orientated ones and algorithm-driven ones. The former, under an umbrella term, "internet content service providers", refers to content service platforms, news and media platforms, online forums, searching, e-commerce platforms, online public accounts service, etc. Algorithm-driven platforms include algorithm recommendation service providers and deep synthesis services, which enable the creation of social bots, the fabrication of fake news, or the manipulation of search results and traffic. Also, in contrast to the United States' (proposed) policies, the Chinese policies usually included precise requirements and punishments regarding all of these different types of platforms.

Government actions

Although we identified multiple agents from the policy documents, in this chapter we only include the analysis of government actions, as limited by space. Drawing from the literature on policy design (Pal, 2014) and based on our open coding in the framework development stage, we identified four categories of policy instruments for misinformation—direct actions, expenditure-based actions, information-based actions, and policymaking actions.

Direct action by the government is usually narrowly understood as governmental agencies or their collaborative partners providing a direct service to achieve an outcome, instead of working through citizens or organizations to achieve public goals (Pal, 2014). In this study, however, it is defined as the various actions that government agencies take or plan to take to prevent or control misinformation directly. The Chinese policy documents showed more direct actions. In almost all categories (see Table 1.7 for specific actions), the Chinese policies had higher percentages than the US ones. One type of action is especially noteworthy in China—governments mobilizing citizens to file reports/complaints and handling these complaints directly. Encouraging the public to report misinformation is not unique—for example, the US' Trump administration introduced a "Tech Bias Reporting tool" to solicit "online censorship" reporting (Executive Order 13925, 2020), but citizen reporting has served as arguably one of the most effective measures in the Chinese government's rumor control.

The element of serving directly (providing information and services), is a special type of action unique to misinformation policies, and should not be confused with direct actions or information-based actions. Because of the nature of misinformation, the direct actions of governments include providing facts or correct information to counteract misinformation. Therefore, we defined *serving directly* as information, tools, or services provided directly by the government or by a third-party partnership or contract. In China, the government directly engaged in fact-checking practices by operating the state-owned Refute-the-Rumor Platform and

Table 1.7 Frequency and percentage of actions elements in policy documents from the United States and China

Actions	United States		China	
	Occurrence	Percentage	Occurrence	Percentage
Direct actions	39	42.4	29	61.7
Court actions	15	16.3	10	21.3
Direct moderation	6	6.5	16	34.0
Encouraging and handling citizen complaints	2	2.2	8	17.0
Making warning	0	0.0	4	8.5
Requirements or orders	5	5.4	9	19.1
Serving directly (providing information and services)	8	8.7	3	6.4
Shutting down business	10	10.9	11	23.4
Oversight	3	3.3	7	14.9
Expenditure-based	8	8.7	7	14.9
Appropriation or allocation	8	8.7	0	0.0
Fine	8	8.7	7	14.9
Information-based	41	44.6	23	48.9
Condemning or criticizing	7	7.6	4	8.9
Other information-based actions	10	10.9	0	0.0
Promoting media literacy	21	22.8	9	19.1
Raising awareness	23	25.0	2	4.3
Publicity[4]	0	0	15	31.9
Policymaking	43	46.7	17	36.2
Developing plans, programs, and strategies	29	31.5	9	19.1
Investigation and research	18	19.6	7	14.9
Rulemaking or lawmaking	13	14.1	2	4.3

collaborating with commercial companies to build fact-checking websites. Governments serving the public directly by providing information and services has been prevalent worldwide since the beginning of the pandemic, and the numbers in our analysis of policy documents are by no means an accurate depiction of such services, because they were not often mentioned in the policy documents we collected.

Expenditure-based actions consist of both affirmative and negative actions. Some of the United States' policy documents mention expenditure-based actions, such as congressional appropriations, agency budget justifications, and awarding grants, for the purpose of supporting various governmental and nongovernmental misinformation countermeasures. None of the Chinese policies we analyzed, however, mentioned such actions. This does not mean China did not have this type of action; rather, this was possibly due to the distinctive government financial practices and reflects another limitation of our data collection and document analysis. In Chinese policies, fines were widely adopted as an administrative punishment to prevent misinformation creation and sharing.

Information-based actions are efforts to influence people through the transfer of knowledge, communication of reasoned argument, and moral persuasion to achieve a policy result (Vedung & van der Doelen, 1998, p. 103). As with many other governments, the United States and China both prioritized promoting media and information literacy programs. They were also similar in issuing proclamations or announcements that criticized other countries' disinformation behavior. But the differences between the two countries are apparent. First, more of the United States policies were aimed at or emphasized raising the public's awareness of misinformation. Second, the United States had more types of information-based actions, such as making suggestions, issuing advisories, reaffirming certain values, expressing concerns, calling on other governments to correct misinformation, etc. In contrast, China's actions appeared more coherent and uniform. Third, a general observation is the diplomatic nature of these information-based actions—blaming other countries, consistent with the United States' overall emphasis on foreign disinformation. In comparison, China's emphasis on publicity, with a focus on mainstream values and themes, indicated a priority of domestic control on public opinions—often referred to as unified thought or unity of thinking.

In this study, policymaking is a category we used to capture the purpose or proposition of certain government actions. These actions were more evident in the United States, since many policies demanded or suggested government agencies or other agents perform research to understand misinformation, and make tools to prevent its dissemination, develop plans to battle misinformation in its various aspects and sectors, and make laws or rules to regulate misinformation-related issues. Overall, the United States' policies were more tentative and investigative. They had much more law-making and rulemaking requests than China did, possibly because China already had quite comprehensive, detailed, and mature laws and regulations to command and prohibit these behaviors.

Discussion and Conclusion: A Framework for the Future

As information and communication technologies are fast developing and widely used, the scope and spreading speed of misinformation are also increasing. Today, the misinformation phenomenon has expanded from a pre-COVID politics-focused social issue to a more pervasive social challenge. Governments worldwide have adopted or are designing a variety of regulatory strategies and tools to cope with this challenge. To understand the complexity and nuanced realities of government misinformation regulatory practices, in this study we developed an analytical framework by connecting policy design studies and the social informatics perspectives. Our framework emphasized two aspects of misinformation policies. First, we identified agents, actions, and target groups. These essential components of policy design reflect the logic of governmental regulations that aim to change human behaviors. In addition, drawing from the social informatics tradition, we incorporated several sociopolitical dimensions related to misinformation—the contexts where misinformation policies are devised; the specific issues, topics, and forms of misinformation; and the channels for its creation and spread. We demonstrated misinformation in today's information environment as a sociotechnical phenomenon with social groups/human actors/stakeholders, ICT, and information itself, and proved the usefulness of these analytical dimensions from policy analysis.

Methodologically, we employed the content analysis and comparative case study methods as a combined analytical approach to unpacking government-initiated misinformation-fighting policies. Additionally, we systematically collected misinformation-related policies in each country and reported both numerical results and qualitative descriptions. This approach fills research gaps in the existing literature that had mainly focused on single cases, and lacked systematic research design and data collection for comparative work.

Empirically, we tested this tech-socio-political framework in the United States and Chinese contexts separately. Our findings suggested that the differences between those two countries are much more than the ideological debate, which is predominantly discussed or taken for granted in the existing literature. As shown in our coding scheme of "issues", "contexts", and "channels", misinformation regulation is embedded in the broader social, technological, and political context. In addition, different from previous misinformation policy studies that tended to focus on either social media or misinformation content, this study revealed and identified a wide range of elements in the misinformation policy content, which can provide useful evidence for policymakers. The complexity of the contexts, issues, and social norms determines the diversity and complexity of the misinformation policies and policymaking in different settings. For example, through the United States-China comparison, we found that, while political actors in the United States are still proposing and discussing the adoption of misinformation-related policies, the Chinese policies related to misinformation have been embedded in the comprehensive and sophisticated ICT regulatory and legislative system under centralized control.

Admittedly, we found the policies in the two countries fit well with their well-known, respective political narratives. The US policies have a strong political (especially international relationship) focus, and their (proposed) actions are often diplomatic in nature. China's policies are more domestic-focused and often mention "publicity" of mainstream values and "directing" public opinions. However, quite different from the stereotypical views of the Chinese information policies, we found that the Chinese government's regulatory actions regarding misinformation are not merely about censorship (even though "purifying" online discourses is one of the main components). Rather, they are more frequently used to protect and promote their digital-driven domestic economy. These results echoed Creemers' (2017) statement that digital technology is placed at the center of an ambitious agenda for comprehensive reform of social and economic governance in China. Correspondingly, digital platforms have been placed at the center of the misinformation regulations and have played a dual role. On the one hand, they are the policy targets to be governed in the existing regulatory framework. On the other hand, they are the agents of regulators to take responsibility for online content moderation and control. The pressures from the government will probably make the platforms in China act differently from their counterparts in the United States, which are still enjoying autonomy and conducting content moderation voluntarily or for profit.

This framework is also useful for identifying nuanced differences between countries that are at different stages of policymaking. The majority of US policies are still in the discussion, negotiation, or planning stages. The regulatory system of social media platforms is still in its infancy. In contrast, China's policies are much more mature. The Chinese government has established a sophisticated legislative system consisting of overarching laws and domain-specific policies that cover the regulatory practices related to misinformation and evolving digital platforms.

This United States-China comparison sheds light on the potential of our framework. It can serve as an analytical tool to identify nuanced characteristics of misinformation regulation in different countries. Built upon this, we can deepen our understanding of and expand our knowledge of this global phenomenon.

Based on the analytical framework and findings presented in this chapter, we conceptualize misinformation policy analysis using Figure 1.1. This model captures the main analytical dimensions and can help researchers understand the misinformation phenomenon from a policymaking point of view. As stated in the *Methodology* section, agents and targets often overlap, but this overlap is not shown in the diagram. This conceptual model presents a sociotechnical network beyond loosely connected components, as it reveals some of the relationships among the components. Although this current revelation of these relationships may be too rudimentary at this point, it provides a start for future investigation.

Our framework is neither individual behavior-focused at a micro-level, nor the macro-level discussion of regulatory models per se. Instead, this meso-level framework expands information distribution-focused studies by embracing both human and nonhuman agents and their related context, situated from the perspective of governments. This overarching framework might guide researchers to pursue questions in different geographic settings through various element combinations. By unpacking the *context, issues, and actions*, we can identify the foci and priorities related to distinct regulatory systems. What matters to the governments

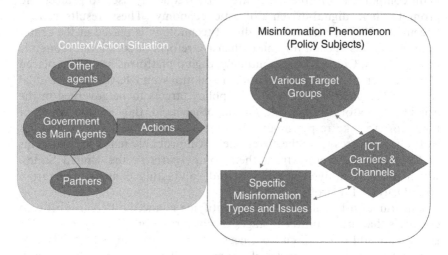

Figure 1.1 Misinformation policy analytical conceptual model.

most as they confront such social challenges? What are the underlying logic and core values of the regulation? For instance, domestic-focused and diplomacy-focused misinformation regulation in China and the United States implied divergent concerns about the consequences of misinformation. Under what kind of conditions do governments design different regulatory actions? What does it mean if similar misinformation issues are regulated differently in different countries? Next, unfolding the *agents and target groups* might also expand our understanding of how stakeholders engage in the regulation and the boundaries among them. For instance, we could further examine what kind of roles digital platforms play, as they might be both the agents and targets related to certain issues and in certain contexts. Moreover, the complexity of misinformation increased because of the diversified material features of technology. We use *channels* to indicate technology characteristics in the framework. One relevant question is how different technological carriers affect the misinformation spread and the consequences. Last, regulations include a set of practice-based activities. These elements might also provide policymakers with toolkits to evaluate practices in different regions for developing and optimizing their own responses to misinformation.

There are some limitations to this study. First, we selected two extreme cases in this study to test the feasibility and flexibility of our analytical framework. The trade-off of this approach is that the entire framework is built upon case-specific elements. Thus, more studies in different countries are necessary to verify the usefulness of this framework in a broader context and enhance its robustness. Second, we should notice the limitation caused by the difficulty in data collection and comparability. Governmental decision-making data are seldom open to the public in China. The data limitation might have constrained our understanding and comparison of policymaking. For future studies, it is critical to develop more feasible and compatible methods for data collection. Last but not the least, limited by space, we only report the findings regarding major actors and their actions. The nuanced differences between the two policy systems can be described and discussed in more detail.

Notes

1 We thank the first author's students in her Government Information Sources course for their help in the initial filtering of about 900 of these documents. We also thank her graduate assistants Elan Sandler and Joseph Winberry for searching and filtering several hundred of these documents.
2 GEC is an agency under the United States Department of State. It was established through the collaboration of multiple agencies, including the United States Department of State and the United States Department of Defense, according to the *2017 National Defense Authorization Act*, bipartisan legislation that requires government agencies to fight against propaganda from foreign governments.
3 Public accounts refer to verified official accounts used by an entity or individual. They are public in the sense of 'public figures'.
4 Propaganda may be a more direct translation of the Chinese term "宣传". We chose another frequently used term, publicity, when coding Chinese documents to avoid potential negative connotation in the English language context.

References

Abdali, S. (2022, March 25). Multi-modal misinformation detection: Approaches, challenges and opportunities. *arXiv*. https://doi.org/10.48550/arXiv.2203.13883

Adams, T. (2017, June 16). AI-powered social bots. *arXiv*. https://doi.org/10.48550/arXiv.1706.05143

Alam, F., Cresci, S., Chakraborty, T., Silvestri, F., Dimitrov, D., Martino, G.D.S., Shaar, S., Firooz, H., & Nakov, P. (2021). A survey on multimodal disinformation detection (arXiv:2103.12541). *arXiv*. 10.48550/arXiv.2103.12541

Altheide, D.L. (1987). Ethnographic content analysis. *Qualitative Sociology, 10*(1), 65–77. https://www.public.asu.edu/~atdla/ethnographiccontentanalysis.pdf

Altheide, D.L. (1996). *Qualitative media analysis*. Thousand Oaks, CA: Sage Publications.

Anti-CCP Espionage via Social Media Act, H. R. 3057, 117th Cong. (2021). https://www.congress.gov/bill/117th-congress/house-bill/3057

Algorithmic Justice and Online Platform Transparency Act, H.R.3611, 117th Cong. (2021). https://www.congress.gov/bill/117th-congress/house-bill/3611

Associated Press (2022, April 25). Elon Musk buys Twitter for $44 billon, will privatize company. *Wttw.com*. https://news.wttw.com/2022/04/25/elon-musk-buys-twitter-44-billion-will-privatize-company

Baade, B. (2018). Fake news and international law. *European Journal of International Law, 29*(4), 1357–1376. 10.1093/ejil/chy071

Cassese, E.C., Farhart, C.E., & Miller, J.M. (2020). Gender differences in COVID-19 conspiracy theory beliefs. *Politics & Gender, 16*(4), 1009–1018. 10.1017/S1743923 X20000409

CBS Sacramento. (2018, September 27). Governor Brown vetoes fake news bill, calls it 'not necessary'. *CBS Sacramento.* https://sacramento.cbslocal.com/2018/09/27/california-fake-news-bill-veto/.

Chayka, K. (2022, March 3). Watching the world's "first Tiktok war". *New Yorker.* https://www.newyorker.com/culture/infinite-scroll/watching-the-worlds-first-tiktok-war

Creemers, R. (2017). Cyber China: Upgrading propaganda, public opinion work and social management for the twenty-first century. *Journal of Contemporary China, 26*(103), 85–100. 10.1080/10670564.2016.1206281

China's State Council Information Office. (2020). *White Paper: Fighting COVID-19: China in Action.* https://english.www.gov.cn/news/topnews/202006/07/content_WS5edc559ac6d066592a449030.html

CNN Editorial Research. (2016, December 26). *2016 presidential campaign hacking fast facts.* CNN. https://www.cnn.com/2016/12/26/us/2016-presidential-campaign-hacking-fast-facts/index.html

COVID-19 Misinformation and Disinformation Task Force Act of 2020, S. 4499, 116th Cong. (2020). https://www.congress.gov/bill/116th-congress/senate-bill/4499

COVID-19 Disinformation Research and Reporting Act, S.913, 117th Cong. (2021). https://www.congress.gov/bill/117th-congress/senate-bill/913

Cyberspace Administration of China. (2020a). *Wǎngluò xìnxī nèiróng shēngtài zhìlǐ guiding.* http://www.cac.gov.cn/2019-12/20/c_1578375159509309.htm

Cyberspace Administration of China. (2020b). *Guójiā wǎng xìn bàn quánmiàn bùshǔ jiā dà "zì méitǐ" guīfàn guǎnlǐ gōngzuò.* http://www.cac.gov.cn/2020-07/29/c_1597578778783428.htm

Cyberspace Administration of China. (2021a). *Guānyú jìnyībù yā shí wǎngzhàn píngtái xìnxī nèiróng guǎnlǐ zhǔtǐ zérèn de yìjiàn.* http://www.cac.gov.cn/2021-09/15/c_1633296790051342.htm

Cyberspace Administration of China. (2021b). *Hùliánwǎng yònghù Gōngzhòng Zhànghào Xìnxī fúwù guǎnlǐ guiding.* http://www.cac.gov.cn/2021-01/22/c_161288 7880656609.htm

Cyberspace Administration of China. (2021c). *Zhōngyāng wǎng xìn bàn bùshǔ "qīnglǎng·dǎjí chuánbò zàojiǎ, hēi gōngguān, wǎngluò shuǐ jūn" zhuānxiàng xíngdòng.* http://www.cac.gov.cn/2021-12/23/c_1641859284732677.htm

Cyberspace Administration of China. (2021d). *Wǎngluò zhíbò yíngxiāo guǎnlǐ bànfǎ (shìxíng).* http://www.cac.gov.cn/2021-04/22/c_1620670982794847.htm

Cyberspace Administration of China. (2021e). *Hùliánwǎng xìnxī fúwù suànfǎ tuījiàn guǎnlǐ guiding.* http://www.gov.cn/zhengce/zhengceku/2022-01/04/content_5666429.htm

de Gregorio, G., & Radu, R. (2019, November 24). Counter-disinformation around the world: Comparing state actions [Conference session]. *2019 Global Internet Governance Academic Network Annual Symposium, Berlin, Germany.* https://www.giga-net.org/2019symposiumPapers/25_DeGregorio_Counter-disinformation-around-the-World.pdf

Deep Fakes Accountability Act, H.R.3230, 116th Cong. (2020). https://www.congress.gov/bill/116th-congress/house-bill/3230

Durach, F., Bargaoanu, A., & Nastasiu, C. (2020). Tackling disinformation: EU regulation of the digital space. *Romanian Journal of European Affairs, 20*(1), 5–20.

Dye, T.R. (1976). *Policy analysis: What governments do, why they do it, and what difference it makes.* Tuscaloosa, AL: University of Alabama Press.

European Union. (2018). *A draft code of practice on online disinformation.* https://digital-strategy.ec.europa.eu/en/library/draft-code-practice-online-disinformation

European Union. (2022). *The digital services act package.* https://digital-strategy.ec.europa.eu/en/policies/digital-services-act-package

Exec. Order No. 13848, 83 FR 46843 (September 12, 2018). https://www.govinfo.gov/app/details/DCPD-201800593

Exec. Order No. 13925, 85 FR 34079 (June 2, 2020). https://www.govinfo.gov/app/details/DCPD-202000404

European Commission. (2020). *Assessment of the code of practice on disinformation – Achievements and areas for further improvement.* https://digital-strategy.ec.europa.eu/en/library/assessment-code-practice-disinformation-achievements-and-areas-further-improvement

Funke, D., & Flamini, D. (n.d.). A guide to anti-misinformation actions around the world. *Poynter.org.* from https://www.poynter.org/ifcn/anti-misinformation-actions/

Gerbic, P. & Stacey, E. (2005). A purposive approach to content analysis: Designing analytical frameworks. *The Internet and Higher Education, 8*, 45–59.

Gillespie, T. (2010). The politics of 'platforms'. *New Media & Society, 12*(3), 347–364. 10.1177/1461444809342738

Gillespie, T. (2018). Platforms are not intermediaries. *Georgetown Law Technology Review, 2*(2), 198–216.

Girard, P., Mohr, R.D., Deller, S.C., & Halstead, J.M. (2009). Public-private partnerships and cooperative agreements in municipal service delivery. *International Journal of Public Administration, 32*(5), 370–392. 10.1080/01900690902827267

Glaser, B.G. (1978). *Advances in the methodology of grounded theory: Theoretical sensitivity.* Mill Valley, CA: The Sociology Press.

Glaser, B., & Strauss, A. (1967). *The discovery of grounded theory strategies of qualitative research.* London, UK: Wiedenfeld and Nicholson.

Global Engagement Center. (2020). *Pillars of Russia's disinformation and propaganda ecosystem.* US Department of State. https://www.state.gov/wp-content/uploads/2020/08/Pillars-of-Russia%E2%80%99s-Disinformation-and-Propaganda-Ecosystem_08-04-20.pdf

Global Engagement Center. (2022). *Kremlin-funded media: RT and Sputnik's role in Russia's disinformation and propaganda ecosystem.* US Department of State. https://www.state.gov/wp-content/uploads/2022/01/Kremlin-Funded-Media_January_update-19.pdf

Gorwa, R. (2019). What is platform governance? *Information, Communication & Society, 22*(6), 854–871. 10.1080/1369118X.2019.1573914

Hatred going viral in 'dangerous epidemic of misinformation' during COVID-19 pandemic. (2020, April 14). UN News. https://news.un.org/en/story/2020/04/1061682

Health Misinformation Act of 2021, S.2448, 117th Cong. (2021). https://www.congress.gov/bill/117th-congress/senate-bill/2448

Honest Ads Act, S.1989, 115th Cong. (2018). https://www.congress.gov/bill/115th-congress/senate-bill/1989

Hossain, T., Logan IV, R.L., Ugarte, A., Matsubara, Y., Young, S., & Singh, S. (2020). COVIDLies: Detecting COVID-19 misinformation on social media. *Proceedings of the 1st Workshop on NLP for COVID-19 (Part 2)*. EMNLP 2020, Online.

Howlett, M. (2011). *Designing Public Policies: Principles and Instruments*. New York: Routledge.

Humprecht, E. (2019). Where 'fake news' flourishes: A comparison across four Western democracies. *Information, Communication & Society, 22*(13), 1973–1988. 10.1080/1369118X.2018.1474241

Imhoff, R., & Lamberty, P. (2020). A bioweapon or a hoax? The link between distinct conspiracy beliefs about the coronavirus disease (COVID-19) outbreak and pandemic behavior. *Social Psychological and Personality Science, 11*(8), 1110–1118. 10.1177/1948550620934692

Jaeger, P.T., & Taylor, N.G. (2019). *Foundations of information policy*. Chicago, IL: ALA Neal-Schuman.

Kling, R., Rosenbaum, H., & Sawyer, S. (2005). *Understanding and communicating social informatics: A framework for studying and teaching the human contexts of information and communication technologies*. Information Today, Inc.

Kolluri, N.L., & Murthy, D. (2021). CoVerifi: A COVID-19 news verification system. *Online Social Networks and Media, 22*, 100123. 10.1016/j.osnem.2021.100123

Magnier, M. (2015, June 1). China's internet police step out of the shadows. *The Wall Street Journal*. https://www.wsj.com/articles/BL-CJB-26989

Miller, J.M. (2020). Psychological, political, and situational factors combine to boost COVID-19 conspiracy theory beliefs. *Canadian Journal of Political Science/ Revue Canadienne de Science Politique, 53*(2), 327–334. 10.1017/S000842392 000058X

National Commission on Online Platforms and Homeland Security Act, H.R.4782, 116th Cong. (2020). https://www.congress.gov/bill/116th-congress/house-bill/4782

National Intelligence Council. (2021). *Foreign threats to the 2020 US federal election*. Office of the Director of National Intelligence. https://www.dni.gov/files/ODNI/ documents/assessments/ICA-declass-16MAR21.pdf

Neuendorf, K.A. (2002). *The content analysis guidebook*. Thousand Oaks, CA: Sage Publications.

No Social Media Accounts for Terrorist and State Sponsors of Terrorism Act, H.R.1543, 117th Cong. (2021). https://www.congress.gov/bill/117th-congress/house-bill/1543

Notice: Continuation of the National Emergency with Respect to Foreign Interference in or Undermining Public Confidence in United States Elections, 84 FR 48039 (September 11, 2019). https://www.govinfo.gov/app/details/FR-2019-09-11/2019-19849

Notice: Continuation of the National Emergency with Respect to Foreign Interference in or Undermining Public Confidence in the United States Elections, 85 FR 56469 (September 11, 2020). https://www.govinfo.gov/app/details/FR-2020-09-11/2020-20315

Notice: Continuation of the National Emergency with Respect to Foreign Interference in or Undermining Public Confidence in United States Elections, 86

FR 50601 (September 9, 2021). https://www.govinfo.gov/app/details/FR-2021-09-09/2021-19625

Office of the Surgeon General (OSG). (2021). Confronting health misinformation: The U.S. Surgeon General's advisory on building a healthy information environment. https://www.hhs.gov/sites/default/files/surgeon-general-misinformation-advisory.pdf

Ostrom, E. (2005). *Understanding institutional diversity*. Princeton, NJ: Princeton University Press.

Pal, L. (2014). *Beyond policy analysis: Public issue management in turbulent times* (5th edition). Nelson College Indigenous.

Park Advisors. (2019). *Weapons of mass distraction: Foreign state-sponsored disinformation in the digital age*. US Department of State. https://www.state.gov/wp-content/uploads/2019/05/Weapons-of-Mass-Distraction-Foreign-State-Sponsored-Disinformation-in-the-Digital-Age.pdf

Pielemeier, J. (2020). Disentangling disinformation: What makes regulating disinformation so difficult? *Utah Law Review, 4*, 917–940.

Powers, S. & Kounalakis, M. (2017). *Can public diplomacy survive the internet? Bots, echo chambers, and disinformation*. The US Advisory Commission on Public Diplomacy. https://www.state.gov/wp-content/uploads/2019/05/2017-ACPD-Internet.pdf

Protect Against Public Safety Disinformation Act, H.R.7282, 116th Cong. (2020). https://www.congress.gov/bill/116th-congress/house-bill/7282

Protecting Democracy from Disinformation Act, H.R.7012, 116th Cong. (2020). https://www.congress.gov/bill/116th-congress/house-bill/7012

Pummerer, L., Böhm, R., Lilleholt, L., Winter, K., Zettler, I., & Sassenberg, K. (2022). Conspiracy theories and their societal effects during the COVID-19 pandemic. *Social Psychological and Personality Science, 13*(1), 49–59. 10.1177/194855 06211000217

Radu, R. (2020). Fighting the 'Infodemic': Legal responses to COVID-19 disinformation. *Social Media + Society, 6*(3). 10.1177/2056305120948190

Rochefort, A. (2020). Regulating social media platforms: A comparative policy analysis. *Communication Law and Policy, 25*(2), 225–260.

Rodrigues, U.M., & Xu, J. (2020). Regulation of COVID-19 fake news infodemic in China and India. *Media International Australia, 177*(1), 125–131. 10.1177/132 9878X20948202

Schmitt, S. (2012). Comparative approaches to the study of public policy-making. In E. Araral et al. (Eds.) *Routledge Handbook of Public Policy*. London, UK: Taylor & Francis Group.

Schneider, A., & Ingram, H. (1990). Behavioral assumptions of policy tools. *The Journal of Politics, 52*(2), 510–529. 10.2307/2131904

Security Clearance Act, H.R.353, 117th Cong. (2021). https://www.congress.gov/bill/117th-congress/house-bill/353

Shattock, E. (2021). Self-regulation 2:0? A critical reflection of the European fight against disinformation. *Harvard Kennedy School Misinformation Review*. 10.37016/mr-2020-73

Shao, C., Ciampaglia, G.L., Varol, O., Yang, K., Flammini, A., & Menczer, F. (2018). The spread of low-credibility content by social bots. *Nature Communications, 9*(1), 4787. 10.1038/s41467-018-06930-7

Social Media Fraud Mitigation Act, H.R.4654, 117th Cong. (2021). https://www. congress.gov/bill/117th-congress/house-bill/4654

State Council Information Office of China. (2020). *Fighting COVID-19: China in Action* [White Paper]. https://english.www.gov.cn/news/topnews/202006/07/ content_WS5edc559ac6d066592a449030.html

Tenove, C. (2020). Protecting democracy from disinformation: Normative threats and policy responses. *The International Journal of Press/Politics, 25*(3), 517–537. https://doi.org/10.1177/1940161220918740

The Guardian. (2017, October 30). Facebook, Google and Twitter grilled by Congress over Russian meddling. *The Guardian.* https://www.theguardian.com/ technology/live/2017/oct/31/facebook-google-twitter-congress-russian-election-meddling-live

US Department of Justice, & US Department of Homeland Security. (2021). *Key findings and recommendations from the Joint Report of the Department of Justice and the Department of Homeland Security on Foreign Interference Targeting Election Infrastructure or Political Organization, Campaign, or Candidate Infrastructure Related to the 2020 US Federal Elections.* https://www.justice. gov/opa/press-release/file/1376761/download

Van Dijck, J. (2020). Seeing the forest for the trees: Visualizing platformization and its governance. *New Media & Society,* 1–19. https://doi.org/10.1177/1461444 820940293

Vedung, E., & van der Doelen, F.C.J. (1998). The sermon: Information programs in the public policy process: Choice, effects and evaluation. In M.-L. Bemelmans-Videc, R.C. Rist, & E. Vedung (Eds.), *Carrots, sticks, and sermons: Policy instruments and their evaluation* (pp. 103–128). New Brunswick, New Jersey and London: Transaction Publishers.

Vériter, S.L., Bjola, C., & Koops, J.A. (2020). Tackling COVID-19 disinformation: Internal and external challenges for the European Union. *The Hague Journal of Diplomacy, 15*(4), 569–582. 10.1163/1871191X-BJA10046

Vosoughi, S., Roy, D., & Aral, S. (2018). The spread of true and false news online. *Science, 359,* 1146–1151. 10.1126/science.aap9559

Walker V.S., & Walsh, R.E. (2020). *Public diplomacy and the new "old" war: Countering state-sponsored disinformation.* U.S. Advisory Commission on Public Diplomacy. https://www.state.gov/wp-content/uploads/2020/09/Public-Diplomacy-and-the-New-Old-War-Countering-State-Sponsored-Disinformation.pdf

Wimberly, C. (2021). The birth of the post-truth era: A genealogy of corporate public relations, propaganda, and Trump. *The Journal of Speculative Philosophy, 35*(2), 130–146. 10.5325/jspecphil.35.2.0130

Williamson, S., & Magaloni, B. (2020). Legislatures and policy making in Authoritarian regimes. *Comparative Political Studies, 53*(9), 1525–1543. 10.1177/ 0010414020912288

Xi, J. (2014, February 27). Bǎ wǒguó cóng wǎngluò dàguó jiànshè chéngwéi wǎngluò qiángguó. *Xinhua net.* http://news.xinhuanet.com/politics/2014-02/27/c_ 119538788.htm

Xi, J. (2020, February 5). Quánmiàn tígāo shīgōng fúwù zhīhuī nénglì, wèi qǐyè tígōng ānquán bǎozhàng. *Xinhua net.* http://www.xinhuanet.com/politics/leaders/ 2020-02/05/c_1125535239.htm

Yang, G. (2012). A Chinese internet? History, practice, and globalization. *Chinese Journal of Communication, 5*(1), 49–54.

Zhou, X., & Zafarani, R. (2020). A survey of fake news: Fundamental theories, detection methods, and opportunities. *ACM Computing Surveys, 53*(5), 1–40. 10.1145/3395046

Zhu, X., Yang, S., & Allen, S. (2022, January). A comparison of false-information policies in five countries before and during the COVID-19 Pandemic. *In Proceedings of the 55th Hawaii International Conference on System Sciences.* 2629–2638. https://hdl.handle.net/10125/7966

2 Governing Privacy as Contexts Overlap during Crisis

Madelyn Rose Sanfilippo and Chang Liu

Introduction

Throughout the COVID-19 pandemic, schools, clinics, businesses, churches, and community organizations have struggled to provide services, support social interaction and communication, and simply make things work, depending on ever-changing sociotechnical systems and public health guidelines. Technological adoption—often of technologies previously unfamiliar to their users—supported social and interpersonal interactions to a greater extent than ever before, to achieve safe social distancing. Parents were encouraged to download apps they had never heard of before to communicate with teachers; they were told, "Don't worry; it's really easy to use!" Elderly parishioners made Facebook accounts to try to stream church services. Overworked and overexposed nurses struggled to keep track of which video chat each patients' family used to communicate, as hospitals and clinics were locked down to avoid visitors' contracting or further spreading the out-of-control virus. These brief video conversations were often the only way families could say goodbye to dying loved ones through one last Zoom call. Survivors later used the same account to host distant and inadequate celebrations of life, to conduct work meetings, or to attend online classes.

As many people lived and worked at a social distance over the past two years, using technology to connect to one another in all aspects of their lives, contexts of use are increasingly conflated or collapsed (Marwick & boyd, 2011). Often, we speak of or study how social norms in discrete domains or contexts impact the use of technology, or expectations of privacy within that context (e.g., Nissenbaum, 2009; Schonscheck, 1997). For example, we have specific privacy expectations or preferences with respect to health or education, work, or social interactions. We make an important differentiation between work and social life, including how we conceive of the balance between them. As depicted in Figure 2.1a, we imagine and govern them as separate spheres.

However, in the pandemic, these contexts increasingly overlap, as for example when considering an individual's need to disclose medical information in order to obtain permission to work from home or to gain

DOI: 10.4324/9781003231769-4

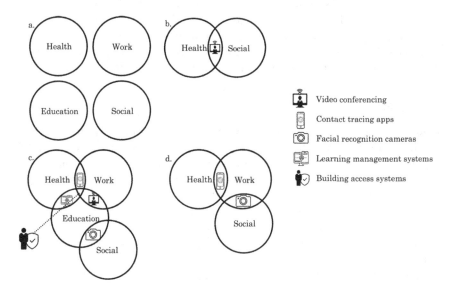

Figure 2.1 Overlapping contexts.

clearance to enter buildings, as depicted in Figures 2.1c and 2.1d. These are not simply matters of socially important contact tracing, including in work contexts, but rather are a merging of health and work contexts (Riva et al., 2021). Additionally, for students and academics, as well as all employees and staff on university campuses and in schools worldwide, the boundaries are blurred with respect to educational information and privacy norms (Paris et al., 2021), as in the complex and overlapping arrangements seen in Figure 2.1c.

In many places, the contextual complexity increases as we all engage in work, health, education, and social activities, using the same devices, in the same friendliest-to-video-conferencing spaces in our homes, and challenging expectations and norms about the privacy of our homes in the process. In this sense, previous norms do not necessarily guide us toward what good governance might be, with respect to ICTs (Dwivedi et al., 2020; Kant & Norman, 2021). In this sense, the pandemic not only raises normative contextual boundary management challenges, but also conflates and collapses contexts, introducing new normative challenges. Emergency circumstances enhance and exacerbate constraints, as well as change the nature of ICT use and further challenge status quo efforts to regulate data and privacy within contexts, already limited in efficacy by the nature of social digital technologies (Sanfilippo et al., 2020).

As the COVID-19 pandemic unfolded and dependence upon digital infrastructures increased, these normative challenges arose, and the general public learned a lot about the fragility and limitations of both platforms and governance of ICTs. Suddenly people's social lives and healthcare needs were met using the same platforms, which didn't necessarily differentiate between the privacy nuances of specific information types or contexts, as illustrated in Figure 2.1b. This chapter will explore privacy governance and enforcement in the domains of health, education, and labor.

Background

Under emergency circumstances, privacy is especially important to consider. While we both anticipate expanded information flows, especially to relief organizations, and embrace the promises of ICTs to facilitate improved responses, we also recognize the sensitive nature of information about victims of natural disasters, pandemics, and other emergencies such as fires or crimes. The general public expects that information is shared to help these individuals, and that we safeguard against inappropriate disclosures in order to protect vulnerable individuals from information harms in the future.

Privacy during and around crises is thus conceived of in terms of contextual integrity. We therefore understand privacy as the appropriate flow of personal information in context, as defined by contextual norms (Nissenbaum, 2009).

If, for the purposes of this discussion, we focus on contextual governance in the United States, we might look to regulation as a guide for what practices ought to be, as they are typically less extensive and more directed than norms, as well as more path-dependent. Generally, the Privacy Act tells us how federal agencies and contractors must engage with and protect personal information, but says little about platforms and practices for non-civil service interactions. Instead, regulations at the national level provide some targeted interventions, including the Family Educational Rights and Privacy Act (FERPA) for the educational context, and the Health Insurance Portability and Accountability Act (HIPAA) for the health context, while the Children's Online Privacy Protection Act (COPPA) intersects with both in protecting children's privacy. Yet it is the complex patchwork system at the state and local level which provides more interesting and extensive interventions.

We also must look beyond regulation, as governance is fundamentally an assemblage of institutions that are at once intentional and unintentional, formal and informal. This chapter builds upon the social informatics conceptualization of assemblage (e.g., Davenport, 2008; Jarrahi et al., 2021; Meyer et al., 2019) to offer an applied conceptualization of governance assemblages, in order to address the ways in which design, management, infrastructure, use, practice, and regulation all intersect to impact privacy as experienced by people, going beyond how privacy governance is defined on the books, in theory.

Recent targeted state regulations, like the California Consumer Privacy Act (CCPA), formalize rules about privacy and address current technology as intended, while legacy regulations might have unintended impacts or less impact over time, as their enforcement with respect to modern technology and information flows must be reinterpreted. Similarly, while systems often encode norms or rules to address privacy objectives intentionally, they often have unintended privacy implications because of informal, unsystematized choices made in their development or administration. Another relevant governance example to consider is how management choices, particularly with respect to educational data, have intentional but informal impact.

In this sense, we must conceive of governance both as a hierarchy of institutions, in the political-economic sense (e.g., Crawford & Ostrom, 1995), and as an assemblage of laws, norms, markets, and architecture (e.g., Lessig, 1999), in order to understand fully the often unpredictable and inequitable outcomes associated with governance in sociotechnical systems. We must recognize that, while regulations are often path-dependent, other forms of governance are not so entrenched. While technology, and by extension code as law (Lessig, 1999), evolves at a fast pace, the governance assemblages, including markets and norms, entail complex institutional misalignment that leads to externalities, unintended consequences, and gaps at any given time. This is exacerbated by the interactions resulting from crossing individual jurisdictions, when exploring the reality of information flows in a global economy. For example, requirements under the General Data Protection Regulation (GDPR) do not align with those under the CCPA, leading to challenges in international applications of Silicon Valley-based ICTs in Europe.

Governance interventions reflect a hierarchy of institutional structure, depicted in Table 2.1, including underlying strategies as approaches toward particular objectives, norms as strategies embedded with modal language to enforce social pressure or to hedge, and rules as norms enforced with clear consequences for violation (Crawford & Ostrom, 1995). At any given point in time, multiple institutions of different strengths may address the same dilemma or information resource. Further efforts to operationalize (rules-in-use) the rules that are formally written in law or policy (rules-on-the-books) for specific applications may yield results that diverge from the original intent of the rules. We must also recognize that, in an extended state of emergency, the discrepancies between rules-on-the-books and rules-in-use (e.g., Frischmann et al., 2014) are greater than ever, especially around the governance of privacy and technology, both of which evolve at a faster pace than their regulation or oversight elasticity (Sanfilippo et al., 2018; 2021).

Table 2.1 provides an example through which we both see how to apply the grammar and understand how strategies can be institutionalized into norms, and norms can subsequently be institutionalized into rules. We begin with the strategy that health insurers share an individual's personally identifiable information (PII) with contracted third parties when they are processing claims, or when the information is necessary for services. As we coalesce around these strategic practices and reach consensus, we modify

Table 2.1 Institutional grammar as applied to privacy governance

Institutional Hierarchy			Component	Definition	Example
			Attributes	To whom does this apply? Individual, organizational variables	Health Insurers
		Strategies	Aims	Specific actions	Share an individual's PII with contracted third-parties
	Norms		Conditions	When, where, how aims apply	When they are processing claims; when the information is necessary for services
Rules			Modality	Operators implying pressure (deontics) or hedging Examples: Permitted, obliged, forbidden, may, etc.	May only
			Consequences	Sanctions for noncompliance; penalties in absence of consent	Or else fines ($100–$25,000) will be applied per violation

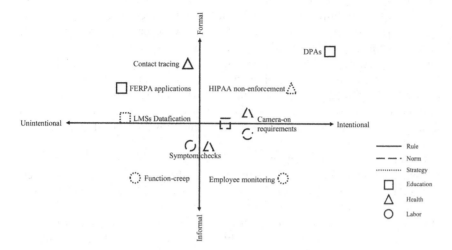

Figure 2.2 Sociotechnical governance assemblages.

this strategy to say that health insurers MAY ONLY share an individual's PII with contracted third parties when they are processing claims or when the information is necessary for services. Eventually, we enforce this norm by appending it with a clear consequence to establish the rule: health insurers may only share an individual's PII with contracted third parties, when they are processing claims or when the information is necessary for services, or else fines ($100–$25,000) will be applied per each violation.

We can apply this structured approach to analyze privacy governance of ICTs used in multiple domains during the pandemic, maintaining the ability to make comparisons. The conclusion of this chapter maps case analysis and institutional assemblages onto this typology in Figure 2.2.

Cases

Healthcare

The first case in which we examine contextual privacy governance challenges is a product of the significant changes in medical interactions during the pandemic. As COVID-19 outbreaks spread around the world in early 2020, telemedicine was more rapidly and widely adopted than at any previous point in history, beginning with its expansion in China in January 2020 (Hong et al., 2020) and spreading worldwide (Ohannessian et al., 2020).

This broad global trend was also evident within the United States, with a rapid shift toward medical consultations via phone or video-conferencing, concurrent with the March 2020 shutdowns (e.g., Patel et al., 2021). Not only are telemedicine platforms considerably more prevalent now, but so too are uses of generalist technology for medical interactions and the exchange of medical information, including FaceTime, Google Hangouts, and Skype. These systems support interactions between providers and high-risk patients who need to avoid exposure in more conventional, physical healthcare settings, by using technologies with which patients are likely to be already familiar. Further, platforms such as Zoom and WebEx connect providers distributed in different places from their patients who need care in hot spots. These platforms also allow family members of COVID patients to interact with providers and loved ones when they cannot safely visit them in hospitals.

Concurrent with these changes, the federal government announced that it would "exercise discretion" in enforcing health privacy regulations, given the emergency circumstances (HHS Press Office, 2020), raising yet another dimension of context: what constitutes an emergency? Note that the official statement on enforcement discretion was interpreted in many different ways, with some hospitals informally deciding that this statement paved the way for delaying decision-making, and others acting quickly to announce more flexible solutions for patients and their families, recognizing the pandemic as an emergency circumstance. In contrast, many more well-funded or institutionally supported hospitals and clinic systems, as well as many university hospitals and clinics, did not appear to change their behavior based on this discretion, responding instead to the need for expanded video communication channels by licensing appropriate HIPAA-compliant platforms.

Recent research has sought to understand the impact of changes in both ICT use and privacy governance, relative to pandemic sociotechnical systems (e.g., Carvalho et al., 2021; Yang et al., 2020). In specifically exploring the statements released by hospital systems about the use of technology to meet telehealth needs, and examining documentation around technology practices in the same hospitals throughout the pandemic, there is evidence that: (1) the norms of the emergency context overrode rules about privacy; (2) the impact of the enforcement decision was bifurcated between compliance with HIPAA privacy standards and leveraging of the loophole to satisfice the telehealth need by using any available channels; and (3) the privacy implications of ICT use in healthcare during the pandemic were highly inequitable.

Even outside of crisis or emergency circumstances, the US healthcare context is extremely complex. Given the largely private healthcare system—augmented by Veteran's Administration (VA) hospitals and clinics, Medicare, and Medicaid—and the extensive networks of intermediaries for insurance and record-keeping, there are numerous actors with distinct roles and interests, many of which compete with the values and needs of patients. This is especially true with respect to privacy. Individuals have different preferences and understandings about how their personal information is collected, used, retained, and shared over time, which also do not necessarily match with reality. Recent events have shown, for example, how little the average person understands about what information HIPAA protects (e.g., Bodie, 2022; Lo et al., 2005). Add to the situation vast amounts of technology to mediate information flows, and an extended state of emergency with no end in sight, and constant pressure to control the spread of disease and meet wildly different expectations, and the resultant sociotechnical system is complex and rife with governance challenges that decision-makers struggle to address.

Changes within the sociotechnical systems employed for healthcare, and the governance of those systems, were simultaneous, rather than indicative of clear cause and effect. While some hospitals and clinics responded to this governance change by expanding the usage of technologies, both formally and informally, the federal governments' decisions responded primarily to emergency needs-based decisions, and new practices that were already happening. In this sense, the norms—or perhaps lack of norms—for emergencies overrode health privacy norms. Many hospitals and clinics had already moved numerous interactions, services, and communications to digital or distributed platforms. Some did so formally, depending on costly telemedicine services or extensive contracting with Zoom or Webex, often through public or university contracting. Others did so informally, out of desperation, depending on whatever means individual patients or families could facilitate, lacking any organizational support, systematic plan, or centralized directive.

The federal governments' initial response to this was a temporary legal absolution of the patchwork of practices in the short term, with a decision to waive sanctions and penalties against covered hospitals that do not comply with the following provisions of the HIPAA Privacy Rule:

- The requirements to obtain a patient's agreement to speak with family members or friends involved in the patient's care. See 45 CFR 164.510(b).
- The requirement to honor a request to opt out of the facility directory. See 45 CFR 164.510(a).
- The requirement to distribute a notice of privacy practices. See 45 CFR 164.520.
- The patient's right to request privacy restrictions. See 45 CFR 164.522(a).
- The patient's right to request confidential communications. See 45 CFR 164.522(b).[1]

This was notably not a temporary suspension, but rather forgiveness during this window of time for any standards violations or other rule-breaking associated with PII and available communication channels during the emergency circumstances. Yet, the 72 hours grace period defined by HHS was insufficient, and a series of decisions were made in March and April 2020 by the Office for Civil Rights (OCR) at the US Department of Health and Human Services (HHS) to promote flexibility and waive fines and enforcement for digital communications,[2] public health, and health oversight purposes.[3]

The result was a moratorium on enforcement of rules for an unspecified duration, rather than clear strategies, norms, or rules from the federal government to establish emergency standards of information privacy. This presented a long-term problem, as the governance void might only temporarily impact information flows, but the information itself would not be protected against re-use or retention by new and inappropriate data holders. Further, a problem has emerged as individual hospitals, clinics, and patients had to improvise and develop rules or standards for themselves, as the burden of complying with long-term enforcement rested with them. This has come at a time when healthcare providers are experiencing high stress and many other demands on their decision-making and problem-solving abilities, leading to an array of strategies ranging from complete deferment, to passing the burden of decision-making onto patients and their families, to temporarily satisficing with a plan toward longer-term data minimization, to contracting to address telemedicine privacy immediately.

Not only do different grassroot strategies emerge in the absence of shared norms or enforced rules, but there is also the negative consequence that the privacy impacts of distinct strategies are extremely unequal and are inequitably distributed across the US population. Well-resourced hospitals and clinics are much more likely to negotiate new contracts with Cisco, Microsoft, or Zoom, obtaining protective data use agreements that include HIPAA-sensitive and proactive clauses and conditions, such as data localization in the case of university hospitals, or data minimization. By contrast, rural, low-income, and non-white majority communities are much more likely to have hospitals and clinics that either choose inaction (i.e., no telemedicine or no policy whatsoever) or adopt a policy that places the burden of privacy protection on patients and their families, by instructing them to choose whichever platform they feel most comfortable using, and preempting liability with dubious policies, statements, or disclaimers.

While there are very real tradeoffs documented between prioritizing vulnerable populations and satisficing with available technology, privacy sacrifices in turn also impact these populations. The enforcement action is limited to healthcare providers, excluding insurance companies. Analysis of hospital practices relative to socioeconomic status of communities served illustrates that more affluent medical systems use health-specific technologies or negotiate appropriate features and terms of use to protect patient data, than do those hospitals and clinics that serve lower-income communities. There are significant variations in privacy protections by platform, and much of the burden of protecting sensitive medical information falls on individuals as, in their haste to connect, hospitals and healthcare providers turn to non-contextually configured platforms.

Education

There are parallel issues and practices in education, as recently revealed in a large collaborative study of 25 video conferencing platforms used in K12 and higher education (Cohney 2021). In this project, in addition to examining security issues empirically, we compare gaps between empirical privacy practices, platform privacy policies, user expectations, and rules, enforced via contracts and regulation, including the 140 state educational privacy laws found around the United States to date, as documented by the Student Privacy Compass guide to state educational laws (2022).[4]

In comparison to the health context, higher education has done a much better job of negotiating privacy obligations and protections via Data Protection Addenda (DPA). Default settings do not meet state educational laws or social norms, making the use of general video conferencing platforms inappropriate, without additional effort to enforce norms. Rather than placing the burden of the protection on patients or health care professionals, who are analogous to students and educators in this case, universities are re-negotiating and hosting platforms locally, to control data flows in ways consistent with rules and norms. While many adopted platforms provided some generalist educational addenda, which were immediately adopted, universities have made changes throughout this pandemic through contractual changes that are more effective than traditional purpose limitations (e.g., Zeide, 2016).

In this project, we surveyed both educators and IT administrators in higher education, with a corresponding survey for K12 administered in parallel by another group, with which we eventually plan to make comparisons. Social expectations and the educational norms that were revealed include the expectation that practices are consistent by platform, not by use, meaning from university to university, as well as in free consumer versions. In addition, educators and IT administrators felt they should control video data themselves, without the possibility that anyone else could control or access it. In keeping with many state laws, advertising on the platforms is strongly opposed. There is also a pervasive expectation that platforms will automatically comply with laws, which implies that privacy protection burdens should not fall on students as individuals. Compliance burdens on schools and universities with respect to advertising vary across states.

The practices across the platforms in this study vary just like their uses in health contexts did. Education technology platform practices were often more compliant with regulations, but did not comply with norms. Regulations are more fixed and clearly defined than contexts, norms, and technology are over time, providing easier points of reference for compliance. This is especially true regarding educational privacy, yet does not provide an explanation for the persistent and ubiquitous confusion about what regulations like FERPA actually impact. Many general video platforms violated their own privacy policies by sharing location information immediately, thereby also violating laws about student and family control over directory information. Additionally, those platforms, such as Jitsi,[5] that were the most normative, were so because they provided flexibility, with their default settings not necessarily aligned with regulations. This may indicate that the use of locally hosted, open-source platforms provides the contextual flexibility and scalability necessary during emergency circumstances.

These findings are also contextualized by a variety of recent educational technology and student privacy research (e.g., Jones et al., 2021; Paris et al., 2021; Zeide, 2020), which address the proliferation of datafication, automation, and surveillance within the complex contexts of pandemic era education. In addition to the use of video conferencing to meet distributed educational challenges, and the expanded use of learning management systems (LMSs), various attempts at techno-solutionism dramatically challenged established norms, such as with virtual proctoring technologies like Proctorio (Swauger, 2020). These systems attempted to automate or digitize conventional in-person techniques to prevent cheating, when in reality they introduced significantly more data collection and potential information harm, that were unanticipated and disproportionately borne by female, low-income, and students of color, as well as those with disabilities.

The invasive nature of surveillance in the home—both in virtual classroom and virtual assessment settings—garnered significant push-back by students around the world (e.g., Bailey et al., 2021; Jones et al., 2020), and in some cases from instructors, in instances where universities imposed burdensome requirements (e.g., Wong & Moorhouse, 2020). As universities and schools introduced new top-down rules to maintain operations amid the pandemic, they dramatically challenged existing norms and rules about student privacy, and exacerbated longstanding tensions between students, educators, administrators, educational technology support, and vendors.

In addition to the social outcry—such as from anti-Proctorio petitions in the United States and Canada, to the "F*** the Algorithm" movement in the United Kingdom—various sociotechnical approaches to subvert intrusive technologies and supplement perceived inadequate regulation, policy, and management emerged. Students worldwide found ways to obfuscate surveillance and to game data collection that they perceived as malicious compliance; their actions constituted a form of grassroots governance in practice.

Labor

The COVID-19 outbreaks led to widespread office closures and a broad shift to remote work, while many jobs have had to continue in person, including those based in hospitals, nursing homes, schools, grocery stores, logistics, factories, and warehouses. Maintaining productivity and ensuring safety have been primary challenges faced by employers and employees around the world.

Digital technology has played a critical role in the response to this challenge (e.g., Bodie & McMahon, 2021). Contact-tracing and exposure notification measures have been widely used to manage health risks at on-site workplaces. Interactions on communication and collaboration applications, such as Zoom and Slack, have become a centerpiece of everyday work for remote workers. The "success" of the technology-driven responses has been facilitated by multiple factors. In the United States, the use of technology to respond to the pandemic has been enabled by, among other factors, US law that gives employers wide latitude in work-related monitoring and tracking for workplace safety purposes (e.g., Rosenblat et al., 2014), and the public's willingness to adapt to health precautions that involve the intrusive use of technology, despite the skepticism and concerns that have persisted (Auxier, 2020). In addition, technologies and practices have been developed that purposefully do not collect certain data about individuals, in order to preserve privacy. For example, Bluetooth-enabled contact-tracing and exposure notification are considered privacy-aware for not gathering location data. Computer vision technologies used in some workplaces to enforce real-time social distancing are said to not collect any personal data. But technology has also given rise to privacy challenges and highlighted the fragility and limitations of the existing privacy protection approaches.

Current privacy regulations rest on certain preconceptions of contexts and boundaries. During the pandemic, organizations have relied on the Centers for Disease Control's (CDC) guidelines and a patchwork of other regulations and guidelines intended for specific contexts, to navigate the use of wellness monitoring and other surveillance technology. But the pandemic has shown that preconceived contexts and boundaries can collapse. For instance, while US employers are allowed to have wide latitude in mandating work-related monitoring and tracking, especially to promote workplace safety, remote work has made it impossible for employees to maintain even a fine line dividing the workplace and off-duty spheres. How should privacy be preserved to keep the employer-employee power imbalance in check, and protect individuals while they are working for organizations in highly private places? As things stand now, both organizations and individuals must answer tough questions like this. In the absence of comprehensive data protection guidelines, organizations and individuals are left to navigate privacy challenges arising from the rapid shifts in technology use in uncertain times.

This situation gives rise to privacy concerns as businesses' and organizations' motivation increases to avoid disruptions, enhance productivity, and establish control in the altered work environment. While many workers enjoy working from home because of not having to commute, and having more flexibility for personal and family responsibilities, surveillance is catching up to the point where employers look to bring workplaces back under their control. Some employers are constantly checking-in via instant messaging and emails, as well as monitoring webcams, displays, and keyboards to extend managerial reach to employees working from home. With organizations enforcing extensive surveillance of remote workers, individual workers now carry the burden of proof of their productivity, and must offer transparency to their organizations while working from home. These scenarios illustrate where surveillance deviates from the meaningful tradeoffs between safety and privacy, violating norms and expectations. Increased monitoring for productivity has long been known to impact employees' experiences and mental health negatively (Smith et al., 1992). It also makes individual employees more vulnerable to organizational decisions made on the basis of systematic and intrusive surveillance.

The invisible, easily-transmitted COVID-19 virus, as a workplace hazard once unimaginable to many, has raised an expanded notion of safety measures, and a renegotiation of what are acceptable tradeoffs between privacy and safety as both a social response and an externality. For in-person workplaces, where surveillance itself is considered to be the primary safety measure against the pandemic, expanded safety measures can become a potential umbrella for broader surveillance via function creep. Pandemic-motivated surveillance could be repurposed for non-safety-related uses, and become tools for organizations to assess productivity and performance, though health precautions may be proffered as their justification. During the pandemic, many employees have become accustomed to invasive health precautions to allow for timely responses to the outbreaks. Even worse, society is just as poorly prepared to end the emergency status and start reclaiming the privacy that employees, among other citizens, have given up. Now, the growing consensus among experts that COVID-19 will become endemic and is here to stay (Phillips, 2021), suggests that the end of the pandemic will not be clear-cut. But failing to roll back surveillance would be socially expensive, despite incentives for organizations to keep these technologies in place. In the long term, even technologies that claim to be less intrusive (such as Bluetooth-enabled contact tracing and exposure notification, or computer vision technology for real-time social distancing) can pave the way for the normalization of a greater level of surveillance.

The COVID-19 pandemic has shown that the lack of comprehensive data protection guidelines in the United States has given rise to privacy risks in a time when labor protection is a priority. This makes yet another case for new legislation providing comprehensive protection for personal information. Robust governance that works in shifting contexts, serves democratic values, and maintains expectations of privacy in both emergency and usual times, will help prevent undesirable privacy harms. Privacy cannot remain an individual responsibility. Workers who experienced the 1918–1919 influenza pandemic lacked a safety net, in the absence of progressive labor protection regulations that were only introduced afterwards. The current pandemic has again highlighted the need to protect workers, and urges us to expand the protection of their rights, including their privacy, in the face of the extensive use of technology. Businesses and organizations are likely to make critical choices moving forward, debating what considerations need to be made to retain a competitive workforce. Acknowledging that things will not simply return to the pre-pandemic state, it is imperative to renegotiate contexts and boundaries to better reflect values and norms as we emerge from the pandemic.

Implications

Overall, society cannot simply use ICTs in a manner that is reflexively responding to emergencies like the current COVID-19 pandemic, without considering governance. Rather, it is necessary to find ways to ensure privacy, especially across contexts, through creative and wholistic governance assemblages, when responding to emergency circumstances. We, as information professionals, must evaluate and plan for social norms and expectations in context, and across them, as well as specifically for emergencies and crises, including natural disasters and public health crises. Regulation alone is not sufficient, particularly when it is not enforced.

Looking at the three cases explored in this chapter, information flows are not discrete and current governance is insufficient. Despite popular misconceptions about medical privacy rights and obligations, the reality of healthcare during the pandemic being overly burdened and under-supported, coupled with the pervasive impact of medical information on other contexts, leaves people in a worse position. Normalization of surveillance, dependence upon platform-as-a-service vendors, and education's transcendence from traditional classroom spaces to occurring in every location from bedrooms to parking lots with free wi-fi, illustrate that we are also overdue for new student privacy protections. Labor surveillance and intrusions by employers for the sake of essential business extend similar concerns, along with raising new intrusion privacy harms. These cases indicate that current privacy protection, whether portrayed as an individual responsibility, or lacking control and transparency, is not only unsustainable, but also not meaningful. Governance must be more than notice and consent.

There is a lot to learn from pandemic ICT use about global and domestic privacy governance challenges and needs. Figure 2.2 depicts some of the strategies, norms, and, to a lesser extent, rules that have shaped pandemic era privacy around ICTs. The next three paragraphs summarize and explain the formal and informal, and intentional and unintentional, governance of strategies, norms, and rules crossing educational, health, and labor contexts, that were explored in this chapter.

Strategies for employee monitoring varied from organization to organization, with different expectations for in-person essential workers and work-from-home employees, by industry, and across municipalities, states, and countries. While most strategies were intentional, they were often highly informal, and the lack of consensus prevented their acceptance by those whom they impacted and resulted in further institutionalization to support these practices. The discrepancies between essential workers and others contributed to digital divide dimensions that are very distinct from traditional patterns, as suddenly highly educated healthcare workers, for example, experienced some of the challenges typically associated with lower-income and less informed professions. Further, strategies for ICT governance regarding labor give us the clearest foreshadowing of how seemingly innocuous or temporary choices, made to address emergency needs, can impact governance by their effects. As use-cases creep and functions are re-purposed within organizations to satisfice urgent needs in challenging circumstances, temporary solutions linger and expand, allowing organizations to surveil simply because it is possible.

Norms have emerged around some technologies such as Zoom—crossing contexts, or within domain specific needs—as with symptom tracking for public health purposes, despite the implications for other contexts. The camera-on requirement across all three cases illustrates how the same directive could be institutionalized in quite different ways; many healthcare and telemedicine examples depended on formalized camera-on norms to approximate analogous face-to-face interactions. While education was split between formal and informal approaches to this norm, their approaches were often less intentional than those in healthcare.

Notably, the most established rules of FERPA have significant unintended consequences, such as delimiting educational privacy issues with traditional educational records, and placing the burden of compliance on schools and universities, based on a model that does not account for modern educational data flows, thereby overlooking the worst privacy harms to students. In general, many unintentional facets of ICT governance choices and failures throughout the pandemic, summarized regarding key implications from each case, have had a dominant impact. We see distinct and contextual impacts, despite the overlap in contextual conflation and ICTs used, as well as the need for proactive governance efforts.

Policymakers, organizational decision-makers, and information professionals must recognize that privacy is contextual and, therefore, governance must also be contextual. Privacy is normative and must correspond with social expectations to be appropriate. Emergency circumstances challenge contextual boundaries, yet the nature of emergency is itself a context, necessitating an assemblage of governance features that address social, technological, and contextual facets. Further, regulations are not sufficient governance to protect privacy. Rather, governance must also encompass flexible and contextually responsive design, management, and contracts.

Some may read this chapter, or other academic perspectives, on the privacy governance worldwide associated with pandemic era ICT use, and dismiss concerns as relics of temporary emergency circumstances, and therefore irrelevant, since contact tracing apps and remote proctoring will not persist forever. Yet, even if we are not concerned with these specific technologies in the long term, they have irrevocably changed the nature of interactions, information lifecycles, and contexts for the long term, including the nature of work, healthcare and the last mile problem (Hasson, 2010), and the datafication of students. It is important to consider how we will govern ICT use and associated data for ordinate and emergency times as we develop, adopt, and adapt sociotechnical systems. It is equally as important to consider how ICTs are governing our behaviors, via intentional strategies and unintentional implications from design choices.

These cases, along with the concept of sociotechnical governance assemblages, have meaningful implications for practice. Co-production of governance and sociotechnical systems should be intentional, with responsive governance accompanying technological change (Frischmann et al., 2014; Sanfilippo et al., 2021). All too often governance is an afterthought, intentionally distinct from technology and occurring after the fact from design, implementation, and use, as a social form of compliance and oversight. Designers, policymakers, and information professionals need to consider the implications of data flows within systems as they are created and used, allowing governance to evolve and respond to emergency and everyday needs, as a combination of policy, management, market, and design institutions.

Social informatics scholarship implications also emerge from this chapter. Research cannot continue to limit consideration of governance to a single facet of context, but instead should explore governance as intended and experienced with respect to people, technology, and their contexts. Governance is just as central to outcomes, expected or not, as are underlying values, preferences, history, and design.

Notes

1 https://www.hhs.gov/sites/default/files/hipaa-and-COVID-19-limited-hipaa-waiver-bulletin-508.pdf
2 https://www.hhs.gov/about/news/2020/03/17/ocr-announces-notification-of-enforcement-discretion-for-telehealth-remote-communications-during-the-COVID-19.html
3 https://www.hhs.gov/about/news/2020/04/02/ocr-announces-notification-of-enforcement-discretion.html
4 https://studentprivacycompass.org/state-laws/
5 https://jitsi.org/

References

Auxier, B. (2020, December 18). How Americans view tech in the time of COVID-19. *Pew Research Center.* https://www.pewresearch.org/fact-tank/2020/12/18/what-weve-learned-about-americans-views-of-technology-during-the-time-of-covid-19/

Bailey, J., Flynn, A., & Henry, N. (2021). Pandemics and systemic discrimination: Technology-facilitated violence and abuse in an era of COVID-19 and antiracist protest. In *The Emerald International Handbook of Technology-Facilitated Violence and Abuse.* Emerald Publishing Limited.

Bodie, M.T. (2022). HIPPA. *Cardozo Law Review de-novo*, 2022, pp. 118–128.

Bodie, M.T., & McMahon, M. (2021). Employee testing, tracing, and disclosure as a response to the coronavirus pandemic. *Wash. UJL & Pol'y*, *64*, 31.

Carvalho, T., Faria, P., Antunes, L., & Moniz, N. (2021). Fundamental privacy rights in a pandemic state. *PLOS One*, *16*(6), e0252169.

Cohney, S., Teixeira, R., Kohlbrenner, A., Narayanan, A., Kshirsagar, M., Shvartzshnaider, Y., & Sanfilippo, M. (2021). Virtual classrooms and real harms: Remote learning at US universities. In *Seventeenth Symposium on Usable Privacy and Security* (SOUPS 2021) (pp. 653–674).

Crawford, S.E., & Ostrom, E. (1995). A grammar of institutions. *American political science review*, *89*(3), 582–600.

Davenport, E. (2008). Social informatics and sociotechnical research—a view from the UK. *Journal of information science*, *34*(4), 519–530.

Dwivedi, Y.K., Hughes, D.L., Coombs, C., Constantiou, I., Duan, Y., Edwards, J.S., Gupta, B., Lal, B., Misra, S., Prashant, P., & Upadhyay, N. (2020). Impact of COVID-19 pandemic on information management research and practice: Transforming education, work, and life. *International Journal of Information Management*, *55*, 102211.

Frischmann, B.M., Madison, M.J., & Strandburg, K.J. (Eds.). (2014). *Governing knowledge commons*. Oxford University Press.

Hasson, A.A. (2010, September). The last inch of the last mile challenge. In *Proceedings of the 5th ACM workshop on Challenged networks* (pp. 1–4).

Hong, Z., Li, N., Li, D., Li, J., Li, B., Xiong, W., Lu, L., Li, W., & Zhou, D. (2020). Telemedicine during the COVID-19 pandemic: Experiences from western China. *Journal of Medical Internet Research*, *22*(5), e19577. 10.2196/19577

HHS Press Office. (2020, April 2). OCR announces notification of enforcement discretion to allow uses and disclosures of protected health information by business associates for public health and health oversight activities during the COVID-19 nationwide public health emergency. *Office of Civil Rights, Department of Health and Human Services*. https://public3.pagefreezer.com/content/HHS.gov/31-12-2020T08:51/https://www.hhs.gov/about/news/2020/04/02/ocr-announces-notification-of-enforcement-discretion.html

Jarrahi, M.H., Sawyer, S., & Erickson, I. (2021). Digital assemblages, information infrastructures, and mobile knowledge work. *Journal of Information Technology*, *37*(3), 02683962211050943.

Jones, K.M., Asher, A., Goben, A., Perry, M.R., Salo, D., Briney, K.A., & Robertshaw, M.B. (2020). "We're being tracked at all times": Student perspectives of their privacy in relation to learning analytics in higher education. *Journal of the Association for Information Science and Technology*, *71*(9), 1044–1059.

Jones, K., VanScoy, A., Bright, K., & Harding, A. (2021, January). Do they even care? Measuring instructor value of student privacy in the context of learning analytics. In *Proceedings of the 54th Hawaii International Conference on System Sciences* (p. 1529).

Kant, L., & Norman, E. (2021). Working under the gun: A theoretical analysis of stressors associated with the re-negotiation of norms and control of work tasks during COVID-19. *Frontiers in Psychology*, *12*.

Lessig, L. (1999). *Code and other laws of cyberspace*. Basic Books.

Lo, B., Dornbrand, L., & Dubler, N.N. (2005). HIPAA and patient care: the role for professional judgment. *JAMA, 293*(14), 1766–1771.

Marwick, A.E., & boyd, d. (2011). I tweet honestly, I tweet passionately: Twitter users, context collapse, and the imagined audience. *New media & society, 13*(1), 114–133.

Meyer, E.T., Shankar, K., Willis, M., Sharma, S., & Sawyer, S. (2019). The social informatics of knowledge. *Journal of the Association for Information Science and Technology, 70*(4), 307–312.

Nissenbaum, H. (2009). *Privacy in context: Technology, policy, and the integrity of social life.* Stanford University Press.

Ohannessian, R., Duong, T.A., & Odone, A. (2020). Global telemedicine implementation and integration within health systems to fight the COVID-19 pandemic: A call to action. *JMIR public health and surveillance, 6*(2), e18810.

Paris, B., Reynolds, R., & McGowan, C. (2021). Sins of omission: Critical informatics perspectives on privacy in e-learning systems in higher education. *Journal of the Association for Information Science and Technology, 73*(5), 708–725.

Patel, S.Y., Mehrotra, A., Huskamp, H.A., Uscher-Pines, L., Ganguli, I., & Barnett, M.L. (2021). Trends in outpatient care delivery and telemedicine during the COVID-19 pandemic in the US. *JAMA Internal Medicine, 181*(3), 388–391.

Phillips, N. (2021). The coronavirus is here to stay—Here's what that means. *Nature, 590*(7846), 382–384. 10.1038/d41586-021-00396-2

Riva, M.A., Paladino, M.E., Paleari, A., & Belingheri, M. (2021). Workplace COVID-19 vaccination, challenges, and opportunities. *Occupational Medicine,* 72 (4). pp. 235–237.

Rosenblat, A., Kneese, T., & boyd, d. (2014). Workplace surveillance. *Open Society Foundations' Future of Work Commissioned Research Papers.*

Sanfilippo, M., Frischmann, B., & Standburg, K. (2018). Privacy as commons: Case evaluation through the Governing Knowledge Commons framework. *Journal of Information Policy, 8*, 116–166.

Sanfilippo, M.R., Frischmann, B.M., & Strandburg, K.J. (Eds.). (2021). *Governing privacy in knowledge commons.* Cambridge University Press.

Sanfilippo, M.R., Shvartzshnaider, Y., Reyes, I., Nissenbaum, H., & Egelman, S. (2020). Disaster privacy/privacy disaster. *Journal of the Association for Information Science and Technology, 71*(9), 1002–1014.

Schonscheck, J. (1997). Privacy and Discrete "Social Spheres". *Ethics & Behavior, 7*(3), 221–228.

Smith, M.J., Carayon, P., Sanders, K.J., Lim, S.-Y., & LeGrande, D. (1992). Employee stress and health complaints in jobs with and without electronic performance monitoring. *Applied Ergonomics, 23*(1), 17–27. 10.1016/0003-6870(92)90006-H

Swauger, S. (2020). Our bodies encoded: Algorithmic test proctoring in higher education. In R. Benjamin (Ed.), *Critical Digital Pedagogy* (Chapter 6). Pressbooks.

Wong, K.M., & Moorhouse, B.L. (2020). The impact of social uncertainty, protests, and COVID-19 on Hong Kong teachers. *Journal of Loss and Trauma, 25*(8), 649–655.

Yang, S., Fichman, P., Zhu, X., Sanfilippo, M., Li, S., & Fleischmann, K.R. (2020). The use of ICT during COVID-19. *Proceedings of the Association for Information Science and Technology, 57*(1), e297.

Zeide, E. (2016). The limits of education purpose limitations. *U. Miami L. Rev., 71*, 494.

Zeide, E. (2020). Robot teaching, pedagogy, and policy. In M.D. Dubber, F. Pasquale, & S. Das (Eds.), *The Oxford Handbook of Ethics of AI* (pp. 789–804). Oxford University Press.

Part II
Community

3 A Social Informatics Approach to Online Communities of Practice of the Art Recreation Challenge on Instagram during COVID-19

Pnina Fichman and Meredith Dedema

Introduction

When the COVID-19 pandemic forced people all over the world into lockdowns, the roles of technology in society shifted and became a necessary part of every aspect of life. This could be the ultimate realization of the utopian future in terms of information and communication technology (ICT) use that early information technology scholars envisioned. In 1992, Hollan and Stornetta proposed an innovative and somewhat futuristic idea of "beyond being there". At the time, they argued that the motivation behind much of the research that focused on the design, implementation, and use of ICTs was the faith in the ability of ICTs to imitate face-to-face communication in order to increase work efficiency. However, they claimed this belief would be problematic, because it limits the possibility to explore how ICTs could provide an experience that is richer than face-to-face communication, and enhance communication among individuals and groups to a level that is "beyond being there". Building on this idea, Shachaf and Hara (2007), for example, introduced the notion that the simultaneous use of multiple communication channels would both introduce situational complexity (in which behavioral choices of channels were, at times, paradoxical), and provide communication experiences that are "beyond being there", as communication is facilitated across structural barriers among global virtual team members. These early writings brought a critical view to the deterministic vision of mainstream research on ICTs. The deterministic approach assumed that the introduction and increased use of ICTs in society would improve people's lives; delivering experiences that are "beyond being there" would then be possible (e.g., Hollan & Stornetta, 1992). This approach to ICT research proposed an ideal utopian future, in which the use of widespread ICT positively enhances people's work and lives. However, it wasn't until the COVID-19 global pandemic and lockdown that the use of ICTs significantly expanded: people had to conduct almost all of their daily activities and interactions with the outside world utilizing ICTs.

This dystopian reality of COVID-19 quarantine pushed ICT use from what was perceived to be technological determinism's utopia, to a new level

DOI: 10.4324/9781003231769-6

of ICT use where blurred boundaries of context provided new and imaginative communication opportunities. This took the idea of "beyond being there" one step further. In an attempt to explore how the dystopian context during COVID-19 quarantine promotes these early conceptions of the utopian future, we illustrate how the pandemic-driven use of ICTs allowed for the realization of the utopian use of ICTs to go past the idea of "beyond being there". We incorporate these two opposing forces, dystopian and utopian, that create a complex contextual setting for ICT use to illustrate the type of relationships between people and technology that are informed by and contribute to social informatics (Fichman et al., 2015). For that purpose, we develop a case study in which we concentrate on one social media challenge of art recreation on Instagram that began during COVID-19; four online communities of practice (CoPs) formed around this challenge, using unique hashtags (#) in three languages and two scripts, Latin and Cyrillic.

During the COVID-19 lockdown, while visitors could not physically visit art collections in museums, the museums' use of digital art collections increased. Museum employees devised new ways of reaching out to their constituencies by enhancing their online interactions with their communities, offering through social media new ways to consume, interpret, share, and interact with art. Inspired by the Rijksmuseum (the national museum of the Netherlands in Amsterdam), the Getty Museum also started a social media challenge on Wednesday, March 25, 2020 for Instagram, Facebook, and Twitter users. In this challenge, they asked users to recreate works of art from the Getty Museum's online collection using three household items, and to post their recreations on social media, along with the hashtag #gettymuseumchallenge (Waldorf & Stephan, 2020). As a result, many social media users posted their creations, tagging these museums or using hashtags such as #tussenkunstenquarantaine in Dutch, #изоизоляция in Russian, and #gettymuseumchallenge or #betweenartandquarantine in English. This challenge was also entered by art teachers in elementary school, who saw it as a fun and engaging activity (e.g., Wantagh Elementary School, 2020).

We approach the exploration of this challenge by interpreting it as an online community of practice (CoP), bounded by the four hashtags, and then examining the boundaries and overlap of these four CoPs, focusing on users who act as "boundary spanners" or "brokers", and on users' art recreation posts that act as "boundary objects". Boundary spanners are individuals who are engaged in information and knowledge dissemination, as well as in relationship and capacity building; Lave and Wenger (1991) suggest that this is a leader's role in a CoP. Boundary objects are entities that can link communities together, as they allow different groups to collaborate on a common task (Wenger, 1998); these boundary objects are shared within and across these four CoPs. Online CoPs are composed of members that share common interests and interact with each other to discuss topics, exchange ideas, and seek support (Rosenbaum & Shachaf, 2010). We argue that this challenge is a social activity that involves people with a shared interest in art recreation on social media platforms, who utilize the platforms' unique affordances (e.g., hashtags and following) for their shared social practice and identity. Four common hashtags in three languages were utilized as part of this Instagram challenge, with each constituting one CoP, with more than 50,000 posts: #betweenartandquarantine, #gettymuseumchallenge, #tussenkunstenquarantaine, and #изоизоляция. Many posts included more than one of these hashtags, crossing CoPs boundaries.

To illustrate the relationships between ICTs and people during this dystopian period of time, we use Wenger's (1998) theoretical framework of CoPs, and respond to the need for more research boundary maintenance proposed by Hara and Fichman (2014). We aim to make a specific contribution to this domain. While there is a lot of discussion about boundaries in the CoP literature, our objective is to investigate Instagram's textual and visual affordances in relation to boundary maintenance, and to observe the role that these textual and visual practices play in four different CoPs. Specifically, we explore the overlap between these CoPs as it relates to their social practice (as it is manifested through text, image, and other social media features, such as hashtags), and to their identity (as it is manifested through their nationality, language, and community hashtags). To gain a better understanding of boundary maintenance, we have compared: 1) the posts that serve as boundary objects and have been shared across the boundaries of a single community, with those that have not; and 2) the highly visible posts with those that are less visible. Thus, we aim to address the following three research questions:

1   What is the overlap between the four online CoPs?
2   What are the differences between posts that belong to a single community and those that cross boundaries?
3   What are the differences between posts with high and low visibility?

Background

We first provide background about art recreation and replication; then, using Wenger's (1998) CoP framework, we describe the ways in which our case study of the art recreation challenge serves as a useful template for studying boundary maintenance in online CoPs.

Art recreation

Art recreation and replication is a common practice among artists. Replication is the process of reproducing something, and it is distinct from forgery, which is "the attempt to acquire prestige through the attachment to a famous name" (Anguissola, 2007, p. 100). Forgery is harmful because it forces the focus about the painting to be not on the value of the painting's subject itself, but more on its monetary value. There is also attention spent on distinguishing the differences between the fake and the original (Ravasio, 2018). Recreations themselves are created not so that the little differences can be identified, but rather with the purpose of emphasizing the meaning of the piece as a whole. Replications, on the other hand, do not try to pretend to be the original; therefore, there is less harm done to the artwork (Ravasio, 2018). In Greek and Roman times, art was sometimes replicated to protect a sacred talisman from thieves or to substitute for the original (Anguissola, 2007). While these replications were being used to mirror the original, they were done for the sake of protecting the original from being taken and sold. Currently, works of art are displayed in their original forms in museums, and though they are at some risk of being stolen, it is not enough of a reason for the museum to display replicas in their place. Replicas are more commonly made to allow the average person to display a popular painting, without taking the original or paying as high a price as the original would command.

Thanks to digital technologies, more and more artworks can be recreated and replicated online, without temporal and spatial limitations (Gultepe et al., 2018). As an example, the Getty Museum uploaded digital images from their collections of artworks, allowing people to see these works of art online (Zia, 2019). Thanks to information technologies, a variety of information can also be easily integrated and presented alongside the digital images of the artworks. This allows museums to provide insights into artworks and offer new perspectives on their elements, creation, and history. Digital images can be used to "mechanically index the original" (Geismar, 2018, p. 108), so the original is not forgotten or lost, as was the case in 2016, when the Institute of Digital Archaeology printed a 3D replica of the fallen structure the Triumphal Arch of the Temple of Bel in Palmyra, Syria, after ISIS destroyed it. As a digital recreation of a fallen arch, the media "focus [ed] on the redemptive power of digital imaging to reproduce lost heritage" (Geismar, 2018, p.109). Social media platforms are also playing an important role in the dissemination of digital representations of artworks, where not only museums, but also many artists, are presenting their artworks online (Kang & Chen, 2017). Consequently, more attention is drawn to the included artwork. The increased exposure of the museums' collections and activities enhances their influence over current and future art creations, art movements, and artistic trends. Digitized online artworks are especially important at a time when many museums and galleries are closed to the public for various reasons, including the pandemic.

Between art and quarantine as a CoP

Online CoPs are composed of members that share common interests and interact regularly with each other to discuss topics, exchange ideas, seek support, and learn how to do things better. The concept of a CoP was introduced by Lave and Wenger (1991), and Wenger (1998) further developed it, discussing the two axes of relevant tradition. The horizontal axis connects theories of social practice and theories of identity. He explains that, "Theories of social practice address the production and reproduction of specific ways of engaging with the world ... [and] Theories of identity are concerned with the social formation of the person, the cultural interpretation of the body, and the creation and use of markers of membership such as rites of passage and social categories ... [that help us] understand the person as formed through complex relations of mutual constitution between individuals and groups" (1998, p. 13). Online CoPs are phenomena that have attracted social informatics scholars (e.g., Hara & Fichman, 2014; Rosenbaum & Shachaf, 2010), and as such we choose to approach the Instagram challenge as an online CoP. In the context of our CoPs, practice involves posting unique art recreations along with text and relevant hashtags on Instagram, as well as commenting on, liking and sharing these posts. More specifically, a piece of art is chosen, and then materials and methods for the recreation are selected. Finally, the recreation is captured in a digital photo and shared along with an image of the original. The level of appropriateness of the piece of art, the use of tools and materials, and how people capture and share the recreations, are crucial elements of the CoP. Then, the type of text the post includes, and the kinds of comments CoP members post, are added to the mix, constituting a shared practice.

Wenger (1998) suggests that practice is the source of not only coherence in a community, but also defines the boundaries of the community. He then argues that identity can be understood through the inherent characteristics of practice, and that membership of a community can be achieved through engagement or other modes of belonging, such as alignment and imagination (Wenger, 1998). In the context of our CoPs, identity is expressed first through the shared practice of the art recreation challenge, and then by the specific hashtag for each of the CoPs. Language can serve as the basis for group identity, and can define membership in a particular CoP and also be used for boundary maintenance. This doesn't seem to be an issue in this study's CoPs; the language of the posts and hashtags used for each CoPs is not limited to English, but rather includes languages such as Dutch and Russian. In addition to engagement through posting, liking, and commenting, using Instagram features, such as following a particular hashtag, can be interpreted as belonging to a community. Wenger's (1998) two main concepts, identity and practice, were further discussed and developed later; for example, Murillo (2008) adopted five constitutive dimensions as key characteristics of virtual CoP: mutual engagement, joint enterprise, shared repertoire, community, and learning or identity acquisition. We describe the #betweenartandquarantine Instagram challenge as an online CoP, using these five dimensions.

Mutual engagement among a group of people will form a CoP. The #betweenartandquarantine challenge consists of members' practice-related interactions to produce artifacts, provide feedback, and discuss other topics. From the beginning, the shared artifacts that were posted were joined by textual posts and hashtags, the latter of which linked the posts to the community of those who shared the same interest. People used household items to recreate or replicate the artwork, and posted them on social media platforms using similar hashtags. The posts' comments involved supportive text and emojis, and discussions about the technique and materials used, composition of the artifact and/or its recreation, in addition to other contextual comments. Many posters described the story behind the original artwork or elaborated on the process of making the recreation work, and they also replied to comments made on their original posts. Mutual engagement is one of the most critical building blocks of an online CoP. Over time, sustained mutual engagement results in the development of resources and repertoire that the community shares with its members, "includ[ing] routines, words, tools, ways of doing things, stories, gestures, symbols, genres, actions or concepts that the community has produced or adopted". (Wenger, 1998, p.83)

This *shared repertoire* included the use of specific hashtags or even more outrageous ways of replicating artwork. For example, many members paired up with their pets (dogs or cats) or their siblings, and used food or fabrics they found at home; some participants used COVID-19-related items, such as toilet paper or masks, adding a satirical flavor to their recreations. This type of artwork was found easily, given the name of the hashtags. The #betweenartandquarantine challenge has become one of the most popular hashtags, just one example of the affordance Instagram provides for the online community (Bryant et al., 2005). Adding to the creation of the shared repertoire, from which participants could draw tools and inspiration, were two institutional Instagram accounts: The Getty Museum and the Rijksmuseum—the initiator of this challenge (user_id: tussenkunstenquarantaine). Both have been collecting recreation and replication work for other online users. These institutional accounts contributed to another important aspect of a CoP, *joint enterprise,* which involves building a shared understanding of the nature of the community's activities, as well as creating a differentiated atmosphere for the community. The Getty Museum and Rijksmuseum accounts played major roles in creating and disseminating the challenge from the start, announcing it and encouraging their followers to take part in this joint endeavor, while the museums were closed to the public.

The #betweenartandquarantine challenge enabled the formation of a stable and persistent virtual *community.* The members of the community started to develop strong personal interrelationships online, following or tagging other members in their posts. In this community of like-minded peers, members started to feel valued by other participants, through likes and comments. Many who appreciate fine art found a welcoming and supportive community to release their creativity and relieve their stress and/

or boredom from social isolation during COVID-19. This outlet provided members with temporary relief from the isolation and boredom of the pandemic. *Learning or identity acquisition* took several paths in these CoPs, manifesting different ways of belonging, including identity in practice (Wenger, 1998), where participants identify with the community by sharing recreations or utilizing other sociotechnical affordances of the platform. Some individuals who posted frequently became leaders of the CoP, setting up the tone for what are acceptable behavior and posts, and for some of these individuals it became their professional identities as artists. As for other participants, rather than sharing recreations, they identified with the community solely by liking, following, sharing, and commenting on those posts, demonstrating other modes of belonging to the CoP.

One of the building blocks of online CoPs is their boundary maintenance, upheld by boundary-crossing and boundary brokers (Wenger, 1998). Often boundary objects are the technology that connects CoP members—Instagram hashtags, in our case—and facilitate boundary-crossing among different CoPs, while enforcing the boundaries of each CoP. Boundary brokers are members of more than one CoP, who make effective connections between them (Brown & Duguid, 1998). Wenger (1998, p. 109) describes the broker's role in the following way: "It requires the ability to link practices by facilitating transactions between them and to cause learning by introducing into a practice, elements of another". Brokers are CoP leaders (Lave & Wenger, 1991). In our case, these are users who utilized multiple hashtags, posted their recreations regularly, and typically engaged with the CoPs more frequently than others, with their posts, comments, likes, and follows. CoPs' boundary maintenance processes have received some attention, but scholars call for the need for further research on boundary-crossing (Hara & Fichman, 2014). When language barriers between communities are evident, unpacking the role of boundary brokers and boundary objects is necessary; it is particularly important to understand the boundary-crossing that occurs on Instagram's CoPs, given the platform's visual affordances. Thus, we examine the overlap across four CoPs that were part of the same art recreation challenge during COVID-19 lockdown. We also compare posts that were part of only one of the four CoPs (#betweenartandquarantine, #gettymuseumchallenge, #tussenkunstenquarantaine, and #изоизоляция.) with those that are part of more than one CoP. Then, because according to Lave and Wenger (1991), CoP leaders are brokers, facilitating the boundary spanning process, we compare posts with high and low visibility to see if higher visibility is aligned with CoP boundary maintenance.

Methodology

We conducted this study on Instagram, because of its visual affordance, hashtags, and tagging features. We collected and analyzed data from four CoPs that were formed around four common hashtags (in three languages), that have been used during the COVID-19 pandemic for art recreation and replication.

Data collection

On April 2 and 4 in 2021, using *Phantombuster's Instagram Hashtag Collector*, we collected the Instagram posts with each of the hashtags #betweenartandquarantine, #gettymuseumchallenge, #tussenkunstenquarantaine, and #изоизоляция. These four hashtags attracted thousands of posts each, around the art recreation challenge on Instagram, during the COVID-19 lockdown. Screening the hashtags of the posts that we have collected did not reveal additional hashtags for this art recreation challenge that were as popular; we identified hashtags in languages (e.g., French, German), but these attracted a much lower participation. The data included URL, published date, description, comments count, like count, and account username per post. While there were 233,876 posts on Instagram with these four hashtags, the crawler agent stopped when it hit Instagram's rate limit of at most 5,000 posts per hour (Lam, 2015), thereby collecting 107,698 rather than the 233,876 posts. After cleaning the data and removing empty, damaged or unformatted posts, our included data set went from 107,698 to 107,517 posts (Table 3.1). #tussenkunstenquarantaine, the first hashtag in the challenge, is the most popular hashtag with 71,009 posts.

To further understand the overlap between the four online CoPs, we sampled 400 posts, 100 posts from each CoP. We excluded some posts during the sampling stage based on the following criteria: 1) Posts from institutional accounts (e.g., museums and media outlets) were excluded, as institutional accounts may be more influential than others; 2) Posts that didn't include images of art recreation, or included more than one recreation were excluded to simplify the coding interpretation; 3) Posts that included recreations of scenes from films or magazine covers were excluded to allow for systematic analysis and contextualization within fine art. Furthermore, because we wanted to ensure the inclusion of a more representative sample rather than a sample biased toward less popular posts, we limited our sample to posts with at least 50 comments. Then, we ranked the posts in each hashtag based on the number of likes they attracted and chose the top 50 posts (highest number of likes) and bottom 50 posts (lowest number of likes) from each. In other words, our sample included posts with at least 50 comments that were the most liked and least liked posts in each CoP.

Data analysis

To gain a better knowledge of the boundary-crossing process, a coding scheme was developed from the data (Table 3.2). The coding scheme was refined and iterated by two authors in accordance with the data from the "between art and quarantine" hashtag. Coding was done at the individual

Table 3.1 Posts collected from each hashtag

Hashtag	Posted	Collected	Cleaned	Comment: Maximum	Comment: Mean	Like: Maximum	Like: Mean
#betweenartandquarantine	53,607	22,209	22,158	1,111	9.9	54,271	282
#tussenkunstenquarantaine	71,009	29,402	29,361	850	9.5	59,398	272
#gettymuseumchallenge	56,207	27,974	27,948	1,060	8.3	59,398	171
#изоизоляция	53,053	28,113	28,050	3,052	11.8	95,842	208
Total	233,876	107,698	107,517	1,518	9.9	66,977	233

Table 3.2 Codebook

Category	Code	Description
Use of community relevant hashtags	Single community	Post includes only one out of the four hashtags
	Multiple communities	Post includes more than one out of the four hashtags
Use of language	Single language or script	Post written in only one language or script
	Multiple languages and script	Post written in more than one language and script
Nationality	The nationality of the user	The location in the user's profile
	The nationality of the artist of original artwork	Google information about the original artwork
	The country of the collection/museum of original artwork	Google information about the collection/museum of original artwork
Post norms in the text	Info about original masterpiece	The text of the posts includes information about original artwork, for example, name of artist, and name of picture, year, collection, style and so on
	Personal motivation/story with original/recreation work	The text of the posts includes something personal about the user
Recreation norms in the image	Recreation of composition	Recreation artwork replaces objects/people/pets compared to original artwork
	Recreation iconography goes beyond the original	The iconography of recreation artwork goes beyond original artwork, for example, use of COVID-19 items, change main character's race/gender, use of modern technology and so on
Social media features	Hashtag	The number of hashtags used in the posts
	Tagging	The number of tagging used in the posts
	Followers	The number of followers of posting users
	Comment	The number of comments the posts get
	Like	The number of likes the posts get

post level, and intercoder reliability reached 87.5%, with Cohen's kappa at 0.60. For the analysis of the social media features, averages were calculated for the number of the user's followers, the number of hashtags used in each post, and the amount of tagging used in each post at the time of coding, along with the number of comments and likes per post.

To answer our research questions, we conducted a comparative content analysis, as well as statistical analysis to test if the code frequency variations between and within the four groups of posts we identified were significant. Using SPSS 28, we performed Chi-square tests, Gamma coefficient, and *t*-test, as well as one-way and two-way ANOVA.

Among the limitations of our study are the use of a single case of one art recreation challenge (with four CoPs' hashtags) on one platform (Instagram), the relatively small sample of posts analyzed, and the limited variability in practices and languages. Thus, transferability of findings should be made with great caution. Still, our analysis allows for a better understanding of boundary maintenance and boundary-crossing processes that involve the unique sociotechnical visual and textual affordances of Instagram.

Findings

We answer the research questions by first describing the overlap between the four CoPs in terms of their social practice and identity, and then by comparing posts that cross single community boundaries with those that do not. Next, we describe the differences between highly visible posts versus less visible posts. We examine these differences both as a whole and within each CoP. In each section, we describe the findings in regard to our codes, and then in regard to the social media features. We achieve this by first describing the findings in the sample as a whole, and then following up with an examination of each CoP.

1   The overlap between the four CoPs.

We start by describing the overlap among the four CoPs in our sample, illustrating it with a Venn diagram (Figure 3.1). We found that only three posts in our entire sample included all four hashtags (1%), while 143 posts (36%) included only one hashtag. Further, most of the posts with the Russian hashtag (74%) were unique to the Russian CoP, and only one quarter of the posts with the Russian hashtag included hashtags in other languages. In each of the other CoPs, only about one quarter or fewer of the posts were unique to one of the other communities (24 with #betweenartandquarantine, 20 with #gettymuseumchallenge, and 25 with #tussenkunstenquarantaine). We also found that the overlap between the Russian CoP and the other CoPs was smaller (fewer than five posts with each combination of hashtags, included the Russian hashtag) than the overlap between each of the other CoPs (more than 15 posts in each combination of hashtags excluded the Russian hashtag).Thus, it is clear that 1) the boundaries of the Russian online CoP were less permeable than the three other CoPs; 2) the overlap across all four CoPs is significant, with only one third of the posts (36%) in our sample including a single hashtag.

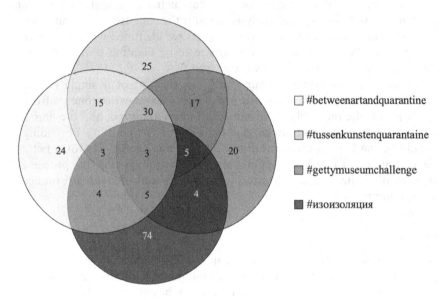

Figure 3.1 The overlap between the four CoPs.

While there is some overlap between the four CoPs, we examined if and how the use of various Instagram social media features also varies across the four CoPs. As shown in Table 3.3, the highest average number of hashtags were seen in the two English CoPs, while posts in the Russian CoP included half as many hashtags. A similar pattern was observed for the average tagging in each CoP measure. Interestingly, posts in the Russian CoP resulted in more likes, more comments, and had an average of almost five times more followers than did posts in the English CoPs. The variations across the four CoPs were statistically significant for tagging, according to the one-way ANOVA statistic (see the second and third column of Table 3.4). Despite the common practice of posting art recreations on Instagram, users in each of these four CoPs demonstrated significantly different social media behaviors.

In the Russian CoP, the use of only one of the four CoPs hashtags was higher than in any other CoPs (Table 3.5), and according to Chi Square

Table 3.3 Average numbers of social media features in each of the four CoPs

Average per post for each CoP	Hashtag	Tagging	Follower	Comment	Like
#betweenartandquarantine	13.37	1.60	23,942	88	1,826
#tussenkunstenquarantaine	10.39	1.62	77,071	111	3,458
#gettymuseumchallenge	12.77	1.68	27,491	100	2,423
#изоизоляция	5.71	0.79	154,392	168	4,326

Table 3.4 ANOVA results for social media features across four CoPs, and between single and multiple communities across four CoPs

Social media features	One-way ANOVA across four CoPs		Two-way ANOVA between single/multiple community across four CoPs		Two-way ANOVA of posts with high/low visibility across four CoPs	
	Levene's Statistic	F (N=3)	Levene's Statistic	F (N=3)	Levene's Statistic	F (N=3)
Hashtag	14.140***	12.291***	7.923***	2.302	7.071***	0.575
Tagging	2.135	2.347	2.419*	3.417	2.990**	0.278
Follower	6.575***	2.582	4.627***	2.304	9.265***	2.693*
Comment	19.694***	10.642***	9.707***	4.371**	17.277***	15.704***
Like	4.336**	3.117*	2.596*	2.061	11.840***	4.025**

Sig. (*$p < 0.05$; **$p < .001$; ***$p < 0.001$).

statistics (Table 3.6), this difference was significant. The Russian hashtag was more likely to be used in a post without any of the other three hashtags.

Interestingly, as shown in Table 3.5, posts in all four communities were mostly written in one language (87%), and we didn't find any significant differences between the four when comparing the use of single or multiple languages. Furthermore, the only significant difference between the four CoPs was the use of a single hashtag (first column of Table 3.6). In all four CoPs, more often than not (86%), the nationality of the original painter and the user did not match, nor did the location/museum of the original art and user's nationality (88%). The frequency of disclosure of information about the original artwork was at about the same level (88%), and the inclusion of a personal story in posts was similar across the four communities (61%). The frequency of the use of objects varying from those in the original artwork was as common across the four CoPs (28%). Posting recreations with iconography that went beyond the original was low overall (21%), yet was slightly higher in the two English CoPs compared with the other two (25% and 24% compared with 19% and 17%, respectively).

2   The difference between posts in single community and those that cross boundaries.

To answer our second research question, we compared posts that belong to a single community—those that include only one of the four hashtags—with those that bridge CoPs boundaries—they include more than one hashtag. As can be seen in Figure 3.2, the frequency of each of the codes is higher in posts with multiple communities. However, these differences between single communities and multiple communities were statistically

Table 3.5 Code frequency and percent per CoP

Code/CoP	#betweenartandquarantine (N=100)	#tussenkunstenquarantaine (N=100)	#gettymuseumchallenge (N=100)	#изоизоляция (N=100)	All four CoPs (N=400)
Single community	24	25	20	74	143 (36%)
Single language	91	84	85	89	349 (87%)
Nationality: Painter=User	14	16	14	13	57 (14%)
Nationality: Museum=User	14	13	12	8	47 (12%)
Info of original work	89	88	86	88	351 (88%)
Personal story	61	61	62	59	243 (61%)
Replace the object	29	27	27	27	110 (28%)
Iconography beyond original	25	19	24	17	85 (21%)

Table 3.6 Results of cross tabulation across four CoPs, between single and multiple communities, and between high and low visibility posts

Code/Chi Square Statistics	Four CoPs (hashtags) χ^2 (N=400, df=3)	Single/multiple community χ^2 (N=400, df=1)	High/low visibility χ^2 (N=400, df=1)
Single community	85.538***	/	2.449
Single language	2.944	0.488	5.056*
Nationality: Painter=User	0.389	0.503	7.386**
Nationality: Museum=User	2.001	1.518	1.181
Info of original work	0.442	11.126***	0.023
Personal story	0.199	10.097***	27.271***
Replace the object	0.150	0.153	0.000
Iconography beyond original	2.674	0.125	1.210

Sig. (*p < 0.05; **p < 0.01; ***p < 0.001).

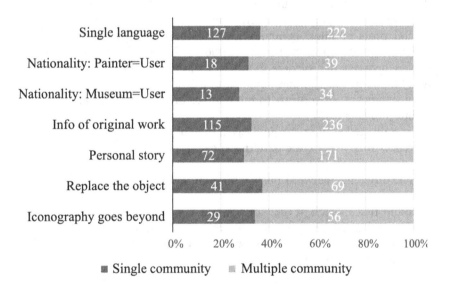

Figure 3.2 Code frequency in single and multiple communities.

significant for only two codes, the inclusion of a personal story (χ^2 = 11.126, $p < 0.001$), and information about the original work (χ^2 = 10.097, $p < 0.001$) (second column of Table 3.6). As can be seen in Figure 3.2, posts in multiple communities were significantly more likely to include a personal story and information about the original work than were posts in a single community (236 vs. 115 and 171 vs. 72, respectively).

We conducted a follow-up analysis in each of the CoPs to observe whether they follow the same pattern. Surprisingly, the percentage of Russian hashtags accompanying posts divulging information about the original work was the same in single community posts as it was in multiple communities' posts (88%). But for the other three hashtags, the percentage of posts in multiple communities including such information was higher, compared with posts in each single community (92% vs. 79%, 92% vs. 76%, and 93% vs. 60%, respectively) (Table 3.7). This was significant in only one of the CoPs, the #gettymuseumchallenge ($G = -0.783$, $p < 0.01$) (Table 3.8). Although for each CoP, the percentage of posts that included a personal story was higher in multiple community posts than in single community posts, these differences were significant in only two CoPs, #betweenartandquarantine ($G = -0.481$, $p < 0.01$) and #gettymuseumchallenge ($G = -0.607$, $p < 0.01$).

When it came to Instagram's features, we found variations between the posts in single and multiple communities, including the average number of hashtags, tags, followers, and comments per post (Table 3.9). We found a higher average number of hashtags and tags for posts in multiple communities than in single communities (13.44 vs. 5.38 and 1.83 vs. 0.69, respectively), but we found a higher average number of followers, comments, and likes on posts in single communities than those in multiple communities (91,754 vs. 59,022, 150 vs. 97, and 3,706 vs. 2,628, respectively). The differences between the average number of hashtags ($F = 37.531$, $p < 0.001$), tags (14.068, $p < 0.001$), and comments ($F = 36.209$, $p < 0.001$) were statistically significant, in contrast to the number of followers and likes (second column of Table 3.10).

We conducted a follow-up analysis in each of the CoPs to examine if these differences follow the same pattern (Table 3.11).

3   The difference between posts with high and low visibility.

We found that in each of the CoPs, all the compared social media features significantly varied between posts in both single and multiple communities and followed the same pattern as we had identified in the sample as a whole (fourth and fifth columns of Table 3.4).

Our sample included the 50 most visible posts and 50 least visible posts—based on the number of likes a post received—in each CoP, in order for us to answer the third research question effectively, and identify the differences between posts with high and low visibility in our sample and within each of the four CoPs. Figure 3.3 illustrates the differences in code frequency based on post visibility, showing that, unlike our expectations, posts with high visibility were more commonly included in only one of the four CoPs. Posts with lower visibility were more likely written in one language, paired with a personal story, or associated with artwork by an artist who does not have the same nationality as the user—nor does the artwork

Table 3.7 Code frequency and percentage of single and multiple communities per CoP

Code/Single and multiple community per CoP	#betweenartandquarantine		#tussenkunstenquarantaine		#gettymuseumchallenge		#изоизоляция	
	Single (N=24)	Multiple (N=76)	Single (N=25)	Multiple (N=75)	Single (N=20)	Multiple (N=80)	Single (N=74)	Multiple (N=26)
Single language	21 (88%)	70 (92%)	21 (84%)	63 (84%)	18 (90%)	67 (84%)	67 (91%)	22 (85%)
Nationality: Painter=User	3 (13%)	11 (14%)	4 (16%)	12 (16%)	3 (15%)	11 (14%)	8 (11%)	5 (19%)
Nationality: Museum=User	3 (13%)	11 (14%)	2 (8%)	11 (15%)	3 (15%)	9 (11%)	5 (7%)	3 (12%)
Info of original work	19 (79%)	70 (92%)	19 (76%)	69 (92%)	12 (60%)	74 (93%)	65 (88%)	23 (88%)
Personal story	10 (42%)	51 (67%)	12 (48%)	49 (65%)	7 (35%)	55 (69%)	43 (58%)	16 (62%)
Replace the object	6 (25%)	23 (30%)	10 (40%)	17 (23%)	7 (35%)	20 (25%)	18 (24%)	9 (35%)
Iconography beyond original	6 (25%)	19 (25%)	6 (24%)	13 (17%)	6 (30%)	18 (23%)	11 (15%)	6 (23%)
Total	24 (100%)	76 (100%)	25 (100%)	75 (100%)	20 (100%)	80 (100%)	74 (100%)	26 (100%)

Table 3.8 Results of cross-tabulation per code between single and multiple communities in each CoP

Code/G statistics	G (N = 100) #betweenartandquarantine	G (N = 100) #tussenkunstenquarantaine	G (N = 100) #gettymuseumchallenge	G (N = 100) #изонзоляция	G (N = 400) Total
Single language	-0.250	0.000	0.272	0.270	0.112
Nationality: Painter = User	-0.085	0.000	0.051	-0.325	-0.108
Nationality: Museum = User	-0.085	-0.328	0.164	-0.286	-0.208
Info of original work	-0.509	-0.568	-0.783**	-0.030	-0.465**
Personal story	-0.481*	-0.342	-0.607**	-0.071	-0.324**
Replace the object	-0.131	0.389	0.235	-0.244	0.045
Iconography beyond original	0.000	0.202	0.192	-0.264	-0.045

Sig. (* < 0.05; ** p < 0.01; *** p < 0.001).

Table 3.9 Average number of social media features in single and multiple communities

Average per post for single and multiple community	Hashtag	Tagging	Follower	Comment	Like
Single community	5.38	0.69	91,754	150	3,706
Multiple communities	13.44	1.83	59,022	97	2,628

Table 3.10 *t*-Test results for social media features of single/multiple community and high/low visibility posts

Social media features	Single/multiple community F (N = 400, df = 398)	High/low visibility F (N = 400, df = 398)
Hashtag	37.531***	10.989***
Tagging	14.068***	12.260***
Follower	0.092	27.359***
Comment	36.209***	114.507***
Like	1.683	42.059***

Sig. (*p < 0.05; **p < 0.01; ***p < 0.001).

Table 3.11 Average numbers of social media features in single and multiple community across four CoPs

Average per post for single and multiple community in each CoP		Hashtag	Tagging	Follower	Comment	Like
#betweenartandquarantine	Single	5.92	1.04	63,304	112	3,282
	Multiple	15.72	1.78	11,512	80	1,366
#tussenkunstenquarantaine	Single	7.28	0.60	37,304	116	3,812
	Multiple	11.43	1.96	90,327	110	3,366
#gettymuseumchallenge	Single	7.05	0.45	53,435	130	3,304
	Multiple	14.20	1.99	21,005	92	2,203
#изоизоляция	Single	4.12	0.66	129,734	180	3,916
	Multiple	10.23	1.15	224,573	133	5,495

belong to a museum nearby. In addition, the poster is likely to have experimented with iconography that goes beyond the original. However, only some of these differences were statistically significant (fourth column of Table 3.6). It was surprising to see that visible posts were significantly less likely to include a personal story, more than one language, or reflect an artwork by an artist from another nation than low visibility posts. As can be seen in Figure 3.3, among the top three most frequent codes is the inclusion of a personal story (147 vs. 96). However, only about half of the highly visible posts included a personal story (96 out of 200), while about three quarters of the less visible posts included a personal story (147 out of 200).

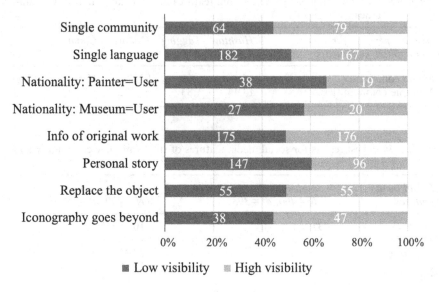

Figure 3.3 Frequency of codes in posts with high and low visibility.

When we further compared posts with varying levels of visibility in each of the CoPs (Table 3.12), we found that the difference in the inclusion of a personal story in less visible posts was greater in each of the four CoPs, and statistically significant in three of them (Table 3.13). Interestingly, regarding the Russian CoP, highly visible posts were less likely to include photos with replaced objects than were the less visible posts. Furthermore, posts with high visibility using the two English hashtags were more likely to be included in only one CoP than posts with low visibility (17 vs. 7 and 13 vs. 7, respectively), whereas highly visible and less visible posts within the Dutch or Russian CoPs were as likely to be posted in single communities as they were in multiple communities (12 vs. 13 and 37 vs. 37, respectively). However, these differences were statistically significant only for the #betweenartandquarantine CoP ($G = 0.520$, $p < 0.05$). While our sample indicated that highly visible posts were significantly more likely to use one language than were less visible posts, these differences were statistically significant only for posts within the #gettymuseumchallenge community ($G = -0.529$, $p < 0.05$). Furthermore, highly visible posts within the Dutch community were significantly less likely to use an artwork for which the nationality of its artist matches the user's ($G = -0.568$, $p < 0.05$).

As we examined the variations in use of social media features between posts with high visibility and those with low visibility (Table 3.14), we found that for each measure we examined, highly visible posts had a significantly different pattern from the less visible posts (third column of Tables 3.10).

Table 3.12 Code frequency and percentage of posts with high and low visibility per CoP

Code/high low visibility per CoP	#betweenartandquarantine		#tussenkunstenquarantaine		#gettymuseumchallenge		#изоизоляция	
	High (N=50)	Low (N=50)	High (N=50)	Low (N=50)	High (N=50)	Low (N=50)	High (N=50)	Low (N=50)
Single community	17	7	12	13	13	7	37	37
Single language	44	47	40	44	39	46	44	45
Nationality: Painter=User	5	9	4	12	4	10	6	7
Nationality: Museum=User	7	7	4	9	5	7	4	4
Info of original work	43	46	46	42	40	46	47	41
Personal story	22	39	27	34	24	38	23	36
Replace the object	17	12	13	14	16	11	9	18
Iconography beyond original	16	9	9	10	16	8	6	11

Table 3.13 Results of cross-tabulation per code of posts with high and low visibility in each CoP

Codel G statistics	G (N=100) #betweenartandquarantine	G (N=100) #tussenkunstenquarantaine	G (N=100) #gettymuseumchallenge	G (N=100) #изозоляция	G (N=400) Total
Single community	0.520*	−0.053	0.367	0.000	0.162
Single language	−0.362	−0.294	−0.529*	−0.102	−0.333
Nationality: Painter=User	−0.328	−0.568*	0.484	−0.088	−0.382**
Nationality: Museum=User	0.000	−0.433	−0.189	0.000	−0.168
Info of original work	−0.304	0.373	−0.484	0.549	0.023
Personal story	−0.637***	−0.288	−0.549**	−0.502**	−0.501***
Replace the object	0.240	−0.051	0.251	−0.439*	0.000
Iconography beyond original	0.364	−0.065	0.424	−0.348	0.134

Sig. (*p < 0.05; **p < 0.01; ***p < 0.001).

Table 3.14 Average frequency of use of social media features in posts with high and low visibility

Average per post for posts with high and low visibility	Hashtag	Tagging	Follower	Comment	Like
High visibility	7.92	1.54	138,018	162	5,817
Low visibility	13.21	1.31	3,429	71	209

As expected, posts with high visibility received significantly more likes and comments, included more tags, and were posted by users with significantly more followers, but they have used significantly fewer hashtags.

When we examined whether these differences were evident in each of the CoPs (Table 3.15), we found that three CoPs follow a similar pattern of social media features use, but differed from the Russian CoP; these were significant differences (fourth column of Table 3.4). We found that posts in the Russian community use fewer hashtags than the other three, regardless of high or low post visibility (3.16 compared with 9.88, 8.66., and 9.96; and 8.26 compared with 16.86, 12.12, and 15.58). In posts with low visibility in the Russian community, we found more tagging on average per post (0.84 compared with 0.74), in contrast to the three other CoPs, where the more visible posts had a greater number of tags than posts with lower visibility (1.56 compared with 1.64, 1.38 compared with 1.86, 1.44 compared with 1.92). Furthermore, in the Russian community's posts with high visibility, we found more comments (304,972) and likes (8,458) on average than in any of the three other CoPs. Still, while the follower count of users who post highly visible posts in the Dutch CoP is not as high as the Russian average, it is not as low as the other two English CoPs (151,546 compared with 43,770 and 51,786). Furthermore, the Dutch CoPs' most visible posts receive a higher average of likes than those of the most visible posts in the English CoPs (6,734 compared with 3,434 and 4,642).

Table 3.15 Average numbers of social media features in posts with high and low visibility across four CoPs

Average per post for high and low visibility per each CoP		Hashtag	Tagging	Follower	Comment	Like
#betweenartandquarantine	High	9.88	1.64	43,770	103	3,434
	Low	16.86	1.56	4,114	72	217
#tussenkunstenquarantaine	High	8.66	1.86	151,546	149	6,734
	Low	12.12	1.38	2,596	74	221
#gettymuseumchallenge	High	9.96	1.92	51,786	129	4,642
	Low	15.58	1.44	3,196	70	206
#изоизоляция	High	3.16	0.74	304,972	267	8,458
	Low	8.26	0.84	3,812	68	194

Discussion and Conclusions

We begin by discussing boundary maintenance, and then boundary-crossing; we explain our findings in light of existing knowledge on CoPs and within the specific sociocultural context of the four observed CoPs, drawing on cross-cultural communication theories (Barna, 1994; Hall, 1989; Hofstede et al., 2010; and Trompenaars & Hampden-Turner, 2012).

As a result of our attempt to understand if and how Instagram's visual affordances play a role in boundary maintenance processes (Dedema & Fichman, 2021), we have noticed specific sociotechnical practices that aim at maintaining the boundaries of a given CoP, consequently creating a homogeneity within the CoP and strengthening the CoP members' identities in practice. In particular, we observed that the hashtag's language served as a boundary maintenance tool, especially when the Cyrillic script in the Russian hashtag was used. The Latin script, on the other hand, was utilized in the three other hashtags. In fact, the use of a different script, rather than just the use of a different language, seems to enforce boundaries that are the least permeable, and the Russian/Cyrillic hashtag was significantly more likely to be used in a post without any of the three other Latin hashtags. This Instagram feature, the hashtag's script, aligns strongly with the separation and overlap between the four CoPs; we found that the vast majority of the posts in the Russian CoP did not overlap with any of the three other CoPs, while the vast majority of the posts in each of the three other CoPs overlapped with at least one other CoP.

The differences between the Russian CoP and the other three were evident in the comparison of almost all of Instagram's social media features that we examined, but any significant differences in regard to art recreation practice were unnoticeable. Specifically, on average, the Russian posts received more likes and comments, and had many more followers, yet fewer hashtags than did posts in each of the three Latin-script CoPs. Thus, we conclude that, despite the common practice of posting visual images of art recreations on Instagram, users in each of these four CoPs exhibit various social media behaviors. While the art recreations were shared across CoPs boundaries, the posts were shared almost exclusively among the segments of the community that used the same script. The hashtag, which is a textual representation of the post's topic, serves as a stronger form of identity in practice than do the images of art recreation. It is perhaps not a surprise that the script used to write a language creates barriers between the four observed CoPs, given that language barrier is one of the six most basic stumbling blocks in intercultural communication (Barna, 1994). What is noteworthy here is the extent to which chosen script dictates the permeability of a community even on Instagram, a platform known for its visual affordances, and within the context of a challenge that focuses on fine art. While an image is worth a thousand words and the art recreation practice was shared across CoPs, the least permeable boundaries between the CoPs have been maintained through the different hashtags' scripts. Future research should further explore and compare the extent of the textual versus the visual boundary maintenance practices.

Indeed, while hashtags' scripts served as a significant boundary between CoPs, making the Russian CoP more distinct from the other three, most of the posts in our data set were common to multiple CoPs, demonstrating permeable boundaries where boundary-crossing practices are common. These posts that facilitated the boundary-crossing process and belonged to more than one CoP (multiple communities) differed from those that did not facilitate the boundary-crossing process and only belonged to one CoP (single community). Most of the posts that crossed boundaries employed the Latin script, while the majority of the posts that used the Cyrillic script did not cross the boundaries of a single CoP.

We found that, more often than not, the ways in which the platform's social media features were utilized for boundary-crossing were expected. For example, posts that crossed CoP boundaries had, on average, a significantly larger number of hashtags and tags. Interestingly, however, posts in more than one CoP had significantly lower average numbers of followers, comments, and likes compared with posts that did not cross boundaries. This suggests that perhaps brokers function at the periphery of each CoP. Boundary brokers are "members who are particularly adept at maintaining a presence at the boundary of their community, while sustaining their own engagement in practice" (Thommons, 2017, p.12). Lave and Wenger (1991) describe how newcomers become experienced members of a CoP, starting with low-risk contributions at the margin of the community, in what the authors call *legitimate peripheral participation*. In a similar way, art historians have frequently traced deviations and innovations in style and techniques at the margins of masterpieces; these margins were often left to the artist's students and apprentices, some of whom later became established artists, pushing art forward through a continued chain of development (Gombrich, 1995). We observed that the social media practices differed between posts that served for boundary-crossing and those that did not, placing the Russian CoP as an outlier again.

The differences between the boundary-crossing posts and non-boundary-crossing posts were also noticeable in our content analysis, as boundary-crossing posts were significantly more likely to include information about the original work and/or to include a personal story than were posts in single communities that did not cross boundaries. Yet again, this boundary-crossing practice was not as common in posts within the Russian CoP, where posts were equally likely to include information of the original work in the Russian CoP, whether they were posted to one or more CoPs. Furthermore, while the percentage of posts that included a personal story was higher in boundary-crossing posts in each CoP, there was a significant difference when comparing them with the English non-boundary-crossing posts, #betweenartandquarantine and #gettymuseumchallenge. This may suggest that the language of the post, in addition to scripts, plays an important role in boundary-crossing practices; other cultural norms may affect this boundary-crossing practice (inclusion of a personal story), making it more common in Anglo-Saxon cultures than in other cultures.

It is possible that in Anglo-Saxon cultures, sharing personal information with strangers in online CoPs is more common, and that in these individualistic cultures, people are more likely to trust strangers enough to share with them their personal stories, in order to connect and gain sympathy. This practice of sharing information with strangers varies across cultures (e.g., Trompenaars & Hampden-Turner, 2012). For example, small talk across cultural barriers between Russians (coconut culture) and Americans (peach culture) is tricky in part because of their cultural differences (Meyer, 2014). Meyer (2014) explains that in peach cultures, "people tend to be friendly ("soft") with new acquaintances ... share information about themselves and ask personal questions of those they hardly know. ... [then] they suddenly get to the hard shell of the pit where the peach protects his real self and the relationship suddenly stops". Meyer (2014) continues and claims that in contrast, in coconut cultures, "people are initially more closed off from those they don't have friendships with. They rarely smile at strangers, ask casual acquaintances personal questions, or offer personal information to those they don't know intimately. But over time, as coconuts get to know you, they become gradually warmer and friendlier. And while relationships are built up slowly, they also tend to last longer". Meyer's (2014) idea comes from the difference between cultures based on the diffuse-specific dimension of culture (Trompenaars & Hampden-Turner, 2012) or the differences between high-low context cultures (Hall, 1989). Russian's diffuse and high context culture impacts their communication pattern, as they don't talk with strangers and are more conservative in general, whereas individuals from Anglo-Saxon cultures are less conservative and more likely to talk with strangers. These cultural differences can explain why the Russians' CoPs posts included less personal information than posts in the three other CoPs, and also why sharing personal information in posts in the Russian CoP was low both in boundary-crossing and non-boundary-crossing posts.

More generally, we found that the Dutch CoP most of the time was similar to the two English CoPs, and frequently in between the Russian and English CoPs, and this might be explained by the relative rank of these countries on Hofstede's six dimension of national culture (Hofstede et al., 2010). Furthermore, these cultural differences can explain why the Russian CoP boundaries were less permeable more generally, in addition to the differences in the use of Cyrillic vs. Latin script, and why we found different boundary maintenance practices between the Russian CoP and the three other CoPs. Russia differs from the Dutch and the other Anglo-Saxon cultures also on each of Hofstede's cultural dimensions (Hofstede et al., 2010),[1] which can help explain the general similarity between the three CoPs in English and Dutch, and the differences between the Russian CoP and the three other CoPs. Future research may benefit from a more thorough exploration of variations across cultures in other CoPs, beyond the specific cultures that we cover.

It is important to note here, however, that the frequency of sharing personal information in posts in the art recreation challenge may further be intensified online, compared with offline information sharing due to the disinhibition effect (Suller, 2004). When people communicate on social media platforms, they are more likely to open up and share personal information than they would be offline. As a result of benign online disinhibition (Suller, 2004), people might self-disclose more on the Internet than they would in real life, or go out of their way to help someone or show kindness online. The effect of cultural variations in toxic online disinhibition has been documented, (Fichman & Rathi, 2022), but the impact of culture on benign disinhibition has yet to be explored.

Because we initially thought post visibility (# of likes) may be a good indicator of boundary-crossing processes, we examined the differences between posts with high and low visibility and found that, following the same pattern we have identified earlier, the Russian CoP was also an outlier when it came to differences between posts with high or low visibility. Contrary to our expectations, posts with high visibility were more likely to belong to just one CoP, and when compared to less visible posts, the latter were significantly less likely to include a personal story, more than one language, or an artwork by an artist from another nation. Only about half of the visible posts included a personal story and about three quarters of the less visible posts included a personal story. Furthermore, posts with high visibility, as expected, received significantly more likes and comments, included more tags, and were posted by users with significantly more followers. These posts included significantly fewer hashtags, consequently minimizing the likelihood of crossing boundaries, which is counter-intuitive. All but the Russian CoP followed the same patterns when it came to social media features use; posts in the Russian community used fewer hashtags than the three other CoPs, regardless of visibility. Less visible posts in the Russian community included more tags on average per post, in contrast to the three other CoPs, where more visible posts had more tags than posts with lower visibility. Posts with high visibility in the Russian community had on average more comments and likes than visible posts in any of the three other CoPs. Surprisingly, visible posts in the Dutch community were posted by accounts with more followers and received more likes on average than visible posts in any of the two English CoPs. The challenge was very popular in the Netherlands, and the Dutch CoP, which also created an active Instagram account, was nominated for social media influencer of the year for 2020 in the country, and was awarded second place (The Best Social Awards, 2021). The variations between the Russian CoP and the three other CoPs only add to the differences we have already identified and explained in regard to boundary maintenance and boundary-crossing processes across and within these four CoPs.

Beyond the specific contribution that our study makes to the body of literature on online CoPs, our study also adds to the understanding of the relationships between technology and society more broadly, and to social informatics research in particular. We provide an example of an Instagram challenge to illustrate how the dystopian context of COVID-19 quarantine promoted early conceptions of the utopian future, in which ICTs are used everywhere in ways that go past the idea of "beyond being there". Two opposing ideals, dystopia and utopia, are merging to create a complex and even paradoxical contextual setting for ICT use. It is this combination that allows for the use of ICTs in new and innovative ways. As we observed, in all four CoPs, practices involved sociotechnical manifestations that are "beyond being there", not only in terms of specific technological affordances, but also by creating a new form of art that combines 1) the past and the present in pushing into the future; 2) fine art of the great masters and folk art that is created by anyone through repetition, the latter of which is enabled and encouraged on social media in general, including Instagram, with the help of its visual affordances; 3) the real artifact and its digital representation or the digital manipulation of the recreation that only exists in digital format. As a form of art, the recreation exists only in light of the original; its existence, however, pushes the boundaries of the original into new contexts in which new artists and amateurs utilize other materials, objects, and style to create new pieces of art. The recreated art then has a life of its own, as it is easily shareable; it can be further manipulated and shared and duplicated like any other meme, regardless of size, medium, materials, or location of the original.

The art recreation challenge has attracted amateurs and professional artists, motivated to engage in this social media challenge for many reasons, one of which is the desire to overcome anxiety and trauma that were introduced to many by the COVID-19 lockdown. One of the most active participants in this challenge, Eliza Reinhardt, writes: "These works search for selfhood and a reclamation of lost memories resulting from a traumatic brain injury. The sedimentary addition and subtraction of paint functions both as a literal and metaphorical archaeology of memory. Faces are fragmented, broken, and hidden; ambiguous, but sincere. A violent collision between my own physicality, paint, and image, the resulting canvases house a rich eruption of painting – a record of my re-genesis of self". (Reinhardt, 2021) The recreations later began to spill over outside the confinement of their existence as a shareable digital image on a social media platform, and back into the physical world, bringing some recreations into museums' buildings or turning some into commercialized artifacts. Not only did museums promote the challenge early on (e.g., The Getty and the Rijksmuseum—the national museum of the Netherlands), but also later, in response to its popularity, they reinforced the idea that art recreations in this challenge exist as a legitimate form of contemporary art by curating exhibitions of recreations within the museums in real life. For example, the Palais des Beaux-Arts de Lille—an art museum in France—curated the first official exhibition of these recreations in real life; the exhibition was open to visitors from September 19, 2020 to November 30, 2020. The exhibition referred to the recreations as interpretations that were presented by the masterpieces from their collection, and in some instances provided the physical setting for visitors to recreate their own interpretations of museum masterpieces. Another spillover of these recreations from Instagram to real life involves the commercialization of some art recreations by artists (e.g., Eliza Reinhardt) in the form of prints, postcards, and calendars.

In conclusion, we contribute in this chapter a nuanced understanding of CoP boundary maintenance within the context of Instagram's art recreation challenge during the COVID-19 crisis. We emphasize the sociotechnical affordances of the platform, and highlight how these sociotechnical affordances pushed the relationships between ICT and society to new levels "beyond being there". By doing so, we contribute to social informatics research.

Note

1 Based on Hofstede et al. (2010) the scores of the Netherland, Russia, and USA, respectively are: PDI 39-93-40; IDV 80-39-91; MAS 14-36-62; UAI 53-95-46; LTO 67-81-26; and IND 68-20-68.

References

Anguissola, A. (2007). Retaining the function: Sacred copies in Greek and Roman art. *Res: Anthropology and Aesthetics, 51*, 98–107. 10.1086/RESv51n1ms20167718

Barna, L.M. (1994). Stumbling blocks in intercultural communication. In R. Porter, & L. Samovar (Eds.), *Intercultural communication: A reader* (pp. 337–346). Wadsworth Publishing Company.

Bryant, S.L., Forte, A., & Bruckman, A. (2005). Becoming Wikipedian: Transformation of participation in a collaborative online encyclopedia. In K. Schmidt, M. Pendergast, M. Ackerman, & G. Mark (Eds.), *Proceedings of GROUP International Conference on Supporting Group Work.* (pp. 11–20). ACM Press.

Brown, J.S., & Duguid, P. (1998). Organizing knowledge. *California Management Review, 40*(3), 90–111.

Dedema, M., & Fichman, P. (2021). Boundary-crossing in online community of practice: "Between Art and Quarantine". *Proceedings of the Association for Information Science and Technology, 58*(1), 697–699.

Fichman, P., Sanfilippo, M.R., & Rosenbaum, H. (2015). Social informatics evolving. *Synthesis lectures on information concepts, retrieval, and services, 7*(5), 1–108. 10.2200/S00668ED1V01Y201509ICR046

Fichman, P., & Rathi, M. (2022). *The impact of culture on online toxic disinhibition: Trolling in India and the USA. Hawaii International Conference on System Sciences.* 10.24251/HICSS.2022.357

Geismar, H. (2018). Mimesis, replication, and reality. In *Museum Object Lessons for the Digital Age* (pp. 105–113). UCL Press. 10.2307/j.ctv1xz0wz.11

Gombrich, E. (1995). *The story of art* (16th ed.). Phaidon Press.

Gultepe, E., Conturo, T.E., & Makrehchi, M. (2018). Predicting and grouping digitized paintings by style using unsupervised feature learning. *Journal of Cultural Heritage, 31*, 13–23. 10.1016/j.culher.2017.11.008

Hall, E.T. (1989). *Beyond culture*. Anchor Books.

Hara, N., & Fichman, P. (2014). Frameworks for understanding knowledge sharing in open online communities: Boundaries and boundary-crossing. In P. Fichman, & H. Rosenbaum (Eds.), *Social Informatics: Past, Present and Future* (pp. 89–100). Cambridge Scholars Publishing.

Hofstede, G., Hofstede, G.J., & Minkov. M. (2010). *Cultures and organizations: Software of the mind* (3rd ed.). McGraw Hill.

Hollan, J., & Stornetta, S. (1992). Beyond being there. *Proceedings of the SIGCHI Conference on Human Factors in Computing Systems*, 119–125. 10.1145/142750. 142769

Kang, X., & Chen, W. (2017). The like economy: The impact of interaction between artists and fans on social media in art market. *Proceedings of the International Conference on Business and Information Management*, 45–49. 10.1145/31342 713134281

Lam, M.L.K. (2015). *Collaborative #Sunrise: A computational art installation that uses Instagram photos from around the world to create an "Eternal Sunrise"* [M.S., Dartmouth College].

Lave, J., & Wenger, E. (1991). *Situated learning: Legitimate peripheral participation*. Cambridge University Press.

Murillo, E. (2008). Searching Usenet for virtual communities of practice: Using mixed methods to identify the constructs of Wenger's theory. *Information Research: An International Electronic Journal, 13*(4).

Meyer, E. (2014, May 30). One reason cross cultural small talk is so tricky. *Harvard Business Review*. Retrieved from https://hbr.org/2014/05/one-reason-cross-cultural-small-talk-is-so-tricky

Ravasio, M. (2018, March 8). *Replicating paintings*. Retrieved from https://contempaesthetics.org/newvolume/pages/article.php?articleID=826

Reinhardt, E. (2021). About page from personal website. Retrieved from https://elizareinhardt.com/About

Rosenbaum, H., & Shachaf, P. (2010). A structuration approach to online communities of practice: The case of Q&A communities. *Journal of the American Society for Information Science and Technology, 61*(9), 1933–1944.

Shachaf, P., & Hara, N. (2007). Behavioral complexity theory of media selection: A proposed theory for global virtual teams. *Journal of Information Science, 33*(1), 63–75. 10.1177/0165551506068145

Suller, J. (2004). The online disinhibition effect. *CyberPsychology and Behaviors, 7*(3), 321–326. 10.1089/1094931041291295

The Best Social Award. (2021). Retrieved from https://thebestsocialawards.nl/

Thommons, J. (2017). *Learning architectures in higher education: Beyond communities of practice*. Bloomsbury Academic Collection. Ch.1, pp. 1–16. 10.5040/97814742 61722.ch-001

Trompenaars, F., & Hampden-Turner, C. (2012). *Riding the waves of culture: Understanding diversity in global business* (3rd ed.). McGraw Hill.

Waldorf, S., & Stephan, A. (2020, March 30). Getty artworks recreated with household items by creative geniuses the world over. Retrieved from https://blogs.getty.edu/iris/getty-artworks-recreated-with-household-items-by-creative-geniuses-the-world-over/

Wantagh Elementary School. (2020). Students participate in viral Getty challenge. Retrieved from https://wes.wantaghschools.org/news/what_s_new/students_participate_in_viral_getty_challenge

Wenger, E. (1998). *Communities of practice: Learning, meaning, and identity*. Cambridge University Press.

Zia, A. (2019, July 30). Digitizing art history. Retrieved from https://hermitagemuseum.wordpress.com/2019/07/30/digitizing-art-history/

4 Treating a Viral Culture: Using Cultural Competency and Social Informatics to Design Contextualized Information Literacy Efforts for Specific Social Information Cultures

Rachel N. Simons and Aaron J. Elkins

Introduction

Information does not exist in a void; it is created by people, for people, in specific contexts and for specific purposes. These contexts and purposes also shape how information is shared between individuals and within groups. Researchers have long argued for the importance of understanding information behavior in context (Agarwal, 2017; Courtright, 2007), including the role of sociocultural factors (Savolainen, 2016; Shin et al., 2007). Yet, even given that information behaviors are performed in the context of sociocultural belonging, the shifting approach to understanding the "post-truth" nature of information literacy (Cooke, 2018) starkly underlines that information behaviors within a single context may be far from homogenous. A single larger sociocultural context (e.g., the population of the United States) can contain multiple different social information cultures; members of one information culture can even find another information culture to be completely incomprehensible.

Thus far, little research has focused particularly on how shared socio-cultural frameworks shape information behavior within groups or communities as a culture. In this chapter, we develop a novel framework for understanding "social information cultures" (SICs) as unique subjects of study. We argue that developing an understanding of how people interact with information, as contextualized within a specific SIC, can enable information literacy (IL) efforts that more effectively address members of that culture. This process requires information professionals to focus on increasing their social information cultural competency (SICC).

In order to understand fully any social information culture, we must also examine how a culture is shaped by and reflected in its usage of information and communication technologies (ICTs). In today's global information society ICTs, such as social media platforms, bring together individuals from different geographic areas and allow them to create distinct social

DOI: 10.4324/9781003231769-7

information cultures that leverage both social and technical aspects to maintain a community. The field of social informatics (SI) focuses on using a sociotechnical approach to understanding the "design, uses, and consequences of information technologies" while "[taking] into account their interaction with institutional and cultural contexts" (Kling, 2007, p. 205). Accordingly, SI provides a crucial framework for using cultural competency to understand a particular social information culture in context.

After describing the SICC framework, we illustrate how SICC can be used to analyze a case study of the COVID-19 misinformation SICs engaged with through social media during the current pandemic. In particular, we examine three current IL intervention approaches for addressing COVID-19 misinformation (inoculation or "prebunking" efforts, accuracy prompts before posting or sharing, and online conversation groups). During this examination, we consider how each approach compares to key features of the SICC framework, and how adopting the SICC framework might enhance such IL efforts. Finally, we conclude with some suggestions for how IL and SI researchers might employ the SICC framework to help information professionals treat and inoculate those infected by viral misinformation cultures.

Social Information Cultural Competency: A Sociotechnical Approach to Understanding Information Behaviors in Context

In this section, we discuss the different frameworks that contribute to our novel approach to understanding SICs, by bringing together theoretical perspectives on psychosocial understandings of information behavior, cultural competence, and SI. We then discuss how information professionals might better design contextualized information literacy efforts by applying SICC.

Contextualizing information behavior within social information cultures

We define culture (Jahoda, 2012) here primarily as a socially constructed, systematic set of beliefs and concomitant behaviors to which individuals may adhere—and in which they may engage to various extents—in order to experience social belonging. A key part of those beliefs and behaviors is determined by their relationship to narratives within the culture (Bruner, 2014; Miller et al., 2007), including both shared and personal narratives (Hammack, 2008). All human beings need to feel a sense of belonging to/in a sociocultural context (Allen et al., 2021); increasingly, many people use online interactions to foster a sense of social belonging (Meshi et al., 2020). Social media is an important tool for fostering belonging in educational settings (Vaccaro et al., 2015), work settings (Eren & Vardarlier, 2013), and for older adults (Sum et al., 2009).

In addition to culture, a variety of psychosocial factors interact to create information contexts that influence peoples' information behavior (Hollister et al., 2020). Identity performance is one way to indicate belonging to a given culture; identity performance is the purposive expression of certain behaviors and suppression of other behaviors (O. Klein et al., 2007). Identity performance also includes information behavior (O. Klein et al., 2007; Mahmud & Wong, 2021; S-O'Brien et al., 2011; Torres, 2010; Vignoles et al., 2006). As individuals participate in both information and cultural contexts, they engage in particular information behaviors guided by beliefs that provide them with comfort and moral direction; they additionally hope their beliefs and subsequent actions will provide them with a better life (Shermer, 2002).

While research on information worlds (Burnett & Jaeger, 2008), social media culture (Cino & Formenti, 2021; Megarry, 2018; Odii, 2020), conspiracy culture (De Maeyer, 2019; Grodzicka & Harambam, 2021), and communities of practice (Wenger & Snyder, 2000) address some aspects of information behavior in particular sociocultural contexts, they have not necessarily considered the relationship between information behavior and identity performance as situated within a sociotechnical context. In particular, very little research has considered this relationship within the context of cultures whose information behaviors are intertwined with information and communication technologies (ICTs); such social information cultures may exist in hybrid online and physical spaces, primarily online, or even shift between spaces.

The concept of an information culture is a particularly powerful tool for interrogating information behaviors performed in a situated context. Current uses of the term "information culture" typically focus on knowledge management and sharing behaviors within an organizational work context, often in relation to productivity (Choo, 2013; Oliver, 2017). This concept of information culture is important, as it provides a tool to interrogate information behaviors performed in the particular context of an organizational environment. However, because of its critical value, we argue that the term "information culture" should be extended to contexts beyond the traditional organizational model, to include other groups and communities of practice. We therefore propose the term "social information culture" (SIC) to understand better the information behaviors that are performed in the context of sociocultural belonging, and within a specific sociotechnical community that includes ICT use as an integral feature.

Social information cultural competency

A single larger sociocultural context (e.g., the population of the United States) can contain multiple different SICs. In particular, the growing need for information professionals to address a "posttruth era" (Baer, 2018; Cooke, 2018; Lewandowsky, 2019; Lewandowsky et al., 2017) starkly underlines that social information culture is far from homogenous. However, very few of the researchers examining the information behaviors of such cultures have discussed in depth just how information professionals attempting to work with these SICs (but who are not themselves part of the SIC) can develop an understanding of how to approach them. One approach to understanding the information behaviors of such cultures—after recognizing them as cultures—is to develop a nuanced cultural competency.

Cultural competence is an important framework within the fields of library and information studies (LIS) (Cooke, 2017), although authors have criticized the lack of critical awareness and theoretical rigor around the term (Blackburn, 2020). Broadly defined as the ability to interact respectfully with people from other cultures, and sometimes framed in terms of "cultural humility" (Hodge, 2019; Hodge & Mowdood, 2016; Hurley et al., 2019), cultural competence is partially developed by understanding the intersectional nature of identity, and how our identities variously privilege or oppress us within the systems of power of a culture (Blackburn, 2020; Montiel-Overall, 2009). In particular, an understanding of such cultural hierarchies and beliefs may be facilitated by analyzing both the dominant cultural narratives and counternarratives within the culture (Cooke, 2017). Accordingly, developing a nuanced cultural competence for a specific culture requires significant time and critical reflection, usually including developing a meaningful relationship with the culture/community (Cooke, 2017).

Intellectual empathy is one tool that information professionals may use while developing cultural competence (Hollister et al., 2020). Intellectual empathy asks us to consider how the affective and cognitive factors that comprise social identity interact to affect reasoning and belief (Baer, 2018, 2019; Linker, 2011, 2015). The five skills essential for intellectual empathy are: "[U]nderstanding the invisibility of privilege; knowing that social identity is intersectional; using the model of cooperative reasoning; applying the principal of conditional trust; [and] recognizing our mutual vulnerability" (Linker, 2015, p. 14). Along with these five skills, we may use the "web of belief" model (van Orman Quine, 1975) to understand how beliefs exist in relation to their importance to identity; as people adopt some beliefs into the core of their identities, those beliefs become highly resistant to change, even in the face of overwhelming counter-evidence. Developing an understanding of what beliefs people have adopted as core to their identities, and why they have so internalized those beliefs over others, can provide part of the blueprint to build a bridge of intercultural understanding successfully.

Accordingly, we propose that Social Information Cultural Competence (SICC) is the ability to respectfully interact with people from different SICs formed through a deeper relationship with the community, an understanding of the privileges and oppressions resulting from the intersectional nature of identity, and intellectual empathy. Additionally, a foundational aspect of SICC is the expectation both to analyze dominant cultural narratives of an SIC, and to make space for counternarratives.

Social informatics and SICC

While the application of cultural competence is an important framework of practice and instruction within the field of LIS more broadly, the framework is not frequently applied to research in the area of SI. Yet SI shares several relevant principles with cultural competence, including encouraging careful attention to the details of practice and identity as they are enacted within a specific context.

An integral part of the SICC approach, SI "emphasizes the core relationships among people, ICT, and organizational and social life from perspectives that integrate aspects of social theory" (Fichman & Rosenbaum, 2014, p. xviii). Through close examination of these relationships, "the invisible can be made visible and its hidden assumptions brought to light for careful critical examination" (Fichman & Rosenbaum, 2014, p. xviii). This ability is incredibly important for developing SICC for a specific SIC. SI has also discussed the importance of looking at cultural norms, such as around interactions with intellectual property through ICTs (Eschenfelder, 2014).

The field of SI is not only well-attuned to examining closely both the sociocultural and technical details of how an SIC engages with ICTs, but is also useful for considering "embodied, culturally situated knowledge" performed by users of specific ICTs (Simons et al., 2020, p. 183). The significance of sociocultural context is a core principle of SI (Goggins & Mascaro, 2013; Sawyer & Tapia, 2007), wherein "the situated nature and uses of computing means that context and use are bound up through practice" (Sawyer & Tapia, 2007, p. 274). Moreover, SI emphasizes that, because "the design, implementation, and uses of ICT have reciprocal relationships with the larger social context", we cannot ignore the larger societal consequences of "the differential effects of the design, implementation, and uses of ICTs" (Sawyer & Tapia, 2007, p. 274).

SICC is particularly informed by previous SI theory examining the practices of knowledge sharing in online communities (Hara & Fichman, 2014). Much like the concept of SICs, Hara and Fichman (2014) similarly emphasize the need to examine the practices of communities outside of traditional organizations. Similar in some ways to the idea of using boundary objects or boundary spanners (Hara & Fichman, 2014), SICC provides a perhaps more contextualized approach for communicating and understanding information behaviors between those who may not fully share SIC memberships. In recent years, the rise of "posttruth" conceptualizations of information have only increased the importance for SI to consider such frameworks of knowledge sharing.

Integrating an SICC approach into the field of SI accordingly has potential impacts for both research and practice in a number of areas. In our case study within this chapter, we show both how SICs can be analyzed as a sociotechnical subject of study by SI researchers, and how SICC can guide the direct practice of information professionals engaging in information literacy interventions with a particular SIC.

SICC-informed information literacy interventions

Although the field of IL has historically focused on developing skills focused on traditional methods of reading (i.e., books and other authoritative written documents), some authors have argued that IL must adopt a sociotechnical approach to theory and practice, as well as integrating social context into IL education and practice (Tuominen et al., 2005). While research in the areas of digital literacy, ICT literacy, information literacy, and media literacy frequently overlap among many different disciplines when considering ICTs (Park et al., 2020), the field of LIS has a particular interest in addressing the topic through community instruction led by information institutions (Lloyd, 2010). Accordingly, the field of LIS has traditionally discussed IL as "more of a practical and strategic concept used by librarians and information specialists" that should be implemented through direct education practice or curriculum development (Tuominen et al., 2005, p. 330).

In particular, social media literacy (or competence) has become a priority for such efforts (Zhu et al., 2021). The focus on social media within the field of IL has increased rapidly over the past ten years, especially because of rising public concern about the increasing spread of "fake news" and misinformation through these ICTs (Jaeger & Taylor, 2021). In response to these growing concerns, researchers have called for IL interventions for addressing misinformation on social media (Rubin, 2019). Rubin (2019), for example, has proposed a sociocultural and sociotechnical framework for IL interventions, which follows the epidemiological disease triangle model and focuses on causal factors, virulent pathogens, and susceptible hosts. Rubin asserts that automated interventions should only "assist (but not replace) human judgments" and "require further in-depth understanding of the phenomenon and interdisciplinary collaboration" (2019, p. 1013).

The SICC framework is well-suited to build on previous IL theory and research, while better informing such attempts to address misinformation through interventions with specific SICs (which necessarily include ICTs). Currently, only some IL approaches focus on sociocultural factors as a critical aspect of tailoring literacy development and instruction (Budd & Lloyd, 2014) or integrate a cultural competency/humility framework (Cobus, 2008; Hodge & Mowdood, 2016; Montiel-Overall, 2007). While researchers have looked at the relationship between IL and social capital (Widén et al., 2021), and how social structures outside of the control of individuals can impact the development of IL skills (Lin, 2010), IL frameworks continue to struggle between a desire to highlight individual agency by promoting "the knowledge and skills to battle the complexity of the modern information world", and the tendency to frame individuals through a "deficit perception" of their current agency and perceived lack of appropriate literacies (Hicks & Lloyd, 2020, p. 363). Despite making great progress, IL interventions generally fail to account for the full complexity of the context of information behaviors. Instead, IL interventions need to recognize that "knowledge is not located in texts as such—or in the individual's head", and focus on the "co-construction of situated meanings and takes place in networks of actors and artifacts" (Tuominen et al., 2005, p. 338).

An SICC-informed approach aims to honor the focus on agency and skill development that is central to most IL interventions within the field of LIS. An important part of this process is an emphasis on critical reflective practice (Corrall, 2017) for everyone involved in the intervention. At the same time, an SICC-informed approach shifts the primary focus from the individual to an SIC—thereby allowing for an information professional to better understand the sociocultural and sociotechnical context of that group, before engaging them directly in an intervention. Developing SICC for an IL intervention necessarily requires developing a relationship with the SIC and approaching this relationship with intellectual empathy.

Finally, we again emphasize the importance for an SICC-informed IL intervention to understand and address the significance of cultural narratives within an SIC. As information professionals attempt to grapple with the role of "posttruth" and misinformation, they must address the important role of narrative in creating a sense of meaning and belonging in relation to misinformation (Bessi et al., 2015; Bessi et al., 2015; Dahlstrom, 2021). Researchers looking at the problem of misinformation on social media have discussed the power of conspiracy narratives, for example, as being "a combination of disinformation, misinformation, and rumour that are especially effective in drawing people to believe in post-factual claims and form disinformed social movements" (Darius & Urquhart, 2021, p. 1). In fact, some research indicates that ignoring the relevant narrative during an intervention may have a "backfire effect" that causes members of an SIC to become even more invested in misinformation (Zollo, 2019, p. 1). However, it is worth noting that counterstories can exist even alongside these dominant narratives of misinformation within an SIC (Goldstein, 2018).

We therefore propose that such SICs that become organized around cultural narratives of misinformation may be called "misinformation SICs". These SICs require a careful SICC approach to IL intervention, lest the intervention support the very misinformation it is trying to address. In the rest of this chapter, we develop a specific case study, in order to illustrate both the SICC framework and how it might improve IL interventions with a misinformation SIC.

Case Study: Information Literacy Campaigns Addressing COVID-19 Misinformation on Social Media

In this section, we will use a specific case study on current approaches to addressing the rapid spread of misinformation related to the COVID-19 pandemic through social media. We first discuss the specific context of the COVID-19 misinformation SIC, including developing an understanding of this SIC as a culture, and illuminating some important technical features of social media platforms on which this SIC draws. We then discuss some current frameworks for approaching IL interventions with this SIC. We conclude by discussing three examples of IL interventions and comparing these approaches to the SICC framework.

Background

As the COVID-19 pandemic continues throughout the world, access to accurate and timely information remains a high priority for individuals and global society. Throughout the pandemic, a significant number of people across cultures and demographics have and are searching for, engaging with, and sharing information about the COVID-19 pandemic, specifically through social media platforms (Banerjee & Meena, 2021; Neely et al., 2021). Accordingly, the quick spread of accurate health information over social media can be useful for sharing important and even life-saving information (Venegas-Vera et al., 2020).

Unfortunately, an alarming amount of the information about COVID-19 and the pandemic that is being circulated is "disinformation", "misinformation", "false rumor", or "conspiracy theories" (Cinelli et al., 2020; Islam et al., 2021; Kouzy et al., 2020).[1] In addition to coverage of these topics in several previously established fields of research (Pool et al., 2021), the field of "infodemiology" has rapidly developed after the World Health Organization popularized the term "infodemic" (Purnat et al., 2021; Zielinski, 2021). While not all information contained in the COVID-19 infodemic is inaccurate, the prevalence of inaccurate information can make it even more difficult for individuals to access or assess the accurate information (Calleja et al., 2021). Even a well-intentioned rush to share academic knowledge about the COVID-19 pandemic has led to a boom of preprint articles, including many that have been later retracted or revised (Fraser et al., 2021; Tentolouris et al., 2021). At least one systematic review identified "social media usage, [a] low level of health/eHealth literacy, and [the] fast publication process and preprint service" to be "the major causes" of our current COVID-19 infodemic (Pian et al., 2021, p. 1).

Researchers are alarmed at both the rapid spread and sheer quantity of misinformation being shared over social media (N. Ahmed et al., 2020; Banerjee & Meena, 2021; Bin Naeem et al., 2021). One recent study found, for example, that roughly 25% of tweets with COVID-19 health information contained inaccurate information (Swetland et al., 2021). What makes this particular kind of dis/misinformation especially concerning is the seriousness of the consequences for not only those individuals who engage with this dis/misinformation (Barua et al., 2020; De Coninck et al., 2021; Pian et al., 2021), but also for those in the same physical communities who do not actively engage with this misinformation (Calleja et al., 2021; Hornik et al., 2021).

Understanding COVID-19 misinformation networks as social information cultures

In order to address effectively the negative impacts of COVID-19 dis/misinformation spread through social media, we must first better understand who is sharing this content, how and where networks of sharing develop, and—perhaps most importantly—why individuals engage with COVID-19 dis/misinformation content and choose to share it with others in their social networks. Previous research on "fake news" and dis/misinformation has identified several different psychosocial factors for why individuals engage with and share this content on social media, including a lack of deliberation in evaluating the content (Bago et al., 2020), a reliance on emotion (Martel et al., 2020), a "laziness" in utilizing analytic thinking (Pennycook & Rand, 2019, p. 2521), and using heuristics of familiarity when encountering information, without a depth of personal knowledge on the topic (Pennycook & Rand, 2021).

While the research on COVID-19 dis/misinformation engagement and sharing on social media is still (rapidly) developing, there is compelling evidence that a cultural model is an appropriate approach for understanding this information behavior (Rampersad & Althiyabi, 2020). Similar to previous examinations of groups such as the "antivax" or "vaccine hesitant" communities on social media (Koltai, 2020a, 2020b; Wawrzuta et al., 2021), preliminary research indicates that people who go beyond simply reading and decide to share COVID-19 "fake news" or dis/misinformation, do so for complex sociocultural reasons. While individual differences may predict a particular user's likelihood of sharing certain kinds of COVID-19 misinformation, such as conspiracy theories (Lobato et al., 2020), research has found that the general motivation for sharing COVID-19 dis/misinformation is greatly determined by tie strength to others in the sharing network (Apuke & Omar, 2020), along with a value of altruism (Apuke & Omar, 2021). These shared beliefs may lead social media users into closed networks of COVID-19 dis/misinformation that further their ties to the group through "echo chambers" that promote "confirmation bias" (Modgil et al., 2021).

In short, an individual's reasoning for whether or not to share COVID-19 misinformation goes beyond individual psychological factors, and is influenced by their connections to others with similar beliefs and values.

These connections form a unique SIC that is both mediated by and reflected in the use of social media. There are indications that content sharing networks are not necessarily bound by the same traditional geographical, national, or demographic divisions as traditional cultures. Within boundaries such as the United States, for example, COVID-19 dis/misinformation is spreading across traditional racial, socioeconomic, and gender lines (Collins-Dexter, 2020; Ross, 2020). Or at least, dis/misinformation narratives can be taken and repurposed for different groups, so that "concepts similar enough to pass as first cousins on the misinformation family tree have proliferated in social media spaces that do not usually cross or blend" (Ross, 2020, para. 5).

This COVID-19 misinformation SIC represents a culture that is unique to and shaped by the specific context of COVID-19, while also drawing on preexisting SICs such as the "alternative medicine community" (Soveri et al., 2021) and "antivax" or "vaccine hesitant community" (Koltai, 2020b). For example, dedicated sharers of COVID-19 dis/misinformation have begun employing shared "secret codes" and alternative words to get around bans on misinformation designed by social media platforms—a tactic that is particularly well-documented among the previously existing "antivax" SIC (Collins & Zadrozny, 2021). This shared language not only provides the SIC with a valuable tool for using social media platforms on their own terms, but also solidifies their shared sense of group identity as a culture.

Members of the COVID-19 dis/misinformation SIC accordingly draw on these overlapping SICs to learn both social media tactics (Kalichman et al., 2021), and how to frame compelling narratives rhetorically (Martin & Vanderslott, 2021), both of which are key aspects for the SIC to grow and flourish. Research indicates that, while antivaccine cultural narratives on social media have tended to coalesce around a few prevalent themes such as freedom of choice and harm prevention from vaccine-related injuries (Wawrzuta et al., 2021), antivaccine narratives are increasingly able to incorporate more diversity and flexibility, and thus to draw in individuals with more diverse interests (Johnson et al., 2020). Furthermore, antivaccine content is better able to present and use rhetorical message framings that are known to be persuasive and engaging, while provaccine content on social media may not use such compelling rhetoric (Argyris et al., 2021).

This greater cohesion of narrative and rhetorical framing on one side of the debate may be explained by the fact that people who engage with provaccine content on social media do not necessarily consider themselves to be part of a "provaccine" social group, and do not perceive their information behaviors to be within the context of such an SIC. For example, there are far fewer "provaccine" groups on Facebook than "antivaccine" or "vaccine hesitant" groups; on average, antivaccine groups not only create more content but also stay active for a longer period of time than provaccine groups (Kim & Kim, 2021). Previous research has shown that antivaccine groups on platforms such as Facebook foster a sense of community and belonging among members, and form "network ties due to homophily through values", with those values being consistent between different groups (Koltai, 2020b, p. 3). These connections indicate a larger sense of culture that goes beyond specific groups or content. At least one study has shown that any two local clusters of antivaccine groups on Facebook (e.g., within two US states) are "typically interconnected through an ether of global clusters and so feel part of both a local and global campaign" (Johnson et al., 2020, p. 231).

As this SIC continues to coalesce, it produces a feedback loop that amplifies its own presence. With many of their normal cognitive and social structures disrupted by the pandemic, individuals look for alternative sociocultural structures on social media, and may find a compelling one in the COVID-19 misinformation SIC. As they become socialized into this SIC, they begin acting in the "real" world based on these cultural beliefs, and sharing the results of their actions back on social media—which then amplifies the cultural narratives even more and draws greater attention (and new members) to the SIC (Dow et al., 2021). Significantly, the Center for Countering Digital Hate (CCDH) claims that a number of "leading antivaxxers" met secretly in person in October 2020 to share their approaches to using social media and—among other goals—to coordinate around a "master narrative" (CCDH, 2020, p. 4).

Relevant technical features and understanding the role of platforms

As the CCDH additionally points out (CCDH, 2020), antivax leaders and average sharers must successfully leverage the technical features of social media platforms to propagate cultural narratives effectively. It is worth noting, however, that even the broad use of the term "social media" may erase important distinctions in how the affordances of each specific platform interact with the information behaviors of an SIC. For example, "echo chambers" may look and function very differently on different social media platforms, based on the features of those platforms (Cinelli et al., 2021). The use of private groups, the inability for users to curate highly their own "feed" of posts shared by "friends", and other sharing features, may create more highly segregated "homophilic clusters" on Facebook than on a platform such as Reddit (Cinelli et al., 2021).

At the same time, social media users are capable of translating dis/misinformation narratives successfully across platforms and adapting to leveraging the different affordances of these platforms. For example, the organization First Draft has a number of guides and "recipes" to help researchers and journalists understand the spread of specific dis/misinformation across different platforms (First Draft, 2022). The guide to "tracking the cross-platform spread of harmful and misleading narratives" asserts that "misinformation and conspiracy theories are not static" and "move from one platform to another, often promulgated by organized online communities that seed this information across the web" (Smith & De Keulenaar, 2021, para. 1). One example of a particularly contagious piece of disinformation is the Plandemic "documentary", which continued to be shared across multiple platforms, even as individual platforms attempted to ban the video and discussion (Graham, 2020).

Several researchers studying the spread of COVID-19 dis/misinformation on social media have urged that attempts to address this problem must consider the deliberate use of "media manipulation" on these platforms by conscious actors (Donovan et al., 2021; Nazar & Pieters, 2021). Donovan et al. (2021) argue that not only is such "media manipulation" an understudied aspect of the COVID-19 infodemic, but also that it is specifically "a sociotechnical process, whereby motivated actors leverage conditions or features within an information ecosystem to [...] advance their agenda" (p. 6). Their advice "is designed to work within any cultural context", is "fluid", and relies on "the method of research known as investigative digital ethnography, which takes into account the differences in geography, culture, language, law, and demographic diversity, so that these recommendations can be tailored to specific environments as per the needs of the locale and situation" (Donovan et al., 2021, pp. 4–5). Notably, they also identify the sharing of specific narratives as an important component of the "seeding" of a dis/misinformation campaign through social media (Donovan et al., 2021, p. 20).

Donovan et al. discuss several specific features of the use of social media to distribute narratives, including attempting to dominate conversations on specific platforms "where they believe they can reach a target audience", for example, by identifying specific Facebook pages, or engaging with a particular Twitter hashtag (2021, p. 20). The CCDH has identified similar tactics around the spread of dis/misinformation, with the goal of advancing narratives, as well the use of social media deliberately to create spaces for confused or uncertain individuals to receive misinformation under the guise of getting "answers", including misleadingly named Facebook groups and misleading hashtags on Instagram and Twitter (CCDH, 2020, p. 10). By achieving a "critical mass in conversation that will lead to a campaign['s] becoming newsworthy or result in a false perception of massive public concern", seeded dis/misinformation ultimately lends authority to narratives that become increasingly compelling (Donovan et al., 2021, p. 20). Once "a particular piece of disinformation has spread beyond a core group of media manipulation campaign operators, resulting in trending topics on social media, uptake by influential social media accounts, and coverage by fringe websites with little or no editorial oversight", this dis/misinformation has been successfully integrated into wider discussions on social media beyond the initial group doing the "seeding" (Donovan et al., 2021, p. 20). These narratives may then engage both core members of the SIC and other users of social media.

Significantly, some researchers have argued that the solution to such deliberate manipulation of the specific affordances of social media platforms is not simply to increase technical or digital literacy for all people who may interact with dis/misinformation narratives. For example, Sirlin et al.'s (2021) study of social media users who were presented with a set of true and false news posts, found significant differences in the factors associated with believing false posts versus sharing false posts. While this study supports previous research associating lower digital literacy with "less ability to tell truth from falsehood", it simultaneously contradicts the prevalent belief that this same relationship explains sharing behaviors around dis/misinformation (Sirlin et al., 2021, p. 3). In fact, the authors argue that "the pattern is strikingly different" for sharing intentions, whereby "[no] digital literacy measure is consistently associated with sharing discernment—the tendency to share true news more than false news—nor are they significantly associated with the fraction of headlines the subject shared that are true (an alternative metric of information sharing quality)". Sirlin and colleagues also noted that "analytic thinking is also not significantly associated with either sharing quality measure" (Sirlin et al., 2021, p. 3).

Researchers, politicians, and concerned users have all called for greater transparency from social media platforms (Donovan et al., 2021), and for these companies to take greater responsibility for the spread of COVID-19 dis/misinformation (CCDH, 2021; B. Klein et al., 2021). Over the past year and a half, several platforms have made efforts to control this aspect of the infodemic, primarily by banning certain misinformation (Stelter & Pellico, 2021), and occasionally by banning the accounts of well-known "super-spreaders" (De Vynck, 2021; Pietsch, 2021). However, these efforts have been criticized as still lacking transparency or unity across platforms (Krishnan et al., 2021).

Such platform-driven efforts have had only limited success in controlling either the spread of dis/misinformation narratives or the growth of the COVID-19 misinformation SIC (N. Ahmed et al., 2020; De Vynck & Lerman, 2021). As evidenced by the Plandemic video (Graham, 2020) and other narratives, such as the "#FilmYourHospital" conspiracy (W. Ahmed 2020), specific narratives may easily circumvent moderation by any one platform (Cruickshank et al., 2021). To get around bans of specific links known to contain misinformation, users may develop workarounds such as using the WayBack Machine digital archive to point to links of since-removed (or debunked) articles that are now banned on platforms (Donovan, 2020). Posts may also use "co-tagging" with multiple hashtags to circumvent bans on specific misinformation-related hashtags (Quinn et al., 2021). Automatic flagging on platforms like Twitter has had mixed results and may even backfire, as members of such misinformation SICs may be influenced by narratives alleging that these efforts are "political" attempts to control them, and become even more firm in their beliefs (Lanius et al., 2021). Notably, many of these moderation approaches are largely automated. While automated moderation does show some promise, it still struggles to follow both the role of psychosocial factors and the way that SICs continue to amend and adapt narratives across platforms—especially as misinformation narratives evolve and change over time (Gerts et al., 2021).

Accordingly, we argue that there is still a significant need for information professionals to intervene and to address the spread of harmful dis/misinformation on social media platforms, especially within the dedicated COVID-19 dis/misinformation SIC.

COVID-19 misinformation IL interventions

Because of their long history with similar IL efforts, and their sophisticated understanding of "information", information professionals are not only well-suited to these interventions, but also should feel obligated to intervene. Bin Naeem and Bhatti (2020), for example, refer to the current COVID-19 infodemic as a "new front for information professionals" and document existing guides that librarians have assembled to combat misinformation (p. 233).

Researchers and platforms have tried several approaches to ban or otherwise label COVID-19 dis/misinformation content on social media, including fact-checking (Roitero et al., 2021) and de-bunking (Wang et al., 2021) strategies. As mentioned above, many of these approaches are automated. However, most such attempts to control dis/misinformation content do not really attempt to improve the IL within the COVID-19 dis/misinformation SIC. Instead, such approaches focused on limiting the spread of the content itself, and therefore do not really correspond to IL frameworks in LIS, which focus on developing the agency and skills of users. Accordingly, researchers have argued that interventions need to go beyond "fact-checking" approaches (Burel et al., 2021; Chou et al., 2021; Shahi et al., 2021) to developing long-term eHealth and science literacy (Eysenbach, 2020). Yet these literacy interventions are still framed in terms of individual users, rather than the SIC as a whole.

Of the approaches aimed at individual users, many COVID-19 dis/misinformation interventions are framed as media (Melki et al., 2021; Su et al., 2022) or communication literacy (Mheidly & Fares, 2020) approaches. Some may be called health literacy (Bin Naeem & Kamel Boulos, 2021; Silva & Santos, 2021) or digital health literacy (Dadaczynski et al., 2021; Nguyen et al., 2021; Patil et al., 2021; Vrdelja et al., 2021) interventions. Others have focused on proactively increasing trust in science (Agley et al., 2020; Agley & Xiao, 2021), including by using infographics (Crutcher & Seidler, 2021; Rotolo et al., 2021). Despite the differences in names, nearly all of these approaches share an interest in trying to automate the intervention and to scale it up in order to reach as many people as possible.

Next, we analyze three specific types of intervention efforts that have recently been gaining significant research and media coverage in more detail. In our analysis, we discuss both similarities with our proposed SICC framework, and where possible gaps in these approaches might be better addressed by incorporating an SICC approach. To develop our analysis, we have closely read these processes (Feinberg, 2012) through online documentation, research articles, and interviews that discuss these approaches. Our analysis is also informed by the approach of Critical Technocultural Discourse Analysis (CTDA), which "applies critical cultural and, importantly, technocultural theories to ICT artifacts" (Sweeney & Brock, 2014, p. 3). We discuss these specific intervention approaches merely as examples, not as a comprehensive review of all approaches.

Inoculation or prebunking

A growing body of research indicates that approaches focusing on fact-checking or de-bunking dis/misinformation that has already been extensively shared on social media are not particularly effective in changing the minds of users who have already been exposed. Even a single exposure may form an "illusory truth effect" that is hard to combat (Pennycook et al., 2018, p. 1865). Additionally, debunks "don't reach as many people as misinformation, and they don't spread nearly as quickly" (Garcia & Shane, 2021, para. 3). "Inoculation" or "prebunking" efforts therefore attempt to catch users at (or before) the first time they encounter a new piece of dis/misinformation (Lewandowsky & van der Linden, 2021). In a guide developed for First Draft, Garcia and Shane (2021) list three main types of prebunking efforts: fact-based (focused on correcting a specific false claim or narrative), logic-based (focused on explaining tactics used to manipulate), or source-based (pointing out bad sources of information). While the approach can be used for different types of dis/misinformation, the guide particularly emphasizes COVID-19 dis/misinformation.

Focusing primarily on a combination of "fact" and "logic" based approaches, First Draft offers a guide to designing prebunking efforts. Notably, the first step is to "figure out what information people need"; the authors encourage those designing an intervention to "anticipate [their] audience's questions" by not assuming "that [their] questions are the same as [their] audience's" (Garcia & Shane, 2021, sec. What to prebunk). The authors encourage the use of "tools such as Google Trends to figure out trending questions or issues", as well as "[checking] in with community figures and [thinking] about creating a space where people can submit their questions" (Garcia & Shane, 2021, sec. What to prebunk). This step involves asking questions such as "What preexisting narratives might bad actors exploit?" and "How can you help people identify these tactics and narratives so that they are less likely to fall for them?" (Garcia & Shane, 2021, sec. What to prebunk).

The tenth (and final) step is "Find where your audience is and publish there", in which "successful prebunks will join and be integrated in online spaces and platforms where your audience is already spending time" (Garcia & Shane, 2021, sec. How and where to share). Those designing interventions are encouraged to "use social listening and monitoring tools to figure out the digital spaces where "the party" is happening and join in", after "[reading] the room before [jumping] into the conversation" (Garcia & Shane, 2021, sec. How and where to share). This final step involves "[thinking] about the culture of the specific online space or platform you have identified" by asking questions such as "What are the trends or styles that people use to communicate?" and "How can you use those in a way that effectively communicates the information you want people to have?" (Garcia & Shane, 2021, sec. How and where to share).

This approach to addressing dis/misinformation is mostly in line with a true IL approach, as it aims to develop the agency and skills of individuals by teaching them to "be better equipped to spot it and question it" (Garcia & Shane, 2021, sec. The basics). The process described here includes several other qualities that are integral to the SICC framework, most notably a nascent understanding of the importance of targeting prebunking efforts at communities that have their own "cultures". Focusing on listening and understanding existing narratives are also key components of developing cultural competency/humility for a specific SIC.

Integrating the SICC framework into this prebunking process would encourage intervention designers to think more deeply in a few key areas. In particular, the SICC framework would encourage a deeper approach to understanding the target SIC, beyond using more shallow tools such as Google Trends. In particular, developing a better understanding of why members of the SIC value and share certain narratives would further deepen the approach to supporting members' ability to spot and question these narratives—as well as to evaluate more critically their membership in the SIC as a whole. Teaching intervention designers more clearly how to engage in the process of developing cultural competency/humility, such as how to employ an "investigative digital ethnography" (Donovan et al., 2021, p. 4), would be particularly helpful.

Finally, while preventative dis/misinformation IL interventions are a great approach in theory, it is worth considering how cultural competency should be applied to understanding who is likely to participate in such interventions. It seems unlikely that core or deeply invested members of the COVID-19 dis/misinformation SIC would be eager to approach such interventions without a preexisting value for spotting and questioning dis/misinformation—which seems especially unlikely given the values of this SIC. Accordingly, a pre-prebunking effort might be necessary just to build trust with the SIC and to entice such members to participate in the intervention. As the primary tool for engaging individuals in these interventions is often automated games that are aimed at reaching as many people in a general population as possible (e.g., DROG, 2022; Social Decision-Making Lab, 2022; Warner, 2022), it may be difficult to build this kind of pretrust through a relationship specifically with the SIC.

Accuracy prompts

Based on prior research that indicates a boost in critical thinking reduces "inattentive" sharing of fake news and misinformation, the intervention approach of "accuracy reminders" (also called prompts or nudges) aims to encourage social media users to evaluate COVID-19 dis/misinformation more closely before sharing it (Pennycook et al., 2020, p. 777). Pennycook et al. (2020) argue that this approach is effective for fighting COVID-19 dis/misinformation because "people generally wish to avoid spreading misinformation and, in fact, are often able to tell truth from falsehood; however, they nonetheless share false and misleading content because the social media context focuses their attention on factors other than accuracy" (p. 771). Accordingly, the approach focuses on applying "subtle nudges" to make the "concept of accuracy more salient" in users' minds as they interact with social media content. Several researchers in this area believe that this approach can be widely applied, because the analytical thinking mechanism can work independently from users' "political ideology" or personal background (Pennycook & Rand, 2019, p. 39).

In particular, recent research by Epstein et al. (2021) examined several different accuracy prompt interventions, using survey experiments with US social media users "quota-matched to the national distribution on age, gender, ethnicity, and geographic region" (p. 2). As with previous studies, this study focused primarily on judging the content of headlines (some with misinformation and some with accurate information), and asking participants about their sharing intentions. The authors found that the most effective intervention into reducing participants' stated intention to share false headlines incorporated a multistep approach before asking them about their sharing intentions for the specific headlines of the study: "(i) asking participants to judge the accuracy of a non-COVID-19 related headline, (ii) providing minimal digital literacy tips, (iii) asking participants how important it was to them to share only accurate news, [...] (iv) asking participants to judge the accuracy of a series of [four] non-COVID-19–related headlines (and providing corrective feedback on their responses), [and] (v) informing participants that other people thought it was important to share only accurate news (providing "descriptive norm" information)" (Epstein et al., 2021, p. 3).

The authors argue that certain forms of this multistep accuracy prompt intervention are "particularly appealing" because of the following factors: the approach does not "require technology companies to decide (e.g., via machine learning or human moderators) what is true versus false"; the approach allows users to "exercise [their] desire to avoid sharing inaccurate content, preserving user autonomy"; and because "accuracy prompts are scalable (unlike, for example, professional fact-checking, which is typically slow and only covers a small fraction of all news content)" (Epstein et al., 2021, p. 2). They additionally argue that "gender, race, partisanship, and concern about COVID-19 did not moderate effectiveness, suggesting that the accuracy prompts will be effective for a wide range of demographic subgroups" (p. 2). Yet the authors do conclude that "the prompts were more effective for participants who were more attentive, reflective, engaged with COVID-related news, concerned about accuracy, college-educated, and middle-aged" (Epstein et al., 2021, p. 2). Finally, they do indicate some areas for future research, including assessing "how long the effects last" and understanding how their results "would generalize cross-culturally" (Epstein et al., 2021, p. 3).

Again, there are several aspects of this approach that could work well in an SICC-informed IL intervention. In particular, the SICC framework is roughly in line with the authors' emphasis on including a complex approach that incorporates both digital literacy skills and a connection to psychosocial factors of belonging (such as discussing values of the user and of others they may consider to be in their "community"). Additionally, the approach specifically values "user autonomy" (Epstein et al., 2021, p. 2) and users' ability to develop and use their own judgement and IL skills.

At the same time, the SICC framework would indicate some potential gaps in this approach. First, this is (again) a very individual-centered approach that explicitly aims to be generally effective across demographics, cultures, and groups (rather than working with a specific SIC and building a relationship). However, it is worth noting that even the authors indicated that the results were most effective for participants with certain characteristics (namely: attentive, reflective, engaged with COVID-related news, concerned about accuracy, college-educated, and middle-aged) and that "the effect was also stronger among people who placed greater importance on sharing only accurate news, consistent with the idea that shifting attention to accuracy should increase sharing discernment only insofar as the user actually cares about accuracy" (Epstein et al., 2021, p. 3). The SICC framework would suggest that some additional investigation and building of cultural competency is likely necessary to understand fully if this set of "characteristics" and "values" indicates the presence of a distinct SIC(s) with whom this approach will particularly resonate, and if there are other SICs for whom the approach does not work. While the authors briefly address the limitation of generalizing across cultures, they likely mean the more traditional sense of geographic/national or ethnic/racial cultures.

Additionally, there is little nuance in the approach toward understanding how a "preference for accuracy" may be balanced with other psychosocial factors of belonging and belief, including other values of the SIC. Adopting the SICC framework could potentially help information professionals looking to use this approach to target certain cultural values better and make them even more salient, by more fully understanding the relationships of other values and the cultural narratives of the SIC. Why and when do certain "foci" become more "salient" for members of the COVID-19 dis/misinformation SIC? For example, are all headlines and topics equally culturally important to the SIC? Are headlines even of primary interest to members of this SIC when they make sharing decisions?

Finally, as with many current COVID-19 misinformation IL approaches, this approach particularly emphasizes scalability and generalizability. This is certainly an understandable goal, and the approach may indeed work well for the majority of social media users who casually interact with COVID-19 dis/misinformation. While researchers have proposed integrating this approach into social media platforms, the platforms have not yet adopted this intervention. Like with the prebunking approach, the current primary mechanism for this type of intervention is the use of online "training" games (e.g., Social Decision-Making Lab, 2022). Similar to the prebunking approach, however, it may be necessary to develop a longer-term relationship directly with the COVID-19 dis/misinformation SIC, in order to encourage members of the SIC actually to engage with this intervention.

Conversation groups

In contrast to more large-scale and automatable interventions, several grassroots "conversation group" approaches have developed, that encourage a more interpersonal and human-focused framework for addressing COVID-19 dis/misinformation. Among these, arguably the most successful is the grassroots effort "Vaccine Talk". Vaccine Talk focuses on engaging with individual users on social media platforms—especially the vaccine "skeptical" and those with vaccine skeptics in their personal lives. While not focused exclusively on the COVID-19 vaccine, the group has been greatly focused on discussing this particular vaccine within the context of the pandemic (Dwoskin et al., 2021).

Although members may venture out into other social media platforms such as the Reddit discussion forum (Dwoskin et al., 2021), the movement's main home is a private Facebook group (meaning that users must request and be given access by a group moderator), with almost 79,000 current members (Vaccine Talk, 2022). The group describes itself as a "group for vaccine debate and discussion" where "PV [Pro-Vaccine], AV [Anti-Vaccine], and undecided are all welcome" (para. 1). The group has ten stated rules, including: "No misrepresentation and no medical advice"; "No doxing or harassment, civility is required"; "Please provide evidence when asked for it"; and "Please include a discussion or debate topic" (Vaccine Talk, 2022, sec. Group rules from the admins). As of August 2021, the group had twenty-five moderators/administrators who represented six different countries (Dwoskin et al., 2021) and were collectively available 24 hours a day (Simon, 2021).

In interviews, one of the group's co-founders (Kate Bilowitz) stresses that the group is moderated "by real people" (para. 5) who "want to get people out of their echo chambers and start talking to each other" (Simon, 2021, para. 6). Bilowitz describes "the process to engage somebody who is concerned about vaccines" as beginning with "[encouraging] them to make a post in the group expressing what it is that they're concerned about, why they're feeling that way and what specific questions they have"; then the other group members are encouraged "to provide [the poster] with either evidence showing that, you know, what they're concerned about is not true or evidence showing that there's nothing to be concerned about" (Simon, 2021, para. 9). Not only do posters need to provide some kind of link to "evidence" within 24 hours upon the request of any single other group member, but they must also give "a little bit of commentary about it" in order to "[cut] down on spamming" (Simon, 2021, para. 10). Once "evidence" has been provided, "it's up to the members in the group to evaluate that source and tell the member who provided it why it's a good source or why it's a bad source" (Simon, 2021, para. 10). Bilowitz adds that this reflective engagement process with both the information and the other group members is "really educational for a lot of people who have maybe never been challenged in that way before" (Simon, 2021, para. 10).

Unlike the other interventions, which can quantitatively measure the amount of times that certain misinformation content is shared, or whether or not recipients of the intervention choose to share sampled misinformation, the outcome metrics of a conversation group like Vaccine Talk are more qualitative. The post-by-post approach focuses on each individual and their own "discussion or debate topic"; there is no external evaluation of the outcome of the conversation sparked by posts, of the objective truth of the claims made, or of the impact on the individuals involved. Yet, while the primary goal of the group is not necessarily to convert as many vaccine skeptics as possible, Bilowitz claims that the group administrators loosely monitor the sentiment of people who join the group (as "antivaccine or on the fence") and that they have documented over 400 cases of group members remarking that the group has changed their mind (Simon, 2021, para. 12).

The group deliberately uses different tactics than the automated approaches that social media platforms are using, focusing on fostering nuanced conversations instead of simply banning certain key words, topics, or sources (Dwoskin et al., 2021). In fact, Bilowitz expresses frustration that Facebook's tactics to control dis/misinformation frequently hinder the group's own efforts, saying that "the biggest challenge that we face right now is dealing with Facebook's content moderation" because "Facebook's algorithm can't understand the difference between something that's posted with the intention of spreading misinformation and something that's posted with the intention of debunking or critiquing it" (Simon, 2021, para. 12). Furthermore, Bilowitz argues that Facebook's "inconsistent" flagging makes it hard for the group to avoid complete (temporary) deactivation—an occasional occurrence that "keeps [her] up at night [worrying] about what's going to happen to the group" (Simon, 2021, para. 11). She expresses a deep concern with the "banning" approach, saying, "Facebook is attempting to shut down misinformation by shutting down all conversation entirely, [but] I strongly believe that civil, evidence-based discussion works, and Facebook's policies make it extremely difficult for that to happen" (Dwoskin et al., 2021, para. 5). A critical part of making these discussions work, she emphasizes, is empathy for all of the members of the group: "Empathy is critical to this work. I don't think you could do this if you didn't care about people. I think all of our moderators and myself [care] very deeply about what we're doing" (Simon, 2021, para. 13). The goal of this "care" is to acknowledge realistically that the "conversation about vaccines" is not easily solved universally with a one-time intervention, and to "continue the group and to grow it to help get the correct information to people to help them feel confident in their decision to get vaccinated" (Simon, 2021, para. 13). Bilowitz adds that this approach to getting people to accept the COVID-19 vaccine is "how we're going to end this pandemic" (Simon, 2021, para. 13).

Although the Vaccine Talk group would not necessarily describe themselves as an "information literacy" intervention, this grassroots movement has several important features of the SICC IL approach. First, the organizers of the group have an explicit focus on intellectual empathy and on allowing members of the group to express their own values/beliefs and to be respectfully heard. Second, the organizers are invested in cultivating an environment in which members can productively cultivate their own evaluations and interpretations, rather than forcing an externally defined goal and understanding of the context. From its own description, the group is ostensibly not concerned either with determining an absolute truth or with defending a particular side in the debate. However, comments made by Bilowitz clearly indicate that the group's main purpose is to "get the correct information to people to help them feel confident in their decision to get vaccinated" (Simon, 2021, para. 13). Similarly, while a culturally competent or humble IL approach should be empathetic and respect participants' agency, information professionals do not necessarily have to adopt a "neutral" approach without specific desired outcomes—especially when dealing with SICs of misinformation. Finally, the organizers, while themselves not necessarily part of the antivaccine SIC, have taken (and continue to take) considerable time to engage with this SIC and to understand it.

There are also some aspects of this approach that do not completely line up with an SICC IL intervention. Most notably, the approach somewhat deliberately avoids placing posters' "discussion or debate topic" into full cultural context, and instead establishes a post-by-post or individual focus. While the group does leave some room for personal narrative and counternarratives, it still very heavily privileges—in fact, requires—the presence of "evidence" and labels itself as an "Evidence Based Discussion Forum".

However, the group does leave the validation and interpretation of what makes something definitively "evidence" up to each individual (which does, in turn, support the agency of members in developing their own critical thinking and information literacy skills). Finally, while this approach has some implications for integrating counternarratives, it does not do so explicitly; we may also question whether such a group will ever appeal to core members of the COVID-19 dis/misinformation SIC, or whether it can only appeal to less-engaged or tentative members.

Discussion: Suggestions for Treating a Viral Misinformation SIC

Our case study analysis supports previous work indicating that a focus on individual deficiencies in information literacy skills is not sufficient to explain why or how misinformation narratives become viral and are shared within an SIC (Sirlin et al., 2021)—and may even risk creating a "backfire effect" (Zollo, 2019). Accordingly, we propose that the SICC framework can guide information professionals in learning to understand information behaviors and social information cultural narratives in a sociotechnical context—without that full context, IL interventions with SICs are not likely to be as successful, particularly in the case of such viral misinformation cultures.

First, we argue that IL intervention efforts need to better understand who is most deeply engaging with dis/misinformation content on social media (i.e., the actual SIC members), versus focusing exclusively on the behaviors of non-SIC members who happen to be interacting with misinformation narratives. It is true that many people engaging in these narratives, while not actively members of the SIC, may be inadvertently supporting and raising the profile of these narratives. Yet while there is still value in interventions that prompt non-SIC members to think carefully about sharing misinformation, these users may not represent the most "viral" sharers. While more generalized prebunking and accuracy prompt interventions may be easier to scale, they will also likely be less effective at improving IL for the most core members of a misinformation SIC.

Accordingly, at least some IL interventions should be tailored to those who have become deeply invested in the specific cultural narratives of the dis/misinformation SIC. For example, one study found that individuals' belief in COVID-19 misinformation does not necessarily stem from a lack of trust in the narrative of scientific consensus, so much as a simultaneous support for other narratives (Agley & Xiao, 2021). This finding indicates that simply presenting these individuals with consensus-based scientific "fact" may not be as useful for changing a belief in misinformation, as making this narrative more compelling than other misinformation cultural narratives. Using an SICC framework helps information professionals to assess and address actual SIC members meaningfully.

Second, we argue that IL interventions need to understand better why the members of an SIC (especially a misinformation SIC) engage in certain information behaviors and are invested in certain cultural narratives. There is compelling evidence, for example, that people fall back on shared cultural values and narratives even more in times of crisis and informational uncertainty or overload. Darius and Urquhart argue that, during the COVID-19 pandemic, conspiracy narratives "provide a pseudo-epistemic background for disinformed social movements that allow for self-identification and cognitive certainty in a rapidly changing information environment" (2021, p. 1). The exponentially growing – and sometimes legitimately conflicting – information from official and academic sources about COVID-19 makes many individuals particularly reliant on trusting compelling narratives and voices (Purvis et al., 2021).

However, the goal of IL interventions should not simply be to purge an SIC of all cultural narratives: adopting an SICC approach includes recognizing that narratives are a key part of any culture, and that both narratives and counternarratives are an important tool to engage both individuals and the group. Previous research has shown, for example, that narrative approaches can be highly successful in delivering accurate COVID-19 health information tailored to diverse subgroups across social media (Gesser-Edelsburg, 2021; Ngai et al., 2020). Currently, the small body of research on using narratives in conjunction with health information on social media is focused more on subgroups or personas (e.g., Massey et al., 2021), and is primarily focused on conveying accurate information—as opposed to cultivating IL skill development through intervention with an SIC. We suggest that SICC IL approaches to COVID-19 dis/misinformation might consider building on such research by, for example, integrating personal and affective narratives from culturally competent health professionals. While some research has indicated that personal narratives from healthcare professionals is effective in promoting accurate COVID-19 information (Topf & Williams, 2021), these approaches are often still lacking specific cultural competency for the SICs they are targeting. Integrating celebrity or other influential voices might be a similar approach.

Similarly, while SICC IL approaches can build on other interventions that encourage critical reflection, they should integrate an understanding of how to encourage members of a particular SIC to engage in these behaviors. While the literature emphasizes the importance of critical reflection, few studies address the all-important question of how to get individuals to engage in this practice if reflection (or reflection in this way) is not already a valued part of their SIC. For this reason, it may also be helpful to engage current or former members of the SIC in sharing counternarratives from within the SIC itself that may support the ultimate goal of developing IL skills. Conversation group approaches such as Vaccine Talk offer one possible way to engage such counternarratives, if deliberately cultivated and supported. When using such an approach, we must be aware of how super-spreaders use similar groups to achieve the opposite goals, and further pull in uncertain SIC members (and potential members) by doubling-down on and tailoring compelling narratives (CCDH, 2020). Yet the very success of this approach in drawing individuals into SICs may indicate the potential for successfully using the same approach to help draw them out of it again.

Finally, we argue that IL interventions must understand how dis/misinformation is shared within and outside of SICs, specifically by understanding the technical affordances of the ICTs that are an integral part of the SIC. Building on advice given by Donovan et al. (2021) that is "designed to work within any cultural context" (p. 4) and "can be tailored to specific environments as per the needs of the locale and situation" (p. 5), we argue that an SICC approach can go one step further by understanding the COVID-19 dis/misinformation SIC is the cultural context itself to which it should be tailored. Accordingly, information professionals attempting an information literacy intervention for this (or any) SIC can employ the approach of "investigative digital ethnography" (Donovan et al., 2021, p. 4) as part of their development of cultural competency. This approach also includes developing familiarity with the specific ICTs (and their affordances) used by the SIC, as an integral part of the SIC.

Notably, as Donovan et al. (2021) argue, "Observing online communities properly takes time, and the ethnographic process requires a commitment to observation during breaking news events and also during the downtime in between" (p. 47). Similarly, we posit that perhaps the most defining feature of an SICC approach is the deliberate avoidance of haste in deploying (particularly automated) interventions; time is required to develop both cultural competency and a meaningful relationship with the SIC, with which an information professional seeks to work. Time and relationship building are important features, for example, of the Vaccine Talk conversation group. While these features are also largely absent from current automated approaches (such as the prebunking and accuracy prompt interventions), we argue that automated approaches might find greater success within the core dis/misinformation SIC if these approaches were designed after fully developing cultural competency.

Information professionals—particularly those who are used to engaging with the field of social informatics—are particularly well-situated to appreciate the effort necessary to understand fully both the sociocultural and technical aspects of an SIC before designing anything. We propose that the SICC framework provides a valuable approach to understanding the who, why, and how of successfully treating a viral misinformation culture.

Conclusion

In this chapter, we have proposed a novel framework for designing contextualized information literacy interventions using the approach of SICC.

While developing a case study of dis/misinformation spread through social media during the COVID-19 pandemic, we argue that current information literacy efforts to address COVID-19 misinformation—while promising— are incomplete because they currently fail to fundamentally understand and address why, how, and through whom cultures of dis/misinformation continue to flourish online. We propose that adopting an SICC framework will better allow existing and future information literacy efforts (such as those aimed at combatting COVID-19 misinformation) to assist individuals in developing their information literacy skills within the context of their social information culture.

In addition to advancing IL practice and research, our SICC framework contributes to the field of SI research by introducing the novel concept of SICs. The field of SI is a foundational aspect of the SICC framework and guides the principle of understanding SICs as inherently and deeply sociotechnical "subjects" that are deserving of study. Additionally, we encourage the field of SI to embrace the conceptual and methodological framework of cultural competency when investigating SICs; while cultural competency (or cultural humility) is becoming increasingly relevant within the practice of many information professionals, it has not yet been adopted within the research (or practice) specifically of SI. Accordingly, our case study examination offers one starting example of how SI research might adopt the SICC framework.

In order to "treat" viral misinformation cultures, information professionals must develop both a sociotechnical and sociocultural understanding: they must become empathetic "doctors" who take the time necessary to understand fully where their "patients" are coming from, or risk administering ineffective or even harmful treatments.

Note

1 Because we are not interested here in distinguishing between the sources and/or intentions of the creators of inaccurate COVID-19 information, for the purposes of this case study, we primarily refer to inaccurate information as "misinformation" or "dis/misinformation".

References

Agarwal, N.K. (2017). Exploring context in information behavior: Seeker, situation, surroundings, and shared identities. *Synthesis Lectures on Information Concepts, Retrieval, and Services, 9*(7), i–163. 10.2200/S00807ED1V01Y201710ICR061

Agley, J., & Xiao, Y. (2021). Misinformation about COVID-19: Evidence for differential latent profiles and a strong association with trust in science. *BMC Public Health, 21*(1), 89. 10.1186/s12889-020-10103-x

Agley, J., Xiao, Y., Thompson, E.E., & Golzarri-Arroyo, L. (2020). COVID-19 misinformation prophylaxis: Protocol for a randomized trial of a brief informational intervention. *JMIR Research Protocols, 9*(12), e24383. 10.2196/24383

Ahmed, N., Shahbaz, T., Shamim, A., Shafiq Khan, K., Hussain, S.M., & Usman, A. (2020). The COVID-19 infodemic: A quantitative analysis through Facebook. *Cureus, 12*(11), e11346. 10.7759/cureus.11346

Ahmed, W., López Seguí, F., Vidal-Alaball, J., & Katz, M.S. (2020). COVID-19 and the "Film Your Hospital" conspiracy theory: Social network analysis of Twitter data. *Journal of Medical Internet Research, 22*(10), e22374. 10.2196/22374

Allen, K., Kern, M.L., Rozek, C.S., Mcinerney, D.M., & Slavich, G.M. (2021). Belonging: A review of conceptual issues, an integrative framework, and directions for future research. *Australian Journal of Psychology, 73*(1), 87–102. 10.1080/0004 9530.2021.1883409

Apuke, O.D., & Omar, B. (2020). Modelling the antecedent factors that affect online fake news sharing on COVID-19: The moderating role of fake news knowledge. *Health Education Research, 35*(5), 490–503. 10.1093/her/cyaa030

Apuke, O.D., & Omar, B. (2021). Fake news and COVID-19: Modelling the predictors of fake news sharing among social media users. *Telematics and Informatics, 56*, 101475. 10.1016/j.tele.2020.101475

Argyris, Y.A., Monu, K., Tan, P.-N., Aarts, C., Jiang, F., & Wiseley, K.A. (2021). Using machine learning to compare provaccine and antivaccine discourse among the public on social media: Algorithm development study. *JMIR Public Health and Surveillance, 7*(6), e23105. 10.2196/23105

Baer, A. (2018). It's all relative? Post-truth rhetoric, relativism, and teaching on "Authority as Constructed and Contextual". *College & Research Libraries News, 79*(2), 72. 10.5860/crln.79.2.72

Baer, A. (2019). What intellectual empathy can offer information literacy education. In S. Goldstein (Ed.), *Informed Societies: Why information literacy matters for citizenship, participation and democracy* (pp. 47–68). Facet. 10.29085/9781783303922.005

Bago, B., Rand, D.G., & Pennycook, G. (2020). Fake news, fast and slow: Deliberation reduces belief in false (but not true) news headlines. *Journal of Experimental Psychology. General, 149*(8), 1608–1613. 10.1037/xge0000729

Banerjee, D., & Meena, K.S. (2021). COVID-19 as an "infodemic" in public health: Critical role of the social media. *Frontiers in Public Health, 9*, 610623. 10.3389/fpubh.2021.610623

Barua, Z., Barua, S., Aktar, S., Kabir, N., & Li, M. (2020). Effects of misinformation on COVID-19 individual responses and recommendations for resilience of disastrous consequences of misinformation. *Progress in Disaster Science, 8*, 100119. 10.1016/j.pdisas.2020.100119

Bessi, A., Coletto, M., Davidescu, G.A., Scala, A., Caldarelli, G., & Quattrociocchi, W. (2015). Science vs conspiracy: Collective narratives in the age of misinformation. *PloS One, 10*(2), e0118093. 10.1371/journal.pone.0118093

Bessi, A., Zollo, F., Del Vicario, M., Scala, A., Caldarelli, G., & Quattrociocchi, W. (2015). Trend of narratives in the age of misinformation. *PloS One, 10*(8), e0134641. 10.1371/journal.pone.0134641

Bin Naeem, S., & Bhatti, R. (2020). The COVID-19 "infodemic": A new front for information professionals. *Health Information and Libraries Journal, 37*(3), 233–239. 10.1111/hir.12311

Bin Naeem, S., Bhatti, R., & Khan, A. (2021). An exploration of how fake news is taking over social media and putting public health at risk. *Health Information and Libraries Journal, 38*(2), 143–149. 10.1111/hir.12320

Bin Naeem, S., & Kamel Boulos, M.N. (2021). COVID-19 misinformation online and health literacy: A brief overview. *International Journal of Environmental Research and Public Health, 18*(15), 8091. 10.3390/ijerph18158091

Blackburn, F. (2020). Cultural competence: Toward a more robust conceptualisation. *Public Library Quarterly, 39*(3), 229–245. 10.1080/01616846.2019.1636750

Bruner, J. (2014). Narrative, culture, and psychology. In A. Antonietti, E. Confalonieri, & A. Marchetti (Eds.), *Reflective Thinking in Educational Settings: A Cultural Framework.* Cambridge University Press.

Budd, J.M., & Lloyd, A. (2014). Theoretical foundations for information literacy: A plan for action. *Proceedings of the Association for Information Science & Technology, 51*(1), 82–87. 10.1002/meet.2014.14505101001

Burel, G., Farrell, T., & Alani, H. (2021). Demographics and topics impact on the co-spread of COVID-19 misinformation and fact-checks on Twitter. *Information Processing & Management, 58*(6), 102732. 10.1016/j.ipm.2021.102732

Burnett, G., & Jaeger, P.T. (2008). Small worlds, lifeworlds, and information: The ramifications of the information behaviors of social groups in public policy and the public sphere. *Information Research, 13*(2), 1–18.

Calleja, N., AbdAllah, A., Abad, N., Ahmed, N., Albarracin, D., Altieri, E., Anoko, J.N., Arcos, R., Azlan, A.A., Bayer, J., Bechmann, A., Bezbaruah, S., Briand, S.C., Brooks, I., Bucci, L.M., Burzo, S., Czerniak, C., De Domenico, M., Dunn, A.G., ...Purnat, T.D. (2021). A public health research agenda for managing infodemics: Methods and results of the first WHO infodemiology conference. *JMIR Infodemiology, 1*(1). 10.2196/30979

CCDH. (2020). The anti-vaxx playbook. CCDH. https://www.counterhate.com/playbook

CCDH. (2021). Disinformation dozen: The sequel. CCDH. https://www.counterhate.com/disinfosequel

Choo, C.W. (2013). Information culture and organizational effectiveness. *International Journal of Information Management, 33*(5), 775–779. 10.1016/j.ijinfomgt.2013.05.009

Chou, W.-Y.S., Gaysynsky, A., & Vanderpool, R.C. (2021). The COVID-19 mis-infodemic: Moving beyond fact-checking. *Health Education & Behavior: The Official Publication of the Society for Public Health Education, 48*(1), 9–13. 10.1177/1090198120980675

Cinelli, M., De Francisci Morales, G., Galeazzi, A., Quattrociocchi, W., & Starnini, M. (2021). The echo chamber effect on social media. *Proceedings of the National Academy of Sciences of the United States of America, 118*(9), e2023301118. 10.1073/pnas.2023301118

Cinelli, M., Quattrociocchi, W., Galeazzi, A., Valensise, C.M., Brugnoli, E., Schmidt, A.L., Zola, P., Zollo, F., & Scala, A. (2020). The COVID-19 social media infodemic. *Scientific Reports, 10*(1), 16598. 10.1038/s41598-020-73510-5

Cino, D., & Formenti, L. (2021). To share or not to share? That is the (social media) dilemma. Expectant mothers questioning and making sense of performing pregnancy on social media. *Convergence, 27*(2), 491–507. 10.1177/1354856521990299

Cobus, L. (2008). Integrating information literacy into the education of public health professionals: Roles for librarians and the library. *Journal of the Medical Library Association: JMLA, 96*(1), 28–33. 10.3163/1536-5050.96.1.28

Collins, B., & Zadrozny, B. (2021, July 21). Who is the "pizza king"? The secret language being used by anti-vaccine groups to skirt detection. NBC News. https://www.nbcnews.com/tech/tech-news/anti-vaccine-groups-changing-dance-parties-facebook-avoid-detection-rcna1480

Collins-Dexter, B. (2020). Canaries in the coal mine: COVID-19 misinformation and Black communities. https://shorensteincenter.org/canaries-in-the-coal-mine/

Cooke, N.A. (2017). *Information services to diverse populations: Developing culturally competent library professionals.* Libraries Unlimited. https://ebookcentral.proquest.com/lib/texaswu/detail.action?docID=4742121

Cooke, N.A. (2018). *Fake news and alternative facts: Information literacy in a post-truth era.* American Library Association. http://ebookcentral.proquest.com/lib/texaswu/detail.action?docID=5491295

Corrall, S. (2017). Crossing the threshold: Reflective practice in information literacy development. *Journal of Information Literacy, 11*(1), 23–53. http://d-scholarship.pitt.edu/28240/

Courtright, C. (2007). Context in information behavior research. *Annual Review of Information Science and Technology, 41*(1), 273–306. 10.1002/aris.2007.1440410113

Cruickshank, I., Ginossar, T., Sulskis, J., Zheleva, E., & Berger-Wolf, T. (2021). Content and dynamics of websites shared over vaccine-related tweets in COVID-19 conversations: Computational analysis. *Journal of Medical Internet Research, 23*(12), e29127. 10.2196/29127

Crutcher, M., & Seidler, P.M. (2021). Maximizing completion of the two-dose COVID-19 vaccine series with aid from infographics. *Vaccines, 9*(11), 1229. 10.3390/vaccines9111229

Dadaczynski, K., Okan, O., Messer, M., Leung, A.Y.M., Rosário, R., Darlington, E., & Rathmann, K. (2021). Digital health literacy and web-based information-seeking behaviors of university students in Germany during the COVID-19 pandemic: Cross-sectional survey study. *Journal of Medical Internet Research, 23*(1), e24097. 10.2196/24097

Dahlstrom, M.F. (2021). The narrative truth about scientific misinformation. *Proceedings of the National Academy of Sciences of the United States of America, 118*(15), e1914085117. 10.1073/pnas.1914085117

Darius, P., & Urquhart, M. (2021). Disinformed social movements: A large-scale mapping of conspiracy narratives as online harms during the COVID-19 pandemic. *Online Social Networks and Media, 26,* 100174. 10.1016/j.osnem.2021.100174

De Coninck, D., Frissen, T., Matthijs, K., d'Haenens, L., Lits, G., Champagne-Poirier, O., Carignan, M.-E., David, M.D., Pignard-Cheynel, N., Salerno, S., & Généreux, M. (2021). Beliefs in conspiracy theories and misinformation about COVID-19: Comparative perspectives on the role of anxiety, depression and exposure to and trust in information sources. *Frontiers in Psychology, 12,* 646394. 10.3389/fpsyg.2021.646394

De Maeyer, J. (2019). Taking conspiracy culture seriously: Journalism needs to face its epistemological trouble. *Journalism, 20*(1), 21–23. 10.1177/1464884918807037

De Vynck, G. (2021). YouTube is banning prominent anti-vaccine activists and blocking all anti-vaccine content. *Washington Post.* https://www.washingtonpost.com/technology/2021/09/29/youtube-ban-joseph-mercola/

De Vynck, G., & Lerman, R. (2021). Facebook and YouTube spent a year fighting COVID misinformation. It's still spreading. *Washington Post.* https://www.washingtonpost. com/technology/2021/07/22/facebook-youtube-vaccine-misinformation/

Donovan, J. (2020, April 30). Covid hoaxes are using a loophole to stay alive—Even after content is deleted. *MIT Technology Review.* https://www.technologyreview. com/2020/04/30/1000881/covid-hoaxes-zombie-content-wayback-machine-disinformation/

Donovan, J., Friedberg, B., Lim, G., Leaver, N., Nilsen, J., & Dreyfuss, E. (2021). Mitigating medical misinformation: A whole-of-society approach to countering spam, scams, and hoaxes. *Technology and Social Change Research Project.* 10.3701 6/TASC-2021-03

Dow, B.J., Johnson, A.L., Wang, C.S., Whitson, J., & Menon, T. (2021). The COVID-19 pandemic and the search for structure: Social media and conspiracy theories. *Social and Personality Psychology Compass,* e12636. 10.1111/spc3.12636

DROG. (2022). Bad News. *Bad News.* https://www.getbadnews.com/

Dwoskin, E., Oremus, W., & De Vynck, G. (2021, August 24). A group of moms on Facebook built an island of good-faith vaccine debate in a sea of misinformation. *Washington Post.* https://www.washingtonpost.com/technology/2021/08/23/facebook-vaccine-talk-group/

Epstein, Z., Berinsky, A.J., Cole, R., Gully, A., Pennycook, G., & Rand, D.G. (2021). Developing an accuracy-prompt toolkit to reduce COVID-19 misinformation online. *Harvard Kennedy School Misinformation Review.* 10.37016/ mr-2020-71

Eren, E., & Vardarlıer, P. (2013). Social media's role in developing an employee's sense of belonging in the work place as an HRM strategy. *Procedia - Social and Behavioral Sciences, 99,* 852–860. 10.1016/j.sbspro.2013.10.557

Eschenfelder, K. (2014). Use regimes: A theoretical framework for social informatics research on intellectual and cultural property. In P. Fichman, & H. Rosenbaum (Eds.), *Social informatics: Past, present and future* (pp. 89–101). Cambridge Scholars Publishing.

Eysenbach, G. (2020). How to fight an infodemic: The four pillars of infodemic management. *Journal of Medical Internet Research, 22*(6), e21820. 10.2196/ 21820

Feinberg, M. (2012). Synthetic ethos: The believability of collections at the inter-section of classification and curation. *The Information Society, 28*(5), 329–339. 10.1080/01972243.2012.708709

Fichman, P., & Rosenbaum, H. (Eds.). (2014). *Social informatics: Past, present and future.* Cambridge Scholars Publishing.

First Draft. (2022). Training. *First Draft.* https://firstdraftnews.org:443/training/

Fraser, N., Brierley, L., Dey, G., Polka, J.K., Pálfy, M., Nanni, F., & Coates, J.A. (2021). The evolving role of preprints in the dissemination of COVID-19 research and their impact on the science communication landscape. *PLoS Biology, 19*(4), e3000959. 10.1371/journal.pbio.3000959

Garcia, L., & Shane, T. (2021, June 29). A guide to prebunking: A promising way to inoculate against misinformation. *First Draft.* https://firstdraftnews.org:443/articles/ a-guide-to-prebunking-a-promising-way-to-inoculate-against-misinformation/

Gerts, D., Shelley, C.D., Parikh, N., Pitts, T., Watson Ross, C., Fairchild, G., Vaquera Chavez, N.Y., & Daughton, A.R. (2021). "Thought I'd share first" and other conspiracy theory tweets from the COVID-19 infodemic: Exploratory study. *JMIR Public Health and Surveillance, 7*(4), e26527. 10.2196/26527

Gesser-Edelsburg, A. (2021). Using narrative evidence to convey health information on social media: The case of COVID-19. *Journal of Medical Internet Research, 23*(3), e24948. 10.2196/24948

Goggins, S.P., & Mascaro, C. (2013). Context matters: The experience of physical, informational, and cultural distance in a rural IT firm. *The Information Society, 29*(2), 113–127. 10.1080/01972243.2012.758212

Goldstein, D.E. (2018). Never remember: Fake news turning points and vernacular critiques of bad faith communication. *Journal of American Folklore, 131*(522), 471–481.

Graham, M. (2020, May 7). Facebook, YouTube and other platforms are struggling to remove new pandemic conspiracy video. *CNBC*. https://www.cnbc.com/2020/05/07/facebook-youtube-struggling-to-remove-plandemic-conspiracy-video.html

Grodzicka, E.D., & Harambam, J. (2021). What should academics do about conspiracy theories? Moving beyond debunking to better deal with conspiratorial movements, misinformation and post-truth. *Journal for Cultural Research, 25*(1), 1–11. 10.1080/14797585.2021.1886420

Hammack, P.L. (2008). Narrative and the cultural psychology of identity. *Personality and Social Psychology Review, 12*(3), 222–247. 10.1177/108886830831 6892

Hara, N., & Fichman, P. (2014). Frameworks for understanding knowledge sharing in online communities: Boundaries and boundary crossing. In P. Fichman & H. Rosenbaum (Eds.), *Social informatics: Past, present and future* (pp. 89–101). Cambridge Scholars Publishing.

Hicks, A., & Lloyd, A. (2020). Peeling back the layers: Deconstructing information literacy discourse in higher education. In A. Sundqvist, G. Berget, J. Nolin, & K.I. Skjerdingstad (Eds.), *Sustainable Digital Communities* (pp. 363–372). Springer International Publishing. 10.1007/978-3-030-43687-2_28

Hodge, T. (2019). Integrating cultural humility into public services librarianship. *International Information & Library Review, 51*(3), 268–274. 10.1080/10572317.201 9.1629070

Hodge, T., & Mowdood, A. (2016). Addressing cultural humility and implicit bias in information literacy sessions. *Library Instruction West, 2016*. https://digitalcommons.usu.edu/liw16/Libraryinstructionwest2016/FridayJune10/14

Hollister, J.M., Lee, J., Elkins, A.J., & Latham, D. (2020). Potential implications and applications of terror management theory for library and information science. *Journal of the Korean Society for Library and Information Science, 54*(4), 317–349. 10.4275/KSLIS.2020.54.4.317

Hornik, R., Kikut, A., Jesch, E., Woko, C., Siegel, L., & Kim, K. (2021). Association of COVID-19 misinformation with face mask wearing and social distancing in a nationally representative US sample. *Health Communication, 36*(1), 6–14. 10.1 080/10410236.2020.1847437

Hurley, D.A., Kostelecky, S.R., & Townsend, L. (2019). Cultural humility in libraries. *Reference Services Review, 47*(4), 544–555. 10.1108/RSR-06-2019-0042

Islam, M.S., Kamal, A.-H.M., Kabir, A., Southern, D.L., Khan, S.H., Hasan, S.M.M., Sarkar, T., Sharmin, S., Das, S., Roy, T., Harun, M.G.D., Chughtai, A.A., Homaira, N., & Seale, H. (2021). COVID-19 vaccine rumors and conspiracy theories: The need for cognitive inoculation against misinformation to improve vaccine adherence. *PloS One, 16*(5), e0251605. 10.1371/journal.pone.0251605

Jaeger, P.T., & Taylor, N.G. (2021). Arsenals of lifelong information literacy: Educating users to navigate political and current events information in world of ever-evolving misinformation. *The Library Quarterly, 91*(1), 19–31. 10.1086/711632

Jahoda, G. (2012). Critical reflections on some recent definitions of "culture". *Culture & Psychology, 18*(3), 289–303. 10.1177/1354067X12446229

Johnson, N.F., Velásquez, N., Restrepo, N.J., Leahy, R., Gabriel, N., El Oud, S., Zheng, M., Manrique, P., Wuchty, S., & Lupu, Y. (2020). The online competition between pro- and anti-vaccination views. *Nature, 582*(7811), 230–233. 10.1038/s41586-020-2281-1

Kalichman, S.C., Eaton, L.A., Earnshaw, V.A., & Brousseau, N. (2021). Faster than warp speed: Early attention to COVD-19 by anti-vaccine groups on Facebook. *Journal of Public Health (Oxford, England)*, fdab093. 10.1093/pubmed/fdab093

Kim, S., & Kim, K. (2021). The information ecosystem of online groups with anti- and pro-vaccine views on Facebook. *ArXiv*:2108.06641 [Cs]. http://arxiv.org/abs/2108.06641

Klein, B., Vazquez, M., & Collins, K. (2021, July 19). Biden backs away from his claim that Facebook is "killing people" by allowing COVID misinformation. *CNN.* https://www.cnn.com/2021/07/19/politics/joe-biden-facebook/index.html

Klein, O., Spears, R., & Reicher, S. (2007). Social identity performance: Extending the strategic side of SIDE. *Personality and Social Psychology Review, 11*(1), 28–45. 10.1177/1088868306294588

Kling, R. (2007). What is social informatics and why does it matter?. *The Information Society, 23*(4), 205–220.

Koltai, K.S. (2020a). *Human values and scientific controversies: Studying vaccine information behavior on social networking sites* [Thesis]. 10.26153/tsw/12582

Koltai, K.S. (2020b). Vaccine information seeking and sharing: How private Facebook groups contributed to the anti-vaccine movement online. *AoIR Selected Papers of Internet Research.* 10.5210/spir.v2020i0.11252

Kouzy, R., Abi Jaoude, J., Kraitem, A., El Alam, M.B., Karam, B., Adib, E., Zarka, J., Traboulsi, C., Akl, E.W., & Baddour, K. (2020). Coronavirus goes viral: Quantifying the COVID-19 misinformation epidemic on Twitter. *Cureus, 12*(3), e7255. 10.7759/cureus.7255

Krishnan, N., Gu, J., Tromble, R., & Abroms, L.C. (2021). Research note: Examining how various social media platforms have responded to COVID-19 misinformation. *Harvard Kennedy School Misinformation Review.* 10.37016/mr-2020-85

Lanius, C., Weber, R., & MacKenzie, W.I. (2021). Use of bot and content flags to limit the spread of misinformation among social networks: A behavior and attitude survey. *Social Network Analysis and Mining, 11*(1), 32. 10.1007/s13278-021-00739-x

Lewandowsky, S. (2019). The 'post-truth' world, misinformation, and information literacy: A perspective from cognitive science. In S. Goldstein (Ed.), *Informed societies: Why information literacy matters for citizenship, participation and democracy* (pp. 69–88). Facet. 10.29085/9781783303922.006

Lewandowsky, S., Cook, J., & Ecker, U.K.H. (2017). Letting the gorilla emerge from the mist: Getting past post-truth. *Journal of Applied Research in Memory and Cognition, 6*(4), 418–424. 10.1016/j.jarmac.2017.11.002

Lewandowsky, S., & van der Linden, S. (2021). Countering misinformation and fake news through inoculation and prebunking. *European Review of Social Psychology, 32*(2), 348–384. 10.1080/10463283.2021.1876983

Lin, P. (2010). Information literacy barriers: Language use and social structure. *Library Hi Tech.* 10.1108/07378831011096222

Linker, M. (2011). Do squirrels eat hamburgers? Intellectual empathy as a remedy for residual prejudice. *Informal Logic, 31*(2), 110–138. 10.22329/il.v31i2. 3063

Linker, M. (2015). *Intellectual empathy: Critical thinking for social justice.* University of Michigan Press.

Lloyd, A. (2010). *Information literacy landscapes: Information literacy in education, workplace and everyday contexts.* Elsevier.

Lobato, E.J.C., Powell, M., Padilla, L.M.K., & Holbrook, C. (2020). Factors predicting willingness to share COVID-19 misinformation. *Frontiers in Psychology, 11*, 566108. 10.3389/fpsyg.2020.566108

Mahmud, M.M., & Wong, S.F. (2021). Social media blueprints: A study of self-representation and identity management. *International Journal of Asian Social Science, 11*(6), 286–299. 10.18488/journal.1.2021.116.286.299

Martel, C., Pennycook, G., & Rand, D.G. (2020). Reliance on emotion promotes belief in fake news. *Cognitive Research: Principles and Implications, 5*(1), 47. 10.11 86/s41235-020-00252-3

Martin, S., & Vanderslott, S. (2021). "Any idea how fast 'It's just a mask!' can turn into 'It's just a vaccine!'": From mask mandates to vaccine mandates during the COVID-19 pandemic. *Vaccine,* S0264-410X(21)01351-7. 10.1016/j.vaccine.2021 .10.031

Massey, P.M., Chiang, S.C., Rose, M., Murray, R.M., Rockett, M., Togo, E., Klassen, A.C., Manganello, J.A., & Leader, A.E. (2021). Development of personas to communicate narrative-based information about the HPV vaccine on Twitter. *Frontiers in Digital Health, 3*, 682639. 10.3389/fdgth.2021.682639

Megarry, J. (2018). Under the watchful eyes of men: Theorising the implications of male surveillance practices for feminist activism on social media. *Feminist Media Studies, 18*(6), 1070–1085. 10.1080/14680777.2017.1387584

Melki, J., Tamim, H., Hadid, D., Makki, M., El Amine, J., & Hitti, E. (2021). Mitigating infodemics: The relationship between news exposure and trust and belief in COVID-19 fake news and social media spreading. *PloS One, 16*(6), e0252830. 10.1371/journal.pone.0252830

Meshi, D., Cotten, S.R., & Bender, A.R. (2020). Problematic social media use and perceived social isolation in older adults: A cross-sectional study. *Gerontology, 66*(2), 160–168. 10.1159/000502577

Mheidly, N., & Fares, J. (2020). Leveraging media and health communication strategies to overcome the COVID-19 infodemic. *Journal of Public Health Policy, 41*(4), 410–420. 10.1057/s41271-020-00247-w

Miller, P.J., Fung, H., & Koven, M. (2007). Narrative reverberations: How participation in narrative practices co-creates persons and cultures. In *Handbook of cultural psychology* (pp. 595–614). The Guilford Press.

Modgil, S., Singh, R.K., Gupta, S., & Dennehy, D. (2021). A confirmation bias view on social media induced polarisation during COVID-19. *Information Systems Frontiers: A Journal of Research and Innovation*, 1–25. 10.1007/s10796-021-10222-9

Montiel-Overall, P. (2007). Information literacy: Toward a cultural model. *Canadian Journal of Information & Library Sciences*, *31*(1), 43–68.

Montiel-Overall, P. (2009). Cultural competence: A conceptual framework for library and information science professionals. *The Library Quarterly*, *79*(2), 175–204. 10.1086/597080

Nazar, S., & Pieters, T. (2021). Plandemic revisited: A product of planned disinformation amplifying the COVID-19 "infodemic". *Frontiers in Public Health*, *9*, 649930. 10.3389/fpubh.2021.649930

Neely, S.R., Eldredge, C., & Sanders, R. (2021). Health information seeking behaviors on social media during the COVID-19 pandemic among American social networking site users: Survey study. *Journal of Medical Internet Research*, *23*(6), e29802. 10.2196/29802

Ngai, C.S.B., Singh, R.G., Lu, W., & Koon, A.C. (2020). Grappling with the COVID-19 health crisis: Content analysis of communication strategies and their effects on public engagement on social media. *Journal of Medical Internet Research*, *22*(8), e21360. 10.2196/21360

Nguyen, L.H.T., Vo, M.T.H., Tran, L.T.M., Dadaczynski, K., Okan, O., Murray, L., & Van Vo, T. (2021). Digital health literacy about COVID-19 as a factor mediating the association between the importance of online information search and subjective well-being among university students in Vietnam. *Frontiers in Digital Health*, *3*, 739476. 10.3389/fdgth.2021.739476

Odii, A. (2020). Social media culture: Change and resistance, a tool for change management. *The Creative Artist: A Journal of Theatre and Media Studies*, *11*(3), Article 3. https://journals.ezenwaohaetorc.org/index.php/TCA/article/view/385

Oliver, G. (2017). Understanding information culture: Conceptual and implementation issues. *Journal of Information Science Theory and Practice*, *5*(1), 6–14. 10.1633/JISTaP.2017.5.1.1

Park, H., Kim, H.S., & Park, H.W. (2020). A scientometric study of digital literacy, ICT literacy, information literacy, and media literacy. *Journal of Data and Information Science*, *6*(2), 116–138.

Patil, U., Kostareva, U., Hadley, M., Manganello, J.A., Okan, O., Dadaczynski, K., Massey, P.M., Agner, J., & Sentell, T. (2021). Health literacy, digital health literacy, and COVID-19 pandemic attitudes and behaviors in U.S. college students: Implications for interventions. *International Journal of Environmental Research and Public Health*, *18*(6), 3301. 10.3390/ijerph18063301

Pennycook, G., Cannon, T.D., & Rand, D.G. (2018). Prior exposure increases perceived accuracy of fake news. *Journal of Experimental Psychology. General*, *147*(12), 1865–1880. 10.1037/xge0000465

Pennycook, G., McPhetres, J., Zhang, Y., Lu, J.G., & Rand, D.G. (2020). Fighting COVID-19 misinformation on social media: Experimental evidence for a scalable accuracy-nudge intervention. *Psychological Science*, *31*(7), 770–780. 10.1177/095 6797620939054

Pennycook, G., & Rand, D.G. (2019). Lazy, not biased: Susceptibility to partisan fake news is better explained by lack of reasoning than by motivated reasoning. *Cognition*, *188*, 39–50. 10.1016/j.cognition.2018.06.011

Pennycook, G., & Rand, D.G. (2021). The psychology of fake news. *Trends in Cognitive Sciences*, *25*(5), 388–402. 10.1016/j.tics.2021.02.007

Pian, W., Chi, J., & Ma, F. (2021). The causes, impacts and countermeasures of COVID-19 "infodemic": A systematic review using narrative synthesis. *Information Processing & Management*, *58*(6), 102713. 10.1016/j.ipm.2021.102713

Pietsch, B. (2021, July 20). Twitter suspends Rep. Marjorie Taylor Greene for spreading COVID-19 misinformation. *Washington Post*. https://www.washingtonpost.com/politics/2021/07/20/marjorie-taylor-green-twitter-suspended-covid/

Pool, J., Fatehi, F., & Akhlaghpour, S. (2021). Infodemic, misinformation and disinformation in pandemics: Scientific landscape and the road ahead for public health informatics research. *Studies in Health Technology and Informatics*, *281*, 764–768. 10.3233/SHTI210278

Purnat, T.D., Vacca, P., Burzo, S., Zecchin, T., Wright, A., Briand, S., & Nguyen, T. (2021). WHO digital intelligence analysis for tracking narratives and information voids in the COVID-19 infodemic. *Studies in Health Technology and Informatics*, *281*, 989–993. 10.3233/SHTI210326

Purvis, R.S., Willis, D.E., Moore, R., Bogulski, C., & McElfish, P.A. (2021). Perceptions of adult Arkansans regarding trusted sources of information about the COVID-19 pandemic. *BMC Public Health*, *21*(1), 2306. 10.1186/s12889-021-12385-1

Quinn, E.K., Fazel, S.S., & Peters, C.E. (2021). The Instagram infodemic: Cobranding of conspiracy theories, coronavirus disease 2019 and authority-questioning beliefs. *Facebook group Cyberpsychology, Behavior and Social Networking*, *24*(8), 573–577. 10.1089/cyber.2020.0663

Rampersad, G., & Althiyabi, T. (2020). Fake news: Acceptance by demographics and culture on social media. *Journal of Information Technology & Politics*, *17*(1), 1–11. 10.1080/19331681.2019.1686676

Roitero, K., Soprano, M., Portelli, B., De Luise, M., Spina, D., Mea, V.D., Serra, G., Mizzaro, S., & Demartini, G. (2021). Can the crowd judge truthfulness? A longitudinal study on recent misinformation about COVID-19. *Personal and Ubiquitous Computing*, 1–31. 10.1007/s00779-021-01604-6

Ross, J. (2020, May 2). From white conservatives to Black liberals, coronavirus misinformation poses serious risks. *NBC News*. https://www.nbcnews.com/news/nbcblk/coronavirus-misinformation-crosses-divides-infect-black-social-media-n1198226

Rotolo, S.M., Jain, S., Dhaon, S., Dokhanchi, J.K., Kalata, E., Shah, T., Mordell, L.J., Clayman, M.L., Kenefake, A., Zimmermann, L.J., Bloomgarden, E., & Arora, V.M. (2021). A coordinated strategy to develop and distribute infographics addressing COVID-19 vaccine hesitancy and misinformation. *Journal of the American Pharmacists Association: JAPhA*, S1544-3191(21)00357-5. 10.1016/j.japh.2021.08.016

Rubin, V.L. (2019). Disinformation and misinformation triangle: A conceptual model for "fake news" epidemic, causal factors and interventions. *Journal of Documentation*, *75*(5), 1013–1034. 10.1108/JD-12-2018-0209

Savolainen, R. (2016). Approaches to socio-cultural barriers to information seeking. *Library & Information Science Research*, *38*(1), 52–59. 10.1016/j.lisr.2016.01.007

Sawyer, S., & Tapia, A. (2007). From findings to theories: Institutionalizing social informatics. *The Information Society*, *23*(4), 263–275. 10.1080/01972240701444196

Shahi, G.K., Dirkson, A., & Majchrzak, T.A. (2021). An exploratory study of COVID-19 misinformation on Twitter. *Online Social Networks and Media, 22,* 100104. 10.1016/j.osnem.2020.100104

Shermer, M. (2002). *Why people believe weird things: Pseudoscience, superstition, and other confusions of our time.* St. Martin's Griffin.

Shin, S.K., Ishman, M., & Sanders, G.L. (2007). An empirical investigation of socio-cultural factors of information sharing in China. *Information & Management, 44*(2), 165–174. 10.1016/j.im.2006.11.004

Silva, M.J., & Santos, P. (2021). The impact of health literacy on knowledge and attitudes towards preventive strategies against COVID-19: A cross-sectional study. *International Journal of Environmental Research and Public Health, 18*(10), 5421. 10.3390/ijerph18105421

Simon, S. (2021, September 18). "Vaccine Talk" Facebook group is a carefully moderated forum for vaccine questions. *NPR.* https://www.npr.org/2021/09/18/1038533086/vaccine-talk-facebook-group-is-a-carefully-moderated-forum-for-vaccine-questions

Simons, R.N., Fleischmann, K.R., & Roy, L. (2020). Leveling the playing field in ICT design: Transcending knowledge roles by balancing division and privileging of knowledges. *The Information Society, 36*(4), 183–198. 10.1080/01972243.2020.1762270

Sirlin, N., Epstein, Z., Arechar, A.A., & Rand, D.G. (2021). Digital literacy is associated with more discerning accuracy judgments but not sharing intentions. *Harvard Kennedy School Misinformation Review.* 10.37016/mr-2020-83

Smith, R., & De Keulenaar, E. (2021, March 31). Track misinformation across platforms on 4chan, 8kun and Reddit. *First Draft.* https://firstdraftnews.org:443/long-form-article/tracking-cross-platform-spread/

S-O'Brien, L., Read, P., Woolcott, J., & Shah, C. (2011). Understanding privacy behaviors of Millennials within social networking sites. *Proceedings of the ASIST Annual Meeting, 48.* 10.1002/meet.2011.14504801198

Social Decision-Making Lab. (2022). GO VIRAL! Go Viral! https://www.goviralgame.com/books/go-viral/

Soveri, A., Karlsson, L.C., Antfolk, J., Lindfelt, M., & Lewandowsky, S. (2021). Unwillingness to engage in behaviors that protect against COVID-19: The role of conspiracy beliefs, trust, and endorsement of complementary and alternative medicine. *BMC Public Health, 21*(1), 684. 10.1186/s12889-021-10643-w

Stelter, B., & Pellico, K. (2021, July 21). Instagram blocked the #VaccinesKill hashtag two years ago. Facebook only just now got around to doing it. *CNN.* https://www.cnn.com/2021/07/21/tech/facebook-vaccineskill-hashtag/index.html

Su, Y., Lee, D.K.L., & Xiao, X. (2022). "I enjoy thinking critically, and I'm in control": Examining the influences of media literacy factors on misperceptions amidst the COVID-19 infodemic. *Computers in Human Behavior, 128,* 107111. 10.1016/j.chb.2021.107111

Sum, S., Mathews, R.M., Pourghasem, M., & Hughes, I. (2009). Internet use as a predictor of sense of community in older people. *CyberPsychology & Behavior, 12*(2), 235–239.

Sweeney, M.E., & Brock, A. (2014). Critical informatics: New methods and practices. *Proceedings of the American Society for Information Science and Technology, 51*(1), 1–8. 10.1002/meet.2014.14505101032

Swetland, S.B., Rothrock, A.N., Andris, H., Davis, B., Nguyen, L., Davis, P., & Rothrock, S.G. (2021). Accuracy of health-related information regarding COVID-19 on Twitter during a global pandemic. *World Medical & Health Policy.* 10.1002/wmh3.468

Tentolouris, A., Ntanasis-Stathopoulos, I., Vlachakis, P.K., Tsilimigras, D.I., Gavriatopoulou, M., & Dimopoulos, M.A. (2021). COVID-19: Time to flatten the infodemic curve. *Clinical and Experimental Medicine, 21*(2), 161–165. 10.1007/s1 0238-020-00680-x

Topf, J.M., & Williams, P.N. (2021). COVID-19, social media, and the role of the public physician. *Blood Purification, 50*(4–5), 595–601. 10.1159/ 000512707

Torres, V. (2010). Perspectives on identity development. In J.H. Schuh, S.R. Jones, & S.R. Harper (Eds.), *Student Services: A Handbook for the Profession* (pp. 187–206). John Wiley & Sons.

Tuominen, K., Savolainen, R., & Talja, S. (2005). Information literacy as a socio-technical practice. *The Library Quarterly, 75*(3), 329–345. 10.1086/497311

Vaccaro, A., Adams, S.K., Kisler, T.S., & Newman, B.M. (2015). The use of social media for navigating the transitions into and through the first year of college. *Journal of the First-Year Experience & Students in Transition, 27*(2), 29–48.

Vaccine Talk: An evidence based discussion forum. (2022). https://www.facebook. com/groups/vaccinetalkforum/about/

van Orman Quine, W. (1975). Two dogmas of empiricism. In *Can Theories be Refuted?* (pp. 41–64). Dordrecht- Holland.

Venegas-Vera, A.V., Colbert, G.B., & Lerma, E.V. (2020). Positive and negative impact of social media in the COVID-19 era. *Reviews in Cardiovascular Medicine, 21*(4), 561–564. 10.31083/j.rcm.2020.04.195

Vignoles, V.L., Regalia, C., Manzi, C., Golledge, J., & Scabini, E. (2006). Beyond self-esteem: Influence of multiple motives on identity construction. *Journal of Personality and Social Psychology, 90*(2), 308–333. 10.1037/0022-3514. 90.2.308

Vrdelja, M., Vrbovšek, S., Klopčič, V., Dadaczynski, K., & Okan, O. (2021). Facing the growing COVID-19 infodemic: Digital health literacy and information-seeking behaviour of university students in Slovenia. *International Journal of Environmental Research and Public Health, 18*(16), 8507. 10.3390/ ijerph18168507

Wang, X., Chao, F., & Yu, G. (2021). Evaluating rumor debunking effectiveness during the COVID-19 pandemic crisis: Utilizing user stance in comments on Sina Weibo. *Frontiers in Public Health, 9*, 770111. 10.3389/fpubh.2021.770111

Warner, A. (2022). Fake It To Make It. http://www.fakeittomakeitgame.com/

Wawrzuta, D., Jaworski, M., Gotlib, J., & Panczyk, M. (2021). Characteristics of antivaccine messages on social media: Systematic review. *Journal of Medical Internet Research, 23*(6), e24564. 10.2196/24564

Wenger, E.C., & Snyder, W.M. (2000). Communities of practice: The organizational frontier. *Harvard Business Review, 78*(1), 139–146.

Widén, G., Ahmad, F., & Huvila, I. (2021). Connecting information literacy and social capital to better utilise knowledge resources in the workplace. *Journal of Information Science*, 01655515211060531. 10.1177/01655515211060531

Zhu, S., Yang, H.H., Wu, D., & Chen, F. (2021). Investigating the relationship between information literacy and social media competence among university students. *Journal of Educational Computing Research, 59*(7), 1425–1449. 10.1177/ 0735633121997360

Zielinski, C. (2021). Infodemics and infodemiology: A short history, a long future. *Revista Panamericana De Salud Publica = Pan American Journal of Public Health, 45*, e40. 10.26633/RPSP.2021.40

Zollo, F. (2019). Dealing with digital misinformation: A polarised context of narratives and tribes. *EFSA Journal. European Food Safety Authority, 17*(Suppl 1). 10.2903/j.efsa.2019.e170720

Part III
Information Behavior

5 Information Behavior and Emotion Change during a Public Health Emergency of International Concern: A Case Study of Middle-Aged People

Shijuan Li, Xiaolong Chen, Hui Lin, and Xinmei Hu

Introduction

With the rapid application of the Internet to daily life and the acceleration of the pace of life, social media has become an indispensable part of modern life, while playing an essential role in information acquisition and sharing. It is reported that there were 4.62 billion social media users around the world as of January 2022, which is equal to 58.4% of the world's total population (Kemp, 2022). Social media, such as WeChat and Weibo, have become main channels for people to communicate online in the Internet era. The WeChat official accounts have been shown to be the most popular social media in China, and are reported to be one of the health information sources most frequently used in China. Weibo is a Chinese platform for microblogs. During home quarantine in a Public Health Emergency of International Concern (PHEIC), such as COVID-19, people regard social media to be a vital instrument to search health information and communicate with each other. Ho et al. (2020) investigated Chinese participants over 20 years old and found that 80.5% of them used social media as their important information sources for health information. An online survey of US adults found that doctors who shared advice on Twitter were considered more effective at delivering COVID-19 health advice (Solnick et al., 2021). Studies in Egyptian and Spanish populations have confirmed the widespread use of social media in the context of the PHEIC (Montesi, 2020; Shehata, 2021) too. The public can receive relevant and fact-checked information from reliable institutions on social media, and these institutions can understand the public's attitudes, concerns, and needs via social media (Roy et al., 2020; Zhu et al., 2020).

A public health emergency (PHE) is defined as "an occurrence or imminent threat of an illness or health condition, caused by bioterrorism, epidemic or pandemic disease, or an infectious agent or biological toxin, that poses a substantial risk to humans by either causing a significant

DOI: 10.4324/9781003231769-9

number of human fatalities or permanent or long-term disability" (Massachusetts Emergency Management Agency, n.d.). The World Health Organization (WHO) declared the novel coronavirus (COVID-19) outbreak a PHEIC on January 30, 2020 (WHO, 2020a), and a global pandemic on March 11, 2020 (WHO, 2020b). According to WHO (2009) and The State Council Information Office of the People's Republic of China (2020), the COVID-19 pandemic can be divided into the outburst period and the normalized period. The fluctuation of pandemic conditions brought crushing burdens to international healthcare systems, and challenged every citizen's health information literacy, with massive amounts of information, misinformation, and disinformation. An infodemic is typically characterized by people making comprehensive use of multiple information sources, with excessive amounts of information made available on a daily basis, which may be far beyond the users' information processing ability and becomes a cognitive burden for them. Thus, it is critical to understand how people use ICT, especially social media, to seek trustworthy, timely, and authoritative information, and to avoid misinformation and disinformation.

The remainder of this chapter is structured as follows. First, a literature review is conducted, followed by research questions. Then we present our research design, outlining the empirical setting and our methodological approach to data collection, coding, and analysis. Next, we illustrate the findings of our empirical data analysis on the changes in information behavior, emotions, and the interaction between them from a dynamic perspective during the process of a PHEIC. Finally, this chapter ends with a discussion and conclusions.

Related work

Information behavior in PHEIC

Research on information behavior in PHEIC focuses on the construction of information behavior models, the exploration of information behaviors, and the associated influential factors, e.g., personal factors and policy factors. The health information behavior model under COVID-19 includes information demand, information acquisition, information dissemination, information evaluation, and information use (Wang et al., 2020). An individual's health information behavior is affected by his/her "personal small world" (personal characteristics, social environment, and the living environment), which can affect his/her reaction to external policy, choice of media channels, and use of information sources (Wang et al., 2020). Moreover, in the health crisis of a PHEIC, the public can be overwhelmed with information, and as a result, tend to display defensive, evasive behavior regarding health information such as information avoidance and information anxiety (Chen et al., 2020). Studies found that the highest level of information anxiety was associated with information quality, the retrieval system environment, and information literacy, and was significantly correlated with the level of psychological stress (Wang & Ma, 2020). Therefore, it is critical to understand the information behavior change throughout the PHEIC, and discover the associated sentiments, which have a vital impact both psychologically and physiologically, as people respond to this worldwide pandemic.

Studies of associated sentiments in the PHEIC

Previous studies have explored the impact of a PHEIC on public sentiments, and the corresponding emotional reactions to information behavior through various methods. Adverse emotions such as fear, and anxiety toward health outcomes from COVID-19, were identified for those using social media (Gao et al., 2020; John-Henderson & Mueller, 2020; Zhang et al., 2020). Emotions have a significant positive impact on a person's willingness to share positive information, which indicates that users are more willing to share information when they are feeling positive emotions (Huo & Zhu, 2020). Studies have shown that adequate health information was significantly associated with a lower psychological impact by the pandemic and lower levels of stress, anxiety, and depression (Tee et al., 2020). Moreover, a sense of coherence had a direct negative effect on anxiety, and mediated the relationship between anxiety and health information behavior (Leung et al., 2021). Zhang et al. (2020) conducted a nationwide online survey on WeChat users in China and found that the positive relationship between WeChat health information-seeking and mental health was mediated by perceived social support. Zhao & Zhang (2017) searched the existing literature on "public health information retrieval in social media" in Web of Science and found that seeking health information on social media can not only satisfy the demands for health information, but also provides social and emotional support from peer-to-peer interaction. Besides the interaction between information behavior and the sentiments of the participants, the perceived social support and sense of coherence mediated the interaction.

Factors influencing health information behavior in various populations

Students, adolescents, the elderly, and patients with chronic diseases are the most researched populations, with regard to their information behavior in searching, sharing, and using both online (including social media) and offline information channels.

Under the assumption that they are a high information literacy and low health literacy group (Kühn et al., 2022), college students were widely studied. During a PHEIC, both personal and social motivations can drive the health information demands of college students, who then paid more attention to the current pandemic situation and trends and disease prevention (Chen et al., 2021). A cross-sectional study of students using an online questionnaire found that health information literacy was related to online information-seeking behavior of college students during COVID-19 (Rosario et al., 2020). Motivations such as "social needs" and "identification seeking" are significantly correlated with information-sharing behavior (Huo & Zhu, 2020). With regard to college students, the factors influencing their information-sharing behavior on social media, e.g., Weibo, are in order of importance: social interaction, privacy protection, information acquisition, personal enhancement, and recreation.

The information literacy of the elderly is relatively weak, and there are many uncertainty factors in social media, which cause the elderly to feel intimidated about obtaining information from social media (Wang et al., 2019). People who are elderly have acquired a wide range of information, from health information to policy information, during the pandemic to maintain social and emotional connections while coping with isolation and loneliness (Lund & Ma, 2022). Low literacy about social media use was an important influencing factor for diabetic patients seeking health information from social media, which thereafter affected the health status of diabetics in the community (Ni et al., 2019). As the largest proportion of the population (Department of Economic and Social Affairs Population Dynamics, n.d.), middle-aged people take on the most responsibilities in life, including taking care of children and family, while balancing work and life at the same time (Lunnay et al., 2021). Therefore, PHEIC increases the psychological burden on middle-aged people trying to satisfy their health information demands, because they have to protect the whole family from infection and earn a living for their family at the same time. In addition, their lack of information literacy leads to the inability to distinguish the authenticity of information, and increases the probability of their being affected by sensationalized headlines and distorted information (OfCom, 2022). They deserve more attention as a neglected population.

Research questions

To study the health information behavior and its interaction with emotions in a PHEIC in a more comprehensive way, this chapter attempts to explore the health information behavior and emotion change, and the interaction between them, during the different dynamic different stages of the PHEIC. In addition to the identification of two periods (outburst and normalized) by WHO, Wang et al. (2020) divided the PHEIC into four stages: the incubation stage, outbreak stage, development stage, and remission stage. In order to identify the factors influencing users, this work refers to the above divisions and uses middle-aged people as an exemplar case. We focus on the outburst period and normalized period, and have modified the first period into the outburst stage, the development stage, and the remission stage (WHO, 2009; The State Council Information Office of the People's Republic of China, 2020). This research aims to provide practical understanding of the relationships between information behavior and associated emotions, from the perspective of dynamic and different stages of the PHEIC, to aid various stakeholders in optimizing health information services.

The main research questions are as follows:

1 What is the health information behavior of middle-aged people at different stages throughout the PHEIC?
2 How do the emotions (e.g., anxiety) of middle-aged people change during the process of the PHEIC?
3 In the context of the PHEIC, what is the interaction between emotions (e.g., anxiety) and the health information behavior of middle-aged people?

Research methods

Research design

As Figure 5.1 shows, this study adopted a semi-structured interview approach, to conduct qualitative research. On the basis of the investigation of relevant literature, the interview outline was designed after the full discussion of the expert group. In order to obtain the emotions and behavior change data of middle-aged people at different stages in PHEIC, the study employed three steps. First, we conducted a pilot study to examine the research design. Secondly, the formal interview followed, to collect qualitative data from middle-aged people about their health information behavior and emotions, based on social media during the process of the PHEIC. Thirdly, inductive data analysis processes (Glaser & Strauss, 1999) were utilized to analyze the qualitative data, consisting of (1) open coding to obtain the initial classification and labeling of codes; (2) axial coding for the identification of the main categories; and (3) selective coding to determine the relationships among categories and to uncover the core categories.

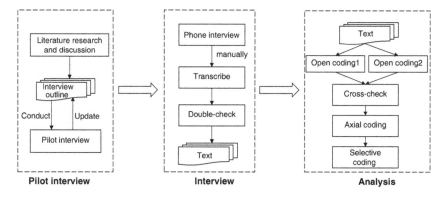

Figure 5.1 Design of the framework of the research.

Data collection

In order to show the characteristics of middle-aged people, the recruitment of interviewees met the following two essential criteria: (1) The age of interviewees should be in the range of middle-age, and (2) The individual has experience in using at least one social media platform such as a WeChat official account or Weibo. The middle-age range is defined by the United Nations as between 45 and 59 years old, while other ranges were discussed that define middle-age as between 35 and 55 years old (Wang et al., 2011), or between 40 and 59 years old (Zhang & Wu, 2013). Based on the above definitions, this study defines middle-age as 39 to 59, to include a wide range of participants for this study. In accordance with the above two criteria, four members of the project team carried out a preliminary investigation with the qualified volunteers. After introducing the research background and obtaining consent from the participants, the project team recruited the individuals meeting the criteria, to experience the full scope of the interview.

In this study, data was obtained by telephone interview to include participants from various regions, without compromising the study quality under the restrictions imposed by the PHEIC. After the literature research and discussion among the group, we determined the interview outline used in the pilot interview. After obtaining the consent of the interviewees, an hour-long interview was conducted and recorded. Twenty-three interviewees were involved in the pilot interview. With the feedback from these interviewees, we revised the interview outline into 52 interview questions, included demographic characteristics, social media usage, health information behavior, emotions, and influencing factors within each stage (for the interview outline, see Appendix 1). Then 24 interviewees (see Table 5.1 for their demographic characteristics) volunteered to tell their stories in the formal semi-structured interview. The gender distribution of the interviewees was even, and the age of most of the interviewees ranged from 41 to 50 years old (96%). Most of the participants live in Northwest China or East China, with a few residing in

Table 5.1 Demographic information of interviewees

Age range		Gender		Regional		Degree		Occupation	
No.	%	No.	%	No.	%	No.	%	No.	%
36–40	4%	Male	50%	East China	42%	High school	8%	Enterprises or Institutions	50%
41–50	71%	Female	50%	Northwest China	54%	Technical secondary school	8%	Freelance	42%
51–59	25%			Southwest China	4%	Junior college	17%	Retired	8%
						Bachelor	67%		

Southwest China. Most of the interviewees have a bachelor's degree or above (67%), and half of the interviewees are employees of enterprises or institutions. Fourteen of the 24 participants attended both rounds of the in-depth interview. The scheme for interviewee selection is designed to obtain the information about emotions and information behavior change of middle-aged people, and to obtain more comprehensive information by two rounds of recruitment of participants. To improve the reliability of these self-reported data, we explained the meaning of each question before the interviewees answered them, and asked them to tell the story in as much detail as possible to verify its rationality logically.

After obtaining the recordings of 24 interviewees, we manually transcribed the recordings to obtain text data for further coding and analysis. As it was difficult to understand dialects in different regions, each researcher double-checked the transcribed text to ensure the accuracy of the transcription.

Data analysis

Based on Grounded Theory, open coding (including 7 first-level codes, 30 second-level codes, and 92 third-level codes), axial coding (8 main categories), and selective coding (abstracted into 3 core categories) were carried out. The texts were coded by two researchers independently when the open coding was conducted. The conformance test result was above 0.85, indicating that the coding results were effective and feasible.

Open coding

In order to reveal with clarity the emotions and health information behavior of middle-aged participants during the pandemic, the open coding process was conducted first to explore the initial codes. Then we combined the initial codes, forming the following 7 first-level codes: information channels, information seeking, information adoption, information usage, reading habits, information needs, and emotions, as well as 30 second-level codes, and 92 third-level codes (see Appendix 2).

Axial coding

The main task of axial coding is to explore the corresponding relationships between codes on the basis of open coding, and to then abstract the main categories. During the axial coding, we combined the 92 initial third-level codes into 40 codes, according to their causal and logical relationships. Then these 40 codes were further classified into 8 main categories: pandemic stage, personal factors, interpersonal factors, positive emotions, negative emotions, neutral emotions, information behavior, and information requirements.

Selective coding

There is an interaction between the main categories obtained after the axial coding. Therefore, we refined the core categories through selective coding to tease out the factors of health information behavior and the emotional expression of middle-aged people at different stages of the pandemic, and explored the interaction between them. After a logical induction process, these 8 main categories were further abstracted into 3 core categories, namely driving factors, emotion types, and health information behavior (see Table 5.2), and the interaction among them was discerned. Driving factors refer to situational, personal, and interpersonal factors that influence middle-aged people to pay attention to pandemic information and evoke their emotions. Emotion types include positive, negative, and neutral emotions of middle-aged people at different stages of the PHEIC. Health information behavior includes information activities such as information channel dependence, information seeking, adoption, and usage as well as various types of information needs.

Findings

Interactive influence model of health information behavior and emotions

Through the refinement and analysis of the original data, based on Grounded Theory, we propose the Interactive Influence Model of middle-aged people's health information behavior and emotion change on social media, as shown in Figure 5.2. The model depicts the interactions among Emotion types, Health information behavior, and Driving factors, with the latter presented in three facets (pandemic stage, personal factors, and interpersonal factors).

This proposed model of interaction between health information behavior and emotions integrates three components: health information behavior, emotions, and driving factors. The analysis demonstrated that interactions existed among these three components. The corresponding factors were identified in detail as well.

Moreover, this model considers these information behaviors from the perspective of PHEIC dynamically. Notably, as WHO has declared the COVID-19 outbreak to be a global pandemic (Cucinotta & Vanelli, 2020), according to the phases of pandemic defined by the WHO, the reaction of the Chinese government, and related research (WHO, 2009; The State Council Information Office of the People's Republic of China, 2020; Wang et al., 2020), the COVID-19 pandemic can be divided into the outburst period (including the outbreak, development, and remission stages) and the normalized (regional) period. Different stages of the pandemic yield distinct performance levels of statistical data, policy regulation, seasonal

Table 5.2 Results of selective coding

1 Driving factors		2 Emotion types		3 Health information behavior	
11 Pandemic stage	111 Pandemic stage	21 Positive	211 Optimistic	31 Information behavior	311 Information channels
	112 Seasonal variation	22 Negative	221 Anxious		312 Information seeking
	113 Data statistics		222 Angry		313 Information adoption
	114 Policy provisions		223 Fearful		314 Information usage
	115 Pandemic map	23 Neutral	231 Indifferent	32 Information requirements	321 Pandemic data
12 Personal factors	121 The pace of life		232 Shock		322 Prevention and control measures
	122 Character orientation		233 Dispassionate		323 Travel information
	123 Cognitive structure		234 Calm		324 Resumption of work, production, and school
	124 Reading habits				325 Source of the pandemic
13 Interpersonal factors	131 Family structure				
	132 Relatives' and friends' attitude				
	133 Relatives' and friends' behavior				
	134 Surrounding people				

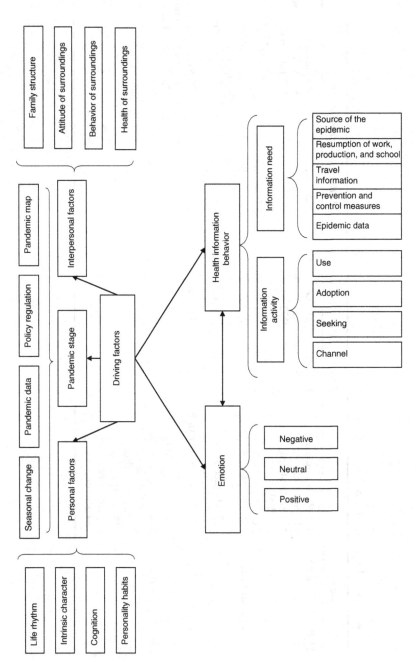

Figure 5.2 A model of interactions between health information behavior and emotions in middle-aged people during the pandemic.

change, and outbreak position and size, affecting individual people's life and health, the attitudes and behavior of people around them, which in turn affect emotions and health information behavior, tempered by individuals' intrinsic character, cognition, personality habits, and family structure.

Through the transition processes along the different pandemic stages, emotional expressions by middle-aged people drove their health information behavior, directly affected their information seeking, information use frequency, and choice of information channels, and affected their needs for different types of information. The reception of different types of pandemic information also caused changes in people's positive, neutral, or negative emotions.

Emotions

Emotion types

In the context of COVID-19, the emotions of middle-aged people ranged from positive (optimism), to neutral (indifferent, calm, and dispassionate), to negative (anxious, fearful, and angry), and the dominant emotion varied in different stages. Individual emotions were basically consistent with the overall intensity of the pandemic, and they would become more anxious when the pandemic was either severe or rebounding. The trends of the pandemic affected emotional changes. During the pandemic, positive emotions accounted for 11% of the emotions expressed by participants, negative emotions accounted for 61%, and neutral emotions accounted for 28%, indicating that in general, negative emotions were the predominant affect during the pandemic.

> The interviewee R said, "At that time (the outburst stage), I didn't feel so anxious, because it was like cold, and I felt it would end quickly."

> The interviewee L said, "When I saw the data of confirmed cases going down, I would be very happy."

> The interviewee J said, "At that time (the development stage), I was not only afraid, but also more nervous, anxious and worried."

The change of anxiety

The stage of the pandemic was an important catalyst for causing middle-aged people to pay attention to information. Data trends, policy orientations, changes in the natural environment, and perceived distance from the pandemic at different stages exerted different pressures on the participants, leading them to adopt different coping methods and life rhythms.

Specifically, during the data collection period, the pandemic can be divided into two periods: the outburst period and the normalized (regional) period (WHO, 2009; Cucinotta & Vanelli, 2020; The State Council Information Office of the People's Republic of China, 2020). The outburst period includes three stages. The outbreak stage refers to when the pandemic had begun, but people knew little about it. The development stage was when the pandemic influenced people's lives heavily, with the number of. confirmed cases surging, and a plethora of information about the pandemic appeared. In the remission stage, there were few and continuously declining numbers of confirmed cases, so the influence of the pandemic degraded, and people began to get their lives back on track. The normalized (regional) period means that the pandemic no longer has broad national influence, but the virus still exists regionally. The pandemic's pattern in Beijing, Dalian, and Xinjiang was aligned with these pandemic periods.

As shown in Figure 5.3, the horizontal axis represents the time series and the vertical axis represents the anxiety ratio, which was a dominant negative emotion throughout the pandemic, according to the interviewees. The anxiety ratio represents the prevalence of anxiety among all participants.

During the outbreak stage, more than half of middle-aged people expressed anxiety, stemming from the fear of unknown viruses and their experience of the SARS pandemic in 2003. At this stage, the COVID-19 pandemic had not yet spread nationally, with its effects limited regionally to Wuhan. Related information was available from few social media platforms, making it unclear whether the virus "has the characteristics of 'human-to-human transmission'". In addition, the degree of harmfulness of the "novel coronavirus" was not clear at that point, so people paid insufficient attention to it.

> The interviewee R said, "At that time, I was calm. I thought the pandemic was far away from my city. I didn't realize that it would be a widespread pandemic".

During the development stage of the COVID-19 pandemic, anxiety reached its peak among middle-aged people. The development stage is when the pandemic had spread nationwide, and research showed that the virus had the characteristics of "human-to-human transmission" (Chan et al., 2020). Middle-aged people perceived danger around them. Thus, their anxiety level continued to climb.

> The interviewee T mentioned, "I was nervous, because the pandemic has come to my side. I used to focus on distant places, but now it has come to my side. I am very nervous".

During the remission stage of the COVID-19 pandemic, the pandemic has been effectively controlled, and the resumption of work, production, and

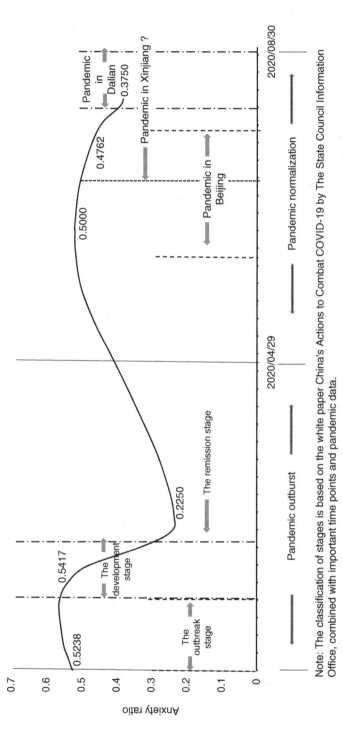

Figure 5.3 Anxiety ratio of middle-aged people at different stages of the pandemic.

school in various regions has recaptured the middle-aged people's attention to study, work, and other basic necessities, reducing their anxiety.

> *The interviewee V mentioned that "I preferred information related to the resumption of work, production, and school. At that stage, my mind would be led away and I wanted to know more about my own work and other industries."*

In addition, the normalization of the pandemic and the adoption of information such as, "The rising temperature decreases the virus activity", have also eased the anxiety of middle-aged people, and made them more optimistic about controlling the pandemic.

Later, the emergence of new cases in Beijing has revived the public's anxiety about the risk of the pandemic rebounding.

> *The interviewee A mentioned that "I was scared when I knew there was another case around me."*

However, by this stage, middle-aged people had already gone through a long time of psychological construction. Beijing's vigorous prevention measures and control of the pandemic gave the public "reassurance", so the middle-aged people's anxiety level in the subsequent regional pandemic did not exceed that of the development stage.

> *The interviewee R mentioned that "I was a bit anxious, but it eased quickly, because Beijing took timely measures to prevent and control the pandemic and made it under control soon."*

Health information behavior

Health information behavior characteristics

Unlike the fluctuation of sentiment that accompanied the ebb and flow of the course of the pandemic, middle-aged people's information behavior, namely information channels, information seeking, information adoption, and information sharing, remained similar to normal pre-pandemic patterns in many aspects. However, a few notable differences in their information behavior emerged, throughout the stages of the pandemic.

1   Access to information was primarily made through the same channels as usual. During the pandemic, the channels for middle-aged people to obtain information can be divided into two groups, online and offline. Online ways mainly included Weibo, WeChat, TV news, and mobile apps, while offline ways included informal sources such as relatives and friends. Among them, WeChat was the most frequently used channel for

information acquisition, with 48% of participants naming this as their source. Interviewees mainly obtained access to information through WeChat official accounts and WeChat group chats. Mobile applications such as Toutiao (an information recommendation application), Tencent News, etc., were used by 28%. At different stages of the pandemic, the health information behavior of middle-aged people remained relatively stable, reflecting the influence of their personalities and established habits. The middle-aged people basically kept stable and consistent when using media.

The interviewee X mentioned that "I used WeChat official accounts at all stages because I used them habitually."

2 Information-seeking behavior remained highly active throughout the PHEIC.

Because of their concern and anxiety about obtaining pandemic information, middle-aged people were more inclined to search actively for information to meet their own information needs. As shown in Figure 5.4, active information collection behavior accounted for 57.14% of their information-seeking activity, while habitual browsing (which is more consistent with ordinary daily behavior) accounted for 28.57%. The ways that middle-aged people obtained information through passive push and friends' recommendations accounted for only 7.14% of their information-seeking behavior.

3 Official information is more favorably regarded, although personal relationships play a role. Information adoption behaviors are influenced by elements such as trust in the source, the origin of the reference, the

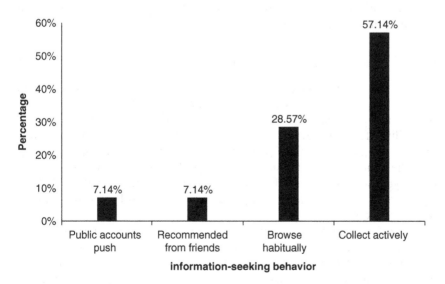

Figure 5.4 Proportion of information-seeking behavior of middle-aged people.

receiver's level of understanding, etc. Fifty-two percent of the middle-aged people said they trusted official information, and 25% of the middle-aged said they didn't trust personal information. Nine percent of middle-aged people admitted that they referenced information that friends recommended. Fourteen percent of middle-aged adults indicated they just made a brief overview of the institutions' information. However, an interesting phenomenon is that middle-aged people were more likely to adopt the information recommended by their friends, versus the information recommended by the WeChat official accounts, indicating that middle-aged people were affected by certain interpersonal relationships when they adopted the information.

4   Participants were cautious about sharing information during the PHEIC. Middle-aged people used information in two ways, either sharing or not sharing. Slightly more than half (56%) were willing to share information, while the others were unwilling to share. According to the interview data, the main reasons for middle-aged people's reluctance to share information are shown in Figure 5.5. Besides their preexisting habit of not sharing, the reasons that they were not willing to share or forward the relevant information fell into two categories: either they were not sure about the quality or trustworthiness of it, or they were unsure whether the information was subject to the regulation of rumors. As for the latter, because of policies to control the spread of rumors, the interviewees were not allowed to share the scary information and faced high risks if they chose to do so. For example, the public were banned from sharing and spreading rumors, or they could face fines, punishments, or dismissal. As a result, middle-aged people were wary of sharing information and may dismiss the information circulating in WeChat that have not been officially verified (Figure 5.5).

Changes in health information behavior

At different stages of the pandemic, data changes, government policies, and the natural environment created psychological implications for middle-aged people, and affected their pace of life, resulting in the necessity for and possibility of various levels of information attention. Figure 5.6 shows how much attention interviewees paid to information related to the pandemic over the course of the COVID-19 pandemic. During the pandemic, the top three types of information that attracted the most attention from middle-aged people were pandemic data, prevention and control measures, and the source of the pandemic.

Figure 5.7 shows the number of interviewees who were concerned about (i.e., paid attention to) each type of information, during each stage of the pandemic. In the outbreak stage, the most concerning information was pandemic data, while the least amount of attention was paid to information about the resumption of work, production, and school. This early reaction

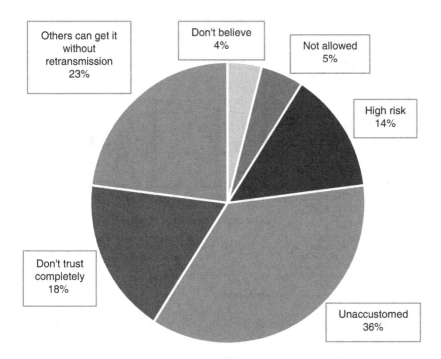

Figure 5.5 Reasons for middle-aged people not sharing information.

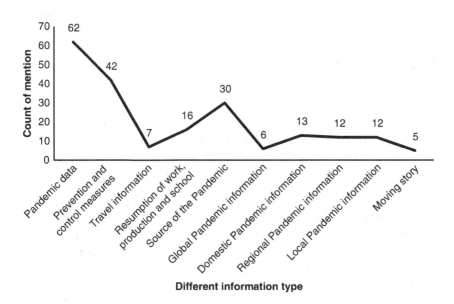

Figure 5.6 Amount of attention interviewees paid to various types of information.

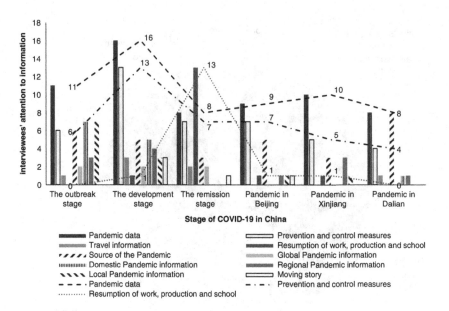

Figure 5.7 Changes in middle-aged people's attention to different information types.

was possibly the result of a limited impact on middle-aged people's daily lives, for the pandemic was not yet severe at this stage.

During the development stage, these middle-aged people paid more attention to pandemic data, and information about pandemic prevention and control measures. This stage included the Lunar New Year holiday, so people's attention to information about the resumption of work, production, and school grew gradually, but was not high. During the remission stage, middle-aged people focused on information about the resumption of work, production, and school, while the topics of pandemic data and prevention and control measures captured less attention. Because of the development of the pandemic, communities were closed off. Students took online classes at home, and middle-aged people worked online from home. In these circumstances, living with families in the same room all the time increased pressure such as conflicts arising from children's education problems. Therefore, middle-aged people were eager to return to work safely as soon as possible, so as to relieve the tension among family members caused by these conflicts during lockdowns. At the normalized (regional) pandemic period, middle-aged people paid more attention to the pandemic data, pandemic prevention and control measures, and regional pandemic situations, and paid less attention to international pandemic information, or information about the resumption of work, production, and school. At this stage, they were worried about pandemic prevention measures such as their community's closed-off management. Therefore, they were not only concerned about the pandemic data, but also about the government's pandemic prevention and control measures, even though, by this stage, they had already acquired knowledge related to pandemic prevention. At the same time, some respondents were located in the center of pandemic hotspots, and were highly concerned about regional pandemic information. Throughout the whole period of the pandemic, the source of the pandemic was the information type to which middle-aged people paid great attention. The original source of the virus was unknown, and the virus itself was highly infectious. Middle-aged people wanted to know the source of the pandemic, in order to carry out more effective daily protection measures.

During the different stages of the pandemic, middle-aged people showed differences in the types of information they were interested in, and their frequency of capturing certain types of information. The intensity of the information needs of these middle-aged participants varied in line with the changes in the severity of the pandemic, during its distinct stages. As shown in Figure 5.8, during the development stage, the largest number of types of information received attention. With the remission of the pandemic, the number of types of pandemic information that participants paid attention to gradually declined. When the pandemic was normalized, the number of information types meriting their attention stabilized. The amount of pandemic information that middle-aged people paid attention to gradually decreased along with the remission of the pandemic, indicating that under the normalization of the pandemic, middle-aged people had less motivation to obtain pandemic information, and their demands for information related to the pandemic decreased.

Association between emotions and health information behavior

With the changes brought about by the pandemic, the emotions and health information behavior of middle-aged people were not only influenced by various external factors, but also interacted with each other. Anxiety over the rapid increases in confirmed cases during the outbreak stage and the development stage led to more frequent information seeking and a greater need for information among middle-aged people.

> *The interviewee I mentioned that "When the pandemic was intense, I checked the information voluntarily, but in the past, I only looked at the information recommended to me."*

During and after the remission stage, the adoption of some information, such as "The rising temperature decreases the virus activity", affected the threat assessment of the pandemic by middle-aged people, and reduced their attention to the pandemic.

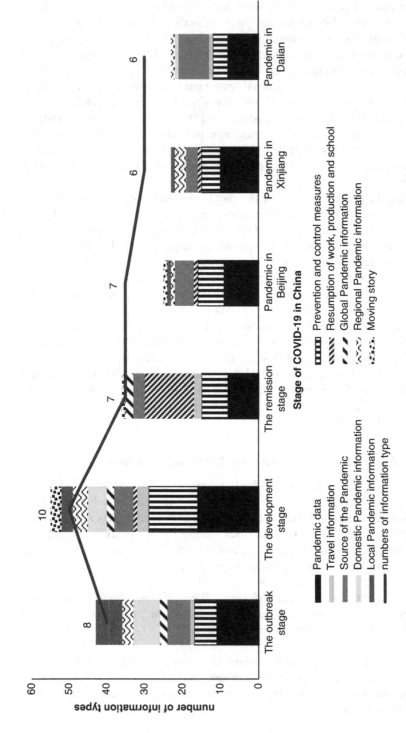

Figure 5.8 Cumulative levels of concern by information types among middle-aged people by pandemic stage.

> The interviewee K mentioned that *"The temperature is rising, I think the pandemic will not have such a big impact, so I pay less attention to it."*

With the rapid growth of confirmed cases, the still-unknown pathogenesis of COVID-19, and being isolated at home, middle-aged people had more time to focus on pandemic information, and to be influenced by the effects of social media. Middle-aged people being exposed to pandemic information were more anxious under this social panic atmosphere.

> The interviewee M mentioned that *"The more relevant information I received, the more panic I have been."*

Discussion and implications

Discussion

An interaction model of middle-aged people's health information behavior and emotion change was constructed, to describe the interaction of health information behavior and emotions under the circumstances of the COVID-19 pandemic. At the beginning of the pandemic, with the accumulation of anxiety emotions, middle-aged people searched health information more frequently and had bountiful information demands. During the remission stage, the anxiety of middle-aged people was alleviated, such that the frequency of health information seeking was reduced, and the scope of information needs was narrowed. Wang Ping and colleagues' research (2020) constructed the process and elements of personal information behavior in the PHEIC, including personal information needs, information acquisition, and information use, which is consistent with the findings of this research. A previous study also mentioned the influence of information acquisition and utilization on individual psychology and cognition; however, interactions among these elements were neglected (Wang et al., 2020). When exploring individual health information behavior patterns, our work focused on the psychological factor of emotions, and clearly expounded the interactive influence of emotions and health information behavior throughout the dynamic process of the pandemic.

During the course of COVID-19, middle-aged people's affect included positive, neutral, and negative emotions. Different dominant emotions would appear at different stages of the pandemic. Individual emotions were basically consistent with the overall intensity of the pandemic in the society, and more anxious emotions emerged while the pandemic was either highly developed or rebounding. At the outbreak stage, more than half of the participants expressed anxiety. During the development stage, an increase in anxiety appeared. Wu and Chen (2021) analyzed the relationship between the fluctuations in COVID-19 and people's psychological security and found that levels of negative emotions changed at different stages of the pandemic. This illustrates that the closer the time is to the serious stages of the pandemic, the stronger the negative emotions experienced by people are. The results of their study are similar to the results regarding emotion change of middle-aged people at different stages of COVID-19 that were found in our study. Moreover, our work analyzed the emotions in a broader range of time windows, which can provide a reference for further study.

During the pandemic, the channels used by middle-aged people to obtain information were the same ones they used in the pre-pandemic context, and their information-seeking behavior was mainly active searching. The research of Niu Jinyu et al. (2020) showed that "information hungry" people tend to pay active attention to and search for risk information, expecting to obtain authentic, reliable, and authoritative information to fill their own "information vacuum", a finding which is corroborated by the proactive information-seeking behavior of middle-aged people found in this research.

During the pandemic, middle-aged people mainly adopted information from official channels, and were cautious about information sharing. The research of Niu and colleagues (2020) showed that the public were more satisfied with risk information obtained from television, newspapers, community publicity, and other traditional channels. Television as a mass medium was still the main way for the public to obtain information. In our work, we found that, because of the convenience of social media, particularly WeChat, its official accounts became the main channel for middle-aged people to access pandemic information. In the study by Niu et al. (2020), it was reported that the proportion of the public obtaining information about the pandemic through the Internet was 89.85%, but the individual channels were not comprehensively compared, which may account for differences from this study.

Anxiety over the rapid increase in pandemic data at the development stage led to more frequent information acquisition, and a greater need for information by middle-aged people. Throughout the stages of the pandemic, middle-aged people paid various levels of attention to particular types of pandemic information, and the changes in the severity of the pandemic were associated with variations in the types of information to which middle-aged people paid attention. Ma & Wang (2020) conducted a study on the health information searching intentions of college students in the case of major infectious diseases, and found that both uncertainty perception and emotions can positively affect their public health information searching intentions. Although the target groups of this and the current study are different, similar conclusions were reached.

Theoretical implications

This work contributes to consumer health information (CHI) literature in several ways. Existing research has paid little attention to middle-aged people's health information behavior. Prior attention to this demographic group mainly reflected middle-aged parents' concern about their children, and middle-aged people's online health information seeking (Gong et al., 2021; Huisman & Biltereyst, 2020; Lee & Oh, 2021; Zhang & Li, 2019). In the context of the pandemic, we comprehensively studied the characteristics of middle-aged people in terms of their health information demands, access, and use, which has expanded the knowledge base of consumer health information. In addition, the existing studies on health information behavior in the context of the pandemic have focused on a fixed point in time, to research a group's health information behavior or psychological emotions. In this study, in-depth semi-structured interviews were used to study the interaction among middle-aged people's health information behavior, emotions, and their development over time, through the dynamic changes throughout pandemic. This work contributes to an understanding of the living state of middle-aged people facing a PHEIC, highlighting their information behavior and emotions, as well as the relationships between these two core concepts.

Practical implications

This study has practical implications for application developers trying to understand the health information behavior of middle-aged people, in order to increase user engagement. For example, we found that the middle aged give high credibility to official information and tend to adjust their pace of life and health information behavior as the official policy changes. This finding can help application designers to determine the most attractive information content, for the different stages of a PHEIC. As this study revealed the changes in health information behavior and emotions in middle-aged people at different stages of the PHEIC, healthcare providers can provide better emotional counseling and other services in the context of the normalization of the pandemic.

Limitations

In this study, although the interviewees were recruited using snowball sampling, the diversity of the sample was still limited. In addition, some interviewees used dialects when communicating. Although we manually transcribed the recordings and double-checked the text used for the analysis, ensuring the reliability of cross-checking remains challenging.

Conclusion

In this chapter, interviews were conducted with middle-aged people in different regions of China to explore their health information behavior and emotions during the different stages of the COVID-19 pandemic, and the data were analyzed using Grounded Theory. An interaction model was proposed, and middle-aged people's demands for health information, as influenced by their changing emotions, and under the fluctuating circumstances of the PHEIC were effectively demonstrated.

The demand for relevant statistics, prevention and control measures, and other information has always been high. However, at the remission stage of the pandemic, the demand for information about the resumption of work, production, and school captured higher attention. The emotions of middle-aged people include positive, neutral, and negative sides, among which anxiety was dominant at different stages, and reached its peak during the development stage. Although anxiety decreased during the remission stage, it rebounded when the pandemic reoccurred regionally. The emotions associated with information have an interactive effect on related information behavior. The more information that middle-aged people received related to the pandemic, the more anxious they became, and in turn, this anxiety drove middle-aged people to access information more frequently. This study brings insights that are useful for optimizing health information services, by exploring the changes in information behavior and related emotions from the perspective of the dynamic and different stages of the PHEIC.

References

Chan, J. F.-W., Yuan, S., Kok, K.-H., To, K. K.-W., Chu, H., Yang, J., Xing, F. Liu, J., Yip, C. C.-Y., Poon, R. W.-S., Tsoi, H.-W., Lo, S. K.-F., Chan, K.-H., Poon, V. K.-M., Chan, W.-M., Ip, J.D., Cai, J.-P., Cheng, V. C.-C., Chen, H., ... , & Yuen, K.-Y. (2020). A familial cluster of pneumonia associated with the 2019 novel coronavirus indicating person-to-person transmission: A study of a family cluster. *Lancet, 395*(10223), 514–523. doi:10.1016/s0140-6736(20)30154-9

Chen, J., Zhang, L., & Lu, Q. (2021). Motivation and topic of college students' health information needs in public health emergencies. *Library and Information Service, 65*(6), 82–92.

Chen, Q., Song, S., & Zhao, Y. (2020). The impact of information overload on user information evasion in public health emergencies: An empirical study based on COVID-19 information prevalence. *Information and Documentation Services, 41*(3), 76–88.

Cucinotta, D., & Vanelli, M. (2020). WHO declares COVID-19 a pandemic. *Acta bio-medica: Atenei Parmensis, 91*(1), 157–160. 10.23750/abm.v91i1.9397

Department of Economic and Social Affairs Population Dynamics, (n.d.). *World Population Prospects 2019.* United Nations. https://population.un.org/wpp/DataQuery/

Glaser, B.G., & Strauss, A.L. (1999). *The discovery of grounded theory: Strategies for qualitative research.* Routledge.

Gao, J., Zheng, P., Jia, Y., Chen, H., Mao, Y., Chen, S., Wang, Y., Fu, H., & Dai, J. (2020). Mental health problems and social media exposure during COVID-19 outbreak. *PLoS One, 15*(4), Article e0231924. doi:10.1371/journal.pone.0231924

Gong, W., Guo, Q., & Jiang, C.L. (2021). Conversation breeds compliance: The role of intergenerational communication in promoting preventive behaviors against COVID-19 among middle-aged parents in China. *International Journal* of *Environmental Research and Public Health, 18*(19), Article 10198. doi:10.3390/ijerph181910198

Ho, H.Y., Chen, Y.L., & Yen, C.F. (2020). Different impacts of COVID-19-related information sources on public worry: An online survey through social media. *Internet Interventions-the Application of Information Technology in Mental and Behavioural Health, 22*(6). Article 100350. doi:10.1016/j.invent.2020.100350

Huisman, M., Joye, S., & Biltereyst, D. (2020). Searching for health: Doctor Google and the shifting dynamics of the middle-aged and older adult patient-physician relationship and interaction. *Journal of Aging and Health, 32*(9), 998–1007. doi:10.1177/0898264319873809

Huo, M., & Zhu, J. (2020). Formation mechanism and management strategy of positive energy information sharing behavior of social network users under the background of emergency public health incidents. *Information Science, 38*(11), 121–127.

John-Henderson, N.A., & Mueller, C.M. (2020). The relationship between health mindsets and health protective behaviors: An exploratory investigation in a convenience sample of American Indian adults during the COVID-19 pandemic. *PLoS One, 15*(11), Article e0242902. doi:10.1371/journal.pone.0242902

Kemp, S. (2022, January 26). *Digital 2022: Global overview report.* Datareportal. https://datareportal.com/reports/digital-2022-global-overview-report

Kühn, L., Bachert, P., Hildebrand, C., Kunkel, J., Reitermayer, J., Wäsche, H., & Woll, A. (2022). Health literacy among university students: A systematic review of cross-sectional studies. *Frontiers in Public Health, 9*, Article 680999. doi:10.3389/fpubh.2021.680999

Lee, H., & Oh, S. (2021). Health consciousness and health information orientation on health information searching behaviors of middle-aged adults. [중년층의 건강관심도와 건강정보추구도가 인터넷 건강정보 검색행동에 미치는 영향]. *Journal of the Korean Society for Information Management, 38*(3), 73–99. doi:10.3743/kosim.2021.38.3.073

Leung, A.Y.M., Parial, L.L., Tolabing, M.C., Sim, T., Mo, P.I., Okan, O., & Dadaczynski, K. (2021). Sense of coherence mediates the relationship between digital health literacy and anxiety about the future in aging population during the COVID-19 pandemic: A path analysis. *Aging & Mental Health, 26*(3), 544–553. doi:10.1080/13607863.2020.1870206

Lund, B., & Ma, J.X. (2022). Exploring information seeking of rural older adults during the COVID-19 pandemic. *Aslib Journal of Information Management, 74*(1), 54–77. doi:10.1108/AJIM-04-2021-0118

Lunnay, B., Foley, K., Meyer, S.B., Warin, M., Wilson, C., Olver, I., Miller, E.R., Thomas, J., & Ward, P.R. (2021). Alcohol consumption and perceptions of health risks during COVID-19: A qualitative study of middle-aged women in South Australia. *Frontiers in Public Health, 9*, Article 616870. doi:10.3389/fpubh.2021.616870

Ma, C., & Wang, D. (2020). Health information seeking intention of university undergraduates during the major epidemic infectious diseases. *Chinese Journal of Medical Library and Information Science, 29*(9), 36–45.

Massachusetts Emergency Management Agency, (n.d.). *Public health emergencies.* Mass.gov. https://www.mass.gov/info-details/public-health-emergencies

Montesi, M. (2020). Situational characteristics of information behavior during confinement by COVID-19: Survey results. *Bid-Textos Universitaris De Biblioteconomia I Documentacio, 45.* doi:10.1344/BiD2020.45.5

Ni, N., Wu, K., Jia, H., Zhou, M., Wei, W., Wang, C., & Peng, X. (2019). Correlation study on health information seeking behavior and health status among patients with diabetes in community. *Chinese Journal of Health Education, 35*(1), 46–49, 53.

Niu, J., Chen, C., Ning, L., Peng, Z., Bi, X., Qunhong, W., & Hao, Y. (2020). Public satisfaction with risk communication during COVID-19 outbreak: The impact of information needs, channel preferences, media trust, and emotions. *Bulletin of National Natural Science Foundation of China, 34*(6), 794–803.

OfCom. (2022, March 30). *Adults' media use and attitudes report.* OfCom. https://www.ofcom.org.uk/research-and-data/media-literacy-research/adults/adults-media-use-and-attitudes

Rosario, R., Martins, M.R.O., Augusto, C., Silva, M.J., Martins, S., Duarte, A., Fronteira, I., Ramos, N., Okan, O., & Dadaczynski, K. (2020). Associations between COVID-19-related digital health literacy and online information-seeking behavior among Portuguese university students. *International Journal of Environmental Research and Public Health, 17*(23), Article 8987. doi:10.3390/ijerph17238987

Roy, K.C., Hasan, S., Sadri, A.M., & Cebrian, M. (2020). Understanding the efficiency of social media based crisis communication during Hurricane Sandy. *International Journal of Information Management, 52,* Article 102060. 10.1016/j.ijinfomgt.2019.102060

Shehata, A. (2021). Health Information behaviour during COVID-19 outbreak among Egyptian library and information science undergraduate students. *Information Development, 37*(3), 417–430. doi:10.1177/0266666920976181

Solnick, R.E., Chao, G., Ross, R.D., Kraft-Todd, G.T., & Kocher, K.E. (2021). Emergency physicians and personal narratives improve the perceived effectiveness of COVID-19 public health recommendations on social media: A randomized experiment. *Academic Emergency Medicine, 28*(2), 172–183. doi:10.1111/acem.14188

Tee, M.L., Tee, C.A., Anlacan, J.P., Aligam, K.J.G., Reyes, P.W.C., Kuruchittham, V., & Ho, R.C. (2020). Psychological impact of COVID-19 pandemic in the Philippines. *Journal of Affective Disorders, 277,* 379–391. doi:10.1016/j.jad.2020.08.043

The State Council Information Office of the People's Republic of China. (2020). *Fighting COVID-19 China in action.* Foreign Languages Press.

Wang, L., & Ma, Z. (2020). Research on information anxiety of university students under the epidemic of COVID-19—from the perspective of stress disorder. *Modern Information, 40*(7), 14–24.

Wang, L., Yang, C., Wang, D., Wang, Q., Li, J., & Zhao, C. (2011). Relationship of BMI to hypertension, blood lipid and glucose in middle-aged adults in Harbin. *Chinese General Practice, 14*(5), 503–505.

Wang, P., Sun, M., & An, Q. (2020). Information behavior of individuals in public health emergencies: Qualitative observation, discussion and enlightenment taking COVID-19 in 2020 as an example. *Library, 48*(7), 92–100.

Wang, X., Li, J., Wang, D., & Wei, Y. (2019). Research on the influencing factors of old-age user boycott behavior in mobile social media: Analysis based on the perspective of Human-System Interaction Theory. *Information and Documentation Services, 40*(1), 81–88.

Wang, Y., Shen, J., & Jiang, Z. (2020). Analysis of the game influence of information behavior on decision makers in public health emergencies: Case study of COVID-19 event. *Information Research, 40*(8), 57–63.

World Health Organization. (2009). *Pandemic influenza preparedness and response: A WHO guidance document.* World Health Organization. https://apps.who.int/iris/handle/10665/44123

World Health Organization. (2020a). *COVID-19 Public Health Emergency of International Concern (PHEIC) global research and innovation forum: Towards a research roadmap.* World Health Organization. https://www.who.int/publications/m/item/covid-19-public-health-emergency-of-international-concern-(pheic)-global-research-and-innovation-forum

World Health Organization. (2020b, August 18). *WHO Director-General's opening remarks at the media briefing on COVID-19.* World Health Organization. https://www.who.int/director-general/speeches/detail/who-director-general-s-opening-remarks-at-the-media-briefing-on-covid-19—18-august-2020

Wu, W., & Chen, L. (2021). Relationship between progress of COVID-19 and psychological security in residents during the epidemic of COVID-19. *Chinese Mental Health Journal, 35*(4), 350–352.

Zhang, C., Ye, M., Fu, Y., Yang, M., Luo, F., Yuan, J., & Tao, Q. (2020). The psychological impact of the COVID-19 pandemic on teenagers in China. *The Journal of adolescent health: Official publication of the Society for Adolescent Medicine, 67*(6), 747–755. doi:10.1016/j.jadohealth.2020.08.026

Zhang, L.S., Jung, E.H., & Chen, Z. (2020). Modeling the pathway linking health information seeking to psychological well-being on WeChat. *Health Communication, 35*(9), 1101–1112. doi:10.1080/10410236.2019.1613479

Zhang, X., & Li, Y. (2019). Ability of users in different age groups to screen health information in social media. [年龄梯度视角下网络用户健康信息甄别能力研究]. *Journal of the China Society for Scientific and Technical Information, 38*(8), 838–848.

Zhang, Z., & Wu, Z. (2013). Study on the use of QQ and its influence on interpersonal relationships between middle-aged people. *Journalism & Communication Review, 84*(1), 104-112, 214, 223.

Zhao, Y.H., & Zhang, J. (2017). Consumer health information seeking in social media: A literature review. *Health Information and Libraries Journal, 34*(4), 268–283. doi:10.1111/hir.12192

Zhu, C., Xu, X., Zhang, W., Chen, J., & Evans, R. (2020). How health communication via Tik Tok makes a difference: A content analysis of Tik Tok accounts run by Chinese Provincial Health Committees. *International Journal of Environmental Research and Public Health, 17*(1), Article 192. https://www.mdpi.com/1660-4601/17/1/192

Appendix 1. Research interview outline

Please provide the following personal information

- Your age
- Your gender
- Your occupation
- Your area
- Your marital status (married/single)
- Do you have an elderly person to support
- Do you have children

Please answer the following questions about the health information behavior on social media and official accounts during the pandemic

Concept explanation: Social media refers to the content production and exchange platform based on user relationships on the Internet. It is a tool and platform for people to share opinions, insights, experiences, and opinions with each other. At this stage, it mainly includes social networking sites, Weibo, WeChat, Blogs, forums, podcasts, etc.

A) What are the channels for you to obtain relevant health information during the pandemic? (TV, Tiktok, WeChat, friends and family, ...)

B) Which social media (Zhihu Q&A platform, Tianya Forum, Weibo, WeChat official accounts, ...) do you prefer to use to capture information during the pandemic? Why is that?

C) Do you know WeChat official accounts release information related to the pandemic (pandemic data, etc.)?

D) Will you actively use your WeChat official accounts to obtain information related to the pandemic? Why is that? (No: not used to; Yes: convenient and quick)

E) What is your attitude towards the pandemic information released by WeChat official accounts? (Trust/distrust)

F) Do you have different levels of attention and trust for different types of WeChat official accounts (official media, individuals and institutions)? What do you feel about different types of WeChat official accounts?

G) Do you subscribe the public health WeChat official accounts to obtain the pandemic information? If so, what do you focus on? What is the reason for using this WeChat official account to obtain information?

H) Do you think the information related to the pandemic provided by your WeChat official account meets your information needs?

I) Do you believe you have the ability to identify correct health information during a pandemic?

J) Do you share or recommend information to others that you think is correct? Why?

K) Whether the WeChat official accounts you subscribe to will publish rumors or refuting rumors? Do you repost or share information when you know it is a rumor or a rumor has been refuted? Why is that?

L) Do you prefer to actively search for information on WeChat official accounts or passively accept information recommended by others?

M) What is your attitude towards the information you obtained from your own WeChat official accounts and the information published by WeChat official accounts others recommended during the pandemic?

(Continued)

N) How do you think the number, frequency and location of the information published by WeChat official accounts will affect you during the pandemic?

O) Please rank the influences of the following factors on your reading experience. Why do you think it is the most important?

I Article title (if this is the most important, ask: length, tone, punctuation, subjective or objective statement)

II Article topic (Follow-up: category, whether the pandemic is related, refuting rumors)

III Source of the article (Follow-up: government, institution, individual)

P) Please rank the importance of the following text presentation methods and your attitude towards each item. Why do you think it/they are the most important?

I The text has sections or subheadings

II Highlight key points in the text

III The body information is presented in multiple ways, and there are many visual elements of charts and audio

IV Keep the text concise and humorous

V There are a lot of technical terms in the text, which is highly academic

VI There are hard ads in the text

VII There are ads in the text

Q) Please make an authoritative order for the following data sources

I specialist

II The hospital

III The official media

IV The enterprises

V Scientific research institutions

VI Other

VII Not paying much attention

R) What is your attitude towards the humorous and concise language of information released by WeChat official accounts during the pandemic? Do you like humorous articles?

S) Do you follow comments on health information articles during the pandemic? How do you think comments that are at odds with the content of the message will affect you?

T) What factors do you think will influence you to change your attitude towards health information obtained during the pandemic?

U) What problems do you think exist in providing information related to the pandemic on WeChat official accounts, and what impact does this have on you?

(*Continued*)

Phase 1 Outbreak stage of the pandemic (January 20–23)	When did you hear about the pandemic? What types of information will you follow on social media at this stage? What is the reason? What emotions do you have when you get information about the pandemic? Why? What kind of information makes you anxious or fearful at this stage? Why is that?
Phase 2 Development stage of the pandemic (January 23–February 20)	When did you hear about the pandemic? What types of information will you follow on social media at this stage? What is the reason? What emotions do you have when you get information about the pandemic? Why? What kind of information makes you anxious or fearful at this stage? Why is that?
Phase 3 Remission stage of the pandemic (February 20–)	When did you hear about the pandemic? What types of information will you follow on social media at this stage? What is the reason? What emotions do you have when you get information about the pandemic? Why? What kind of information makes you anxious or fearful at this stage? Why is that?
New pandemics in Beijing (Since June 11, there have been consecutive confirmed cases of COVID-19.)	When did you hear about the pandemic in Beijing? What types of information will you follow on social media at this stage? What is the reason? What emotions do you have when you get information about the pandemic? Why? What kind of information makes you anxious or fearful at this stage? Why is that?
Pandemic in Xinjiang Production and Construction Corps (A new domestic COVID-19 case was confirmed on June 15)	When did you learn of the pandemic in the Xinjiang Production and Construction Corps? What types of information will you follow on social media at this stage? What is the reason? What emotions do you have when you get information about the pandemic? Why? What kind of information makes you anxious or fearful at this stage? Why is that?
Dalian: A new domestic COVID-19 case was confirmed in Dalian, Liaoning province on July 22.	When did you learn about the pandemic in Dalian? What types of information will you follow on social media at this stage? What is the reason? What emotions do you have when you get information about the pandemic? Why? What kind of information makes you anxious or fearful at this stage? Why is that?
Do you have any suggestions or comments of this interview?	

Appendix 2. Results of open coding

Level 1 coding	Level 2 coding	Level 3 coding
1 Information Channels	11 Weibo	111 Official media
		112 Private Weibo
	12 WeChat	121 Public
		122 Friends
		123 WeChat group chats
		124 WeChat official accounts
	13 TV News	131 News broadcast
		132 Press Conference
	14 Mobile client	141 News APP
		142 Xue xi qiang guo

Level 1 coding	Level 2 coding	Level 3 coding
4 Information Usage	41 Share	411 Be good for others
		412 You think it's important to be right
		413 Care for and comfort those close to you
		414 The object is intimate with oneself
		415 The need for information exchange
	42 Don't share	421 Do not believe and spread rumors
		422 Not be allowed
		423 Others can get it without retransmission
		424 Unaccustomed
		425 High risk

Level 1 coding	Level 2 coding	Level 3 coding
6 Information Requirements	61 Epidemic data	611 Confirmed cases
		612 New cases were reported
		613 Cured cases
		614 Deaths
		616 Asymptomatic cases
	62 Prevention and control Measures	621 National Policies
		622 Local Policies
		623 Personal protection
		624 Vaccine development
		626 Community work

Level 1 coding	Level 2 coding	Level 3 coding
7 Emotions	71 Anxious	711 The virus is highly contagious
		712 Virus is highly survivable
		713 Over publicity
		714 Other people's emotion swings
		715 The epidemic is close
	72 Fearful	721 There is no vaccine
		722 Virus spread
		723 Conceal itinerary
		724 Rumors spread
		725 No effective means or medicine

(Continued)

Level 1 coding	Level 2 coding	Level 3 coding	Level 1 coding	Level 2 coding	Level 3 coding	Level 1 coding	Level 2 coding	Level 3 coding	Level 1 coding	Level 2 coding	Level 3 coding
	15 Relatives and friends	151 Meet and Chat			426 Don't trust completely		63 Travel information	421 Tourism			726 Abnormal festive atmosphere
2 Information Seeking	21 Collect Actively	211 WeChat official accounts articles	5. Reading Habits	51 Article Source	511 Determine the authenticity of the information			422 Visit relatives and friends		73 Calm	731 Anxiety is not conducive to prevention and control
		212 Relevant government pages			512 Represents the article source			423 Information of the community			732 The epidemic has been controlled
	22 Browse habitually	221 News APP			513 There is optional reading		64 Resume work and school	641 Date return to work		74 Dispassionate	741 Believe the epidemic is under control
		222 WeChat small program and official account articles			514 Determine the credibility of the article			642 The school time			742 Expect a vaccine to appear in time
	23 Recommended from friends	231 Share in moments of friends		52 Humor	521 Usually like it very much		65 Source of the epidemic	651 Repeated outbreaks			743 Far from oneself
	24 Official accounts push	241 WeChat official accounts			522 Should be appropriate during the outbreak			652 Source of virus			744 The temperature rises

3 Information Adoption	31 Trust	311 Official Information	53 Authority	531 Experts	653 Route of transmission	745 Long time zero new cases

Reconstructed hierarchical coding table:

Level 1	Level 2	Level 3
3 Information Adoption	31 Trust	311 Official Information
	32 Reference	321 Friends recommend information
		322 Article Comments
	33 Learn about	331 Organization Information
	34 Ignore	341 AD
	35 Don't trust	351 WeChat official accounts by individual
	53 Authority	531 Experts
		532 Hospital
		533 Official media
		534 Enterprises
		535 Scientific research institutions
		653 Route of transmission
	66 The events	661 Touching story
		662 Medical assistance
	75 Optimistic	745 Long time zero new cases
		746 Mortality rate decreased
		747 Technology tracking
		748 Good control effect
		751 Resumption of work and production and school
		752 Fewer new cases
		753 Cured cases increased
		754 Party and government leaders
		755 End home quarantine
		756 National prevention and control is effective

6 Evolution of Discussion Topics in Online Depression Self-Help Groups Before, During, and After COVID-19 Lockdown in China

Honglei Lia Sun and Pnina Fichman

Introduction

As the COVID-19 pandemic rapidly spread across the world, a range of public health measures were gradually adopted by governments to handle the disease before proven cures or effective vaccines were proposed (Nwachukwu et al., 2020); these commonly involved lockdown, isolation, quarantine, and closing of international borders. Lockdown witnessed a steady spread of depression among isolated and quarantined individuals (e.g., Brooks et al. 2020), which resulted in increased socialization on social media platforms by individuals who were desperately seeking to maintain social connections with others (Limaye et al., 2020; Ni et al., 2020; Yu et al., 2021). Now more than ever, we need a better understanding of discussion topics in online depression communities during public health crises. While previous studies focus on mining and analyzing textual content in online depression communities (e.g., Park et al., 2018; Tang et al., 2020; Feldhege et al., 2020), little is known about if and how discussion topics in online health communities evolved over time during the COVID-19 pandemic, and therefore a more nuanced analysis is warranted.

Language use patterns mirror mental states and psychopathological characteristics. Tausczik and Pennebaker (2010) argue that not only is the language the most effective way for individuals to describe themselves, others, and the world, but it is also the most common and reliable way for people to translate their internal thoughts and emotions into a form that others can understand. Language use on social media platforms allows researchers to observe individuals as they freely present themselves in their own words (Schwartz et al., 2013). Research that examines user-generated content in online depression communities pays most attention to the thread length (e.g., Muncer et al., 2000), thematic features (e.g., Feldhege et al., 2020), semantic features of the posts (e.g., Carron-Arthur et al., 2016), and underlying emotion (e.g., Tang et al., 2020). However, despite its importance, longitudinal changes of the language features of user-generated content in online depression communities have not yet been studied. It's necessary to uncover how the fluctuations of internal thoughts and emotions

DOI: 10.4324/9781003231769-10

are related specifically to different stages of the COVID-19 lockdown, and we achieve this by revealing the changes in language features with the progression of the pandemic.

Given the role of context in shaping socio-technical interactions in general (Kling, 2007) and ICT use during the COVID-19 pandemic in particular (Yang et al., 2020), it is important to study user-generated content in online depression communities in various contexts and not overlook its manifestation before, during, and after COVID-19 lockdown. Aiming to address this gap, we collected data from the Chinese platform *Douban Group*'s two online depression self-help groups and traced the evolution of topics and language features over time (before, during, and after the COVID-19 lockdown) to address the following research questions:

1   How did the extent and range of discussion topics in online depression self-help groups in China change over time before, during, and after the COVID-19 lockdown?
2   How did the fluctuations of language use and internal emotions relate to different stages of the COVID-19 lockdown in China?

Background

Language use on social media among people with depression

Language use patterns that involve predispositions to use a range of words can be useful when differentiating between depressed and healthy individuals (Hussain et al., 2020), as well as diagnosing and treating depression. Compared with healthy individuals, those suffering from depression prefer to use *first-person singular pronouns* and negative emotion words, while they are less likely to use *first-person plural pronouns* and positive emotion words (Rude et al., 2004; Molendijk et al., 2010; Zimmermann et al., 2017).

As social media platforms have been increasingly seen as social sensors to detect depression (Fatima et al., 2018), scholars from different disciplines have examined how individuals with depression use languages in social media contexts, such as *Facebook* and *Twitter* (e.g., Leis et al., 2019; Hussain et al., 2020; Huang & Zhou, 2021). Most notably, depressed individuals prefer to use *first-person pronouns* and use *second-* and *third-person pronouns* less often on social media (de Choudhury et al., 2013; Leis et al., 2019). Also, a considerable number of patients expressing suicidal ideation and behavior will employ a larger number of words associated with death (Coppersmith et al., 2015; Preotiuc-Pietro et al., 2015; Li et al., 2019; Hussain et al., 2020). Stimuli or other stressful events that lead to depression may also trigger other emotions besides depression, such as anxiety and anger (Newell et al., 2017), causing individuals with depression to frequently use words that belong to these feelings (Coppersmith et al., 2015; Hussain et al., 2020).

Additionally, Hussain et al. (2020) found that the words that are associated with *negate* and *cause* positively correlated with *depression* on *Facebook* and that individuals with depression frequently employ words that belong to religion and health. Supporting this latter finding is Huang and Zhou's (2021) observation that when depressed individuals seek to escape their unpleasant situation, attract attention, and ask for help, they tend to use extensive health-related words.

The COVID-19 pandemic

Social media use during the COVID-19 pandemic

During COVID-19, social media platforms became a major source of sharing and disseminating information about the pandemic (Malik et al., 2021) and a popular medium through which to socialize with others (Limaye et al., 2020; Ni et al., 2020). Many individuals, while experiencing isolation during hospitalization or quarantining at home, turned to social media as a way to stay in touch with their family and friends and share their personal experiences (Ahmad & Murad, 2020).

Scholars have been paying attention to the social media infodemic caused by COVID-19. For example, Hua and Shaw (2020) argue that in order to reduce the impact of fake news on social media during the COVID-19 Infodemic, there is a need to combine efforts, including different stakeholders' participation as well as stricter regulations. Garfin et al. (2020) suggest that in the age of social media where information so easily goes viral, combatting false information and rumors is extremely important. Ferrucci et al. (2020) argue that during the infodemic, unverified rumors and exaggerated claims not only generated fear and panic, but promoted xenophobic and racist posts.

Additionally, previous studies examined information behaviors on social media during the COVID-19 pandemic. Mi et al. (2021) investigated the psychological health information needs of the public on a social Q&A platform and found that the public was in need of psychological health information related to depression during COVID-19. Malik et al. (2021) illustrate that *Facebook* users who held a positive attitude toward sharing were more likely to share information about COVID-19. Islam et al. (2020) argue that while social status-seeking and socialization are not considered good during crises, socialization and social status are sought by many on social media in order to overcome their fear of being isolated. While doing so, *Facebook* users may indirectly know the updates about their close ones.

Psychological impact of the COVID-19 pandemic

The COVID-19 pandemic as a public health emergency of global concern has caused a huge psychological impact on individuals. Wang et al. (2020)

reported that during the initial phase of the COVID-19 outbreak in China, more than half the respondents rated the psychological impact as moderate-to-severe and about one-third said they experienced moderate-to-severe anxiety. Ferrucci et al. (2020) found that during the epidemic period in Italy, people felt psychologically vulnerable and were afraid of economic crises, falling sick, and dying. Both pre- and post-lockdown, negative feelings contributed to decreased psychological well-being (e.g., decreased sexuality, sleep disturbances, and nutrition-related issues). Hashim et al. (2022) reported that more than half of the participants in their study had depression, anxiety, and stress, and the longer the COVID-19 outbreaks lasted, the more anxious and depressed they—and others less familiar with these feelings—became.

The COVID-19 pandemic not only directly impacted public psychology but also had an indirect psychological impact on the public through a range of public health measures. Some scholars discovered that live statistics and COVID-19-related news tracking the number of confirmed cases, recovered patients, and death toll on social media heighten concerns and uncertainty among populations (Ferrucci et al., 2020). Also, the COVID-19 pandemic caused a range of disease control procedures, including self-isolation, rigorous quarantine, movement restrictions, social distancing, lockdowns, and closing of international borders (Charlson et al., 2016; Nwachukwu et al., 2020) that consequently interfered with most of our routine activities (Li et al., 2020). These measures caused emotional and psychological distress; reports indicate that during or after the quarantine period, many experienced negative emotions, such as fear, frustration, boredom, depression, stress, anger, and low mood (Brooks et al., 2020).

Most of the literature about depression during the COVID-19 pandemic include preliminary reports that focus on depression rates around the world, emphasizing the impact of COVID-19 on depression levels (González-Sanguino et al., 2020; Wang et al., 2020; Nwachukwu et al., 2020). It is essential to examine, however, if and how discussion topics in online health communities evolved during the COVID-19 pandemic in order to promote an understanding of depression during health crises.

The COVID-19 pandemic in China

According to the report "*Fighting COVID-19 China in Action*" (The State Council Information Office of China, 2020), the COVID-19 epidemic in China can be divided into five stages: Stage I: Sudden start of COVID-19 epidemic (December 27, 2019-January 19, 2020, lasting 24 days); Stage II: The rapid spread of the COVID-19 epidemic (January 20-February 20, 2020, lasting 32 days); Stage III: Gradual decline of COVID-19 epidemic (February 21–March 17, 2020, lasting 26 days); Stage IV: Fade of COVID-19 epidemic (March 18-April 28, 2020, lasting 42 days); Stage V: Ongoing prevention and control of COVID-19 epidemic (Since April 29, 2020).

From January 23 to January 29, 2020, all provinces and equivalent administrative units on the Chinese mainland activated a Level 1 public health emergency response, which included self-isolation, rigorous quarantine, and closing borders. On February 21, 2020, most provinces and equivalent administrative units started to downgrade their public health emergency response level in light of the local situation and gradually lifted traffic restrictions. By February 24, 2020, all provincial trunk highways had reopened, and order was restored to the transport networks with the exception of those in Hubei and Beijing. As such, the COVID-19 nationwide lockdown in China lasted about 33 days (from January 23 to February 24, 2020).

Method

To answer our research questions, we focused on analyzing online discussions from two depression self-help groups that were active before, during, and after the COVID-19 lockdown in China.

Data collection

Douban Group is a publicly available forum that provides access to common interest discussion groups. On its homepage, *Douban Group* describes itself as "a place where people of like-mindedness discuss topics together" (Douban Group, 2021). On the forum, there are several depression self-help groups conversing on ways to cope with depression, including for example, "Depression self-help group", "Depression mutual aid clinic group", and "Overcoming depression Group". These groups are moderated by users who ban all missionary and suicide posts and instead ask that members share positive content and encourage each other.

Because the purpose of our study was to investigate the evolution of discussion topics in online depression self-help groups before, during, and after the COVID-19 lockdown in China, our sampling strategy focused on finding the appropriate online depression group. The inclusion criteria of discussion groups were as follows: (1) the group is related to depression self-help; (2) group members are active and located in more than one province or city; (3) the group is long-lived, publicly available, and relatively mature. As a result, only two groups met the criteria and were therefore selected: Group 1: "Depression self-help group" and Group 2: "Depression mutual aid clinic group". Group 1 was *Douban Group*'s largest group for depression self-help; its target members are those with mild-to-moderate depression. Group 2 was *Douban Group*'s oldest group for depression self-help; it was created for users suffering from major depression.

Between June 13, 2021, and June 20, 2021, we used a Python-based web crawler to collect content posted to each of the two groups from December 21, 2019, to March 28, 2020. Given that lockdown in China lasted 33 days, and to facilitate the comparison among the three stages, the duration of each stage was set to 33 days. Thus, stage 1 (pre-lockdown) is from December 21, 2019, to January 22, 2020; stage 2 (during lockdown) is from January 22, 2020, to February 24, 2020; stage 3 (post-lockdown) is from February 25, 2020, to March 28, 2020. The data we collected included username, post title, post, and comment body content, post and comment time, thread to which the post and comment belonged, and timestamp (date and time) of each post and comment. The final dataset consists of 2,999 posts and 25,173 comments (Table 6.1).

Data analysis

LDA topic modeling

First, we prepared the data for the topic modeling. Text preparation mainly consisted of text segmentation and removal of stop words and duplicate entries. We used the segmentation package PyNLPIR to achieve text segmentation and removed stop words according to the stop word database we found through our previous studies (Sun & Fichman, under review). We deleted the duplicate entries posted by the same author at the same time and the feature terms (e.g., "as the title shows") that were unclear and appeared in multiple topics within this dataset.

Many studies have proved the applicability of using the Latent Dirichlet Allocation (LDA) modeling to analyze peer-to-peer conversations about mental health in a variety of online communities (Carron-Arthur et al., 2016; Park et al., 2018; Zhao et al., 2019). To identify the discussion topics in our dataset, we used LDA topic modeling and chose perplexity as the criterion for LDA model evaluation (Blei et al., 2003). As the perplexity value gradually decreases with an increasing number of topics (Dhillon & Modha, 2001), it is crucial to estimate the number of topics contained in the dataset before mining the optimal number of topics (Chi et al., 2021) and to consider the value of perplexity and number of topics comprehensively. Thus, in this study, the value with the smallest perplexity and the fewest number of topics was selected as the optimal number of LDA model training. Based on earlier studies (Zhang et al., 2018; Tian et al., 2018; Tang et al., 2020), we estimated the number of LDA topics to be [3, 7] and then calculated the perplexity of our dataset's content to determine the optimal number of topics. The modeling evaluation process revealed that the perplexity reached the minimum at five, indicating that the best number of discussion topics in our dataset was five. Following the method proposed by Wu and Wang (2019), we then selected 50 featured terms with the highest frequency for each topic's interpretation and adopted the percentage of posts (post frequency in each topic out of all posts) as the representation of each topic intensity.

We further performed LDA topic modeling on the corpus of each group in each stage to identify the discussion topics by each group in each stage

Table 6.1 Description of the dataset

Group	Group name	Depression level	# of members	Stage	# of active members	# of posts	# of comments	Total # of entries
1	Depression self-help group	Mild to moderate	19,874	Stage 1	1,199	793	6,523	7,316
				Stage 2	1,144	727	7,089	7,816
				Stage 3	1,674	1,164	9,846	11,010
				Total	3,047	2,684	23,458	26,142
2	Depression mutual aid clinic group	Major	13,791	Stage 1	212	97	459	556
				Stage 2	227	88	654	742
				Stage 3	250	130	602	732
				Total	580	315	1,715	2,030

along with each topic's intensity and featured terms. We used the six subsets that we created for each condition; each subset contained the textual content generated by each group in each stage. Because the number of identified topics varied between the subsets, ranging between four and seven, and the sum of the top four topics' intensity reached 70% in each, we selected the four topics with the highest topic intensity in each subset as topic representatives. In each subset, we extracted the 50 featured terms of each of the four representative topics and unified these 200 terms as a word set. Overall, we extracted a total of 1,400 featured terms from the main dataset and six subsets. Then, we calculated Jaccard scores between each pair of word sets to provide greater detail on similarity among stages (Park et al., 2018).

To analyze the connection between topics under different subsets, we extracted 50 featured terms of each topic in each subset as a new word set, which included a total of 1,750 featured terms (the number of topics in each stage ranged from four to seven; four in Group 2 Stage 1, Group 1 Stage 3, and Group 2 Stage 3; five in Total and Group 1 Stage 2; six in Group 1 Stage 1; and seven in Group 2 Stage 2). We calculated Jaccard scores between each pair of topics within and across subsets to identify the extent of topic similarity among and within subsets (Yao, Zhang, Ni, & Ma, 2021). Following the similarity analysis, two coders manually assigned labels to each topic in each subset by reviewing posts and comments belonging to each specific topic, in our specific context, and in light of prior research (Nimrod, 2012; Carron-Arthur et al., 2016; Park et al., 2018; Feldhege et al., 2020; Tang et al., 2020), and then two other researchers completed the task of verifying and confirming the labels.

Analysis of language features

To improve the efficiency and reliability of language analysis, Pennebaker and his colleagues started developing computer programs for lexometric analysis in 1990, and eventually created the Linguistic Inquiry and Word Count (LIWC) (Pennebaker et al., 2001). The most important part of LIWC is the dictionary, which defines the categories and the word list related to each category. LIWC quantitatively analyzes the textual content and calculates the word frequency of different categories (e.g., health, religion) in a given text by comparing the words in it with the dictionary (Zhang, 2015). After more than 20 years since its inception, LIWC has been widely used to analyze patterns of language use in a variety of Western contexts (Pennebaker & King, 1999; Schwartz et al., 2013; Zhang, 2015; Yuan et al., 2020). Inspired by the dictionary of LIWC2007 and C-LIWC, TextMind,[1] a Chinese language psychological analysis system, was developed based on the characteristics of the Simplified Chinese language in mainland China, which provides an all-in-one solution from automatic Chinese words segmentation to psychological analysis. Compared with LIWC, the dictionary, text, and punctuation of TextMind are optimized to process Simplified Chinese, and the categories are compatible with LIWC (Gao et al., 2013). The Chinese psychoanalysis dictionary consists of 102 categories (e.g., *first-person singular pronouns, positive emotion,* and *anxiety*) and a total of 6,547 words (Rui Gao et al., 2013).

To explore the language features of individuals with depression before, during, and after the COVID-19 lockdown, we used TextMind to analyze the text of each subset. According to the earlier studies related to language use among people with depression on social media (e.g., Zimmermann et al., 2017; Leis et al., 2019; Hussain et al., 2020), the selected categories from LIWC were as follows: *first-person singular pronouns* (I), *first-person plural pronouns* (We), *second-person pronouns* (You), and *third-person pronouns* (He/She/They), *positive emotions, negative emotions, negate, anxiety, anger, cause, health, religion,* and *death.* We used all the words under the aforementioned categories as the feature set for the depression dictionary. To facilitate a better understanding of the language features, we first calculated the percentage based on how well the words of the given text matched the dictionary categories. Then, we multiplied each percentage by 1,000 to get the frequency of each category, indicating the number of occurrences per 1,000 words.

Findings

We describe our findings, answering our two research questions: (1) How did the extent and range of discussion topics in online depression self-help groups in China change over time before, during, and after the COVID-19 lockdown? (2) How did the fluctuations of language use and internal emotions relate to different stages of the COVID-19 lockdown in China? First, we describe the major discussion topics that we discovered through the LDA topic modeling analysis based on the entire dataset; for each topic, we provide a description and example and indicate their respective intensity (Section 4.1). Next, we present our thematic analysis of the six subsets, including topic similarities and differences across stages and between groups (Section 4.2). Then, we examine the unique language features of the overall discussion topics, as well as in each group in each stage (Section 4.3).

Discussion topics in the entire dataset

Five topics emerged from our topic modeling of the entire dataset (Table 6.2). Following earlier studies (Zhang et al., 2018; Yao, Tang, Fan, & Luan, 2021), we grouped these five topics into two categories: peer support and self-tracking.

The first category, peer support, included the topics *peer diagnosis, emotional support,* and *instrumental support,* accounting for 63.03% of the posts and comments. Specifically, members served in either a peer-seeker role or

Table 6.2 Discussion topics discovered by LDA analysis based on the entire dataset

Topic	Topic intensity	Description	Example
Peer diagnosis	31.14%	Members describe their symptoms, diagnosis, or medications, asking others for assessment and diagnosis (Zhang et al., 2018).	"I have been taking Biolot for more than three months. I started to suffer from night sweats shortly after I started taking the medicine … The doctor said that if you don't feel cold, it's fine … Are there any patients in the same situation? I want to know whether it is a side effect of the medicine and if so, I want to change the medicine." ("我用百洛特三个多月了。我开始服药后不久就开始盗汗……医生说只要不觉得冷就行……有遇到同样情况的患者么? 我想知道这是不是药的副作用, 如果是是想换药。")
Daily record	29.42%	Members keep a public diary of their daily activities and thoughts, recording their treatment (e.g., medication, symptoms) and daily progress (e.g., hours slept, food consumed, exercise) (Carron-Arthur et al., 2016; Zhang et al., 2018).	"2.26, Wednesday, the weather is cloudy, the fourth day of the anti-depression diary, the mood is very bad. … 2.27, Tuesday, the weather is cloudy, the fifth day of the anti-depression diary, the mood is like a roller coaster …" ("2.26, 星期三, 天气阴, 抗抑郁日记的第四天, 心情很不好……"; "2.27, 星期二, 天气阴, 抗抑郁日记的第五天, 心情就像坐过山车……")
			"Baby, I'm here, why are you not feeling well? I see you crying, I feel so sad too!" ("宝贝, 我在这, 你为什么不舒服啊? 看到你哭了, 我也很很难过")
Emotional support	24.48%	Members discuss emotional posts of happiness or sadness and communicate emotional love, concern, caring, or empathy (Yan & Tan, 2014; Zhang et al., 2018; Yao, Tang, Fan, & Luan, 2021).	
Self-reflection	7.55%	Members discuss the mental process one may use to grow their understanding of who they are, what their values are, and why they think, feel, and act the way they do (Feldhege et al., 2020).	"What is the meaning of my existence. Where is the greatness of life? Why cherish life? I really don't understand." ("我存在的意义是什么。生命伟大在哪? 为什么要珍惜生命? 我真的不明白。")
Instrumental support	7.41%	Members provide problem-solving tools or other courses of actions (Yao, Tang, Fan, & Luan, 2021).	"I suggest you fill in a depression self-rating scale to test and search for introductions about depression to see if you have the mental and physical symptoms. If you meet, go to the hospital in time." ("我建议你填写一份抑郁症自评量表测一下, 查查关于抑郁症的介绍, 看看你是否有相应的精神和身体症状。如果符合的话, 及时去医院。")

a peer-provider role, providing or seeking peer support. Among the three topics in this category, *peer diagnosis* made up the highest proportion of posts and comments (31.14%), which accounts for about one in three posts and comments. Often, the replies to these posts included peer diagnosis based on the similar experiences of other group members. With respect to the second topic in this category, *emotional support*, included posts and comments discussing happiness or sadness and communicating emotional love, concern, caring, or empathy, appearing in about one in every four posts and comments. Additionally, members in these groups engaged in problem-solving activities: seeking instrumental support or providing answers as instrumental support.

The second category, self-tracking, included two topics: *daily record* and *self-reflection*, accounting for 36.97% of the posts and comments. Specifically, the entries related to *daily record* accounted for just nearly 30% of the posts and comments in the group. Members of these groups frequently post records of their daily activities (e.g., work, life, and health conditions) with feelings in an attempt to help themselves. Also, some members tracked their thoughts through self-reflection, and part of them described excruciating feelings of depression along with reflecting on the symptoms and causes.

Thematic analysis

To address the first research question, we performed a thematic analysis of the subsets, examining the similarities and differences across stages and between groups. Then, we identified the main topics in each stage by each group.

Topic similarity among stages

While the LDA topic modeling results reflected the uniqueness of each subset, the significant similarity between the core topics discussed at each subset was evident; the thematic similarity across the subsets for the top four topics range was [0.5642, 0.7989] (Table 6.3). This means that the similarities

Table 6.3 Topic similarity across the six subsets

Subsets Similarity	Group 1 Stage 1	Group 1 Stage 2	Group 1 Stage 3	Group 2 Stage 1	Group 2 Stage 2	Group 2 Stage 3
Group 1 Stage 1	1	0	0	0	0	0
Group 1 Stage 2	0.7344	1	0	0	0	0
Group 1 Stage 3	0.7652	0.7989	1	0	0	0
Group 2 Stage 1	0.6350	0.6577	0.6461	1	0	0
Group 2 Stage 2	0.6063	0.6555	0.6823	0.5642	1	0
Group 2 Stage 3	0.6192	0.6576	0.6794	0.6134	0.5888	1

among subsets, in terms of the top four topics that have been discussed in each subset, were between 56.42% and 79.89%. Furthermore, the thematic similarity between the subsets Group 1 Stage 2 and Group 1 Stage 3 for the top four topics was highest, reaching 79.89%; the thematic similarity between the subsets Group 2 Stage 1 and Group 2 Stage 2 for the top four topics was lowest, reaching 56.42%. This result reveals that the highest and lowest thematic similarity across the subsets for the top four topics both emerged in a specific group, rather than across the groups.

To explore the topic similarity among and within subsets in more detail, we examined the similarities among the topics in each subset and compared all topics in each subset to all topics in the other five subsets by creating nine tables; a total of 413 pairs of topics were analyzed for topic similarity. Most of these comparisons (98% of the pairs) showed that the similarity of discussion topics between and within each subset was lower than 0.5 (50%), and only nine pairs were at a higher similarity.

Discussion topics in different stages

Because of the very low topic similarity between the subsets, we wanted to better understand the specific and unique concerns of individuals in each group and stage. Through LDA analysis of each of the six subsets, we identified a total of 10 unique prominent topics, five of which were new topics (Table 6.4), separate from the five in the entire dataset (Table 6.2). Five of the ten topics were common to both groups (i.e., *companionship support, coping skills, emotional support, instrumental support,* and *peer therapy*) and five topics were prominent only in one of the groups: *daily record* (Group 1), *peer diagnosis* (Group 1), *psychological counselling* (Group 2), *self-reflection* (Group 2), and *symptom* (Group 2).

We found that while some topics, like *instrumental support*, prevailed in each group over time, other topics rose and/or faded over time (Figure 6.1). Tracing the changes in discussion prominence over time in each of the groups reveals some interesting patterns. First, in Group 2 (major depression group), the range of topics increased during the COVID-19 lockdown (stage 2) compared with the range before and after the lockdown (from 4 to 7 to 4), but in Group 1 (mild to moderate depression group), the range of topics steadily decreased over time (from 6 to 5 to 4). Second, in both groups, the prominence of *instrumental support* increased over time while that of *emotional support* decreased. Third, *daily record* was the most prominent discussion topics in Group 1 (mild to moderate depression group) before, during, and after lockdown, while in Group 2 (major depression group) *self-reflection* was prominent throughout with a slight decrease over time. Fourth, in both groups, lockdown brought an increase in the frequency of *peer diagnosis*, whose level was not matched before or after lockdown. *Peer diagnosis* was much more prominent during lockdown in Group 1 (mild to moderate depression group) than at any other time in

Table 6.4 Additional five discussion topics based on LDA topic modeling for each subset

Topic	Description	Example
Companionship support	Members ask for companionship or they accompany other members through chatting, group meeting, and other social activities (Yao, Tang, Fan, & Luan, 2021).	"If you want to join the mutual aid activities, add me on *WeChat*, then we can fight depression together" ("如果你想参加互助活动，加我微信，我们一起抗抑郁")
Coping skills	Members discuss strategies or skills for coping with depression (Nimrod, 2012; Zhang et al., 2018; Feldhege et al., 2020).	"If you are diagnosed with depression, you can focus on medicine-based treatment, supplemented by psychological counseling and family support." ("如果被诊断有抑郁症，你可以以药物治疗为主，心理咨询和家庭支持为辅。")
Peer therapy	Members respond to posts expressing negative feelings and point out the problematic thinking that may be behind the poster's problem, as well as offer suggestions for reshaping those thoughts. (Zhang et al., 2018).	"I also started with what you call 'dirty thoughts', but in fact, it is not your thoughts … You're just kidnapped by your own fears. The first step to get out is not to be afraid, especially because of those 'absurd' reasons." ("我也是从你所谓的'肮脏想法'汗始的，但事实是，这不是你的想法……你只是被自己的恐惧绑架了。摆脱的第一步就是不要害怕，尤其是因为那些'荒谬'的理由。")
Psychological counselling	Members discuss the interaction between therapist and client to explore any cognitive or behavioral disorders that may be present in their lives (Feldhege et al., 2020).	"I am a psychologist. If you want to consult, please introduce your basic situation when leaving a message about psychological problems: (1) gender; (2) age; (3) cause; (4) treatment history …" ("我是名心理咨询师。如果你想咨询，请在留言心理问题时介绍一下您的基本情况：(1)性别；(2)年龄；(3)成因；(4)治疗史……")
Symptom	Members discuss the symptoms of depression, including the physical inconveniences (e.g., sickness, hypersensitivity, headaches, nausea, weight change, lack of sexual desire, and so forth) and psychotic features (e.g., anxiety, panic, a sense of loneliness) (Nimrod, 2012).	"I feel my somatization disorder is getting worse, my heart is hurting, and I'm getting more anxious because of various neuralgias" ("我感觉自己躯体化障碍得越来越严重了，心好疼，因为各种神经痛我越来越焦虑了")

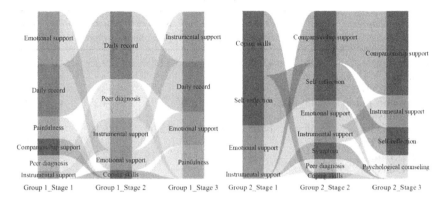

Figure 6.1 Discussion topics of each group at each stage.

Group 2 (major depression group), suggesting that members of this group during lockdown were likely facing symptoms of depression that were new to them. Fifth, members in Group 2 (major depression group) were desperately eager for companionship support during the lockdown, and this need was discussed even more following the lockdown. Finally, it is clear that the nature of discussion shifted significantly in both groups from the pre-lockdown period to the post-lockdown period, suggesting the lockdown's long-lasting impact on both discussion groups.

Language features of each group in each stage

To address the second research question, we applied the LIWC lexicon to examine the language features of the dataset as a whole, and the subsets by each group in each stage. Table 6.5 shows the results of applying the LIWC lexicon to the entire dataset; each column describes the language features of each of the five main discussion topics, and the number in each cell represents the number of words in this category in a specific topic (out of 1,000 words in the entire dataset).

As one would expect, the most frequent words in the dataset were in the emotions category (positive and negative), regardless of the discussion topic. Interestingly, emotional tendency varied between topics; when members posted about peer support topics, such as *peer diagnosis*, *emotional support*, and *instrumental support*, the dominant emotion was positive, with *emotional support* overwhelmingly positive. Posts and comments that involved self-tracking—*daily record* and *self-reflection*—however, were overwhelmingly negative. This might indicate that members' posts and comments were positive when supporting others, but negative about their own struggles, as individuals with depression are more likely to use words expressing *negative emotions* and less likely to use words that express *positive emotions*.

Table 6.5 Language features of each discussion topic

Language/Topic	Peer diagnosis	Daily record	Emotional support	Self-reflection	Instrumental support	Total
First-person singular pronouns (I)	47.98	43.48	43.62	32.88	29.33	42.29
First-person plural pronouns (We)	2.43	2.01	3.17	1.95	4.29	2.65
Second-person pronouns (You)	15.56	14.05	24.56	15.00	16.85	17.38
Third-person pronouns (He/She/They)	2.85	3.41	6.82	3.19	2.17	3.90
Positive emotions	49.99	37.70	88.05	34.32	45.78	53.96
Negative emotions	18.23	44.29	28.33	36.30	17.55	29.33
Negate	2.03	1.98	2.00	2.34	3.79	2.23
Anxiety	3.55	10.37	4.68	4.52	1.73	5.56
Anger	1.94	5.44	5.25	6.33	2.89	4.19
Cause	13.50	11.84	12.12	19.42	8.55	12.75
Health	32.89	24.10	10.37	26.28	24.45	23.63
Religion	4.01	3.11	4.21	6.14	8.11	4.46
Death	4.81	9.47	4.76	5.52	5.29	6.18

Also, as expected in online self-help depression communities, *first-person singular pronouns* were very frequent in each topic, as individuals with depression prefer to use *first-person singular pronouns*, while both *first-person plural pronouns and third-person pronouns* were less frequent, as individuals with depression less likely to use *first-person plural pronouns*. Interestingly, both *second-person pronouns* and *health* were pretty frequent categories across all the topics. The frequent use of *second-person pronouns* may suggest that members in these depression support communities either asked for or provided support to other group members. The frequent use of health-related words is not surprising given that depression is a mental health issue and members joined these online depression support communities to improve their own health. Furthermore, the low frequency of words related to *negate, anger,* and *death* was not anticipated, but this may have been due to the group moderators, who clearly asked members to share only positive content and to encourage each other, and banned all missionary and suicidal posts.

In order to examine if and how the language features of the discussions vary over time and between the two groups, we applied the LIWC lexicon to each of the six subsets, allowing for comparisons across stages and between the two groups (Figure 6.2). We observed that some language categories, such as *first-person singular pronouns* and *positive emotion*, prevailed over time in both groups. We found that the top five language features in the entire dataset (Table 6.5) also prevailed in each of the two

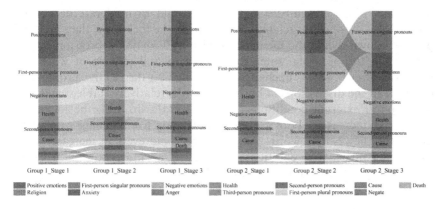

Figure 6.2 Language features of each group in each stage.

groups and three lockdown stages (ranked from most common to least common): *positive emotions, first-person singular pronouns, negative emotions, health,* and *second-person pronouns* (Figure 6.2). Tracing the changes in language use over time in each of the groups reveals some interesting patterns. First, the use of *negative emotions* in both groups increased over time, while the use of *positive emotions* fluctuated. During the lockdown, members in Group 1 (mild to moderate depression group) used fewer *positive emotions* than pre-lockdown, while members in Group 2 (major depression group) used more *positive emotions* during lockdown than pre- and post-lockdown. This may point to differences between the ways the two groups adjusted to coping with the lockdown. Group 2 (major depression group) was replete with individuals who were already accustomed to struggling with depression—they may have provided extra support for fellow members less familiar with depression—while Group 1 (mild to moderate depression group), perhaps a group with more newcomers, witnessed members struggling with new feelings of depression who were not as actively supportive of others. Second, although *first-person singular pronouns* were frequently used in both groups, members in Group 2 (major depression group) employed them significantly more frequently in each of the three stages. Third, in both groups, the lockdown brought an increase in the frequency of *second-person pronouns* and *third-person pronouns*; these frequency levels were not matched by either the first or third stage. Fourth, the use of health-related words steadily increased over time in Group 1 (mild to moderate depression group), while the opposite occurred in Group 2 (major depression group). A possible explanation is that members in Group 1 (mild to moderate depression group) were likely facing symptoms of depression that were new to them and over time they were more eager for attention and help to get them out of their current predicament, while members in Group 2 (major depression group), who were not new to depression, evidently experienced more *negative emotions* over time. Finally, members in Group 1 (mild to moderate depression group) used more cause-related words during the lockdown than pre- and post-lockdown, while the members in Group 2 (major depression group) engaged in the opposite. Interestingly, the overall pattern of word distributions over time was unchanged, meaning that the relative prominence of words in the discussions in both groups was relatively stable, regardless of temporal external conditions, such as lockdown. Still, the lockdown brought an increase in both groups in all the top five language categories, except for the positive words that decreased, and even an increase in the rank order of negative emotions in Group 2, all indicating the negative impact of the lockdown on mental health.

Discussion and conclusion

Thanks to their anonymity, online depression communities reduce depressed individuals' risk of exposure to stigmatization (Zhang, Eschler, and Reddy 2018), improving their self-confidence and control of their treatment (Yao et al., 2021). We describe an evolutionary pattern of discussion topics and analyze the language features in online depression communities, grounded in data from two online depression self-help groups in China that were active before, during, and after the COVID-19 lockdown. In this chapter, we make two major contributions to research on the use of ICT during and after COVID-19. First, this study explores the discussion topics and respective language features in two online depression self-help groups, promoting an understanding of user-generated content in online depression communities in China. Second, informed by social informatics, this study proposes a contextual perspective to explore topic evolution and fluctuations in language use, suggesting that both are related to the different stages of the COVID-19 lockdown. Contextualizing the changes adds a time-based dimension to topic analysis in online health communities, providing a nuanced account of the discussion topics and language use progression over time— before, during, and after the COVID-19 lockdown.

We observed that individuals with depression mainly aim to help themselves and others and do so in two major ways: self-tracking and peer support. When they discuss the topics related to self-tracking—*daily record* and *self-reflection*—they frequently use *negative emotions*, as they write about traumatic experiences (Zhang, 2015). Person pronouns use reflects what people pay attention to, and those who experience physical or emotional pain tend to pay attention to themselves (Rude et al., 2004) more than others. We also found that when individuals track themselves, they frequently use *first-person singular pronouns* and are less likely to use *first-person plural pronouns* and *second-person pronouns*. When members engaged in *daily record*, the highest level of *anxiety* was evident, perhaps because, in these posts and comments, they recorded the stimuli or other stressful events that led to their depression, which in turn triggered anxiety (Coppersmith et al., 2015; Newell et al., 2017; Hussain et al., 2020). Overall, we found that individuals with depression use *negative emotions* when posting about *self-reflection*, and use words related to *cause* and *anger* very frequently. Individuals use more causal and insightful words, when writing about personal traumatic experiences, as they activate the processing of the event, and then this process enables individuals to re-interpret it to improve their mental health (Tausczik & Pennebaker, 2010); words related to *cause* reflect the process by which people re-evaluate events (Zhang, 2015). When individuals with depression discuss topics related to peer support—*peer diagnosis, emotional support,* and *instrumental support*—they frequently use positive words. Furthermore, in line with Hussain et al., (2020), who found that individuals with depression frequently use words that belong to the *health* category, we found that in these two groups, members discuss *peer diagnosis* with high use of *health* words. Poor social relationships (e.g., singleness, living alone, and infrequent social interactions) make depressed individuals less likely to refer to others (Huang & Zhou, 2021). Thus, on social media, depressed individuals use *second-person pronouns* less often than those who are not depressed (de Choudhury et al., 2013; Leis et al., 2019). However, we found that regardless of the changing external conditions, members in these two groups use *second-person pronouns* frequently, especially when they discuss *emotional support*. A reasonable explanation is that in online. depression self-help groups, the social relationships of individuals with depression have been significantly enhanced, and as a result, they tend to use *second-person pronouns* more frequently.

The second research contribution of our study emphasizes the context-dependent changes in discussion topics and language use over time. Inspired by studies that have used evolutionary approaches in the study of communities (Iriberri & Leroy, 2009), groups (Sun, & Fichman, 2020), or organizations (Aldrich, 1999; Shachaf, 2003), we documented how group members with different depression severity changed their discussion topics before, during, and after COVID-19 lockdown in China. It became evident that the range of public health measures—including self-isolation, rigorous quarantine, and closed borders (Charlson et al., 2016)—caused by the COVID-19 pandemic, consequently interfered with people's routine activities (Li et al., 2020). During the lockdown, depression steadily spread among isolated and quarantined individuals (e.g., Brooks et al., 2020), and socialization on social media increased, given individuals' desire to maintain a connection (Limaye et al., 2020; Ni et al., 2020). This, in turn, led to fluctuations in the number of posts and topics over time. Not only were the changes over time noticeable when it came to topics and language use, but we also found that these changes were largely dictated by depression severity (Feldhege et al., 2020; Sun & Fichman, under review).

Although individuals with different depression severity shared a lot of the same concerns, their discussion topics and language use often differed and each of them had a particular pattern related to the evolution of topics/language use.

Specifically, in Group 1, the discussion focus varied significantly (from *emotional support* to *daily record* to *instrumental support*), and the range of discussion topics and *positive emotions* decreased over time, along with the use of *first-person singular pronouns* and health-related words steadily increased over time. With respect to Group 2, the common concerns gradually focused on *companionship support* and *instrumental support*, the range of discussion topics and *positive emotions* increased during the COVID-19 lockdown compared with the range before and after the lockdown, and the use of health-related words steadily decreased over time.

The implications of this work are two-fold. Theoretically, our study provides additional insights into online depression communities during health crises and adds new knowledge to the research on the language use of individuals with depression. Our findings indicated that discussion topics in online communities depend not only on socio-psychological factors but also on other contextual factors, such as a global pandemic and the strict health measures that governments impose on their citizens. Specifically, at times of crisis, such as during the COVID-19 lockdown, topics may significantly shift, as new topics capture the public attention and new participants join the conversations. Also, the findings concerning discussion topics and language use patterns of individuals with different depression severity in China add a nuanced health-based dimension to the research on the content of online depression communities and enhance prior descriptions of user-generated content in these communities. Additionally, this study also suggests that the language use pattern of users' discussion may vary widely within one socio-technical setting as other contextual factors changed. Moreover, as this study provides a deeper analysis of the topic evolutionary pattern and language use pattern of individuals with different depression severity, it offers a better understanding of online support, which is of interest not only to the researchers but also to developers of related mental health communities. Finally, the findings could potentially inform depression therapy and help healthcare professionals understand depression-related issues from depressed individuals' perspectives, especially during health crisis, a lockdown, and the social isolation that these individuals experience.

However, two limitations should be considered when interpreting the results. First, a single case study has limited generalizability, so caution should be taken when generalizing the findings. Future research can expand our results by employing multiple cases to increase the generalizability of the evolutionary pattern. Another limitation is associated with the fact that to improve the efficiency of language analysis and reduce the impact of manual intervention, this study used the software TextMind to quantitative analyze the language features, which makes it impossible to effectively reveal the differences in language use among patients with depression of different genders before, during, and after COVID-19 lockdown. Future studies can combine the qualitative method with a quantitative method to deal with this problem and examine if and how the genders of individuals with depression affect which topics they discuss. In addition, future research may aim to compare and contrast the unique attributes of social media use among depressed individuals in the East and West, extending this work beyond the Chinese context.

Note

1 http://ccpl.psych.ac.cn/textmind/

References

Aldrich, H.E. (1999). *Organizations Evolving*. London, UK: Sage Publications.

Ahmad, A.R., & Murad, H.R. (2020). The impact of social media on panic during the COVID-19 pandemic in Iraqi Kurdistan: Online questionnaire study. *Journal of Medical Internet Research*, 22(5), e19556.

Blei, D., Ng, A., & Jordan, M. (2003). Latent Dirichlet Allocation. *Journal of Machine Learning Research*, 3, 993–1022.

Brooks, S., Webster, R., Smith, L., Woodland, L., Wessely, S., et al. (2020). The psychological impact of quarantine and how to reduce it: Rapid review of the evidence. *Lancet*, 395, 912–920.

Carron-Arthur, B., Reynolds, J., Bennett, K., Bennett, A., & Griffiths, K.M. (2016). What's all the talk about? Topic modelling in a mental health Internet support group. *BMC Psychiatry*, 16(1), e367.

Charlson, F.J., Baxter, A.J., Cheng, H.G., Shidhaye, R., & Whiteford, H.A. (2016). The burden of mental, neurological, and substance use disorders in China and India: A systematic analysis of community representative epidemiological studies. *Lancet*, 388(10042), 376–389.

Chi, M., Pan, M., & Wang, W. (2021). A cross-platform comparative study of reviews on sharing accommodation and hotels reservation platform: combined with LDA- SNA and sentiment analysis. *Library and Information Service*, 65(2), 107–116.

Coppersmith, G., Dredze, M., Harman, C., & Hollingshead, K. (2015). *From ADHD to SAD: Analyzing the language of mental health on Twitter through self-reported diagnoses*. Proceedings of the 2nd Workshop on Computational Linguistics and Clinical Psychology: From Linguistic Signal to Clinical Reality.

de Choudhury, M., Gamon, M., Counts, S., & Horvitz, E. (2013). *Predicting depression via social media*. Proceedings of the 7th International AAAI Conference on Weblogs and Social Media (Vol. 13, pp. 1–10). Palo Alto, CA: Association for the Advancement of Artificial Intelligence.

Dhillon, I., & Modha, D. (2001). Concept decompositions for large sparse text data using clustering. *Machine Learning*, 42(1/2), 143–175.

Douban Group. https://www.douban.com/game/22992396/, last accessed 2021/06/31.

Fatima, I., Mukhtar, H., Ahmad, H.F., & Rajpoot, K. (2018). Analysis of user-generated content from online social communities to characterise and predict depression degree. *Journal of Information Science, 44*(5), 683–695.

Feldhege, J., Moessner, M., & Bauer, S. (2020). Who says what? Content and participation characteristics in an online depression community. *Journal of Affective Disorders, 263*, 521–527.

Ferrucci, R., Averna, A., Marino, D., Reitano, M.R., & Pravettoni, G., et al. (2020). Psychological impact during the first outbreak of COVID-19 in Italy. *Frontiers in Psychiatry, 11*, e559266.

Gao, R., Hao, B., Li, H., Gao, Y., & Zhu, T. (Oct. 2013). Developing simplified Chinese psychological linguistic analysis dictionary for microblog. 2013 International Conference on Brain & Health Informatics (BHI'13). Maebashi, Japan.

Garfin, D.R., Silver, R.C., & Holman, E.A. (2020). The novel coronavirus (COVID-2019) outbreak: amplification of public health consequences by media exposure. *Health Psychology, 39*(5), 355–357.

González-Sanguino, C., Ausín, B., Castellanos, M., Ángel Saiz, J., López-Gómez, A., et al. (2020). Mental health consequences during the initial stage of the 2020 Coronavirus pandemic (COVID-19) in Spain. *Brain Behavior and Immunity, 87*, 172–176.

Hashim, N., Majid, N., Ismail, N.L.N., Anuar, U.N., & Suryanto, S. (2022). Psychological impact and social support received during COVID-19 among nursing students. *Environment-Behaviour Proceedings Journal, 6*(18), 147–154.

Hua, J., & Shaw, R. (2020). Coronavirus (COVID-19) "Infodemic" and emerging issues through a data lens: the case of China. *International Journal of Environmental Research and Public Health, 17*, e2309.

Huang, G., & Zhou, X. (2021). The linguistic patterns of depressed patients. *Advances in Psychological Science, 29*(5), 838–848.

Hussain, J., Satti, F.A., Afzal, M., Khan, W.A., et al. (2020). Exploring the dominant features of social media for depression detection. *Journal of Information Science, 46*(6), 739–759.

Iriberri, A., & Leroy, G. (2009). A life-cycle perspective on online community success. *ACM Computing Surveys, 41*(2), 1–29.

Islam, T., Mahmood, K., Sadiq, M., et al. (2020). Understanding knowledgeable workers' behavior toward COVID-19 information sharing through *WhatsApp* in Pakistan. *Frontiers in Psychology, 11*, e572526.

Kling, R. (2007). What is social informatics and why does it matter? *The Information Society, 23*, 205–220.

Leis, A., Ronzano, F., Mayer, M.A., Furlong, L.I., & Sanz, F. (2019). Detecting signs of depression in tweets in Spanish: Behavioral and linguistic analysis. *Journal of Medical Internet Research, 21*(6), e14199.

Li, A., Jiao, D., Liu, X., Sun, J., & Zhu, T. (2019). A psycholinguistic analysis of responses to live-stream suicides on social media. *International Journal of Environmental Research and Public Health, 16*(16), e2848.

Li, W., Yang, Y., Liu, Z.H., Zhao, Y.J., & Zhang, Q.G., et al. (2020). Progression of mental health services during the COVID-19 outbreak in China. *International Journal of Biological Sciences, 16*(10), 1732–1738.

Limaye, R.J., Sauer, M., Ali, J., Bernstein, J., Wahl, B., Barnhill, A., et al. (2020). Building trust while influencing online COVID-19 content in the social media world. *The Lancet Digital Health*, *2*(6), e277–e278.

Malik, A., Mahmood, K., & Islam, T. (2021). Understanding the *Facebook* users' behavior towards COVID-19 information sharing by integrating the theory of planned behavior and gratifications. *Information Development*, Doi: 10.1177/02 666669211049383 (Early access).

Mi, G., Xian, Z., Wang, L., & Lv, R. (2021). Public psychological health information needs during the COVID-19 pandemic: taking the social Q&A platform *Zhihu* as an example. *Journal of Modern Information*, *41*(6), 108–117.

Molendijk, M.L., Bamelis, L., van Emmerik, A.A.P., Arntz, A., Haringsma, R., et al. (2010). Word use of outpatients with a personality disorder and concurrent or previous major depressive disorder. *Behaviour Research and Therapy*, *48*(1), 44–51.

Muncer, S., Burrows, R., Pleace, N., Loader, B., & Nettleton, S. (2000). Births, deaths, sex and marriage ... but very few presents? A case study of social support in cyberspace. *Critical Public Health*, *10*, 1–18.

Newell, E.E., Mccoy, S.K., Newman, M.L., Wellman, J.D., & Gardner, S.K. (2017). You sound so down: capturing depressed affect through depressed language. *Journal of Language & Social Psychology*, *37*(4), 451–474.

Ni, M.Y., Yang, L., Leung, C.M., et al. (2020). Mental health, risk factors, and social media use during the COVID-19 epidemic and cordon sanitaire among the community and health professionals in Wuhan, China: Cross-sectional survey. *JMIR Mental Health*, *7*(5), e19009.

Nimrod, G. (2012). From knowledge to hope: Online depression communities. *International Journal on Disability & Human Development*, *11*(1), 23–30.

Nwachukwu, I., Nkire, N., Shalaby, R., Hrabok, M., Vuong, W., et al. (2020). COVID-19 pandemic: age-related differences in measures of stress, anxiety and depression in Canada. *International Journal of Environmental Research and Public Health*, *17*(17), e6366.

Park, A., Conway, M., & Chen, A.T. (2018). Examining thematic similarity, difference, and membership in three online mental health communities from *Reddit*: A text mining and visualization approach. *Computers in Human Behavior*, *78*, 98–112.

Pennebaker, J.W., Francis, M.E., & Booth, R.J. (2001). *Linguistic Inquiry and Word Count (LIWC): A Computerized Text Analysis Program* (2nd ed). Mahwah, NJ: Erlbaum.

Pennebaker, J., & King, L. (1999). Linguistic styles: Language use as an individual difference. *Journal of personality and social psychology*, *77*(6), 1296–1312.

Preoiuc-Pietro, D., Eichstaedt, J., Park, G., Sap, M., & Ungar, L. (2015). *The role of personality, age, and gender in tweeting about mental illness*. Proceedings of the 2nd Workshop on Computational Linguistics and Clinical Psychology: From Linguistic Signal to Clinical Reality.

Rude, S., Gortner, E., & Pennebaker, J. (2004). Language use of depressed and depression-vulnerable college students. *Cognition and Emotion*, *18*(8), 1121–1133.

Rui Gao, R., Hao, B., Li, H., Gao, Y., & Zhu, T. (2013). *Developing Simplified Chinese Psychological Linguistic Analysis Dictionary for Microblog*. 2013 International Conference on Brain & Health Informatics (BHI'13). Oct. 2013. Maebashi, Japan.

Schwartz, H.A., Eichstaedt, J.C., Kern, M.L., Dziurzynski, L., Ramones, S.M., et al. (2013). Personality, gender, and age in the language of social media: The open-vocabulary approach. *PLoS One, 8*(9), e73791.

Shachaf, P. (2003). Nationwide consortia life cycle. *LIBRI: International Journal of Libraries and Information Services, 53*(2), 94+102.

Sun, L.H., & Fichman, P. (under review). The impact of depression severity on social media use during public health crises: A comparative analysis between two self-help groups on Douban.

Sun, L.H., & Fichman, P. (2020). The collective trolling lifecycle. *Journal of the Association for Information Science and Technology, 71*(7), 770–783.

Tang, J., Yu, G., & Yao, X. (2020). A Comparative study of online depression communities in China. *International Journal of Environmental Research and Public Health, 17*(14): e5023.

Tausczik, Y., & Pennebaker, J. (2010). The psychological meaning of words: LIWC and computerized text analysis methods. *Journal of Language and Social Psychology, 29*, 24–54.

The State Council Information Office of China. *Full Text: Fighting COVID-19: China in Action.* Retrieved from http://english.scio.gov.cn/whitepapers/2020-06/07/content_76135269_3.htm. Accessed August 3, 2021.

Tian, X., Batterham, P., Shuang, S., Yao, X., & Yu, G. (2018). Characterizing depression issues on Sina Weibo. *International Journal of Environmental Research & Public Health, 15*(4), e764.

Wang, C., Pan, R., Wan, X., Tan, Y., Xu, L., et al. (2020). Immediate psychological responses and associated factors during the initial stage of the 2019 Coronavirus Disease (COVID-19) epidemic among the general population in China. *International Journal of Environmental Research and Public Health, 17*(5), e1729.

Wu, C., & Wang, S. (2019). Research on the theme discovery and evolution of domestic library science research based on LDA. *New Century Library, 7*, 90–96.

Yan, L., & Tan, Y. (2014). Feeling blue? Go online: An empirical study of social support among patients. *Information Systems Research, 25*(4), 690–709.

Yang, S., Fichman, P., Zhu, X., Sanfilippo, M., Li, S., et al. (2020). The use of ICT during COVID-19. *Proceedings of the Association for Information Science and Technology, 57*(1), e297.

Yao, X., Yu, G., Tang, J., & Zhang, J. (2021). Extracting depressive symptoms and their associations from an online depression community. *Computers in Human Behavior, 120*, e106734.

Yao, Z., Tang, P., Fan, J., & Luan, J. (2021). Influence of online social support on the public's belief in overcoming COVID-19. *Information Processing & Management, 58*(6), e102583.

Yao, Z., Zhang, B., Ni, Z., & Ma, F. (2021). What users seek and share in online diabetes communities: Examining similarities and differences in expressions and themes. *Aslib Journal of Information Management, 74*(2), 311–331.

Yu, S.B., Eisenman, D., & Han, Z.Q. (2021). Temporal dynamics of public emotions during the COVID-19 pandemic at the epicenter of the outbreak: Sentiment analysis of Weibo posts from Wuhan. *Journal of Medical Internet Research, 23*(3), e27078.

Yuan, C.X., Hong, Y., & Wu, J.J. (2020). Does *Facebook* activity reveal your dark side? Using online language features to understand an individual's dark triad and needs. *Behaviour & Information Technology, 2*, 1–15.

Zhang, X. (2015). LIWC: A linguistic-based text analysis tool. *Journal of Southwest Minzu University (Humanities and Social Science)*, *36*(4), 101–104.

Zhang, R., Eschler, J., & Reddy, M. (2018). Online support groups for depression in China: Culturally shaped interactions and motivations. *Computer Supported Cooperative Work*, *27*(3-6), 327–354.

Zhao, Y., Zhang, J., & Wu, M. (2019). Finding users' voice on social media: an investigation of online support groups for autism-affected users on Facebook. *International Journal of Environmental Research and Public Health*, *16*(23), e4804.

Zimmermann, J., Brockmeyer, T., Hunn, M., Schauenburg, H., & Wolf, M. (2017). First-person pronoun use in spoken language as a predictor of future depressive symptoms: Preliminary evidence from a clinical sample of depressed patients. *Clinical Psychology and Psychotherapy*, *24*(2), 384–391.

7 Public Engagement with Science During and about COVID-19 via Twitter: Who, When, What, and How

Meredith Dedema and Noriko Hara

Introduction

Effective communication of scientific knowledge encourages the public to take a greater interest in science, value the contributions of scientists, and foster public support for the funding of scientific research (Dudo & Besley, 2016). Presently, traditional models of scientific communication are giving way to new types of public engagement with science as the Internet becomes increasingly ubiquitous. Instead of having scientific findings filtered through traditional intermediaries (journalists, healthcare professionals, government organizations, etc.), scientists have begun to take advantage of social media in order to communicate openly with the public (Collins et al., 2016). Furthermore, the public now directly interacts with scientists on social media platforms, such as Reddit's Ask Me Anything (Hara et al., 2019), and participates in the framing of scientific discoveries and opinions by editing science-related articles on popular websites like Wikipedia (Hara & Sanfilippo, 2016). Brossard (2013) noted that the role of lay participation in online environments has changed the nature of science communication, creating new opportunities for two-way communication. These online environments, however, have created new challenges for scientists—namely, the ability to counterbalance the pseudoscientific and outright false claims that appear in social media, online news outlets, and popular online knowledge depositories like Wikipedia.

Because of the immediate need for scientific information about COVID-19 and its vaccines, more and more people are participating in conversations with scientists online (Garde et al., 2021). Twitter has become one of the most popular platforms for the public to obtain health and science information, and the overall engagement on Twitter with scientists has increased over the last few years (Habibi & Salim, 2021). At the same time, Twitter is one of the major sources of misinformation (Vraga & Bode, 2017). The World Health Organization called the spread of misinformation an "infodemic" and suggested better information management (WHO, 2022). While the recent pandemic created a dire need for scientists and public health organizations to communicate directly and swiftly with the public

DOI: 10.4324/9781003231769-11

(Rufai & Bunce, 2020), effective strategies for such communication are still under development.

In this chapter, we used the social informatics perspective to analyze public engagement with science on Twitter. Some social informatics concepts, such as the unintended consequences of ICTs and the diverse ways of using ICTs by various users (Kling et al., 2005), were informative for the analysis, especially since the chapter addresses the social informatics of knowledge (Meyer et al., 2019). Additionally, the importance of the "context" in which ICTs are used has been highly emphasized as one of the major concepts of social informatics (Fichman et al., 2015; Meyer et al., 2019; Fichman & Rosenbaum, 2014). Twitter use during the global pandemic created an opportunity for us to analyze a sociotechnical system in a unique context. More importantly, we unboxed the use of Twitter by scientists, medical professionals, pseudo-experts, and government health organizations, using a social informatics lens by considering online public engagement with science as a sociotechnical system (Meyer et al., 2019).

Using the social informatics perspective, we investigated the following three research questions in this chapter:

1   What and how are tweets posted during and about COVID-19 by scientists and medical professionals, pseudo-experts, and public health organizations?
2   What and how are tweets posted about COVID-19 in three different periods during COVID-19?
3   What and how do tweets about COVID-19 get different levels of engagement from the public?

Related work

Health communication on social media

With the rapid evolution of the Internet and online social networking, health communication now incorporates dynamic exchanges of information on a global scale. Social media allows for the creation and exchange of user-generated content, providing the means to reach a broad audience rapidly with health information through platforms such as Facebook and Twitter (Barnes et al., 2019). Social media platforms are a place where health information is passively consumed and actively sought. Users can "like", "share", or "comment" on any post, thereby transmitting different types of health information to others (Pilgrim & Bohnet-Joschko, 2019). Scientists, medical professionals, and public health organizations are sharing their research and engaging with the public about health issues online (Harris et al., 2014). Many applications of social media within health contexts exist; for example, medical practitioners and healthcare professionals share videos on YouTube to share their clinical expertise (Drozd et al., 2018).

In addition, Facebook is being used by the public, patients, caretakers, and healthcare professionals to share their experiences with disease management, exploration, and diagnosis (Rosa & Sen, 2019).

Particularly for public health matters, social media can provide communication in real time and at relatively low cost. For example, during the 2009 H1N1 outbreak, Twitter was used to disseminate information from credible sources to the public, and also served as a rich source of opinions and experiences (Chew & Eysenbach, 2010). Twitter could also be used to track users' interests and concerns related to H1N1 influenza, even estimating disease activity in real time (Signorini et al., 2011). A study of online spatio-temporal sentiment toward a new vaccine showed that social media platforms could be used to identify target areas for intervention efforts and to evaluate their effectiveness (Salathé & Khandelwal, 2011). Other than their implementation during specific outbreaks, prior literature shows that social media platforms can be used to disseminate pertinent health information to targeted communities (Reuter et al., 2018) and identify misinformation in health information online (Vraga & Bode, 2017). Moreover, medical professionals can aggregate data about patient experiences from social media platforms and monitor public reactions to public health issues (Deiner et al., 2019).

There are certain benefits of using social media for health communication for the public, scientists, and public health organizations (Moorhead et al., 2013). For example, social media can widen access for those who may not easily access health information via traditional methods, because Twitter use is independent of gender, educational attainment, and income, suggesting it may provide an important new channel for disseminating public health messages to younger people, ethnic minorities, and lower socioeconomic groups (Andrade et al., 2018). Moreover, social media allows information to be presented in forms other than text and can bring health information to audiences with special needs. For example, videos can be used to supplement or replace text and can be useful when literacy is low (Stellefson et al., 2014). However, there are limitations to these benefits. For example, there are concerns over the quality and the lack of reliability of the health information available via social media, as it is difficult for individuals to evaluate the quality and discern the reliability of information found online (Zhou et al., 2021). Prior studies also highlighted concerns about privacy, confidentiality, data security, and the potential harms that emerge when personal data are indexed. Social media users are often unaware of the risks of disclosing personal information online and of communicating harmful or incorrect sources (Sanfilippo et al., 2020).

Public engagement with science via social media

In this chapter, we focused on Public Engagement with Science (PES) on social media, specifically with Twitter in the context of COVID-19. PES generally refers to participation in science engagement activities by scientists and the public, yet multiple definitions exist (Weingart et al., 2021). In this chapter, as we studied the PES on Twitter during the COVID-19 pandemic, we adopted the definition of PES as "meaningful conversation and dialog about scientific issues" (Petersen et al., 2009) online, achieving "greater visibility and transparency of research work" (Watermeyer, 2012), so as to "reduce conflict", "build trust", and lead to a public who is then "more likely to support project goals and implement decisions in the long term" (Sankatsing Nava & Hofman, 2018).

While journalists act as one of the gatekeepers of communicating science to the public through the news media in the past, scientists have more opportunities than ever before to communicate directly with the public, thanks to the development of social media platforms and mobile devices. Science communities considered social media platforms to be a promising tool to help democratize science by enabling two-way communication (Peters, 2013), as laypeople can have more direct, dialogic, personable, and transparent conversations with scientists, sharing their opinions about scientific issues (Delborne et al., 2013). Such two-way communication occurs occasionally on a social media platform such as Reddit's science subreddit (Hara et al., 2019; Chen et al., 2021). However, this type of two-way communication is an exception, partially because scientists have been slow to adopt social media use for communication with the public. Regarding scientists' use of social media, a prior study with 587 scientists from a variety of academic disciplines showed that social media usage had yet to be widely adopted. Twitter, Facebook, and LinkedIn are three dominant platforms in use, however, scientists are mostly using social media platforms to communicate with their peers but not the public (Collins et al., 2016).

At the same time, the public is using social media to access the scientific information. One report from the Pew Research Center showed that millions of people followed science-related pages on Facebook; for instance, as of June 2017, IFLScience had 25.6 million Facebook followers, and NASA had 19.4 million (Hitlin & Olmstead, 2018). Another report asserted that, among social media users, 44% said they at least sometimes saw science news that they wouldn't see elsewhere. However, many were also highly skeptical of the news they were seeing on social media; only about a quarter (26%) of social media users said that they mostly trusted the science posts they found on these sites, compared to twice as many (52%) who mostly distrusted them (Funk et al., 2017). Therefore, scientists' and the public's use of social media for PES demonstrate a significant gap—whereas many scientists show little motivation to use social media for public communication, the public rarely trusts the scientific content on social media.

COVID-19 created a force that changed the situation of social media use for PES by both scientists and the public. The global pandemic was a perfect storm to propel scientists to communicate directly to the public, and for the public to rely on social media to obtain the most current, and hopefully accurate, information related to COVID-19. Under this circumstance, public health scientists and epidemiologists had to increase their use of social media to combat misinformation regarding the effectiveness of mask-wearing, as well as vaccines (Agley & Xiao, 2021).

The level of engagement on social media

For measuring the engagement level of PES via social media, prior studies identified that social media metrics were useful (Muñoz-Expósito et al., 2017). Social media platforms have a unique set of technical features and socially-constructed affordances which could enable communicators to develop new engagement and promotion strategies. For example, Su et al. (2017) mentioned hyperlinks, mentions, retweets, and hashtags as Twitter communication tools. First, communicators may include hyperlinks in their tweets, to direct their followers and other Twitter users to online information on external non-Twitter websites, such as event pages or online articles. Second, communicators can build relationships with individual Twitter users and with one another's Twitter accounts by using the "@" mentions engagement mechanism (Muñoz-Expósito et al., 2017).

Retweets involve a user's reposting another user's tweet while giving acknowledgment to that user. Quote tweets involve the same "@username" syntax, but the reposted tweets are shortened so that the 280-character limit is met, and personal comments can be added. Last but not least, among Twitter's key features are hashtags, represented by the hash symbol (#); this function marks tweets thematically so that users can search for specific types of information and follow conversations about a particular topic. Similarly, Perreault and Mosconi (2018) categorized social media actions and metrics as different types of engagement, as shown in Table 7.1.

A few empirical studies showed evidence that social media features are facilitating science communication and engaging the public. For example, Rus and Cameron's (2016) study of health communication in social media found that specific features predicted different forms of engagement, as the posts with images had higher rates of likes and shares, compared to posts

Table 7.1 Metrics in the level of engagement used on social media platforms (adapted from Perreault & Mosconi, 2018)

Metric	Type of engagement
Like	Expressing their positive feelings of liking content.
Dislike	Expressing their negative feelings about content.
Share	Distributing content to their social network.
Follower	Indicating the influence of accounts in their social network.
Tag	Assigning content to a specific person.
Hashtag	Enabling cross-referencing of content and sharing a topic or theme.
Click	The number of clicks on hyperlink content.

without images. Research about Twitter use in science festivals also found that 86% of the Twitter opinions posted by scientific organizations included hyperlinks that encouraged followers to retrieve more information by following them to external websites (Su et al., 2017). In this study, we used these social media features to measure the type and level of engagement on Twitter.

Methodology

We collected tweets posted by 15 scientists and medical professionals, two pseudo-experts, and six federal government-sponsored public health organizations, over three different periods during the COVID-19 pandemic. Using content analysis, we investigated social media features, content features, social cues, and topics shown in the tweets, sampled from these accounts during each period.

Data collection

Multiple searches were conducted to find the names of scientists and medical professionals for this study. First, a number of articles from established sources (e.g., *Nature* and BBC) identified researchers and scientists whose areas were related to COVID-19 research, COVID-19/pandemic discourse and discussion, and vaccine research/production. These individual Twitter accounts were evaluated if they had a sufficient number of followers (approximately over 20,000) to receive active engagement (Garde et al., 2021). We also confirmed that these accounts had enough posts so that we could obtain relevant data (i.e., at least one post every other day). As a result, 15 scientists and medical professionals (herein called scientists), and their accounts were selected based on their followers, frequency of posts, and the ratio between unique posts and favorites/retweets they receive.

Furthermore, we identified five pseudo-experts who are anti-vaxxers, yet whose Twitter accounts have significant numbers of followers. We used the search terms "Prominent Anti-Vaxxers", "Prominent Anti-Maskers", "COVID Myth", and "COVID Misinformation" on Google. Using various articles from sources such as NPR, CBS News, and the *Washington Post*, we developed a list of individuals who have played a substantial role in promoting COVID-19 misinformation. We finalized the list of five pseudo-experts whose usernames include "doctors" and whose accounts have at least one new post per week. Unfortunately, three of the five pseudo-experts' accounts were suspended and some of their tweets published in the period mentioned below were deleted by the platform.

To select the health organizations, we compared several lists made publicly available on the Internet from online encyclopedias (e.g., Wikipedia) and academic institutions (e.g., the University of Northampton, University of Sheffield) for "majority English-speaking countries". From these lists, we

Table 7.2 Frequency of tweets from three categories in three periods

Category	1st Period	2nd Period	3rd Period	Total
Scientists	910	878	748	2536
Pseudo-experts	54	40	46	140
Public health organizations	215	380	266	861
Total	1179	1298	1060	3537

identified six of the largest nations (Australia, Canada, New Zealand, South Africa, the United Kingdom, United States) that are a part of the "Anglosphere", because of their comparable government structures and quality of life. Then we found the largest government-sponsored public health organization with an active social media presence in each country.

From these 26 Twitter accounts, we collected data from the following time frames using a Twitter Bot. The first period was the beginning of the US lockdowns (March 10–17, 2020); the second period was the week that the Pfizer and Moderna vaccines were given emergency use approval (December 13–20, 2020); and the third period was when the CDC issued updated guidance saying that vaccinated individuals no longer need to wear masks except in certain situations (May 23–30, 2021). For each account, we collected the username and followers for each username. For each tweet, we collected the URL, published date, favorites count, and retweets count. We did not, however, include retweet data this time because retweet data did not contain any additional comments from the Twitter users who were reposting. As a result, 3,537 tweets were collected in the three periods from 23 accounts (15 scientists, two pseudo-experts, and six public health organizations). The frequency of tweets from the three categories in three periods is shown in Table 7.2.

Data analysis

To understand how different scientists and organizations posted on Twitter about COVID-19 within the three periods, and how the public engaged through Twitter's features, based on favorites count and retweets count with these tweets, we conducted a content analysis of tweets, with the codebook shown in Table 7.3.

Content features (Hara et al., 2019) and social cues (Tang et al., 2021) were two variables from prior literature that investigated r/science Ask Me Anything (AMA) sessions on Reddit, on the topic of public engagement with science. Some minor adjustments were made for adapting to this research context, as Reddit is a network formed by communities (i.e., subreddits) and comments, while Twitter is a network formed by individuals and tweets, which are microblogs using fewer than 280 characters. In the content features category, we removed "requesting resources" from the

Table 7.3 Codebook for content analysis of tweets

Codes	Variables	Description
Content features	C1 Providing information	Tweet contains information based on facts or presented as facts, for example, including numbers, dates, anything that could be looked up in a reference source; it could be daily report or weekly briefing that's related to the COVID situation.
	C2 Providing opinions	Tweet contains opinion, sharing a general sense of user's feelings about or reception of any content; text includes expressions such as, "I think …", "I believe …", and "I feel …".
	C3 Providing resources	Tweet shares direct citations or links to external resources; the resources provided can refer to media publications, news stories, or articles from website; these resources are linked directly from the post, or the user provides enough information that the reader will be able to access the resource, for example, citation or URL.
	C4 Providing personal experience	Tweet contains explicit or implicit references to user's personal information such as work experience, area of expertise, life experience, or other types of personal information; tweet is focused on the personal aspect of someone's experience.
	C5 Providing guidance	Tweet contains guidance or suggestion to cope/deal with the COVID-19 situation.
	C6 Making an inquiry	Tweet contains a question that begins a thread and seeks a response.
	C7 Making a reply	Tweet contains a comment specifically replying to previous tweet.
Social cues	SC1 Politeness and comfort	Tweet contains short and warm greetings or polite phrasing that communicates respect; can be attached to either positive or negative feedback; it includes salutations like "hi", "thanks", "congrats", and "good luck".
	SC2 Explicit emotional expression	Tweet includes Internet-specific punctuation (e.g., "!", capitalization, emoticon, and emoji) that emphasizes emotion; emoticons and emoji only include faces and flags.
	SC3 Inviting further contact	Tweet contains a user's contact information or invites others to contact them to engage in further discourse; comment suggests establishing contact with a third party and provides identifying information; contact information also includes phone number and address.
	SC4 Trolling	Tweet does harm toward the sense of community by attempting to derail the conversation; tweet is off-topic in a manner that seems meant to confuse, fluster, or unsettle guests and participants.
	SC5 Humor	Users interjects humorous content into their tweet; intention is to amuse the reader and build a rapport.

(*Continued*)

Table 7.3 (Continued)

Codes	Variables	Description
Social media features	SM1 Link	Tweet contains link, include URL in text, and link to external website.
	SM2 Tagging	Tweet contains tagging "@".
	SM3 Hashtag	Tweet contains hashtag "#".
	SM4 Visualization	Tweet contains image and video.
	SM5 Quote tweet	Tweet contains tweet from another users.
Topics	T1 COVID (virus and disease)	Tweet contains information about COVID as virus and disease, for example, coronavirus, variants, symptoms, diagnosis, how it spread, prevention, type of population, test, treatment, and so on.
	T2 Numbers and statistics	Tweet contains the number of cases, the number of diagnoses, the number of deaths etc., regardless of location or period.
	T3 Vaccine and vaccination	Tweet contains information about vaccines and vaccination, for example, the progress of vaccine studies, how the vaccine works, effective rates of vaccine, the vaccination rates and comments on related biotech company, or other countries, etc.
	T4 Mental Health	Tweet contains information about mental health during the global pandemic, for example, depression and loneliness.
	T5 Governmental intervention	Tweet contains information about policy, regulations, or any governmental intervention regarding the COVID-19 situation, for example, masks, lockdown, social distancing, and financial support.
	T6 Professionals	Tweet contains information about professionals' working status/experience in any occupation during the COVID-19 situation, for example, doctors, nurses, scientists, teachers, public health officers, police officers, and so on.
	T7 Other on-topic	Tweet contains other on-topic comments, for example, location-based outbreaks, politicians, celebrities, research, reports, and misinformation.
	T8 Off-topic	Tweet contains comments not related to the COVID-19 situation.

original codebook, based on a pilot study in which Tweets posted by scientists and government health organizations were largely disseminating resources rather than requesting them. We also added "making a reply" as a new code in this study, because we noticed many tweets replied to specific tweets. Furthermore, social cues can be another indication of engagement, when individuals use social media platforms to participate in science communication. We removed "argumentative or sarcastic tone" because, unlike discussions in Q&A sessions, a microblog is too short to indicate its tone. Additionally, some of the individual tweets randomly selected during the coding process belonged to a larger thread, and as such, these tweets lacked sufficient context to grasp their tones.

Finally, we used a grounded theory approach to develop the codes about social media features and topics as two new categories. We randomly selected a small sample (i.e., 72 tweets) for open coding. Two authors examined all of the tweets and developed a list of codes first. Then we discussed each code and determined if its definition could fit into the example tweets. After a few rounds of iterative coding, social media features and topics were defined and operationalized with their own codes. Then we selected one tweet from each period from 23 accounts for intercoder reliability (Freelon, 2020), and 69 tweets were coded by two coders independently. The results showed that we have achieved adequate percentage agreement (above 90%) for each variable (O'Connor & Joffe, 2020). All of the disagreements in testing the intercoder reliability (under 10%) were discussed and resolved before one of the coders finished the rest of the coding alone.

To understand how the content affects the level of engagement, we included the posts that have both low and high engagement in the sample by calculating the medians of the favorites count and retweets count in each period for each account. In this study, higher engagement means that a post had both a favorites and a retweets count higher than the median number, and lower engagement means both counts were below the median level. We randomly selected five tweets with a higher favorites and retweets count and five tweets with a lower count in each period, from 23 accounts, and 641 tweets were coded in total. With coding results, some descriptive analysis and Chi-square tests have been applied to help explain the difference between tweets posted by different users in three periods with different levels of public engagement.

Findings

RQ1: What and how are tweets posted during and about COVID-19 by scientists, pseudo-experts, and public health organizations?

First, as shown in Figure 7.1, multiple social media features are being used in communication with the public during and about COVID-19. Links (39.9%) were the most frequently used, potentially because Twitter only

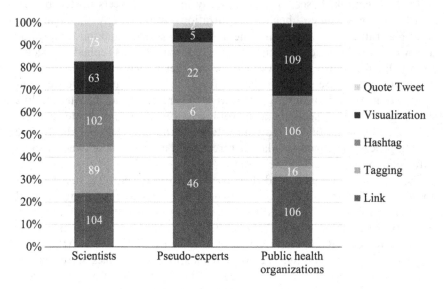

Figure 7.1 Tweets with social media features from different users.

supports tweets under 280 characters; thus, it may be too short for scientists or health organizations to make an argument or a full statement. Therefore, they often gave a link in their tweet, directing the audience to external websites to provide further information. These links included news media, research articles, official websites of health organizations, and retweets. Hashtags (35.9%) were also used more than other features, as they allowed the clustering of tweets thematically so that users could follow conversations about a particular topic. The hashtags most frequently used in these tweets were #COVID19, #StayHome, and #SleeveUp. Visualization (27.6%) was another feature that was used more than others. Images tended to include statistics, while videos were mostly about guidance, e.g., how to wash your hands. Tagging (17.3%) and quote tweeting (12.2%) were used the least. It may be because tagging (with "@") and quote tweeting both facilitate interactions between specific Twitter accounts. They are often used when users are communicating with certain people.

Scientists used more tagging ($\chi^2 = 16.239$, $p < 0.001$) and quote tweeting ($\chi^2 = 41.239$, $p < 0.001$) than pseudo-experts and health organizations did, which showed that scientists used Twitter more to communicate and build relationships with specific people in their social network compared to those in other categories. Pseudo-experts used more links ($\chi^2 = 106.632$, $p < 0.001$) than others. This may be an indication that they attempted to use external evidence to convince people about the reliability of their information. Public health organizations used more hashtags ($\chi^2 = 63.487$, $p < 0.001$) and visualization ($\chi^2 = 138.609$, $p < 0.001$) than other features, which was

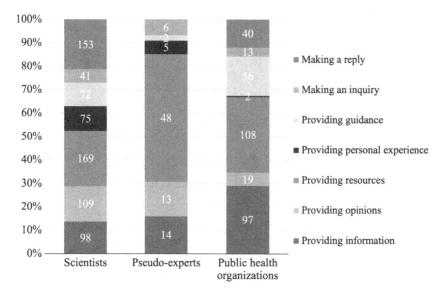

Figure 7.2 Content features of tweets from different users.

considered good practice for user-oriented communication because these features likely allowed the public to get information more conveniently and effectively.

Second, as shown in Figure 7.2, various types of content appeared in the tweets, including providing resources (50.7%), providing information (32.6%), making a reply (30.1%), providing opinions (22%), and providing guidance (20.3%). It indicated that the content and purpose of the tweets were diverse and varied. Scientists and public health organizations did not focus on any specific kinds of content in science communication online.

In terms of the differences among different types of Twitter users, scientists and pseudo-experts provided more opinions than information ($\chi^2 = 138.609$, $p < 0.001$), whereas public health organizations provided more information ($\chi^2 = 52.697$, $p < 0.001$). This possibly is because scientists and pseudo-experts were all individual social media accounts, whereas the public health organizations were representing governments. Similarly, scientists and pseudo-experts provided more personal experiences in their tweets ($\chi^2 = 34.131$, $p < 0.001$), and these personal stories likely made them more relatable to the public, as the stereotypical image of a scientist tends to be distant and rational. Pseudo-experts provided more resources ($\chi^2 = 49.793$, $p < 0.001$) but less guidance ($\chi^2 = 24.520$, $p < 0.001$). Using external resources possibly made them appear more credible while spreading mis/disinformation online. Scientists and public health organizations made more replies ($\chi^2 = 39.650$, $p < 0.001$), which showed that they

Table 7.4 Social cues shown in tweets from different users

Social cues	Scientists	Pseudo-experts	Public health organizations	Total
Politeness and comfort	46 (11.3%)	0 (0.0%)	14 (7.8%)	60 (9.4%)
Explicit emotional expression	98 (24.1%)	13 (23.6%)	23 (12.8%)	134 (20.9%)
Inviting further contact	3 (0.7%)	0 (0.0%)	5 (2.8%)	8 (1.2)
Trolling	18 (4.4%)	4 (7.3%)	0 (0.0%)	22 (3.4%)
Humor	3 (0.7%)	0 (0.0%)	0 (0.0%)	3 (0.5%)
Total	407 (100%)	55 (100%)	179 (100%)	641 (100%)

made an effort to respond directly to, and dialogically interact with the public, even though these activities can be time-consuming.

Third, Table 7.4 presents different social cues that were used in the tweets. While explicit emotional expression (20.9%) and politeness and comfort (9.4%) appeared frequently, inviting further contact (1.2%), trolling (3.4%), and humor (0.5%) seldom occurred in the tweets, which aligns with the results in the prior literature (Tang et al., 2021). Although we did not include "direct message" (DM) as inviting further contact in the codebook, we noticed many users in the sample used DM in their posts later in the coding. Trolling was rather difficult to recognize in the selected tweets. Since a tweet's limit is 280 characters and sampled tweets were randomly selected, the contexts in which the tweets were written were sometimes missing during the coding. The low incidence of humor is not surprising, as COVID-19 is affecting people's lives in overwhelming ways. We speculated that the topic of COVID-19 may be too serious for users to make jokes or use humor while tweeting.

Scientists and public health organizations showed more politeness and comfort in their tweets ($\chi^2 = 7.989$, $p < 0.05$). For example, they used "hi" and "please" to start off their tweets, and they also used many "thanks" and "congrats" when responding to good news or positive tweets. Scientists and pseudo-experts used more explicit emotional expressions in their tweets ($\chi^2 = 9.753$, $p < 0.01$). For example, they used "!" and capital letters to show exclaim and emphasis. They also used many emojis, for example, ***** to suggest people should wear masks, ***** to guide people about washing hands, ***** for sleeving up and getting vaccinated, as well as many arrow symbols ***** and national flags ***** and *****.

Finally, as shown in Table 7.5, topics varied in the tweets as expected. Public health organizations tweeted more about COVID-19 as a virus and a disease, which can be seen as public health education during the global pandemic. Also, public health organizations tweeted more numbers and statistics ($\chi^2 = 22.827$, $p < 0.001$) about COVID-19, which means Twitter can

Table 7.5 Topics of tweets from different users

Topics	Scientists	Pseudo-experts	Public health organizations	Total
COVID-19 (virus and disease)	77 (18.9%)	7 (12.7%)	46 (25.7%)	130 (20.3%)
Numbers or statistics	24 (5.9%)	0 (0.0%)	29 (16.2%)	53 (8.3%)
Vaccines and vaccination	87 (31.4%)	13 (23.6%)	41 (22.9%)	141 (22.0%)
Mental health	2 (0.5%)	0 (0.0%)	6 (3.4%)	8 (1.2%)
Governmental intervention	15 (3.7%)	2 (3.6%)	10 (5.6%)	27 (4.2%)
Professionals	26 (6.4%)	0 (0.0%)	5 (2.8%)	31 (4.8%)
Other on-topic	123 (30.2%)	12 (21.8%)	48 (26.8%)	183 (28.5%)
Off-topic	76 (18.7%)	26 (47.3%)	26 (14.5%)	128 (20.0%)
Total	407 (100%)	55 (100%)	179 (100%)	641 (100%)

serve as an informing tool. Scientists tweeted more information about vaccines and vaccination, as their tweets were often related to their expertise. In return, the public may also have expected such comments from this group of people on social media. Pseudo-experts posted more about off-topic subjects ($\chi^2 = 29.403$, $p < 0.001$), which may have reflected the nature of their tweets' being not helpful or irrelevant to COVID-19.

In other on-topic tweets, public health organizations tweeted about guidance on traveling, tracing applications, COVID-19 impacts on the economy, and epidemiology reports on specific cases. Scientists tweeted about the politicization of COVID-19 topics and progress on COVID-19 relevant research, vaccine development, mis/disinformation issues, facilities (e.g., ventilation and oxygen), and institutions (e.g., public schools and hospitals).

For off-topic tweets, we found that public health organizations also tweeted about other issues such as sleep problems, as May 13 was World Sleep Day, which occurred in the second period of data collection. Another example was that health organizations made announcements about their recent funding resources and plans. Scientists replied to specific tweets, which were sometimes too short to identify the topic, or commented on recent social events not related to COVID-19. Pseudo-experts often tweeted about their new books and interviews as self-promotion; one of them tweeted frequently about climate change as well.

RQ2: What and how are tweets posted about COVID-19 in three different periods during COVID-19?

As shown in Table 7.6, during the first period, which was at the beginning of the US lockdowns, tweet topics were focused more on COVID-19 itself as a new virus and disease ($\chi^2 = 28.791$, $p < 0.001$) causing a global pandemic.

Table 7.6 Topics of tweets in three different periods of time

Topics	1st Period	2nd Period	3rd Period	Total
COVID-19 (virus and disease)	71 (32.0%)	29 (13.7%)	30 (14.4%)	130 (20.3%)
Numbers or statistics	9 (4.1%)	19 (9.0%)	25 (12.0%)	53 (8.3%)
Vaccines and vaccination	4 (1.8%)	62 (29.4%)	75 (36.1%)	141 (22.0%)
Mental health	1 (0.5%)	5 (2.4%)	2 (1.0%)	8 (1.2%)
Governmental intervention	18 (8.1%)	3 (1.4%)	6 (2.9%)	27 (4.2%)
Professionals	15 (6.8%)	7 (3.3%)	9 (4.3%)	31 (4.8%)
Other on-topic	79 (35.5%)	48 (22.7%)	56 (26.9%)	183 (28.5%)
Off-topic	42 (18.9%)	39 (18.5%)	47 (22.6%)	128 (20.0%)
Total	222 (100%)	211 (100%)	208 (100%)	641 (100%)

We expected to find many statistical reports in the first period, but results showed the opposite ($\chi^2 = 9.207$, $p < 0.01$). This might be because the systems to collect and process the numbers had not yet been set up at that time. Moreover, the tools for testing and diagnosing were seldom available at the beginning of the pandemic. As such, we noticed that the incidence of tweets about numbers/statistics increased in each subsequent reporting period. In the second period, when the Pfizer and Moderna vaccines were given emergency use approval, tweets on the topic of vaccines and vaccination ($\chi^2 = 83.445$, $p < 0.001$) were predominant.

Mental health was not mentioned in the data set as much as we originally expected, even though it was one of the major issues during COVID-19 and was discussed frequently on both news media and social media. This may be because most of the scientists in the sample were epidemiologists or medical doctors, not psychologists. Furthermore, governmental interventions like social distancing, 14-day quarantines, travel restrictions, and lockdowns in most of the United States, were mentioned more in the tweets in the first period. We also observed numerous discussions about the working conditions of doctors and nurses across all periods. For example, limited personal protective equipment for healthcare workers in the first period, vaccination priority for healthcare workers in the second period, and a lack of respect for healthcare workers' continuous commitment in the third period.

For other on-topic tweets, we saw many tweets in the first period that were conspiracy theories, such as COVID-19's being created in a Chinese lab. In the second period, tweets about vaccines also referred to the difficulties of administering vaccines in rural areas and among underrepresented groups. In the third period, more comments were about vaccination of children, and the lessons learned from the experience of COVID-19 for public health matters in the future, as they anticipated that COVID-19 was almost over.

RQ3: What and how do tweets about COVID-19 get different levels of engagement from the public?

To answer the third research question, we investigated why tweets with certain social media features, content features, social cues, and topics received different levels of engagement from the public, such as favorite counts and retweet counts.

First, as Figure 7.3 shows, using different social media features could have contributed to different levels of engagement. Tweets using less tagging ($\chi^2 = 9.719$, $p < 0.01$), more hashtags ($\chi^2 = 15.759$, $p < 0.001$), more visualization ($\chi^2 = 17.699$, $p < 0.001$), and more quote tweets ($\chi^2 = 5.489$, $p < 0.05$) received higher numbers of favorites and retweets. The use (or lack of use) of links in the tweets did not make a difference in engagement. This possibly is because using links had already become a norm when tweeting, since the interfaces of online news articles make it convenient to share them via social media platforms by simply clicking on icons. Another feature, tagging, receiving lower levels of favorites and retweets, which was initially surprising. Upon reflection, it made sense, because tagging was used for referring to specific accounts in the tweets, which means that the conversations were targeted to a relatively smaller number of audiences.

As Figure 7.4 shows, tweets with different content features evoked different levels of public engagement. Tweets with higher favorites and retweets counts led to more information ($\chi^2 = 12.151$, $p < 0.001$), opinions ($\chi^2 = 15.963$, $p < 0.001$), resources ($\chi^2 = 7.414$, $p < 0.01$), and guidance ($\chi^2 = 16.210$, $p < 0.001$) being shared. Providing personal experience and

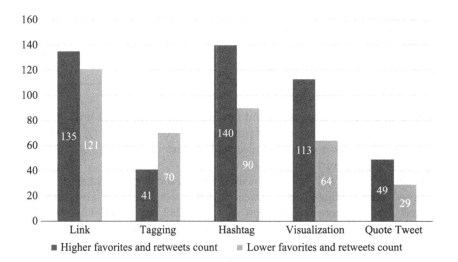

Figure 7.3 Social media features of tweets with different engagement levels.

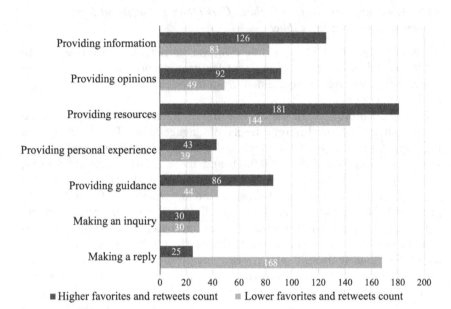

Figure 7.4 Content features of tweets with different engagement levels.

Table 7.7 Social cues shown in tweets with different engagement levels

Social cues	Higher favorites and retweets count	Lower favorites and retweets count	Total
Politeness and comfort	19 (5.9%)	41 (12.9%)	60 (9.4%)
Explicit emotional expression	79 (24.5%)	55 (17.3%)	134 (20.9%)
Inviting further contact	3 (0.9%)	5 (1.6%)	8 (1.2)
Trolling	15 (4.6%)	7 (2.2%)	22 (3.4%)
Humor	1 (0.3%)	2 (0.6%)	3 (0.5%)
Total	323 (100%)	318 (100%)	641 (100%)

making an inquiry in the tweets did not affect the engagement level. Tweets making a reply had lower favorites and retweets counts ($\chi^2 = 154.817$, $p < 0.001$); this was possibly because replies were usually part of a thread, which could have hurt the visibility.

As shown in Table 7.7, Tweets with different social cues evoked different levels of public engagement. Tweets with fewer favorites and retweets showed more politeness and comfort ($\chi^2 = 9.283$, $p < 0.01$). This may be because people used more "hi", "thank you", and "congratulations" salutations when making a reply to specific tweets, which led to less visibility and engagement. Tweets with higher favorites and retweets counts contained more explicit emotional expressions ($\chi^2 = 4.972$, $p < 0.026$), possibly because

Table 7.8 Topics of tweets by different engagement levels

Topics	Higher favorites and retweets count	Lower favorites and retweets count	Total
COVID-19 (virus and disease)	89 (27.6%)	41 (12.9%)	130 (20.3%)
Numbers on statistics	40 (12.4%)	13 (4.1%)	53 (8.3%)
Vaccines and vaccination	101 (31.3%)	40 (12.6%)	141 (22.0%)
Mental health	4 (1.2%)	4 (1.3%)	8 (1.2%)
Governmental intervention	19 (5.9%)	8 (2.5%)	27 (4.2%)
Professionals	19 (5.9%)	12 (3.8%)	31 (4.8%)
Other on-topic	89 (27.6%)	94 (29.6%)	183 (28.5%)
Off-topic	42 (18.9%)	86 (27.0%)	128 (20.0%)
Total	323 (100%)	318 (100%)	641 (100%)

emotional expressions such as emojis and "!" could have solicited more emotional responses from users.

As shown in Table 7.8, different topics in tweets also were related to different engagement levels by the public. Tweets with higher favorites and retweets counts contained more comments on COVID-19 (virus and disease) ($\chi^2 = 21.304$, $p < 0.001$), numbers or statistics ($\chi^2 = 14.540$, $p < 0.001$), vaccines and vaccination ($\chi^2 = 32.625$, $p < 0.001$), and governmental intervention ($\chi^2 = 4.501$, $p < 0.05$). These findings showed that these topics were of more interest to the public than other topics. Especially during the COVID-19 pandemic, information on these topics directly affected their daily lives. The public not only favored those tweets for future use by themselves but also retweeted them so that a larger population of the public could be informed online. Tweets with lower favorites and retweets contained more off-topic comments ($\chi^2 = 19.768$, $p < 0.001$), which means that the public preferred more on-topic comments.

Discussion

In this chapter, we examined public engagement with science (PES) using Twitter as a sociotechnical system by applying a social informatics perspective (Kling, 2007; Meyer et al., 2019). One of the social informatics mantras is that *context matters* (e.g., Kling et al., 2005). By investigating three periods of the COVID-19 pandemic, we uncovered different trends of the supplies (tweets) and responses (engagement) among three types of users: scientists, pseudo-experts, and public health organizations. These three types of users utilized the same tool (i.e., Twitter), for the same purpose (disseminating information about COVID-19), but differently. Obviously, these differences were embedded in existing practices—another concept of social informatics (Agre, 2002; Meyer et al., 2019).

Our analysis of social media features revealed that visualizations and hashtags were used more frequently by public health organizations than by other types of users. Previous research showed that hashtags and visualizations tend to lead to higher user engagement on social media (Wadhwa et al., 2017). This finding suggests that these organizations likely had more resources and ability to disseminate the information widely online than the other user types, as they seemed to be aware of how to present scientific information on Twitter. The scientists may learn from these organizations' Twitter strategies. In terms of content, presenting numbers and statistics was one of the types of content that recorded higher engagement by users than the other types of content. This means that the tweets catered to the information needs of the public.

We also found that scientists and pseudo-experts used more personal stories than public health organizations did. Prior studies indicated that scientists need to make themselves vulnerable for effective science communication (Goodwin & Dahlstrom, 2014) so that the public can relate to them better. While sharing personal stories did not necessarily lead to more engagement in this data set, using explicit emotional expression did translate into higher engagement levels. It is possible that candid expressions of emotion by scientists resonated well with the public. Scientists and public health organizations also tended to reply to comments more often than the pseudo-experts did. Again, making the effort to engage directly with the public is more likely to receive favorable responses from the public (Hara et al., 2019). Although these findings are a start for identifying the different and more effective ways for scientists to connect to the public, further investigation is certainly necessary.

One finding specific to pseudo-experts was that they relied more on external links than the other types of users did. This tendency toward using external sources to legitimize their claims and establish credibility by the anti-establishment was also found in another study that examined online communities' efforts to share and learn information about the MMR vaccine (Hara & Frieh, 2019). This finding has implications for the study of health disinformation in online environments (Agley & Xiao, 2021). As the public searches for information online, one of the indicators of an illegitimate source might be excessively using external resources. If the public is more aware of this type of tendency for illicit sources, it may help them navigate the vast sea of information more safely.

Even though the current study found new insights into online PES, there were some limitations. One limitation of the study is that the numbers of Twitter accounts for scientists and pseudo-experts were not balanced in the sample. Our original intent was to collect data from more pseudo-expert accounts. However, during the data collection period, some of the selected pseudo-expert accounts were deleted from Twitter because they were spreading misinformation. In fact, we were fortunate enough to be able to collect data from these pseudo-expert accounts that were equivalent to scientist accounts in terms of the numbers of posts and followers, even though the data set was small. To address the issue, we used percentages to compare these two types of accounts. Another limitation of the study was related to the sampling method (i.e., random sampling) and the inherent characteristic of tweets (i.e., short texts). The combination of the two conditions made it rather difficult to understand the deeper meanings of some of the posts, as well as to identify trolling. A follow-up study may use a different sampling method to understand the context of the posts more completely.

Throughout the course of analyzing the data, we noticed that encouraging the use of direct messaging occurred relatively frequently. However, we did not include this act in the social cue category (inviting further contact) because the coding of the data at that time was further along. In the future, we should consider coding the direct messaging use. Finally, we did not collect and analyze the replies from the public this time, to keep the scope of the study manageable. However, when discussing online PES, two parties need to be considered: scientists and the public. While the current study scrutinized the scientists, we did not analyze the public side. We plan to examine the replies from the public in a future study.

Conclusion

With a content analysis of tweets posted by scientists, pseudo-experts, and public health organizations, this study shed a light on the black box of PES using Twitter during the COVID-19 pandemic, from a social informatics perspective. The pandemic itself has been a major disruption of society worldwide. At the same time, it created a novel opportunity for scientists to reach out to the public via social media more than ever (Rufai & Bunce, 2020). In a previous study conducted several years ago, scientists were not necessarily taking the initiative to talk to the public via social media (Collins et al., 2016). Communicating science to the public in online environments is complex and involves different factors, such as the types of platforms used, content shared, and the types of social media features available as well as the strategies used by scientists and public organizations. By investigating these aspects of online PES, this study contributed to the literature of online PES, began to develop a means to strategize effective science communication online, and demonstrated the usefulness of applying a social informatics perspective to such a study. Furthermore, social informatics research historically has focused heavily on work and case studies within organizational contexts (Meyer et al., 2019). This current study has added a fresh perspective to social informatics research, with this case of sociotechnical systems use outside of organizations.

Acknowledgment

We would like to acknowledge the assistance provided by Emma Knox with data collection and Grayson Murphy with editing.

References

Agley, J., & Xiao, Y. (2021). Misinformation about COVID-19: Evidence for differential latent profiles and a strong association with trust in science. *BMC Public Health, 21*(1), 89. 10.1186/s12889-020-10103-x

Agre, P.E. (2002). Real-time politics: The internet and the political process. *The Information Society, 18*(5), 311–331. 10.1080/01972240290075174

Andrade, E.L., Evans, W.D., Barrett, N., Edberg, M.C., & Cleary, S.D. (2018). Strategies to increase Latino immigrant youth engagement in health promotion using social media: Mixed-methods study. *JMIR Public Health and Surveillance, 4*(4), e71. 10.2196/publichealth.9332

Barnes, S.S., Kaul, V., & Kudchadkar, S.R. (2019). Social media engagement and the critical care medicine community. *Journal of Intensive Care Medicine, 34*(3), 175–182. 10.1177/0885066618769599

Brossard, D. (2013). New media landscapes and the science information consumer. *Proceedings of the National Academy of Sciences, 110*(Supplement_3), 14096–14101. 10.1073/pnas.1212744110

Chen, H., Hara, N., & McKay, C. (2021). Investigating mediated public engagement with science on the "science" subreddit: From the participants' perspective. *PLoS ONE, 16*(4), e0249181. 10.1371/journal.pone.0249181

Chew, C., & Eysenbach, G. (2010). Pandemics in the age of Twitter: Content analysis of Tweets during the 2009 H1N1 outbreak. *PLoS ONE, 5*(11), e14118. 10.1371/journal.pone.0014118

Collins, K., Shiffman, D., & Rock, J. (2016). How are scientists using social media in the workplace? *PLoS ONE, 11*(10), 1–10. 10.1371/journal.pone.0162680

Deiner, M.S., Fathy, C., Kim, J., Niemeyer, K., Ramirez, D., Ackley, S.F., Liu, F., Lietman, T.M., & Porco, T.C. (2019). Facebook and Twitter vaccine sentiment in response to measles outbreaks. *Health Informatics Journal, 25*(3), 1116–1132. 10.1177/1460458217740723

Delborne, J., Schneider, J., Bal, R., Cozzens, S., & Worthington, R. (2013). Policy pathways, policy networks, and citizen deliberation: Disseminating the results of World Wide Views on Global Warming in the USA. *Science & Public Policy (SPP), 40*(3), 378–392. 10.1093/scipol/scs124

Drozd, B., Couvillon, E., & Suarez, A. (2018). Medical YouTube videos and methods of evaluation: Literature review. *JMIR Medical Education, 4*(1), e8527. 10.2196/mededu.8527

Dudo, A., & Besley, J.C. (2016). Scientists' prioritization of communication objectives for public engagement. *PLoS ONE, 11*(2), 1–18. 10.1371/journal.pone.0148867

Fichman, P., & Rosenbaum, H. (2014). *Social informatics: Past, present and future.* Cambridge Scholars Publishing.

Fichman, P., Sanfilippo, M.R., & Rosenbaum, H. (2015). Social informatics evolving. *Synthesis Lectures on Information Concepts, Retrieval, and Services, 7*(5), 1–108. 10.2200/S00668ED1V01Y201509ICR046

Freelon, D. (2020). *ReCal2: Reliability for 2 Coders – Deen Freelon, Ph.D.* http://dfreelon.org/utils/recalfront/recal2/

Funk, C., Mitchell, A., & Gottfried, J. (2017, September 20). Most Americans see at least some science posts on social media but tend to distrust what they see. *Pew*

Research Center's Journalism Project. https://www.pewresearch.org/journalism/ 2017/09/20/most-americans-see-at-least-some-science-posts-on-social-media-but-tend-to-distrust-what-they-see/

Garde, D., Tirrell, M., & Feuerstein, A. (2021, January 29). Science communication in the Covid-19 era is a brave new world, for better and worse. *STAT.* https:// www.statnews.com/2021/01/29/science-communication-in-the-covid-19-era-is-a-brave-new-world-for-better-and-worse/

Goodwin, J., & Dahlstrom, M.F. (2014). Communication strategies for earning trust in climate change debates. *WIREs Climate Change, 5*(1), 151–160. 10.1002/ wcc.262

Habibi, S.A., & Salim, L. (2021). Static vs. dynamic methods of delivery for science communication: A critical analysis of user engagement with science on social media. *PLoS ONE, 16*(3), 1–15. 10.1371/journal.pone.0248507

Hara, N., Abbazio, J., & Perkins, K. (2019). An emerging form of public engagement with science: Ask Me Anything (AMA) sessions on Reddit r/science. *PLoS ONE, 14*(5), 1–18. 10.1371/journal.pone.0216789

Hara, N., & Frieh, E. (2019). How knowledge contributors are legitimizing their posts on controversial scientific topics: A case of the measles, mumps, and rubella (MMR) vaccine. *First Monday.* 10.5210/fm.v24i11.9594

Hara, N., & Sanfilippo, M.R. (2016). Co-constructing controversy: Content analysis of collaborative knowledge negotiation in online communities. *Information, Communication & Society, 19*(11), 1587–1604. 10.1080/1369118X. 2016.1142595

Harris, J.K., Choucair, B., Maier, R.C., Jolani, N., & Bernhardt, J.M. (2014). Are public health organizations tweeting to the choir? Understanding local health department Twitter followership. *Journal of Medical Internet Research, 16*(2), e2972. 10.2196/jmir.2972

Hitlin, P., & Olmstead, K. (2018, March 21). The science people see on social media. *Pew Research Center Science & Society.* https://www.pewresearch.org/science/ 2018/03/21/the-science-people-see-on-social-media/

Kling, R. (2007). What is social informatics and why does it matter? *The Information Society, 23*(4), 205–220. 10.1080/01972240701441556

Kling, R., Rosenbaum, H., & Sawyer, S. (2005). *Understanding and communicating social informatics: A framework for studying and teaching the human contexts of information and communication technologies.* Information Today, Inc.

Meyer, E.T., Shankar, K., Willis, M., Sharma, S., & Sawyer, S. (2019). The social informatics of knowledge. *Journal of the Association for Information Science and Technology, 70*(4), 307–312. 10.1002/asi.24205

Moorhead, S.A., Hazlett, D.E., Harrison, L., Carroll, J.K., Irwin, A., & Hoving, C. (2013). A new dimension of health care: Systematic review of the uses, benefits, and limitations of social media for health communication. *Journal of Medical Internet Research, 15*(4), e1933. 10.2196/jmir.1933

Muñoz-Expósito, M., Oviedo-García, M. Á., & Castellanos-Verdugo, M. (2017). How to measure engagement in Twitter: Advancing a metric. *Internet Research, 27*(5), 1122–1148. 10.1108/IntR-06-2016-0170

O'Connor, C., & Joffe, H. (2020). Intercoder reliability in qualitative research: Debates and practical guidelines. *International Journal of Qualitative Methods, 19*, 1609406919899220. 10.1177/1609406919899220

Perreault, M.-C., & Mosconi, E. (2018). Social media engagement: Content strategy and metrics research opportunities. *Proceedings of the 51st Hawaii International Conference on System Sciences.* http://hdl.handle.net/10125/50339

Peters, H.P. (2013). Gap between science and media revisited: Scientists as public communicators. *Proceedings of the National Academy of Sciences, 110*(Supplement_3), 14102–14109. 10.1073/pnas.1212745110

Petersen, A., Anderson, A., Allan, S., & Wilkinson, C. (2009). Opening the black box: Scientists' views on the role of the news media in the nanotechnology debate. *Public Understanding of Science, 18*(5), 512–530. 10.1177/09636625 07084202

Pilgrim, K., & Bohnet-Joschko, S. (2019). Selling health and happiness how influencers communicate on Instagram about dieting and exercise: Mixed methods research. *BMC Public Health, 19*(1), 1054. 10.1186/s12889-019-7387-8

Reuter, K., Angyan, P., Le, N., MacLennan, A., Cole, S., Bluthenthal, R.N., Lane, C.J., El-Khoueiry, A.B., & Buchanan, T.A. (2018). Monitoring Twitter conversations for targeted recruitment in cancer trials in Los Angeles county: Protocol for a mixed-methods pilot study. *JMIR Research Protocols, 7*(9), e177. 10.2196/resprot.9762

Rosa, S.D., & Sen, F. (2019). Health topics on Facebook groups: Content analysis of posts in multiple sclerosis communities. *Interactive Journal of Medical Research, 8*(1), e10146. 10.2196/10146

Rufai, S.R., & Bunce, C. (2020). World leaders' usage of Twitter in response to the COVID-19 pandemic: A content analysis. *Journal of Public Health, 42*(3), 510–516. 10.1093/pubmed/fdaa049

Rus, H.M., & Cameron, L.D. (2016). Health communication in social media: Message features predicting user engagement on diabetes-related Facebook pages. *Annals of Behavioral Medicine, 50*(5), 678–689. 10.1007/s12160-016-9793-9

Salathé, M., & Khandelwal, S. (2011). Assessing vaccination sentiments with online social media: Implications for infectious disease dynamics and control. *PLoS Computational Biology, 7*(10), e1002199. 10.1371/journal.pcbi.1002199

Sanfilippo, M.R., Shvartzshnaider, Y., Reyes, I., Nissenbaum, H., & Egelman, S. (2020). Disaster privacy/privacy disaster. *Journal of the Association for Information Science and Technology, 71*(9), 1002–1014. 10.1002/asi.24353

Sankatsing Nava, T., & Hofman, C. (2018). Engaging Caribbean island communities with indigenous heritage and archaeology research. *Journal of Science Communication, 17*(04), C06. 10.22323/2.17040306

Signorini, A., Segre, A.M., & Polgreen, P.M. (2011). The use of Twitter to track levels of disease activity and public concern in the U.S. during the influenza A H1N1 pandemic. *PloS One, 6*(5), e19467. 10.1371/journal.pone.0019467

Stellefson, M., Chaney, B., Ochipa, K., Chaney, D., Haider, Z., Hanik, B., Chavarria, E., & Bernhardt, J.M. (2014). YouTube as a source of chronic obstructive pulmonary disease patient education: A social media content analysis. *Chronic Respiratory Disease, 11*(2), 61–71. 10.1177/1479972314525058

Su, L. Y.-F., Scheufele, D.A., Bell, L., Brossard, D., & Xenos, M.A. (2017). Information-sharing and community-building: Exploring the use of Twitter in science public relations. *Science Communication, 39*(5), 569–597. 10.1177/107554 7017734226

Tang, Y., Abbazio, J.M., Hew, K.F., & Hara, N. (2021). Exploration of social cues in technology-mediated science communication: A multidiscipline analysis on 'Ask Me Anything (AMA)' sessions in Reddit r/science. *Journal of Science Communication, 20*(07), A04. 10.22323/2.20070204

Vraga, E.K., & Bode, L. (2017). Using expert sources to correct health misinformation in social media. *Science Communication, 39*(5), 621–645. 10.1177/1075547017731776

Wadhwa, V., Latimer, E., Chatterjee, K., McCarty, J., & Fitzgerald, R.T. (2017). Maximizing the tweet engagement rate in academia: Analysis of the AJNR Twitter feed. *American Journal of Neuroradiology, 38*(10), 1866–1868. 10.3174/ajnr.A5283

Watermeyer, R. (2012). Measuring the impact values of public engagement in medical contexts. *Science Communication, 34*(6), 752–775. 10.1177/1075547011432804

Weingart, P., Joubert, M., & Connoway, K. (2021). Public engagement with science: Origins, motives and impact in academic literature and science policy. *PLOS ONE, 16*(7), e0254201. 10.1371/journal.pone.0254201

WHO. (2022). *Infodemic.* https://www.who.int/westernpacific/health-topics/infodemic

Zhou, C., Xiu, H., Wang, Y., & Yu, X. (2021). Characterizing the dissemination of misinformation on social media in health emergencies: An empirical study based on COVID-19. *Information Processing & Management, 58*(4), 102554. 10.1016/j.ipm.2021.102554

Part IV
Everyday Life

8 From *Paperless Offices* to *Peopleless Offices*: The Effects of Enforced ICT Usage During Covid-19 Lockdowns on Workplace Information Practices

Katriina Byström

Introduction

Information and communication technology, ICT, has been a major driver of the development of how we have worked for decades. In the early 1980s, Alvin Toffler (1980) coined the notion of *paperless offices* as part of envisioning future workplaces because of the development of personal computers. White-collar workers would be conducting their duties from distributed *electronic cottages* detached from workplace offices. Toffler is perhaps the most well-known workplace futurist, but was certainly not the first, to anticipate a movement away from office buildings. Ten years earlier, Martin and Norman (1970, in Forrester, 1988, p. 227) predicted that a "time will come when the computer terminal is a natural adjunct to daily living" and that "in the future some companies may have almost no offices". There are probably several similar ideas in the previous literature, and often those idealist views were criticized heavily and deemed unrealistic. Among the sceptics, Forrester (1988) writes in response to Toffler's ideas that "[n]obody who has ever worked full-time at home for any length of time could possibly take seriously a statement which overlooks so many practical and psychological problems". In addition to technological infrastructure, several areas of concern in work being carried out from home have been recognized, such as psychological factors related to self-management (e.g., Atkinson, 1985) and relational and material household conditions (e.g., Atkinson, 1985; Forrester, 1988). Jackson and Van der Wielen (1998) conclude that work in virtual environments requires a revision of the social dimension of working to form "a sense of shared enterprise" (p. 340). They emphasize that it is not only a matter of new technologies, but also a social reform involving new attitudes and behaviors, and, consequently, "a wider understanding of issues and work dynamics is required" (Jackson & Van der Wielen, 1998, p. 340).

During the past two decades, the development of workplace information systems and the devices supporting remote access to them has been immense, and in many countries, including the Nordic ones, the technological

DOI: 10.4324/9781003231769-13

infrastructure and use of mobile devices are an inseparable part of everyday life, at work and at home. However, the office building has remained the totemic place of work for white-collar workers. In March 2020, many of these offices were temporarily closed as part of the effort to hinder the spread of the Covid-19 pandemic in societies around the world. Consequently, many white-collar workers initiated a period of remote work that was labelled as an "enforced working from home" by Waizenegger and colleagues (2020). These digital workplaces differed from remote working in the past because this time the entire workforce carried out their duties from somewhere other than their ordinary office spaces. Remote work and remote workers turned from being a complement to the work taking place in company offices, to becoming the new standard in how work is done, making the people working in the office a minority. Studies thereafter have confirmed that the technological infrastructure has proved to have good functionality and that ICT solutions have made it possible for white-collar workers in many countries to fulfil their work duties remotely from home (e.g., Barrero et al., 2021). Whereas the technological development required for fully digital workplaces has been aptly gearing up, it is within the other modalities of work, the social, material and organizational dimensions, where the development has been slower. This is because of either greater resistance to change or underdeveloped alternatives to support "a sense of shared enterprise" (Jackson & Van der Wielen, 1998, p. 340) outside the walls of office buildings. Nevertheless, recent studies indicate that remote work will increase in the future after the experience gained during the Covid-19 pandemic (Barrero et al., 2021).

In this chapter, the focus will be on the effects of the prolonged, temporary all-digital workplace on the development of information practices. A digital workplace is facilitated and enabled by ICT tools and their related infrastructure, and it is independent of any physical framing, such as an office building. A workplace may be considered a digital one when the majority of the workforce is carrying out their work in digitally shared settings instead of physical ones (cf. Byström et al., 2019). Thus, many workplaces became fully digital when the Covid-19 restrictions were introduced, and white-collar workers were given the directive to work from their homes.

Information practices consist of shared understandings and established ways of acting related to needs, management, and uses of the information. They comprise a diversity of mundane activities—tangible and tacit—to handle information and knowledge, such as locating, gathering, sorting, interpreting, valuing, assimilating, producing, and communicating, and cover the epistemological, social, and embodied modalities of information (cf. Lloyd, 2010). During the enforced work-from-home period, some information practices remained the same, whereas others were disrupted completely; a transformation supported by ICT tools primarily accessed from laptops, the portable microcomputers, occurred.

The overall aim is to investigate how and why information practices were affected during the prolonged period of working from home (WFH). Whereas the information practice is seen as an analytical construct emphasizing a conglomeration of social activity, it is the experiences of the actual information exchanges taking place that form the empirical data in this study of everyday WFH. The research questions to be answered are as follows:

1   How have attitudes toward ICT changed during the enforced WFH?
2   How has the use of ICT changed during the enforced WFH?
3   What consequences do these changes imply for information practices at work?

The research questions will be considered from the information perspective, meaning that the examination will be based on the theoretical ideas and conceptual frameworks that either originate from or are revised to adapt to interests within information studies. This means that the purely psychological, social, and organizational examinations fall outside the limits of this analysis.

Previous empirical research

Prior to 2020, virtually no research exists on fully digital workplaces, that is, when the entire workforce primarily works in a digital environment with only limited, if any, connection to the physical workplace (cf. Byström et al., 2017, 2019). The present conditions are fundamentally different from those addressed in the pre-Covid-19 research on remote workers that was carried out beginning in the 1980s. In their seminal review paper on remote work studies, Olson and Olson (2000) found that common ground, independent work tasks, proper skills for collaboration, and the use of collaboration technology were all necessary conditions for successful remote work. They concluded that "[d]eviations from each of these create strain on the relationships among teammates and require changes in the work or processes of collaboration to succeed. Often they do not succeed because distance still matters" (Olson & Olson, 2000, p. 141). Remote work has typically been studied as a (minor) supplement to working in the office; either in the context of virtual teams (e.g., Gilson et al., 2015; Acharya, 2018) or concentrating on work tasks performed independently and requiring concentration (e.g., Messenger & Gschwind, 2016). These more recent research findings imply a more positive view of remote work. For instance, Olaisen and Revang (2017) found that trust and knowledge sharing can be achieved even when co-working in fully virtual settings, in particular when co-operators have both experience and expertise in their task, and have frequent, long-term contacts with each other. Another strand of research focuses on the group of remote workers—often referred to as digital nomads, crowd workers, or gig workers—who are completely detached from a traditional physical workplace. They are described as being mobile, technologically savvy, and entrepreneurial, and were found to have developed their "personal knowledge ecologies" to facilitate their autonomous work (e.g., Jarrahi et al., 2019). Erickson and colleagues (2019) identified the concept of flexibility as a central characteristic for these generally individualistic remote workers, and they forecast that commonalities based on work domain or role become less important in knowledge work. However, the above-mentioned earlier research has focused on only a small proportion of work and the workforce, as only around 5% worked more than three days a week remotely in the United States in 2019 (Brynjolfsson et al., 2020), compared with all work carried out in regular offices.

Currently, research on the consequences of the nearly two years of almost continuous, enforced WFH has exploded in the form of surveys and case studies that report on adjustments to the new working conditions and the rapid adoption of digital technologies. A minor part of these studies has particularly focused on coping with information and knowledge sharing at work. Their findings indicate that workers already from the start had access to a rich amount of digital information supporting their everyday work tasks, whereas other information flows changed gradually. Creative work has continued through contact among teammates (Tønnesen et al., 2021) but "siloed" the labor (Yang et al., 2022). Ad-hoc everyday problems have found new outlets on digital platforms (Lin & Hwang, 2021). Formal information flows have become more inclusive and transparent (Lee et al., 2020) and, at the start of the period, asynchronous communication increased (Yang et al., 2022). Leonardi (2020) uses the expression digital exhaust to describe this accentuated digitalization of work and, along with Tredinnick and Laybats (2021), calls for research on the long-lasting consequences of blended workplaces that combine physical and virtual work environments, allowing hybrid modes of work.

The extraordinary measures broke, at least temporarily, the over-200-year-old hegemony of work offices since the Industrial Revolution, and simultaneously contested the existing work practices and amplified the role of ICT in carrying out work. Understanding the changes in work practices connects to socio-technical research traditions of interconnecting people and technology with each other and their context, highlighting "the social aspects of computerization" (Kling, 2007, p. 205) as part of the organization of social practices in general (cf. Lave & Wenger, 1991; Wenger-Trayner & Wenger-Trayner, 2014) and Lloyd's (2010) information landscapes in particular. Such landscapes are arranged around sociocultural contexts that consist of three intertwined facets of information: epistemic/instrumental (objective, factual and reproducible information), social (unwritten norms and conventions), and corporeal modality (sensations and embodied performances).

In line with this research approach, Taylor (1991) developed Information Use Environments (IUE) as a formation of a defined set of people, their socio-material setting, and the essence of their central problems and typical resolutions, which all are reflected in the use of information resources. Byström et al. (2019) further developed these ideas to accommodate multiple IUE in their Workplace Information Environment (WIE) model. The WIE model focuses on information use as a development over time in relationships between the four original segments of IUE: sets of people, tasks and duties, settings, and legitimized resolutions in the workplace. In a workplace where many different professions interact, the needs, relevance, and uses of information and knowledge are framed by the traditions and values of each professional group (cf. Lloyd, 2010), but are also shared in settings populated by several professions organized in multiple, sometimes professionally mixed, work teams with their specific tasks and duties, as well as material and cultural preconditions (cf. Choo, 2016). Each set of people has duties and work tasks that relate to their specific responsibilities, sometimes coinciding, but oftentimes leading to different needs and uses of information from those of other groups in the work organization. Most work tasks and duties relate to resolutions that are known, not in detail but in general terms; the tasks, duties, and resolutions are legitimized and shared in social interactions, formally or informally, within the set of people, and often also acknowledged by outsiders. Finally, the local settings differentiate the prerequisites for working as its material and cultural context; available tools, regulations, and traditions allow certain kinds of information exchanges but prevent other kinds. Amid the segments, and sensitive to changes in any of them, information flows enable work and display a variety of knowledge. The recognition of multiple communities operating within a workplace provides a consolidated frame for studying ICT that facilitates or impedes information flows.

Method

The research questions are answered based on qualitative, empirical data collected during the spring of 2020, 2021, and 2022 in a Scandinavian university. The research approach has been opportunistic and evolving over time. The first round of data collection was expected to be a one-off occasion as the lockdowns were initially expected to last for only a limited time. As the pandemic continued, the period of enforced WFH was prolonged and the original research plan was ultimately modified to consist of three interview rounds. This material provides an opportunity to investigate how the use of ICT and attitudes toward ICT-supported work have altered during the two-year period.

The participants in the study were ten university employees with work duties mainly in administration (seven participants) or leadership (three participants) capacities. They were recruited through an open email invitation that was distributed twice, in late March 2020 and mid-April 2020. All ten were interviewed on each of the three rounds. Several participants had been employed for many years at the university. Some participants had previous experience with WFH, while others had none, and the common practice, by preference or norm, was to work in the regular office all five days of a working week.

The first interview round focused on the immediate experience of WFH. The interviews were all conducted online. The interview guide consisted of open-ended questions that started with general questions on participants' work duties and their experience with the tasks themselves and remote work. Thereafter, questions concerned the types of information they needed and how they usually collected them, what kinds of information and knowledge exchange they were used to, and how their access to information and knowledge had changed because of WFH. The final questions concerned their overall experience of WFH (surprises, benefits, and challenges) and how they thought this experience would alter their future way of working, if at all. The theme of (co)location-based information flows was identified as central in the first-round data. In particular, topics related to obtaining information for solving everyday work tasks, and the interactivity of information exchanges, were highlighted. These subthemes were returned to in the second- and third-round data collections. In the present analysis, these themes are related to changes in attitudes about and usage of ICT.

The empirical data consist of 21 hours and 37 minutes of interviews. All interviews, originally in Scandinavian languages, were transcribed verbatim and analyzed in three consequent but iterative rounds of manually executed qualitative content analysis. The aim was to identify and analyze variations in information exchanges, not to explain individual behavior. At first, open coding was employed to create an initial understanding of the data on the basis of the identification of significant or interesting characteristics (key word listing). This round was followed by axial coding to create thematic categories (key word clustering). On the third round, the analyses from the two previous rounds were refined in an iterative process to assemble an appropriate set of codes, compile results, and identify illustrative citations. Whereas the analysis was carried out based on the fully transcribed spoken accounts, the selected illustrative excerpts below were condensed and translated into English by the author. Each participant has been anonymized and given an androgynous pseudonym. The excerpts are referred to by each participant's pseudonym and interview round number (1–3).

There are some ethical considerations related to the study. In March 2020, when the lockdowns were put into effect, there was a general expectation that the period would last just a few weeks or months, and thereafter things would get "back to normal". Thus, there was a sense of urgency in launching a study concerning these extraordinary work conditions. This led to recruiting participants in the academic setting that was known to the author, and consequently some of the participants have or have had work-related associations with the author. However, all participants responded to an open invitation, have received and responded to a formal consent form, and been granted a full anonymization. Moreover, the author has had no supervisory role in relation to the participants, nor have there been signs of these relationships affecting the content of the material or having any effect outside of the study. Thus, there are no identified risks or undesirable effects related to the project participation. The project has been assessed and approved by the Norwegian Centre for Research Data (reference number 523594).

Results—changes in information flows in everyday work

There was an immediate disruption of all colocation-based information flows that made visible many mundane information practices, when physical work sites were closed in March 2020. This was a completely new situation, as the participants were used to of working in the regular office. In addition to the cancellation of preplanned, formal onsite meetings and events, many spontaneous conversations that take place in shared office spaces such as by a coffee maker or a printer, on the way to meetings, or coming together for lunch, were all lost overnight. "Brom" explains that "there are a lot of such 'waterholes' at work, at the coffee maker and by the printer, where you meet people and get information. That informal part is gone" (Brom1).

Many activities were transferred surprisingly quickly and with surprisingly good functionality to digital work sites after just a few weeks, and in due time were considered the normal work routine. Among others, "Bobby" and "Bennie" describe the easy transformation. "Bobby" notes early on that "it works very well even for longer periods when everyone works digitally elsewhere rather than in their physical workplace. It is my first time to experience it" (Bobby1). "Bennie" states that "it actually works well. At first it was a bit arduous, but now you almost think that this is normal, and I had not expected that to happen" (Bennie1).

There was also a broad understanding that the all-digital work was not by choice, but rather was a decision imposed on the workplace. In addition, it was not only working conditions that were affected, but also life in general was restricted, with regard to moving around or meeting others. Thus, the usage of and attitudes toward ICT also mirrored the reactions to the overall situation. "Bennie" clarifies that the working mood "has not only to do with work. It also has to do with the whole societal situation, that everyone stays at home, and it affects the way one feels" (Bennie1).

As all-digital work was initiated, there was a realization that for many of the work tasks, it did not matter whether the work was done in the office or elsewhere. Many of the participants' everyday tasks were already relying on ICT tools. "Blaze" points out that "there is nothing I cannot do from home for my work" (Blaze1).

Most information was available, or existed solely, in digital formats, while some was bound to physical objects. However, these printouts and notebooks comprised just a minor part of all the information required for work tasks. Moreover, these material information objects were often easily replaced with digital ones, but the material form was often relied upon by force of habit, preference, or perceived perspicuity and ease of annotation. Becoming all-digital also highlighted some office routines that had remained manual by tradition, and indeed plainly required extra effort to maintain their functionality in the modern information landscape. "Bent" explains that even though they "packed the bag full of papers that I would need, everything is in digital format somewhere. I just need to look it up" (Bent1). "Billie" identified a cumbersome office practice.

> I have started to wonder why we have such old-fashioned systems. For example, we usually produce documents that must be signed by hand and stamped. Often these documents are sent to students by email, so you must first print the document, sign, stamp, and scan in it again.
>
> (Billie1)

Whereas it was possible to manage most work remotely, the material infrastructure of physical offices was often lacking at home. "Boo" states, "I think that no matter how well things work at home, they work better at work" (Boo1). The small screens of participants' personal laptops were immediately perceived as inadequate. As the lockdowns persisted, more dedicated workspaces were set up—a desk, a chair, and a bigger screen, in a separate room when possible.

ICT and individual preferences

Already in the beginning of the enforced WFH, individual preferences and prerequisites surfaced. Some of these were principal approaches, rooted long before the enforced WFH. Whereas "Bevin" was open to new opportunities, "Well, I do not focus on all the problems. I focus much more on the possibilities" (Bevin3), "Brom" was oriented to make the best of the situation and simply stated after returning to the regular office that "when we worked from home, I did not miss the office, and when I sit here, I do not miss the home office. I am fine with both" (Brom3). Yet, for "Blair", who kept a strong preference of full-time onsite office work throughout the two years, WFH was "a kind of inferior variant of a workday" (Blair1).

The mode of consuming information was also viewed differently. Some "prefer to read on paper" (Bent1), instead of reading on screen. Then there were those who made the conscious choice to become more digitally fluent, including reading on screen. During the lockdown period, digital habits were strengthened. "Brom", despite having a printer at home, decided to have fewer documents lying around. "Brom" aimed from the start to "a fully digital office. It has been my goal for a long time. It is not necessary to read on paper, even if you like it best" (Brom1). "Brom's" digital reading practices were reinforced and complemented with new writing practices: "Before I used a notebook. Now I always write directly on the PC. I read everything on screen. That is new too. It is more sustainable in many ways. It is a changed routine" (Brom3). "Bennie" came to rely fully on the digital documentation. After stating that "I had not used that much paper previously, but now I have not used any" (Bennie1) in the first interview, "Bennie" confirms in the last one that "I do not use paper. All documentation is online" (Bennie3).

In general, the participants expressed a preference for a mix of working both on and offsite, depending on the work tasks at hand, and after the restrictions had been removed, most participants opted for one or two days WFH over the typical five-day onsite schedule adhered to prior to the pandemic. "Blair's" preference for full-time onsite office work stayed intact and was coupled with a striving to minimize WFH throughout the period because "that kind of everyday working from home, it is not something I feel for" (Blair1). The rest of the participants revised their views on work location through their experiences during the enforced WFH, and the general expectation was that WFH would increase in the future. "Blaze" reasons "that being able to work from home is important. We will probably have more digital meetings so that people can work wherever, based on their life situation and other things. In my experience, we have not become less efficient by working at home" (Blaze2). To "Bennie" increased WFH seems inevitable, "people are going to have home offices. It seems like a very sensible use of time" (Bennie3).

ICT and altering meeting practices

Whereas ICT use for written exchanges had already been a common practice prior to the pandemic, digital meetings had been used much less often in the past. However, they soon filled the need for synchronous communication as a replacement for onsite office meetings. There were two alternative ICT tools, Zoom and Teams, in use to support synchronous information exchanges, such as one-to-one or group meetings. After a short trial-and-error period and educational efforts, these meetings were considered to have surprisingly good technical functionality. Basic competence was attained quickly and relatively effortlessly, and extended dependence on the use of ICT made it easier to adopt new skills. For "Blaze" adjusting to the new meeting technicalities was easy, "I quickly learned about these meetings, the rules of speaking and muting" (Blaze1), and "Brom" found better replacements for earlier work practices, "it is easy to share a screen, compared with before when you stood next to each other and looked at the same screen. The sharing-screen feature is really useful" (Brom2). "Billie" was pleased with the generally better familiarity with ICT tools:

Everyone has become used to working from home and it is perhaps more structured now compared to how everything was a year ago. Everyone has learned, including myself, to use these digital tools. There are no discussions about how I should technically do something, how Zoom works, or how Teams works.

(Billie2)

The digital meetings were quickly viewed as an ordinary part of WFH. Formal meetings were considered to be more efficient in the digital format, which was seen as both a pro and a con, often because of the same characteristic. For instance, the ease of organizing and joining a meeting offered many the possibility to participate, but then again it also resulted in many meetings of varying relevance and engagement. "Blair" noted that at the regular meetings, "there tends to be full attendance but there are few who speak up" (Blair2), whereas "Billie" experienced that there were "more meetings than before. We used to have a two-hour section meeting once a month. Now we have an hour-long weekly section meeting, which is often not so relevant to everyone attending" (Billie2). Concerning how much room there was for discussion, some felt that the digital meetings kept the content more focused, like "Bevin", "perhaps the meeting activities are more efficient. Maybe you are better at sticking to the point" (Bevin1). "Boo" noted that the meetings had become "very matter-of-fact oriented" (Boo1). Yet others felt that the discussions remained superficial, as was experienced by "Bent" in a recent meeting where "there were some comments, but there were no discussions, no deliberation" (Bent1). In general, digital meetings were shorter and more formal than the physical meetings.

The digital format was better suited for general meetings with an aim to inform, and thus entailed merely one-way communication. The major gain here was that they reached a larger audience. Some meetings, as "Bent" explains, "such as the faculty meetings, they are suitable to have digitally because they are often one-way communication. There is not much dialogue, just a lot of information. More people get an opportunity to join and just listen" (Bent3). "Boo" explains that "it is so nice to have physical meetings again and be able to see each other. You get a different type of communication by being present" (Boo3) but recognizes the value of digital meeting for some purposes, "there are a number of meetings which are just as good to have digitally, such as information meetings, or short meetings" (Boo3).

In addition, meetings that were goal-oriented, factual, practical, and had a clear purpose functioned well for smaller working groups or between colleagues. "Bent" shared a positive experience of group work, "it has worked very well because we are a group that is going to deliver something. There have been working meetings, progress meetings, and we have had a common goal and a deadline" (Bent2). "Bevin" had adopted the format for short meetings, and referred to meetings of the day, "I have had several Teams meetings, status reviews, and meetings about something that needs to be done. It is quick to request and set up a short chat where you can choose to see each other or not. It works great" (Bevin3). "Bobby" too appreciates the digital format for short updates, such as "weekly status meetings on Zoom. We know each other very well and the chat is only for an hour. It is nice to just get a quick update regardless of where you are" (Bobby3).

In the end, the participants considered the onsite meetings to be superior to digital ones as a form of communication. However, the digital meetings provided a good alternative when meeting onsite required more effort in relation to the expected gain. It could be that gathering everyone in the same location was difficult to schedule or that attending the meeting in person was not considered worth the time and effort. "Blaze" sees them as a part of everyday work, "I think that the threshold for having this type of meeting has completely disappeared. It may well be that I will conduct such meetings even if people are on campus. If one is sitting in [one building on campus] and I in [another]" (Blaze1). Such practical issues made the participants appreciate the possibility of meeting digitally, depending on the situation and the matter at hand. Thus, even if the digital meetings were considered less rich as to both content and experience, they were from the start seen as a promising complement to physical meetings, a view that intensified toward the end of enforced WFH.

> If you have a group that knows each other well and you have clear views that you know in advance that you are going to promote, then [a digital meeting] is fine. But if you are going to have a discussion where you have to come up with a result that you do not know in advance, then [a] physical [meeting] is better.
>
> (Bennie3)

> We have digital meetings when collaborating across campus or with external people. It is often difficult to get everyone gathered, so it is much better to arrange digital meetings. Regular staff meetings, project meetings and some team meetings, those we try to have physically. Seeing each other and getting energy from being in the same room, you feel the team pulse. When it is important to meet physically is very dependent on the purpose.
>
> (Bevin3)

When the regular offices were reopened, many meetings were again taking place onsite. However, it was possible to attend many of them remotely. The hybrid formats were often considered less functional, a kind of compromise between the two formats. At this initial stage of reopened offices, there was some confusion over meeting formats. "Boo" explains that "we have section meetings on Zoom and we have ad-hoc meetings on Zoom, and then we have some meetings in Teams, but the big meetings are on Zoom. We have now started to have team meetings as physical meetings again" (Boo3). "Bennie" reflects upon the necessity of hybrid meetings, "there are often some who cannot attend a physical meeting. Then some are on Teams, and some are sitting in the room. And I think we will continue to do so" (Bennie3). "Brom" identifies new difficulties related to these hybrid meetings, "we are back to physical meetings a lot, but they are often hybrid because someone cannot come. We spend time making the technology work. And when it works, I have noticed that the focus is either on those who are on screen or on those who are in the room" (Brom3).

ICT and altering written communication practices

The initial experience of the increased use of ICT for both asynchronous and synchronous information exchange caused an overflow of information, and uncertainty as to where the information, specifically written information, was to be made available. "Billie" experienced that "there was suddenly a lot of information to deal with, lots of channels, and a lot of information came all the time. It was challenging to stay up-to-date on everything, on all that information that was distributed" (Billie1). The initial situation was considered as overwhelming.

> I try to stay informed, but the challenge is that information is now provided on so many different platforms. It is very fragmented. Some information is provided in Teams, Sharepoint, some by email and some on our website. It is a jungle of channels.
>
> (Brom1)

One digital platform in particular established itself during the period: "We have had Teams before. It was not used so actively, but now there is a lot of information that is distributed in Teams" (Billie1). Prior to the pandemic, there was already a plan to introduce Teams as the main communication platform for the workplace, and this development was enhanced by enforced WFH. The establishment of the platform as a standard for general, group-specific, and one-to-one information sharing and contacts happened relatively swiftly. The transformation was successful for several participants, mostly because it was considered to have better functionality than previous information-sharing channels, such as email and university websites. "Bennie" finds that Teams "works. It has become a natural part of everyday work. General information is easier to find in Teams. Before, you had to search [the university's] messy websites and it was not always easy" (Bennie3). Whereas the advantage of channeled documentation was a particular source of appreciation: "Now it is easier to gather information. For example, [a development project] has a specific [group in] Teams. There is a lot of information that is more easily accessible to anyone who is a member of the group" (Blaze2), the platforms coverage of several communication formats was also valued.

> I use [Teams] all the time. I have gotten further and further away [from email]. I am a member of many [groups in] Teams, and I communicate with many of my colleagues in the chat all the time. You can easily add an at-sign and get answers right away. We also share information [there], the log in Teams [is available] all the time. In an email you must search and do much more sorting. Here you have all the information gathered.
>
> (Bevin3)

During the two pandemic years, the Teams platform was found to provide more resilient, although not yet completely agreed upon, forms for both written and oral communication within the group of administrative staff. Thus, the process remained unsettled for the broader information flows at the university. "Boo" reflects upon the dependency between individual and collective views on the ways to communicate: "I am very fond of written communication, so it is very nice to have things on chat. But it requires a chat culture. [Otherwise,] the response time gets long and then the chat falls away" (Boo3). "Bennie" considers email as more engaging format.

> The intention to use [Teams] instead of email does not work because people do not read it as often as email, or it is not as personal. It does not concern me personally when a message is added to the group. But when I receive it as an email, it becomes more personal, even if it is general information.
>
> (Bennie3)

For some, emailing persisted as the main form of communication both among some workmates and in some other parts of the university.

> I prefer information by email. I read the emails first, and when I am done, I go to Teams. So those who think that they get hold of me faster via Teams actually have to wait longer than those who contact me by email. Most colleagues still use email. It is the simpler system. In Teams you must enter into so many different groups to find the information. On email, everything comes into the same stream.
>
> (Brom3)

In addition, there were still uncertainties when it came to structuring information flows.

> There is more information available to me now than before. But it is a struggle to know where to go, which channels, and where it should be.

It is still a challenge. We use [Teams], but there was no actual [decision to do so]. I try to use as little email as possible for information addressing a large group. I have become more and more a fan of Teams and channels [instead of] email; the email file is awful. I have now added the chat function in Teams, but there are not many who have started to use it though it has many positive [effects].

(Bent3)

Nevertheless, as Teams became more familiar, the sharing of written information went through a transformation from being a solely asynchronous form of communication, to being more direct and instant. The chat function came to fill the void for asking quick questions—the everyday small, sometimes trivial problems surfacing during a workday, such as needing help with locating a specific site on the intranet, or with solving a minor problem with a program or application. In the physical office, these questions were smoothly handled in a spontaneous manner by stepping out of one's office, locating a suitable and seemingly available colleague, and approaching them with a question. During WFH, such problems loomed larger, leading to more effort being spent on trying to solve the problem on one's own, or ignoring it when possible: "It happens that I first think, 'Do I need to know this right now? Is this so important that I have to send an email?' I may search the website to find the information there" (Billie1). Moreover, if out of necessity, colleagues were consulted with these questions, the interactions often remained on this more concrete level. After a while, these questions found an outlet in Teams: "First option is the Teams chat. That is where I get inquiries too, which I did not get a year ago" (Blair2). However, after restrictions were removed, the short, informal information exchanges at the office made a quick comeback: "If there is someone in the office, I would rather go over and talk to them instead of sending a chat message" (Boo3).

ICT and information transparency

As informal meeting arenas disappeared, the information flows became more transparent and inclusive through digital platforms. They enabled many to partake of the same written or oral information at the same time. This broke the tradition of letting news spread from mouth to mouth, a change that was considered positive by the participants. According to "Brom", the "written information has improved. Since we are not together, there is more effort invested in internal communication. It has been a weakness [for many years]" (Brom1). "Bevin" agrees that the employees were now provided better updates than before and ponders if this was because of "a better structure for information exchange has been created" (Bevin2). "Billie" provides an example of such improved information flow.

For example, the unit meetings did not used to have any written summary because everyone was expected to attend. Now, if there are any important matters, like assignments for many, there are postings of it in Teams, which is good, and something that should have been done already before.

(Billie3)

This development was hoped to remain, although the reopening of offices caused some uncertainties around these new information flows. "Bent" identifies the potential of the new structures, whereas "Brom" already distinguishes the return of old behaviors.

Since you did not have access to informal information circulating in the hallways, it had to be channelled through more official meetings. I think that was positive. Maybe that will result in an even flatter structure and the hierarchical paths will get shorter, and then it would be the original source conveying the information.

(Bent3)

It is probably more back to the way it was before the pandemic. In the beginning of the pandemic, there were a lot of newsletters and a lot of information from the leadership. But now there is much less of it. What information you get is again more random. You get different pieces of information about the same issue at different meetings. So, what is internally communicated is not standardized; it is a bit arbitrary.

(Brom3)

ICT and time management

In the very beginning of the WFH period, many meetings were cancelled. However, meeting frequency quickly increased again, and was soon considered to be excessive: "The short conversations I had at work, in the corridor or stopping by someone's office, they are now set up as meetings. They fill the calendar" (Blaze1). The high frequency of meetings became a problem that required control measures, which led to better usage of existing tool functionalities. For instance, calendars were used to prohibit fragmentation of workdays by many meetings. "Blend" chose a "quick and dirty" solution: "Now I have simply added to the calendar 'out of office' to show that I am not available for meetings" (Blend2). "Blaze" opted for "own calendar bookings to avoid meetings. I now add to the calendar fixed things, like 'Write a response to this request', or 'Write that memo'" (Blaze1). "Blair" was delighted by two particular suggestions given by the Outlook calendar:

I received a meeting invitation one day. Then [Outlook] notified me, 'It seems that you have a lot of meetings next week. Should I set up some focus time?' The tool has a functionality that protects my working hours. [Outlook] has also suggested to me, 'You have been summoned to a one-hour meeting. Should we suggest 45 minutes?' and I have said yes to that too. This is the first time that I have appreciated [suggestions from the system].

(Blair2)

After a year, some simply recapitulated, and when the meeting topics were of no immediate relevance, the participants used their time more flexibly. This flexibility allowed by spending time together without being in the same location was used for working on individual tasks, and also for low-intensity group activities. "Boo" worked simultaneously on other matters when appropriate, "I have learned to zoom back more in the meetings ... multitasking ..." (Boo2). "Bevin" too kept an eye on several matters concurrently and altered smoothly between them as required.

It is a much more efficient use of time. You can have a joint document open while you are working on other things, and then you can see who is working on a document and where they are in it and write comments to each other. It is a very effective way to have good interaction.

(Bevin3)

"Billie" gave another example of flexible time usage while working together in a workshop format. The project group members were having a digital meeting open all day but would interact only when necessary. When work was carried out independently, the members muted themselves, and when questions arose, they called each other. "Billie" considered this workshop format to have several advantages:

It works better digitally. When you sit at home, you have more peace and quiet. When there was no need to talk with others, we muted ourselves. If there is any noise, like me – I sometimes swear loudly when things get difficult, I do not disturb [the others]. [laughter] If we were to gather in the same room at work, everyone is away from their own office so if they need something from there ..., or if they need to go to the restroom, take a break, or eat ... everything must be more organized. But when you sit at home, you just have to say, 'I'm taking a break now', and you do not disturb others by going out.

(Billie2)

The environment in which the ICT-supported work is carried out appears to have consequences for how work *per se* is perceived. Some participants experienced WFH as being more tiring, as they needed to spend a lot of time being interactive on screen, or simply because of a lack of variation. "Blaze" had "gotten used to it, but it is more tiring" (Blaze2). "Blend" and "Bobby too were used to WFH but finding themselves "so tired of these digital platforms. I get such meeting fatigue" (Blend2), or "very tired of working from home. There was so little variety" (Bobby3).

Individual approaches to WFH differed and appeared to influence the experience of WFH in general and the role of ICT tools as a part of it. The discipline of turning off the laptop was one of the most important individual abilities, for keeping the workdays within normal workhours, and work and private life separated. Some were able to keep the working days intact and turn off the PC at the end of the workday, in much the same way as they would in their regular office. "Bent" is one of them.

> When I work at home, I sit down with the computer at half past seven, then I work until half past four every day. But when I log off in the afternoon, I do not work. I do not read or reply to emails in the evenings or on weekends. Then, I am completely disconnected.
>
> (Bent2)

For others, it was more difficult to avoid prolonging their working hours. However, not all participants considered this type of blending to be a problem, but instead perceived it as a part of the flexibility offered by WFH. "Blend" explains that "when I work from home, it flows much more. I am not so good at setting boundaries and work from eight to four. I have a hard time shutting down the laptop" (Blend1). "Brom" reflects upon the difference in working at home or in the office.

> Separating work and leisure has become more blurred. When I went home from the office, I left the laptop there. If I had not finished a task [at the end of the workday], I often waited until the next day. [At home,] it is easy to turn the PC on again. I might spend more time on it, not so many hours but just to finish the task.
>
> (Brom2)

There was also a different perception of work time. At the office, one could freely move between spaces and get engaged in various discussions, and still feel one was at work, whereas, at home, working time was closely connected to the actual time spent in front of a PC. "Brom" notices that "there is a lot of small talk, which is very nice. But the day becomes less efficient than at home, where one can work focused without so many interruptions" (Brom3). "Boo" reflects upon the difference in experience caused by the location, rather than the content, explicitly:

> When I work at home, I feel that all the time that is not [spent] on the PC is something other than work time. But while at work, I can talk about a cake recipe with a colleague, and I still feel I am at work.
>
> (Boo3)

In addition, there was also the realization that different practical arrangements related to working onsite required time, which had been minimized during WFH. "Brom" become aware of that "in terms of content, [work] is much the same. [But] there is no organizing of refreshments like coffee and water for the meeting delegates in the home office. There is less time spent on those [things]" (Brom2). "Bobby" noticed that organizing physical meetings involves "quite a lot [of] traveling" and "how much more work it is to make travel bookings, how much more time the actual meeting takes" (Bobby3).

ICT and relational information flows

Nevertheless, no matter how functional and practical the digital information exchanges were, they were not able to bridge the entire spectrum of human interaction. Particularly difficult was replacing the context for the informal and spontaneous meetings that would have naturally sprung up at the office. "Bent" explains that "there is something about going to your neighbor's office and having a relaxed conversation. The social part has been completely absent" (Bent3). Such meetings serve both to facilitate work-related matters, and to strengthen the sense of community. From the start and throughout the two-year period, the overall feeling among the participants was that something had gone missing.

> The informal, it disappears. I try to take care of it at these lunches we have, just a chat so that everyone can say how they are doing. But it is something completely different. It gets formal, a bit like staccato ... people mute themselves and the spontaneous disappears.
>
> (Blend1)

The importance of these relationship-oriented information practices that had been taken for granted in the regular office setting become obvious as they become unavailable. The participants noticed that meeting each other at shared locations for coffee or lunch had provided a rich platform for information exchanges, which were now lost. "Blair" ponders over "the daily lunch, the daily conversations we have at work – there is something there that is also about information that you need in your everyday work. It is more casual. I cannot put a finger on it" (Blair1). The longer the enforced WFH became, the clearer the consequences of what had been lost. These discussions provided the possibility of keeping track of matters generally relevant to the workplace, strengthening one's engagement, and receiving and pondering news in one's professional field. "Bennie" states that one gets "a lot of information at the coffee maker, not just gossip. A lot is relevant to your work situation" (Bennie3). "Bevin" emphasizes the motivational aspect and states that "when you are with your colleagues, you get energy to do something instead of needing to problematize everything on your own" (Bevin3). "Boo" misses the opportunity to field-specific discussions:

"It is one thing to do the work tasks that you know you should do. But you do not get the professional conversations in Teams. [For that], you pretty much need to be together with others" (Boo3).

In addition, the spontaneous meetings sometimes offer knowledge support that facilitated work directly. "Brom" reflects upon the informational part of the such meetings and ensures that one gets "more information if you are physically present—the short conversations in the hallways, meeting someone on your way in and out—you snap up information that you would not get otherwise, since it is not part of the formal paths" (Brom3).

Whereas many factual- or technical-matter-oriented tasks were successfully managed in small group or one-to-one digital meetings, other matters were not so easily handled in digital format. Interactions relying on interpersonal relationships did not function satisfactorily in digital format. Examples of these kinds of interactions include getting to know new people, or handling more delicate or personal matters involving feeling the atmosphere in the room or possibly catching several simultaneous reactions, or when reading the body language of the other persons involved is important. "Blaze" used to "feel the atmosphere at lunch, a bit informal, just to soothe the mood. That arena is not there now" (Blaze1). In "Bennie's" opinion, "the performance reviews have been very good online. They are better in person" (Bennie3), and "Boo" finds "it is so much easier to talk about things and take things by email, or whatever, if one has already greeted each other physically" (Boo3).

The interruption of opportunities to meet at the office with colleagues with whom one had no work tasks in common caused lost possibilities for interaction in the broader work context, and made many existing relationships fade away. "Brom" discovered that "updates on how people are doing are now absent" (Brom2), and "Bent" lost many previous contacts.

> Meeting someone from [another section] in the [office], I could say, 'Hello, how are you? What are you working on?' It no longer exists. Now they are just a bunch of people that I have nothing to do with. There are many fewer people that I relate to now than I did before.
>
> (Bent1)

In order to keep the informal relationships active, several digital alternatives were tried out in the beginning of the enforced WFH. Digital coffee breaks and lunches were common and aimed to offer arenas where one could stay in touch, even with colleagues with whom no particular work duties were shared. However, the attendance at these informal gatherings decreased or ceased entirely after a while, as the digital workdays made the participants less interested in spending any more time on digital platforms than necessary: "You are not keen for more Zoom or Teams when you have finished the workday" (Bevin2).

Results summary—changes in ICT usage and attitudes and the development of information practices

For the administrative staff, it became obvious that most of their practical work was carried out with ICT. The participants stated from the start that most of their work tasks were not affected by moving out of their onsite offices. The regular work tasks remained the same and it was possible to carry them out throughout the period (cf. Barrero et al., 2021). They confirmed that all information and administrative systems that they were working with were available for them, in much the same way as when they were in the office. During the WFH period, the participants became more advanced users of many of the different tools that they had had only an elementary, if any, knowledge of at the start (cf. Olson & Olson, 2000). Moreover, they needed to expand the use of ICT into areas where they had earlier been relying on physical interactions, such as meetings and ad-hoc problem solving. Despite the problems with small screens and fatigue resulting from intense virtual communication, the participants were both surprised at and appreciative of the functionality of the ICT tools. Many became more open to utilizing these functionalities even in their onsite office work, indicating that existing information practices related to ICT usage had broadened.

In contrast to carrying out practical work tasks, the social interactions at work went through a profound transformation from in-person, face-to-face contacts to ICT supported interactions. After the first immediate period of adjusting to uncertainties—the increased flow of written information and getting accustomed to digital meeting structures—the new ways of interacting were rapidly established as part of everyday work (cf. Leonardi, 2020). The digital meetings were often shorter and provided increased opportunities to participate, which were viewed as a positive change for all kinds of meetings: meetings with workmates in and outside of their own work organization, or organizational meetings for the unit and the entire workplace. Then again, the number of meetings quickly multiplied and participation in them was sometimes considered to be too time consuming. The meetings were also experienced as being more focused on matters of fact, which made the smaller, goal-oriented meetings more productive, but inhibited in-depth deliberations in the larger meetings and in the meetings where participants did not know each other well. On the other hand, if the aim of the meeting was merely to inform, then digital meetings of any size functioned well. In the end, the participants considered the onsite meetings to be superior to digital ones as a form of communication, especially for creating a broader common ground (cf. Olson & Olson, 2000). However, the digital meetings provided a good alternative when meeting onsite required more effort than the expected gain from meeting physically. In general, the participants adopted a highly practical attitude toward digital meetings during the period, indicating that a new information practice was in the making.

During the WFH period, formal information sharing was channeled through ICT tools and replaced the informal spreading of information in the organization. Overall, as the mouth-to-mouth distribution system of the onsite office collapsed, the new channels of information sharing were considered better in that they were more inclusive and transparent, and information was made available to everyone simultaneously (cf. Lee et al., 2020; Yang et al., 2022). This was seen as a very positive change, which, however, was at risk of weakening as the offices reopened. It remains unclear whether these new information practices will survive the transition back to onsite working.

In addition, a joint virtual communication platform, Teams, that had been introduced shortly before the pandemic, got established in some but not all parts of the workplace, which caused some uncertainties and rivalry between old and new information practices. By the end of the period, general information and work-related material were being shared via several forums, including the re-established solely location-based formats, as the regular offices were reopened. The new ways of using ICT in working with others included sharing material in designated virtual sites, and using chat and video calls/meetings for short clarifications, which partially replaced emailing (cf. Lin & Hwang, 2021). However, email was considered a more personal and intentional form of contact, and persisted as the main communication practice for many, which means that the two partially overlapping information practices will continue to coexist and to require an extra effort by their users, constituting a risk of either misunderstandings or frustration, or both.

Additional new ways of using ICT were adopted for the sake of time management. For instance, calendars were used more actively to manage one's workdays by arranging and prohibiting meetings. In addition, interacting on ICT tools introduced a more effective and flexible use of work time. Multitasking acquired a more positive connotation; one could participate in a meeting and still attend to other matters during the less relevant parts. As with low-intensity collaborative activities, one could interact concurrently or iteratively as required. This type of distributed attention was not experienced as fragmentation, but rather as a more effective use of time. This indicates that information practices during WFH related to ICT usage were viewed differently from those in the regular office.

Replacing the context of informal and spontaneous meetings that occur at the regular office proved to be difficult and was not achieved during the two years of enforced WFH. The physical proximity afforded by the office facilitates these interactions for both work-related matters and for strengthening the sense of community, and the effects of the lack of these arenas grew stronger during the period. Yet, the ICT supported the relationships surprisingly well between colleagues who shared work tasks and duties, and who had regular contact in different work matters (cf. Olaisen & Revang, 2017; Tønnesen et al., 2021). As long as there was joint work to carry out, even new contacts were successfully made using ICT tools. However, the ICT did not succeed in supporting facets of interpersonal relationships without a common denominator on the level of practical work. Interactions between colleagues that depended solely on co-location in the physical office, such as gatherings at breaks or having offices close to each other, vanished to the periphery. This was considered a personal loss, and also hindered opportunities for cross-boundary collaboration (cf. Yang et al., 2022). The lack of a joint physical space was also a hinderance in interactions relying on interpersonal relationships, such as getting to know new people, or handling more delicate or personal matters. Moreover, meeting each other at shared locations had provided a rich platform for information exchanges, both in matters relevant to the workplace, and for participation in professional discussions in general. In addition, recharging one's energy and gaining new angles on different issues were also acknowledged as positive outcomes of collegial togetherness. The attempts to emulate these informal gatherings that take place in a regular office, by adding digital lunches and coffee breaks, lasted only a while before attendance waned. Thus, these information practices remained passive and unfulfilled in the all-digital workplace.

As the mode of work was transferred from regular offices to homes, individual distinctions surfaced (cf. Erickson et al., 2019). Some preferred working in the regular office and found WFH draining. Some preferred regular hours and others preferred more flexible hours. For some, the laptop and other office equipment simply being constantly in sight at home instigated continuous attention to work. For those who strived to keep their private and work lives separated, it became a question of discipline to turn the computer off without the support of changing their location. Additional aspects related to time management surfaced, even in views on work itself. One aspect concerned what is regarded as working; in the office, working was related to the time spent at the location, whereas at home it was defined by the time spent on a PC, thus consisting of a much narrower spectrum of activities, often directly related with work tasks. Time usage became particularly discernible as offices were reopened, and time was again allocated to arranging and attending onsite meetings, as well as to socializing with colleagues. Thus, the many non-actual-work related information (and other) practices carried out in onsite offices were reevaluated as the regular offices were reopened.

All in all, ICT proved effective in supporting practical administrative work, as well as work relationship building for joint activities. The enforced WFH both highlighted the functionality and expanded the use of ICT in performing regular work. The participants discovered new ways of using ICT, which positively affected their attitudes toward ICT. The new ways of using ICT were expected to continue, in both on- and offsite regular offices. However, ICT performed poorly in support of contextual and personal relationships at work. Many information practices related to ICT usage were highlighted during WFH. Some of them, mostly the practical ones, were transformed, while others found no alternative outlets and remained passive during the period. The successful transformations led to increasingly positive attitudes toward ICT, whereas the unsuccessful ones moderated the attitudes toward both ICT and WFH. In sum, the demonstrated ease of accomplishing work remotely, along with the reinforced importance of in-person meetings, were key insights that trigger expectations of altered ways of working in the future.

Discussion

So, what do the results tell us about the usage and attitudes related to ICT during the two years of WFH, and what does it mean for the future development of work? The short answer is that ICT usage increased, and that attitudes grew more positive toward both ICT and remote working, but that does not mean that future ICT use is unproblematic. The results give food for thought for considering the long-term effects. Whereas WFH triggered a huge need for social interaction, and widespread feelings of boredom because of restrictions on activities outside the home, ultimately WFH was still viewed as an anticipated part of future work, closing, if only partially, the gap on Toffler's *electronic cottages* (1980).

The white-collar workers with administrative duties have gained good knowledge of ICT and found novel ways of making use of ICT. Thus, ICT tools have attained an even more profound role in the everyday work of white-collar workers, who by now are more familiar with, more accustomed to, and more relaxed in using ICT in different work situations. There is reason to believe that many of these newly discovered abilities will continue to be used, in both on- and offsite offices: Tutoring on shared screens, having quick digital meetings with colleagues whose offices are in other buildings, having digital meetings with external partners, and keeping the sharing of documents away from email, to mention a few. This indicates an intensified use of ICT in the future. Leonardi (2020) refers to digital exhaust, which is not a negative phenomenon as such, but simply describes how digital information and digital environments become increasingly established in people's lives, including work, making everyone more dependent on these digital interactions.

Whereas the results point to an overall positive attitude toward ICT tools, they also indicate that the difficulties related to WFH are not primarily related to the technology, but instead center around the social facets of working. The findings are in line with Jackson and Van der Wielen's (1998) conclusion about the "sense of shared enterprise". Whereas such a sense of cohesion may be maintained between the closest colleagues when WFH, it seems more difficult to sustain for the workplace at large. Even though the formal information became more transparent and inclusive, the information flows remained more siloed. The interactions tended to be tuned in to shared practical work. The ICT tools served well in such integrated clusters, mediating the flow of both written and oral information, and keeping interpersonal ties activated. While the platforms provided the same capabilities for information sharing more broadly in the workplace, they did not activate the same interest and effort. Thus, the support for serendipitous and cross-boundary interactions remained poorly managed in the all-digital work environment.

The broken office routines left individual workers to organize their workdays themselves, which underscores the importance of developing other individual skills outside of competence in using the ICT tools. As the frequent interruptions of onsite offices were gone during WFH, many felt that they were able to work with greater concentration and be more efficient. However, the lack of interruptions also means that natural breaks disappear, and, if not addressed, this may lead to feelings of both physical and mental fatigue, as Atkinson (1985) cautioned early on. Without reminders from colleagues about things happening at work, one needs to create other ways of staying on top of things. This highlights the need for helping workers to create good work habits, including keeping track of what is going on at work as well as on one's work hours—issues where the use of ICT could be beneficial.

The newly gained experiences call attention to the role of individuals in the transformation of work practices. As the overt view of the office as the place for working has been challenged, there is more room for individual approaches and preferences to surface. This finding aligns with Erickson and colleagues (2019), who predicted that individual approaches would become more significant in shaping future work practices. The prolonged period of offsite office work has made people realize that there are alternative ways of organizing one's work life. While on the one hand, these opportunities may lead to a positively flexible way of working, on the other hand, they may cause conflicts between groups and individuals having different views on how to collaborate and interact at work. In addition, the findings portray remote workers as being, in a sense, the opposite of digital nomads (cf. Jarrahi et al., 2019). Instead of striving toward individualistic independence to work flexibly from wherever, they seem to cherish the work community, including its immediate and peripheral relationships, and thus strive to achieve a blended on- and offsite workplace, characterized by a cohesive coexistence of colocated and remote work.

The hybrid environment concept comes with a new set of challenges for workplaces and for ICT tools to address and is, thus far, met with skepticism. This on-going development introduces novel socio-technical, situated, and socially shaping phenomena to be investigated, opening a new strand of research within social informatics. The present work has demonstrated that addressing the role of ICT in the development of information practices within the WIE framework offers a fertile research approach for examining the interdependencies among people, digital technologies, and their contexts, which are the core foci in social informatics (Sawyer & Jarrahi, 2014).

To conclude, we are amidst a social reformation of work that affects both individual workers and their workplaces. Regardless of the role of WFH in the future, the period of enforced WFH has interrupted many work practices and, by doing so, it has also spotlighted matters that have been taken for granted in the past. The disruption opens work practices for reflection, and indeed necessitates such reflection, on the ways in which work is both looked upon and carried out, being equally relevant no matter whether the work is done offsite or in the regular offices. Moreover, the disruption of information practices has brought them into full view, which offers a rare opportunity to study these practices that are usually imperceptible, deeply embedded, and transforming slowly in their social settlements.

References

Acharya, A. (2018). The factors behind working in virtual community. *Journal of Global Operations & Strategic Sourcing, 12*(2), 246–267. 10.1108/JGOSS-03-2018-0011

Atkinson, W. (1985). *Working at home. Is it for you?* Dow Jones-Irwin.

Barrero, J.M., Bloom, N., & Davis, S. (2021, April). Why working from home will stick. *National bureau of economic research*, No. w28731, 1–68. DOI: 10.3386/w28731

Brynjolfsson, E., Horton, J.J., Ozimek, A., Rock, D., Sharma, G., & TuYe, H.Y. (2020, June). COVID-19 and remote work: An early look at US data. *National bureau of economic research*, No. w27344, 1–26. DOI: 10.3386/w27344

Byström, K., Heinström, J., & Ruthven, I. (2019). Workplace Information Environment – challenges and opportunities for research. In K. Byström, J. Heinström, & I. Ruthven (Eds.), *Information at work: Information management in the workplace* (pp. 147–172). Facet Publishing.

Byström, K., Ruthven, I., & Heinström, J. (2017). Work and information: which workplace models still work in modern digital workplaces?. *Information Research, 22*(1), CoLIS paper 1651.

Choo, C.W. (2016). *The inquiring organization: How organizations acquire knowledge and seek information*. New York, NY: Oxford University Press.

Erickson, I., Menezes, D., Raheja, R., & Shetty, T. (2019). Flexible turtles and elastic octopi: Exploring agile practice in knowledge work. *Computer Supported Cooperative Work, 28*(3), 627–653. 10.1007/s10606-019-09360-1

Forrester, T. (1988). The myth of the electronic cottage. *Futures, 20*(3), 227–240. 10.1016/0016-3287(88)90079-1

Gilson, L.L., Maynard, M.T., Jones Young, N.C., Vartiainen, M., & Hakonen, M. (2015). Virtual teams research: 10 years, 10 themes, and 10 opportunities. *Journal of management, 41*(5), 1313–1337. 10.1177/0149206314559946

Jackson, P.J., & Van der Wielen, J. (1998). Conclusion: New networks and agendas. In P.J. Jackson & J. Van der Wielen (Eds.), *Teleworking: International perspectives: From telecommuting to the virtual organization* (pp. 337–340). Psychology Press. 10.4324/9780203053089

Jarrahi, M.H., Philips, G., Sutherland, W., Sawyer, S., & Erickson, I. (2019). Personalization of knowledge, personal knowledge ecology, and digital nomadism. *Journal of the Association for Information Science and Technology, 70*(4), 313–324. DOI: 10.1002/asi.24134

Kling, R. (2007). What is social informatics and why does it matter? *The Information Society, 23*(4), 205–220. 10.1080/01972240701441556

Lave, J., & Wenger, E. (1991). *Situated learning: Legitimate peripheral participation.* Cambridge University Press. 10.1017/CBO9780511815355

Lee, Y., Tao, W., Li, J.Y.Q., & Sun, R. (2020). Enhancing employees' knowledge sharing through diversity-oriented leadership and strategic internal communication during the COVID-19 outbreak. *Journal of Knowledge Management.* Ahead of print 10.1108/JKM-06-2020-0483.

Leonardi, P.M. (2020). COVID-19 and the new technologies of organizing: digital exhaust, digital footprints, and artificial intelligence in the wake of remote work. *Journal of Management Studies.* 10.1111/joms.12648

Lin, H., & Hwang, Y. (2021). The effects of personal information management capabilities and social-psychological factors on accounting professionals' knowledge-sharing intentions: Pre and post COVID-19. *International Journal of Accounting Information Systems, 42*(C). DOI: 10.1016/j.accinf.2021.100522

Lloyd, A. (2010). *Information literacy landscapes: Information literacy in education, workplace and everyday contexts* [eBook edition]. Elsevier. https://www.elsevier.com/books/information-literacy-landscapes/lloyd/978-1-84334-507-7

Martin, J., & Norman, A.R. (1970). *The computerized society. An appraisal of the impact of the computers on society in the next fifteen years.* Prentice-Hall.

Messenger, J.C., & Gschwind, L. (2016). Three generations of telework: New ICTs and the (r) evolution from home office to virtual office. *New Technology, Work and Employment, 31*(3), 195–208. 10.1111/ntwe.12073

Olaisen, J., & Revang, O. (2017). Working smarter and greener: Collaborative knowledge sharing in virtual global project teams. *International Journal of Information Management, 37*(1), 1441–1448. DOI: 10.1016/j.ijinfomgt.2016.10.002

Olson, G.M., & Olson, J.S. (2000). Distance matters. *Human–computer interaction, 15*(2-3), 139–178. 10.1207/S15327051HCI1523_4

Sawyer, S., & Jarrahi, M.H. (2014). Sociotechnical approaches to the study of information systems. In H. Topi (Ed.), *Computing handbook, third edition: Information systems and information technology* (pp. 5-1–5-27). Boca Raton, FL: CRC Press.

Taylor, R.S. (1991). Information use environments. *Progress in Communication Sciences, 10*, 217–225.

Toffler, A. (1980). *The third wave.* William Morrow.

Tønnessen, Ø., Dhir, A., & Flåten, B. (2021). Digital knowledge sharing and creative performance: Work from home during the COVID-19 pandemic. *Technological Forecasting and Social Change, 170*, 120866. DOI: 10.1016/j.techfore.2021.120866

Tredinnick, L., & Laybats, C. (2021). Editorial: Blended workplaces. *Business Information Review, 38*(3), 108–110. 10.1177/02663821211042474

Waizenegger, L., McKenna, B., Cai, W. & Bendz, T. (2020). An affordance perspective of team collaboration and enforced working from home during COVID-19. *European Journal of Information Systems, 29*(4), 429–442. DOI: 10.1080/0960085X.2020.1800417

Wenger-Trayner, E., & Wenger-Trayner, B. (2014) Learning in Landscapes of Practice: A framework. In E. Wenger-Trayner, M. Fenton-O'Creevy, S. Hutchinson, C. Kubiak & B. Wenger-Trayner (Eds.), *Learning in landscapes of practice: Boundaries, identity, and knowledgeability in practice-based learning* (pp. 13–29). Routledge.

Yang, L., Holtz, D., Jaffe, S., Suri, S., Sinha, S., Weston, J., Joyce, C., Shah, N., Sherman, K., Hecht, B., & Teevan, J. (2022). The effects of remote work on collaboration among information workers. *Nature Human Behaviour*, *6*(1), 43–54. 10.1038/s41562-021-01196-4

9 Algorithmic Assemblages, the Natural Attitude, and the Social Informatics of the Pandemic Lifeworld

Howard Rosenbaum

Introduction

Between 2020 and 2022, as COVID-19 and, at the time of this writing, its Delta and Omicron variants have spread throughout the world, many countries have responded with aggressive containment measures, of which widespread lockdowns have become increasingly common. Schools have been closed and reopened, nonessential workers have been sent home, public events have been cancelled, public gatherings have been limited, and international travel has been curtailed. People were initially advised to stay at home except for essential travel, and have become used to frequent COVID testing, contact tracing, quarantine restrictions, social distancing, masking, and, at the end of 2021, the availability of vaccines.

These mitigation efforts have had varying levels of success and have led to changes in the ways many people are living their domestic, social, and organizational lives (Deb et al., 2020). Of interest here are changes in people's digital lives. For most of 2020 and 2021, Internet use has spiked, a trend that has continued into 2022. People who could, stayed at home for work, school, and personal edification, and spent more time using online platforms and services than in previous years. Roughly a year into the pandemic, De et al. (2020, 1) found that

> Internet services have seen rises in usage from 40% to 100%, compared to pre-lockdown levels. Video conferencing services like Zoom have seen a ten times increase in usage, and content delivery services like Akamai have seen a 30% increase in content usage (Branscombe, 2020).

McClain et al. (2021) reported survey results that show that the "vast majority of [American] adults (90%) say the internet has been at least important to them personally during the pandemic … The share who say it has been *essential* – 58% – is up slightly from 53% in April 2020". Koeze and Popper (2020, April 7) reported that Facebook use increased by 27%, Netflix use by 16%, and YouTube use by 15.3% during the first three months of 2020.

DOI: 10.4324/9781003231769-14

Király et al (2020) found that many people turned to digital social interactions to relieve stress and anxiety caused by the pandemic. Sun et al. (2020) surveyed 6,416 people in China and reported that during the pandemic, "… 46.8% of the subjects reported increased dependence on internet use, and 16.6% had longer hours of internet use". In general, levels of Internet use have risen sharply during the pandemic in what De et al. (2020, 2) call a "digital surge".

What is the significance of this expansion and deepening of people's digital lives? How has this immersion in social media platforms, streaming services, and other digital applications affected the pandemic-dominated social worlds in which we live? Why has it led to the pervasive spread of conflicting and deeply held narratives about the pandemic? How can this phenomenon be accounted for theoretically? These are questions that motivate this chapter, which takes its charge from Willson (2016, 11), who calls for research that poses questions,

> … as to the broader philosophical issues raised around ontological understandings and experiences of the world that are engaged with and developed when the everyday is increasingly algorithmically articulated, or more simply, to ask how this might affect how people see and understand their environment and their relations.

The argument in this chapter develops in three sections. First, algorithms and algorithmic assemblages are introduced. Second, using a framework informed by Schutz's social phenomenology and the work of postphenomenologists, the concepts of the lifeworld and the natural attitude are described. The claim is made that algorithmic assemblages have become a key element of the lifeworld. As Dourish (2016, 1) explains "[w]hen digital processes become more visible as elements that shape our experience, then algorithms in particular become part of the conversation about how our lives are organized". In the third section, these concepts are used to explain how algorithmic assemblages are shaping the lifeworld and the natural attitude and, in doing so, take part in the constitution of social worlds. The claim is made that a key component of the natural attitude is a technological frame that is based on an algorithmic imaginary that underlies and shapes much of the public discourse about the social life of algorithms. This frame grounds people's trust in assemblages and their output. The examples of the algorithmically mediated and polarized responses that have emerged to fundamental issues of the pandemic will be used to illustrate the effects of this social shaping; these will include reactions to the origins of the virus, masking and social distancing, and COVID-19 vaccine hesitancy.

There are two goals for this chapter. The first is to describe a conceptual framework based on social and postphenomenology that can be used to understand how algorithmic assemblages become embedded in the lifeworld and shape the natural attitude. As is well known in the social informatics literature, the introduction of new technologies into social and organizational settings comes with unintended consequences (Kling et al., 2005), one of which, polarization, will be described here. The second goal is to demonstrate that the conceptual foundations of social informatics can be productively informed by the introduction of a perspective based on social and postphenomenology. This approach provides a social ontology, the lifeworld, and a social epistemology, the natural attitude, that can be employed to understand how "technologies can influence the 'worlds of direct experience, of contemporaries, of predecessors and of successors'" (Coeckelbergh & Reijers, 2016, 344).

Algorithms and Algorithmic Assemblages

Except for such digital channels as personal email, direct messaging, and texting, people's routine online social exchanges are mediated by social platforms, services, and their typically hidden and proprietary algorithms. Particularly during the pandemic, people have become "increasingly reliant on online sociotechnical systems that employ algorithmic curation: organizing, selecting, and presenting subsets of a corpus of information for consumption" (Rader & Gray, 2015, 173). As Sundin et al. (2017, 226) explain, even "accidentally encountered information is also always algorithmically framed and often personalised by, for example previous searches and geographical location". Social media news feeds are algorithmically curated based on people's past behaviors; this also is a part of the routine operations of audio streaming, retail, and other companies that employ recommender systems. Algorithmic analyses are increasingly used in a wide range of institutional settings for such activities as hiring decisions, credit scoring, loan decisions, predictive policing, higher education admissions, and parole decisions (O'neil, 2016; Noble, 2018). A common thread running through these activities is that they are mediated by algorithms, which "are widely recognized as playing an increasingly influential role in the political, economic, and cultural spheres" (Napoli, 2013, 3). The nature, extent, and effects of this mediation are not at all clear in large part because much of this algorithmic activity takes place in the deep background of people's digital lives.

Dourish (2016, 2) describes an algorithm as "an abstract, formalized description of a computational procedure" which, when it acts on data structures, becomes a part of a computer program. It is a tool that is part of a computer scientist's professional practice. Algorithms perform several different functions including, but not limited to, counting, sorting, clustering, and performing numerical and probabilistic analyses. These functions are enacted as computer programs are used, making algorithms "code-waiting-to-happen, ready to be deployed and brought to life in programs yet to be written" (Dourish, 2016, 4). An algorithm can be seen as a recipe that takes values (data) and processes them with a goal of "aggregating those assigned values efficiently, or delivering the results rapidly, or identifying the strongest relationships according to some operationalized notion of 'strong'" (Gillespie, 2014a, 3). The analysis of the workings of algorithms, once they are integrated into programs, is very complex for technical reasons explained by Dourish (2016, 4–5). Because the focus of this chapter is on the social life of algorithms in the lifeworld, these complexities will be set aside (or, in the language of social phenomenology, bracketed).

As algorithms are enacted by computer programs, they perform their functions as components in larger sociotechnical assemblages. Sawyer et al. (2014, 40) describe digital assemblages as "distinct patterns of ICT collections that, in use, are functionally equivalent and structurally similar, relying on standardised and commodified ICT and are neither formally designed nor collectively governed". Algorithmic assemblages are technical, including algorithms, software, data structures and data on which the algorithm operates, and material, including the computational and network infrastructures that power algorithmically mediated activity, the platform or interface through which it is available, and the devices used to interact with the service or platform that uses the algorithm. They are also social, involving a range of human participants (Pink et al., 2017, 8; Ananny, 2016, 7; Kavanagh et al., 2015, 8). There are millions interacting with algorithmic assemblages daily, using search engines, social media platforms, ecommerce sites, educational platforms, and others and there are people at the back end "debating the models, cleaning the training data, designing the algorithms, tuning the parameters, deciding on which algorithms to depend on in which context" (Gillespie, 2014a, 5) in a "a global digital assembly line of silent, invisible men and women, often laboring in precarious conditions" (Burrell & Fourcade, 2020, 219).

Lamprou et al. (2014, 5) characterize these assemblages as performative, with "movement and the temporary, socially, materially and discursively accomplished 'coming-together' of heterogeneous entities into social practices". When enacted, an assemblage is intentional and "is not simply a happenstance collocation of people, materials and actions, but the deliberate realisation of a distinctive plan" (Buchanan, 2015, 385). However, this plan is enacted in a dynamic and complex social world, meaning that the assemblage also "involves the 'mess' of its constituent or related parts, as well as that of the institutions, power relations that govern its use, and the conflicting discourses that define it" (Pink et al., 2018; 2). Consequently, assemblages change as access devices evolve, as peoples' practices change when interacting within them and with each other, as the platforms change, and as the data and information people search for, receive, and create regularly and rapidly, enters and leaves assemblages. For example, when searching on a smartphone, people are interacting at one terminus of an algorithmic assemblage. The algorithm is instantiated in a material and performative sense "as a running system, running in a particular place, on a particular computer, connected to a particular network, with a particular hardware configuration" so as they examine the results of the search, their "experience of algorithms can change as infrastructure changes" (Dourish, 2016, 5, 6). The assemblage operates "semi-autonomously, without the need for interaction with, or knowledge of, human users or operators" (Willson, 2016, 3), as it carries out the processes necessary to provide a response. Despite this constant dynamism, an assemblage tends toward "functional stability", meaning that is "able to absorb change—it endures even as it evolves" (Sawyer et al., 2014, 52).

An algorithmic assemblage is a sociotechnical accomplishment and a communication technology, connecting people, groups, companies, governments, and other actors in an ongoing exchange of data, information, and services. Its effects emerge when it is used and this performative enactment involves the whole of the assemblage because "the conditions and consequences of algorithmic rules only come into being through the careful plaiting of relatively unstable associations of people, things, processes, documents and resources" (Neyland & Möllers, 2016, 1). In fact, "[i]t is only through such algorithmic assemblages that any individual process can take place" (Ananny, 2016, 8). This becomes important because, algorithmically mediated activity, while technically sophisticated, is, in fact, a routine social practice and a mundane and mostly invisible part of daily life (Andersen, 2020, 1480; Lomborg & Kapsch, 2020, 747; Sundin et al., 2017, 225).

One approach that can make the invisible visible is based on an integration of Schutz's (1970, 1967) social phenomenology and insights from postphenomenology (Rosenberger & Verbeek, 2015). From this perspective, algorithmic assemblages are not simply the lines of code that define algorithms and the infrastructure that makes them work. They are "'large' spanning time and space, but ... also 'small' coming in contact with routine and everyday practice" (Bowker et al., 2009, 113). The next section introduces two phenomenological concepts, the lifeworld and the natural attitude, the former to describe how algorithmic assemblages have become embedded in people's lives, and the latter to account for the ways in which, through people's routine actions, these assemblages are enacted, maintained, and become powerful actants in the shaping of social worlds.

The lifeworld and the natural attitude

This section explores the question of how to foreground the taken-for-grantedness of algorithmically mediated activity to account for the role of algorithmic assemblages in the constitution of the social world. One way is through Schutz's (1967) social phenomenology and the insights of postphenomenology, an approach to studying people and technology that has emerged over the last three decades. Schutz, in a sense, "socialized" Husserl's philosophical phenomenology by appropriating two central concepts, the "lifeworld", and the "natural attitude". The lifeworld describes the everyday and taken-for-granted world in which we live. According to Husserl, it is "the world in which we find ourselves at every moment of our life, taken exactly as it presents itself to us in our everyday experience" (Gurwitsch, 1962, 51). Within the lifeworld is the natural attitude, a way of being in the world in which people experience each other, the natural and social worlds, and the tangible and intangible objects that constitute these worlds as taken-for-granted, real, and factual. Husserl intends both concepts to serve as points of departure to be transcended when conducting the phenomenological reduction, a goal of his phenomenology. However, rather than setting them aside, Schutz argues that lifeworld and the natural attitude should be foundational objects of study for the social sciences.

Schutz (1945, 549, 553) describes the lifeworld as the "paramount reality" experienced as an "intersubjective world which existed long before our birth, experienced and interpreted by others, our predecessors, as an organized world". It is characterized by pragmatic motives, shared provinces of meaning, and complex interlinked social interactions among individuals, groups, and institutions. It is filled with tangible and intangible natural, cultural, social, and technological objects that, to varying degrees, resist efforts to manipulate them. People routinely act and interact in the lifeworld, carrying out their tasks and projects in ways that both modify the lifeworld and/or are modified by it, producing through these activities a material, and cultural, world characterized by patterns, routines, and interlocking activities of varying degrees of complexity (Butnaru, 2015, 69; Eberle, 2015, 566). The lifeworld is not an objective reality that people confront; it is a social construction and an ongoing practical accomplishment "with the methods for that accomplishment being, for members, known, used, and taken for granted" (Psathas, 1980, 3). According to Schutz (1945, 534),

> The world of everyday life is the scene and also the object of our actions and interactions. We have to dominate it and we have to change it in order to realize the purposes which we pursue within it among our fellow-men. Thus, we work and operate not only within but upon the world.

The assumption of the ontological intersubjectivity of the lifeworld marks Schutz's departure from Husserl and prepares the foundation for his social phenomenology. A contribution of the postphenomenologists that further clarifies the nature of the lifeworld is to foreground the role of technology, explaining that there is no *a priori* relation between the person (subject) and the social world (object), "only an 'indirect one,' and technologies often function as mediators" (Rosenberger & Verbeek, 2015, 12). In this human-technology-world relation, it is mediation that constitutes subject and object (Verbeek, 2015).

The natural attitude is a state of consciousness in which people tacitly accept the reality of their lives as given and taken for granted while suspending doubt and disbelief in the lifeworld (Dreher, 2011, 494). It is a way of being that is "independent of and prior to any scientific or other interpretation" of the world (Hughes & Sharrock, 1997, 96). It is a social epistemology because it is the primary way people come to know their worlds. It is foundational, because it is "the general belief that all our actions, all our life rests on" (Luft, 1998, 163). Further, to live in the natural attitude is an "immersion-in-world", which "refers to the lived fact that human beings are always already inescapably entwined in and subsumed by their worlds that, most of the time, 'just happen' without the intervention of anything or anyone" (Seamon, 2015, 390). Within the natural attitude, one is not aware of being in it, so in phenomenological terms, the natural attitude is hidden from itself (Luft, 1998, 155). In this way, the lifeworld is an ongoing accomplishment of people's routine actions and interactions; it "just happens" while people are engaged in other activities. Therefore, as Psathas (1980, 11) explains:

> Members 'know how' to produce an event or social situation through their actions, but they do not 'know' how they do it; similarly, they 'know how' to recognize a social situation and identify it, but they do not 'know' how they do 'recognizing'.

People are born into preexisting social worlds that they experience as organized with sign and symbol systems, webs of social relationships, sets of rules, guidelines and norms, institutions and roles, power and sanctions, and so on. People learn, understand, and internalize the subtleties of the natural attitude as they are socialized informally in families, social groups, and with the technologies they use; formal socialization occurs in educational and other organizations. Over time, people acquire a "stock of knowledge" about their worlds that for them becomes routine, natural, shared, and taken-for-granted. The lifeworld as defined by this stock of knowledge, "is immediately and intuitively grasped" by people and "endures permanently ... for all of our natural life in a waking state" (Muzzetto, 2015, 261). As we move through the lifeworld, we make frequent use of "at-hand knowledge", which is "acquired through actions, interactions, processes of socialization. It especially concerns the contents of the cultural model of one's social group" (Muzzetto, 2015, 272–273). This type of knowledge is largely social in origin, socially distributed, and shared (Eberle, 2015, 566; Segre, 2016, 94; Costelloe, 1996, 254). Schutz further divides at-hand-knowledge into "knowledge about" and "knowledge of acquaintance". The former includes the clear, distinct, and consistent knowledge people have of some part of the lifeworld that reflects some level of expertise that they have attained. The latter is knowledge that results from more indirect experience, is vaguer, more superficial, and differentiated into dimensions of "well-foundedness, plausibility, likelihood, reliance upon authority, blind acceptance, and complete ignorance" (Dreher, 2011, 498). This is an important distinction because in the natural attitude, most of the knowledge we have about the lifeworld is one or another form of knowledge of acquaintance.

Therefore, the natural attitude is "acquired through, and profoundly influenced by, specific sociocultural practices" (Weiss, 2016, 1). Over the last two decades, one such sociocultural practice involves routine immersion in algorithmic assemblages which "have the capacity to shape social and cultural formations and impact directly on individual lives" (Beer, 2009, 987), including the shaping of the stock of knowledge. These assemblages, then, are "productive elements in co-shaping how people perceive the world, each other and themselves" (Kudina, 2022, 4). As people interact with and within these assemblages, their natural attitude expands to include assumptions of "algorithmic authority", defined by Lustig and Nardi (2015, 743) as "the trust in algorithms to direct human action and to verify information, in place of trusting or preferring human authority". These elements of the stock of knowledge serve a significant purpose because they "eliminate troublesome inquiries by offering ready-made directions for use, to replace truth hard to attain by comfortable truisms, and substitute the self-explanatory for the questionable" (Muzzetto, 2015, 269). The natural attitude then becomes a "schema of interpretation of the common world and a means of mutual agreement and understanding" (Dreher, 2011, 497).

Gurwitsch (1962, 58–59) qualifies the meaning of "assumption" in the context of the natural attitude, explaining that it refers to an "unquestioned belief and certainty, on which we act but which is not made a topic for reflection and is not even rendered explicit, unless we engage in philosophical inquiries". Assumptions of the stability of the lifeworld and shared perspectives are ontological; differences in perspective based for example, on economic class, location, or organizational roles certainly exist but reflect differences in local instantiations of the natural attitude and not the foundational natural attitude itself because there are "features ... common to all social worlds because they are rooted in the human condition" (Schutz, 1970, 79). This is the basis of Muzzetto's (2015, 262–3) claim that the natural attitude has two levels, a "changeable historical-cultural level 'that embraces the certainties that apply to' people living in particular times and places, and "a basic nucleus, an 'invariant structure that is implied not by our way of life but all forms of life in general'" (Spinicci, 2000, 126, quoted in Muzzetto, 2015, 263).

One implication is that at the changeable historical-cultural level, there is a naivety that suffuses the natural attitude, such that people tend to believe that their world views, understandings, and beliefs are natural, right, true, and justified, when in fact, they may only be partial, biased, or even wrong. In the natural attitude, "daily life consists of a set of opinions that do not even make the claim to be exact and absolutely true" (Luft, 1998, 160).

The knowledge most people have of algorithmic assemblages and the knowledge that they derive from them are clearly of this type, described above as knowledge of acquaintance. Search engines, as powerful algorithmic assemblages, play a role in reinforcing this naivety, because their "algorithms do not just impose an order of knowledge on people; people also use searching as a way for strengthening their arguments, to confirm their bias" (Sundin et al., 2017, 233). This is an insight that will be useful when considering the intended and unintended consequences of the pervasiveness of algorithmic assemblages in the lifeworld.

The natural attitude is relatively stable because it "takes the world and its objects for granted until counterproof imposes itself" (Schutz, 1945, 550), meaning that people typically suspend doubt about the existence of the social world and its objects (Eberle, 2015, 572). People live and act within the lifeworld and, while they may question some feature or facet of the world, especially when it provides resistance, they do not typically question the lifeworld itself and this is "an essential precondition of every activity" (Gurwitsch, 1962, 51). The natural attitude persists because it is maintained over time, in part, by people's deep "ontological trust" in the stability of the lifeworld (Giddens, 1984). People have an "uncritical belief in the integrity of the world as it appears" (Costelloe, 1996, 252) and assume that this world is a certain way and has certain characteristics, understanding, without question, that the world was there before they were born and will continue after they die (Zaner, 1970, xii; Schutz, 1970, 79). This is an indication of the extent to which the natural attitude permeates all aspects of social life (Vaitkus, 2005, 112). Schutz (1945, 55) explains one important way in which the natural attitude is collectively maintained:

> As long as the ... established scheme of reference, the system of our and other people's warranted experiences works, as long as the actions and operations performed under its guidance yield the desired results, we trust these experiences. We are not interested in finding out whether this world really does exist or whether it is merely a coherent system of consistent appearances. We have no reason to cast any doubt upon our warranted experiences which, so we believe, give us things as they really are.

Despite its patterned nature, the natural attitude, and the lifeworld of which it is a part, are fragile (Muzzetto, 2015, 248); both can be intentionally or unintentionally disrupted. A terrorist attack, mass shooting, or invasion of another country would be examples of the former, and a pandemic, the latter. However, people do not often experience the fragility of the natural attitude and the lifeworld; the more typical experience of social life is that people are able to carry out their projects, tasks, or interactions successfully, alone or as part of a group, without having to deeply question the nature of the social world, because "our curiosity is satisfied and our inquiry stops if knowledge sufficient for our purpose at hand has been obtained" (Schutz, 1970, 148). The belief that the world exists and will continue to exist, much as it is at any given moment, is the "general thesis of the natural attitude", originally proposed by Husserl (Luft, 1998, 163) and adopted by Schutz.

As people move through the lifeworld and engage in the routine interactions of their domestic, work, and social lives, they are largely unaware that a consequence of their activities is the ongoing reconstitution of the lifeworld. This has a role to play "in determining the meaning of the world that we accept as given, that is, as natural" (Weiss, 2016, 6). This applies as well to our experience with the tools we use, including our digital devices. According to Schutz (1970, 146)

> We live in our present culture surrounded by a world of machines and dominated by institutions, social and technical, of which we have sufficient knowledge to bring about desired effects, without, however, much understanding (if any) of how these effects have been brought about.

The next step in the argument is to use this framework to explore the relationships among algorithmic assemblages, the lifeworld, and the natural attitude. The argument has been foreshadowed with several indications above about the ways in which these assemblages have become taken-for-granted in people's everyday lives. The next section describes the argument in some detail.

Algorithmic assemblages, the lifeworld, and the natural attitude

As the focal point of social media, ecommerce, and educational platforms, public and workplace surveillance systems, smart cities and homes, and other digital services, algorithmic assemblages are an increasingly important part of the lifeworld. When enacted by people as they engage in digital interactions, these assemblages provide algorithmically curated search results, recommendations of all sorts, multimedia artifacts with varying content, and a constant stream of data and information. This data and information flow impacts people's lives in a variety of ways, one of which is that many are becoming increasingly reliant on these systems as primary sources of information about their worlds (Burrell & Fourcade, 2020, 221, 227; Lomborg & Kapsch, 2020, 745–6; Rader & Gray, 2015, 173; Hess, 2014, 10). Another way to phrase this is that, as a part of the lifeworld, algorithmic assemblages shape the natural attitude; this assertion, however, must be unpacked.

In the lifeworld, people engage in many routine, repetitive, and mundane algorithmically mediated interactions that become the contours of their domestic, social, and organizational lives. The more they use digital devices to engage with algorithmically driven online platforms and services, the more the assemblages of which these devices, services, and platforms are a part become embedded in the lifeworld. Feenberg (2015, 230) describes this situation as ontological because technology "is not something added on after the fact ... [it] is as natural to human beings as language and culture; its specific content is historically contingent, but it will always be found wherever there are human beings". As a complex form of technology, an algorithmic assemblage does not "transcend the lifeworld but rather forms a special part of it" (Feenberg, 2015, 234). From the perspective of end users, an assemblage is largely present in and through the devices they use to access it; not as visible are the people working on the back end of the assemblage, the companies that own parts of it, and the hardware, software, and material infrastructure supporting it (Kotliar, 2021, 347).

In their discussion of postphenomenology, Rosenberger and Verbeek, (2015) argue that people can have four different types of relations with complex technologies such as algorithmic assemblages, each affecting the natural attitude in different ways. As people use and integrate digital devices such as smartphones, personal digital assistants, and tablets into their lives, they develop routines and patterns of experience that shape their interactions with their devices and with the lifeworld. These patterns are "embodiment relations", meaning that the device

> ... does not, or hardly, become itself an object of perception. Rather, it 'withdraws' and serves as a (partially) transparent means through which one perceives one's environment, thus engendering a partial symbiosis of oneself and it.
>
> (Brey, 2000, 3)

Transparency is a quality of embodiment relations and is "the degree to which a device (or an aspect of that device) fades into the background of a user's awareness as it is used" (Rosenberger & Verbeek, 2015, 14). The artifacts and the assemblages of which they are a part, become a means by which people carry out their projects and tasks and, as they withdraw, they become extensions of the person. A person may also have a hermeneutic relation with a digital device in which they perceive and interpret the device's output, as when scrolling through a news feed. When this occurs, the person "experiences a transformed encounter with the world via the direct experience and interpretation of the technology itself" (Rosenberger & Verbeek, 2015,17). A third possible relation is "alterity", which refers to an "interface ... devised specifically to mimic the shape of a person-to-person interaction" (Rosenberger & Verbeek, 2015, 18), as in the case of using a device for real-time video meetings. Finally, there is a "background relation" which accounts for the way in which the assemblage typically remains hidden even as people enact it; it operates in the background of everyday life, while being an integral part of it (Gertz, 2019, 68; Rosenberger & Verbeek, 2015, 18). Lomborg and Kapsch, (2020, 754) reinforce this last type of relation:

A central observation in our study is how algorithms often go unnoticed – not just for those who lack a general awareness of them. When users of digital media experience algorithmic operations as smart, convenient, and efficient, they will quickly stop noticing them and maybe even forget about them.

In this way, social phenomenology and postphenomenology have the potential to provide an ontological depiction of the social world and a foundation for social informatics. With the example of algorithmic assemblages, it is possible to understand how technologies "can influence the 'worlds of direct experience, of contemporaries, of predecessors and of successors'" (Coeckelbergh & Reijers, 2016, 344). As a part of the lifeworld and through the four relations they can have with people, algorithmic assemblages are becoming increasingly important in shaping the natural attitude. As people experience these relations, they learn to routinely live with, domesticate, and enact algorithmic assemblages through their digital devices. As they do, algorithmic logic comes to shape and control the data and information flows on which they depend and incorporate into many of their routine activities. In this sense, algorithmic assemblages produce and certify knowledge (Gillespie, 2014b, 2), making them powerful actors in the lifeworld. For this reason, the material and social worlds people produce and reproduce (Eberle, 2015, 295) become imbued with the output of algorithmic assemblages which "become proactive actors in moulding social life" (Raffa & Pronzato, 2021, 295).

Algorithmic assemblages "contribute to shaping our everyday practices and understandings" as "situated artifacts and generative processes" (Willson, 2016, 2, 5) that sort, analyze, manipulate, inform, and predict. They are "built to be embedded into practice in the lived world that produces the information they process, and in the lived world of their users" (Gillespie, 2014a, 17). Burrell and Fourcade (2020, 227) make this point more forcefully, arguing that "[t]he more one interacts with digital systems, the more the course of one's personal and social life becomes dependent on algorithmic operations and choices". Social media newsfeeds are examples of algorithmically curated platforms that become routine parts of daily life. An increasingly common outcome of engagement with these assemblages is that decisions about the relevance of information are being made through technical means that have epistemological consequences. They restrict the domain of what can be known, provide a means by which what is in the domain can be known, and influence the ways in which what is known can be used (Gillespie, 2014b, 1; Raffa & Pronzato, 2021, 296). They "help to bring about particular ways of seeing the world, reproduce stereotypes, reify practices ... and world views, restrict choices or open possibilities previously unidentified" (Willson, 2016, 5). In so doing, algorithmic assemblages shape the natural attitude in ways that are hidden and deeply entangled in people's domestic, social, and work lives, and in their routine information and decision-making practices. This is a novel conceptualization of the relations among people, technologies, and contexts of use.

However, assemblages do more than this. They shape people's knowledge of acquaintance that Schutz argues characterizes much of our stock of knowledge and therefore the natural attitude. This takes place at the level of what Muzzetto (2015, 262–3) calls the "changeable historical cultural level" of the natural attitude and occurs in two ways. First, there is the public discourse about algorithms and algorithmic systems that casts them as objective, efficient, and authoritative (Alvarado et al., 2021, 21), what has been called the myth of algorithmic neutrality (Rosenbaum, 2020, 2; Burrell & Fourcade, 2020, 218). Second, there are the individual experiences that people have with algorithmic assemblages. Together, these form an algorithmic imaginary:

> both in terms of intangible representations and worldviews, such as the one by the producers of algorithmic media, and as worlds constructed by users' perceptions, which then have multifaceted consequences on how users behave and algorithms react within a recursive logic.
>
> (Raffa & Pronzato, 2021, 298)

The algorithmic imaginary describes the ways in which people think about and perceive algorithmic assemblages and their output (Green, 2021; Schwennesen, 2019). As part of the natural attitude, the algorithmic imaginary takes the form of a technological frame, a type of knowledge of acquaintance that has "powerful effects in that people's assumptions, expectations, and knowledge about the purpose, context, importance, and role of technology will strongly influence the choices made regarding the design and use of those technologies" (Orlikowski & Gash, 1994, 179). As it takes hold, it shapes people's experiences in the lifeworld (Alvarado et al., 2021, 3; Bucher, 2017, 41; Spieth et al., 2021, 1964). Research has demonstrated that, for example, social media news feeds are algorithmically curated to reinforce people's beliefs and world views. What has been called a "filter bubble" or an "echo chamber" can be seen as an instantiation of an algorithmically driven world view that people come to believe is factual. The facticity of this level of the natural attitude is strengthened by people's tacit belief in algorithmic authority.

As mentioned above, acquisition of the natural attitude depends in large part on language. As people learn the language of their social groups, they exchange signs and symbols that "are intersubjectively shared and handed down and thereby ensure the cohesion and the meaningfulness of the individual's life-world as a whole" (Dreher, 2011, 502). Language, therefore, is "essential for any understanding of the reality of everyday life" (Berger & Luckmann, 1967, 37) and becomes a repository of meanings, and experiences preserved and passed on to future generations. In the lifeworld, algorithmic assemblages are becoming the digital repositories of a technologically advanced culture's language, signs, symbols, and images, and therefore its meanings. They capture and preserve artifacts and traces of people's, groups' and organization's digital lives, with several of the larger social media platforms claiming never to have deleted anything since they began. In this sense, these assemblages become key actors in the sociomaterial construction of reality, helping to shape the natural attitude and constitute and reconstitute the lifeworld. As people interact with and within these assemblages, the data and information they retrieve and share shapes their "at-hand knowledge" in specific ways that can, for example, reinforce the cultural models of their social and affinity groups. Assemblages therefore play a significant role in defining the "here and now" for distinct social groups, as well as providing the capacity to transcend the present moment, shaping their collective understanding of their pasts and futures (Kudina, 2022, 2). It is important here to understand that, despite assemblages' broad reach in terms of gathering data and information, they "not only promote certain cultural proposals over others, but they also delete some parts of the social world, thereby excluding from the cultural reality contents which are unable to meet the algorithmic flow" (Raffa & Pronzato, 2021, 313).

Accepting the technological frame of algorithmic neutrality, people integrate algorithmic assemblages into their lives, bringing them into their homes and workplaces and "embedding them in their routines, imbuing them with additional meanings that the technology provider could not have anticipated" (Gillespie, 2014b, 20). Over time, people begin to adjust their social actions and interactions in ways that "suit the algorithm they depend on" thereby, in a sense, making themselves "algorithmically available" (Gillespie, 2014a, 2, 18). In terms of the bidirectional relationship between people and technology, this type of adjustment illustrates the material agency of the algorithmic assemblage which can take on gatekeeping and decision support functions through control of the information flow to the individual, shaping the person's "information life" (Napoli, 2013, 8; Musiani, 2013, 1; Beer, 2009, 994).

As people interact with algorithmic assemblages, their activities have another consequence. The data they generate change the algorithms they are using in largely unintentional ways. Gillespie (2014b, 7) argues that "algorithms are made and remade in every instance of their use because every click, every query, changes the tool incrementally". As an algorithm changes, the people who use it are also being changed as it shapes their information spaces and stocks of knowledge. According to Willson (2016), "the ways algorithms are designed and implemented (and their resultant outcomes) help to influence the ways we conduct our friendships (Bucher, 2013), shape our identities (Cheney-Lippold, 2011), and navigate our lives more generally (Beer, 2009)". Gillespie (2014b, 21) describes the potential impacts of the increasing presence of algorithmic assemblages in the lifeworld:

It is easy to theorize, but substantially more difficult to document, how users may shift their world views to accommodate the underlying logics and implicit presumptions of the algorithms they use regularly. There is a case to be made that the working logics of these algorithms not only shape user practices, but [also] lead users to internalize their norms and priorities.

The social informatics of the pandemic lifeworld

The effects of algorithmic assemblages' shaping of the natural attitude can be seen in the ways in which people have responded to the pandemic. In broad terms there has been a clear polarization among large groups in the American population (which is mirrored elsewhere in the world). For example, there are now competing narratives about three main issues related to the pandemic: the origins and severity of COVID-19 and its variants, the efficacy of masking and social distancing, and the push to vaccinate the public. Did the virus escape from a lab? Was it zoonotic? Is it caused by 5G? Is it no more serious than the flu? Can wearing masks increase the chances of becoming infected? What can be done about the tracking nano-devices in vaccines? These are all questions that have been raised over the last two years that have flowed around social media (and some of the mainstream media) (Bunker, 2020, 2). According to Stein et al. (2021, 8)

> In the short time since the beginning of the pandemic, the number of COVID-19-related conspiracy theories increased and propagated on social media. According to some metrics, online sensationalist and conspiratorial sites and articles generate more user engagement than more reputable sources …

Focusing on the genre of narrative that discounts basic facts about the pandemic, the question can be posed as to why people come to believe so strongly in narratives that question science and public health officials and draw heavily on conspiracy theories? One part of the answer is that algorithmic assemblages routinely create, reinforce, and exacerbate polarization, because the "emphasis on objectivity and neutrality leads to algorithmic interventions that reproduce existing social conditions and policies" (Green & Viljoen, 2020, 22). Algorithmic assemblages that are finely tuned to respond to people's online information behaviors deliver the data and information that fills out these narratives. This is good business logic, because the companies that own and manage them "generally find it profitable to exploit viral content and other forms of emergent sociality" (Burrell & Fourcade 2020, 229) to keep people engaged on their platforms. However, over time, the output of these assemblages is forming people's knowledge of acquaintance of the pandemic in what Kotliar (2021, 346) calls the "socioalgorithmic construction of choice". Rather than viewing choice as having origins in individualistic actions, it is more appropriately seen as taking place in a complex information environment composed of social, political, economic, and cultural affordances and constraints. Kotliar (2021, 348) argues that algorithms are carefully designed and implemented to influence people's abilities to choose. Consequently, algorithmic assemblages shape repertoires of choosing in influential ways, one of which is "hyper-nudging", one of the "'subtle, unobtrusive, yet extraordinarily powerful' techniques that recursively refine users' choices" (Yeung, 2017, 2). Peralta et al. (2021, 11) state this plainly:

> Algorithmic bias, an unexpected consequence of the content filtering tools behind most popular social media platforms used today, affects the dynamics of opinion formation and information spreading arising from digital interactions in non-trivial ways, ultimately leading to undesired collective phenomena like group polarization and opinion radicalization.

There is a growing body of research that supports this assertion. Studies of social media use during the pandemic consistently find that significant numbers of people understand the pandemic through misinformation and conspiracy theories, leading to a distrust of science, greater risk to public health, and avoidance of COVID-19-specific health protective behaviors (Allington et al., 2021a, 1768; Choli & Kuss, 2021; Lee, 2021; Rocha et al., 2021; Quinn et al., 2021; Stecula & Pickup, 2021; Bunker, 2020, 2). Stein et al. (2021, 8) find that COVID-19-related conspiracy theories dramatically increased on social media, and that "according to some metrics, online sensationalist and conspiratorial sites and articles generate more user engagement than more reputable sources". Allington et al. (2021b, 11) found an association between social media use and vaccine hesitancy, and Naeem et al. (2021) observed that:

> [T]he COVID-19 infodemic is full of false claims, half-baked conspiracy theories and pseudoscientific therapies, regarding the diagnosis, treatment, prevention, origin and spread of the virus. Fake news is pervasive in social media, putting public health at risk.

Algorithmic assemblages are reshaping the ontological trust that people have in the lifeworld. The trust that the world is as it appears to be is extended to the assemblage and, when taking the form of algorithmic authority, this trust is also directed toward its outputs. Further, the more people engage with these assemblages, the deeper the trust they have in them because "[o]ntological security and routine are intimately connected, via the pervasive influence of habit" (Giddens, 2013, 98). This implies that algorithmic assemblages are constructing diverging types of knowledge of acquaintance about the pandemic, that begin to acquire social ontological status as part of people's sociohistorical lifeworlds. People deeply believe in the pandemic narratives that are flowing through their online and offline social networks and, in the natural attitude, believe in the authority and facticity of the narrative, because "the natural attitude replicates falsehoods as easily as truths—all while atrophying our ability to tell the difference" (Champagne, nd; 7). As algorithmic assemblages routinely spread mis- and disinformation, and as people incorporate it into their knowledges of acquaintance of, in this case, issues related to the pandemic, these assemblages "are transforming the very nature of our moral intuitions—that is, the very nature of our relations to self and others—and what it means to exist in the social world" (Burrell & Fourcade, 2020, 226).

Conclusion

Algorithmically mediated interactions are becoming increasingly important in many people's lives. When using online services and platforms for search, entertainment, and other activities, they are interacting with and within algorithmic assemblages. This routine activity, in a performative sense, brings assemblages to life as people, through their digital devices, enact and become part of algorithmic assemblages. However, as these interactions become more habitual, the assemblages fade from view, becoming hidden in daily life. At the same time, immersion in online digital information-based applications has affected our pandemic-dominated social worlds. It has led to the pervasive spread of conflicting and deeply held narratives about the pandemic. To understand why and how this happens, a framework that draws on Schutzian social phenomenology and the work of post-phenomenologists is proposed to pull back the curtain on these assemblages and their impacts. This framework is timely because the "relevance of phenomenology to the understanding of the social impact of communications technology, particularly the internet, has aroused the interest of many scholars" (Zhao, 2007, 140).

A contribution of this chapter is to provide an initial sketch of a conceptual framework to explore the processes by which algorithmic assemblages play a role in organizing people's lives, opening these assemblages, their inherent power asymmetries, and the algorithmic imaginary of neutrality and authority on which they depend, to sustained critique. This matters because the back end of these assemblages is controlled by powerful corporate actors who take full advantage of the data and information asymmetries that exist in these assemblages (Dalton et al., 2016, 7). According to Burrell and Fourcade (2020, 218):

A cultural circuit made of management gurus, specialized magazines, and tech evangelists (tasked with spreading belief in a particular technology and building a loyal following) further helps [to] organize this myth-making and consolidate[s] power into the hands of those able to implement and understand code and the institutions and individuals who fund them.

The lifeworld is being influenced and shaped by the agendas of these corporate actors in ways that are difficult to see, effectively hiding the "reality making functions of algorithms" (Lomborg & Kapsch, 2020, 747). This chapter, then, aligns well with Willson's (2016, 2)argument that "studies of the everyday are ... partly concerned with rendering the seemingly invisible visible and thereby open to critique and the examination of power relations and practices that are in play".

Using algorithmic assemblages as an example of a modern pervasive and influential technology, the framework posits that they are critically important in shaping the modern lifeworld, as well as the sociocultural level of the natural attitude. As performative and largely invisible actants in the lifeworld, these assemblages are enacted routinely and frequently by people using their embodied digital devices. Using the emergence of competing narratives about pandemic issues, the argument was made that the impact of algorithmic assemblages has been polarization taking place at social, ontological, and epistemological levels. Information and misinformation accessed through algorithmic assemblages become knowledge of acquaintance in people's stock of knowledge, shaping their natural attitude, taking the form of unquestioned and common-sense assumptions about the social world. Interactions with assemblages shape how people come to know their lifeworlds. With widespread acceptance of a technological frame based on an algorithmic imaginary that emphasizes neutrality and algorithmic authority, people develop trust in the assemblage and its output. Consequently, they deeply believe in their chosen narratives and have proven to be intransigent against attempts to challenge narratives based on unfounded claims and conspiracy theories. The contribution of this chapter is that the framework presented here offers an explanation for the depth of this intransigence and, when integrated into a critical social informatics perspective, provides a lens through which to investigate the spread of misinformation and false and dangerous narratives that have accompanied the COVID-19 pandemic.

A second contribution of this chapter is that this framework can potentially strengthen social informatics by providing a grounding for one of its fundamental assumptions—that there is a relationship of mutual shaping among people, technologies, and their contexts of use. The postphenomenological approach recasts the relation between the human subject and the social world as one of emergence based on the mediation provided by technology. From the social phenomenological approach, the concept of the lifeworld offers a social ontology for a socially constructed world, and the natural attitude offers a social epistemology, or the ways in which we come to know this world.

This framework suggests three avenues of investigation of interest to social informatics scholars. First is the micro-level study of the ways in which individuals are immersed in algorithmic assemblages and how their interactions with algorithms shape their natural attitudes. This is in keeping with Couldry and Powell's (2014, 2) call for "a more open inquiry into what actual social actors, and groups of actors, are doing" when engaging in algorithmically mediated interactions". An intriguing avenue for research is opened up by the "broken data" metaphor, which focuses on how people engage with data in mundane settings (Pink et al., 2018, 11); this approach assumes data have materiality and can be broken and repaired as people carry out their algorithmically mediated activities. The second avenue is the study of the structure and functioning of algorithmic assemblages, which can take advantage of the methods used in infrastructure studies. Kitchin (2016, 13) argues that a "way to undertake such research is to conduct ethnographies of how people engage with and are conditioned by algorithmic systems and how such systems reshape how organisations conduct their endeavours and are structured". Third is the critical study of the power and information asymmetries inherent in algorithmic assemblages. An example of this approach is Striphas' (2015, 408) critical evaluation of algorithmic culture, which argues that there has been an entanglement of digital technologies, discourse, big data analytics and political economy, raising the specter of the privatization and algorithmic automation of cultural decision-making. This should also involve an investigation of the organizations in whose platforms and services algorithms are enacted.

References

Allington, D., Duffy, B., Wessely, S., Dhavan, N. & Rubin, J. (2021a). Health-protective behaviour, social media usage and conspiracy belief during the COVID-19 public health emergency. *Psychological Medicine, 51*(10), 1763–1769.

Allington, D., McAndrew, S., Moxham-Hall, V. & Duffy, B. (2021b). Coronavirus conspiracy suspicions, general vaccine attitudes, trust, and coronavirus information source as predictors of vaccine hesitancy among UK residents during the COVID-19 pandemic. *Psychological Medicine*, 1–12.

Alvarado, O., Vanden Abeele, V., Geerts, D., Gutiérrez, F. & Verbert, K. (2021, February). Exploring tangible algorithmic imaginaries in movie recommendations. In *Proceedings of the Fifteenth International Conference on Tangible, Embedded, and Embodied Interaction*. 1–12.

Ananny, M. (2016). Toward an ethics of algorithms: Convening, observation, probability, and timeliness. *Science, Technology, & Human Values, 41*(1), 93–117.

Andersen, J. (2020). Understanding and interpreting algorithms: Toward a hermeneutics of algorithms. *Media, Culture & Society, 42*(7–8), 1479–1494.

Beer, D. (2009). Power through the algorithm? Participatory web cultures and the technological unconscious. *New Media & Society, 11*(6), 985–1002.

Berger, P.L. & Luckmann, T. (1967). *The social construction of reality: A treatise in the sociology of knowledge.* Anchor.

Bowker, G.C., Baker, K., Millerand, F., & Ribes, D. (2009). Toward information infrastructure studies: Ways of knowing in a networked environment. In J. Hunsinger, L. Klastrup, & M. Allen (Eds.). *International Handbook of Internet Research* (pp. 97–117). Dordrecht: Springer.

Branscombe, M. (2020). The network impact of the global COVID-19 pandemic. April 14, Retrieved August 10, 2021, from The New Stack https://thenewstack.io/the-networkimpact-of-the-global-covid-19-pandemic

Buchanan, I. (2015). Assemblage theory and its discontents. *Deleuze Studies, 9*(3), 382–392.

Bucher, T. (2013). The friendship assemblage: Investigating programmed sociality on Facebook. *Television & New Media, 14*(6), 479–493.

Bucher, T. (2017). The algorithmic imaginary: exploring the ordinary affects of Facebook algorithms. *Information, communication & society, 20*(1), 30–44.

Bunker, D. (2020). Who do you trust? The digital destruction of shared situational awareness and the COVID-19 infodemic. *International Journal of Information Management, 55*, 1–6.

Brey, P.A. (2000). Technology and Embodiment in Ihde and Merleau-Ponty. In C. Mitcham, (Ed.), *Metaphysics, Epistemology and Technology (Research in Philosophy and Technology* (vol. 19, pp. 45–58). London: Elsevier/JAI Press.

Burrell, J., & Fourcade, M. (2020). The Society of Algorithms. *Annual Review of Sociology, 47*, 213–237.

Butnaru, D. (2015). Phenomenological alternatives of the lifeworld: Between multiple realities and virtual realities. *SocietàMutamentoPolitica, 6*(12), 67–80.

Champagne, M. (Forthcoming). Putting aside one's natural attitude-and smartphone-to see what matters more clearly. In M. Shafiei, & A.V. Pietarinen, (Ed.), *Phenomenology and Phaneroscopy.* Cham: Springer.

Cheney-Lippold, J. (2011). A new algorithmic identity soft biopolitics and the modulation of control. *Theory, Culture & Society, 28*(6), 164–181.

Choli, M., & Kuss, D.J. (2021). Perceptions of blame on social media during the coronavirus pandemic. *Computers in Human Behavior.* Published online 2021 Jun 4. doi: 10.1016/j.chb.2021.106895

Coeckelbergh, M., & Reijers, W. (2016). Narrative technologies: A philosophical investigation of the narrative capacities of technologies by using Ricoeur's narrative theory. *Human Studies, 39*(3), 325–346.

Costelloe, T.M. (1996). Between the subject and sociology: Alfred Schutz's phenomenology of the lifeworld. *Human Studies, 19*(3), 247–266.

Couldry, N., & Powell, A. (2014). Big data from the bottom up. *Big Data & Society, 1*(2), 1–5.

Dalton, C.M., Taylor, L., & Thatcher, J. (2016). Critical data studies: A dialog on data and space. *Big Data & Society, 3*(1), 1–9.

De, R., Pandey, N., & Pal, A. (2020). Impact of digital surge during Covid-19 pandemic: A viewpoint on research and practice. *International Journal of Information Management, 55*(102171), 1–5.

Deb, P., Furceri, D., Ostry, J.D., & Tawk, N. (2020). The effect of containment measures on the COVID-19 pandemic. IMF Working Paper. *International Monetary Fund.*

Dourish, P. (2016). Algorithms and their others: Algorithmic culture in context. *Big Data & Society, 3*(2), 1–11.

Dreher, J. (2011). Alfred Schutz. In G. Ritzer, & J. Stepnisky, (Eds.), *The Wiley-Blackwell Companion to Major Social Theorists* (Vol. 2, pp. 489–510). Set. John Wiley & Sons.

Eberle, T.S. (2015). Exploring another's subjective life-world: A phenomenological approach. *Journal of Contemporary Ethnography*, *44*(5), 563–579.

Feenberg, A. (2015). Making the gestalt switch. In R. Rosenberger, & P.P. Verbeek, (Eds.), *Postphenomenological Investigations: Essays on Human-Technology Relations* (pp. 229–236). Lanham: Lexington Books.

Gertz, N. (2019). The Four Facebooks. *The New Atlantis*, *58*, 65–70.

Giddens, A. (2013). *The Consequences of Modernity*. John Wiley & Sons.

Giddens, A. (1984). *The constitution of society: Outline of the theory of structuration*. University of California Press.

Gillespie, T. (2014a). Algorithm [draft][# digitalkeywords]. *Culture Digitally*. http://culturedigitally.org/2014/06/algorithm-draft-digitalkeyword/

Gillespie, T. (2014b). The relevance of algorithms. In T. Gillespie, P. Boczkowski, & K. Foot (Eds.), *Media Technologies* (pp. 167–194). Cambridge, MA: MIT Press.

Green, B. (2021). Algorithmic imaginaries: The political limits of legal and computational reasoning. *Law and Political Economy Blog*. https://papers.ssrn.com/sol3/papers.cfm?abstract_id=3926676

Green, B., & Viljoen, S. (2020). Algorithmic realism: expanding the boundaries of algorithmic thought. In *Proceedings of the 2020 Conference on Fairness, Accountability, and Transparency* (pp. 19–31).

Gurwitsch, A. (1962). The common-sense world as social reality: A discourse on Alfred Schutz. *Social Research*, *29*(1), 50–72.

Hess, A. (2014). You are what you compute (and what is computed for you): Considerations of digital rhetorical identification. *Journal of Contemporary Rhetoric*, *4*, 1–18.

Hughes, J.A., & Sharrock, W.W. (1997). *The philosophy of social research*. Routledge.

Kavanagh, D., McGarraghy, S., & Kelly, S. (2015, July). Ethnography in and around an algorithm. In 30th EGOS Colloquium: Sub-theme 15:(SWG) Creativity, Reflexivity and Responsibility in Organizational Ethnography, Athens, Greece, 3–5 July 2015.

Király, O., Potenza, M.N., Stein, D.J., King, D.L., Hodgins, D.C., Saunders, J.B., Griffith, M.D., Gjoneskal, B., Billieux, J., Brand, M., Abbotto, M.W., Chamberlain, S.R., Corazza, O., Burkauskas, J., Sales, C.M.D., Montag, C., Lochner, C., Grünblatt, E., Wegmannn, E., Martinotti, G., Lee, H.K., Rumpf, H-J., Castro-Calvo, J., Rahimi-Movaghar, A., Higuchi, S., Menchon, J.M., Zohar, J., Pellegrini, L., Walitza, S., Fineberg, N.A., & Demetrovics, Z. (2020). Preventing problematic internet use during the COVID-19 pandemic: Consensus guidance. *Comprehensive Psychiatry*, *100*, 152180. 10.1016/j.comppsych.2020.152180

Kitchin, R. (2016). Thinking critically about and researching algorithms. *Information, Communication & Society*, *20*(1), 1–16.

Kling, R., Rosenbaum, H., & Sawyer, S. (2005). *Understanding and communicating social informatics: A framework for studying and teaching the human contexts of information and communication technologies*. Information Today, Inc.

Koeze, E., & Popper, N. (2020, April 7). The virus changed the way we internet. *The New York Times, 7.*

Kotliar, D.M. (2021). Who gets to choose? On the socio-algorithmic construction of choice. *Science, Technology, & Human Values, 46*(2), 346–375.

Kudina, O. (2022). Speak, memory: the postphenomenological analysis of memory-making in the age of algorithmically powered social networks. *Humanities and Social Sciences Communications, 9*(7), 1–16.

Lamprou, E., Mitev, N., & Doolin, B. (2014). Information systems and assemblages. In B. Doolin, E. Lamprou, N. Mitev, L. McLeod (Eds.). *Information systems and global assemblages. (re)configuring actors, artefacts, organizations.* IS&O 2014. IFIP Advances in Information and Communication Technology (Vol. 446, pp. 1–7). Berlin: Springer.

Lee, F. (2021). Enacting the pandemic: Analyzing agency, opacity, and power in algorithmic assemblages. *Science & Technology Studies, 34*(1), 65–90.

Lomborg, S., & Kapsch, P.H. (2020). Decoding algorithms. *Media, Culture & Society, 42*(5), 745–761.

Luft, S. (1998). Husserl's phenomenological discovery of the natural attitude. *Continental Philosophy Review, 31*(2), 153–170.

Lustig, C., & Nardi, B. (2015). Algorithmic authority: The case of Bitcoin. In *System Sciences (HICSS), 2015 48th Hawaii International Conference on* System Sciences (pp. 743–752), IEEE.

McClain, C., Vogels, E.A., Perrin, A., Sechopoulos S., & Rainie, L. (2021). *The Internet and the pandemic.* Pew Research Center.

Musiani, F. (2013). Governance by algorithms. *Internet Policy Review, 2*(3), 1–8.

Muzzetto, L. (2015). Schutz, Berger and Luckmann. The question of the natural attitude. *SocietàMutamentoPolitica, 6*(12), 245–277.

Naeem, S.B., Bhatti, R., & Khan, A. (2021). An exploration of how fake news is taking over social media and putting public health at risk. *Health Information & Libraries Journal, 38*(2), 143–149. https://www.ncbi.nlm.nih.gov/pmc/articles/PMC7404621/

Napoli, P.M. (2013). The algorithm as institution: Toward a theoretical framework for automated media production and consumption. *Media in Transition Conference* (pp. 1–36). Cambridge, MA: Massachusetts Institute of Technology.

Neyland, D., & Möllers, N. (2016). "Algorithmic IF … THEN rules and the conditions and consequences of power. *Information, Communication & Society, 20*(1), 45–62.

Noble, S.U. (2018). *Algorithms of oppression.* New York University Press.

O'neil, C. (2016). *Weapons of math destruction: How big data increases inequality and threatens democracy.* Crown.

Orlikowski, W.J., & Gash, D.C. (1994). Technological frames: making sense of information technology in organizations. *ACM Transactions on Information Systems (TOIS), 12*(2), 174–207.

Peralta, A.F., Neri, M., Kertész, J., & Iñiguez, G. (2021). Effect of algorithmic bias and network structure on coexistence, consensus, and polarization of opinions. *Physical Review E, 104*(4), 1–39.

Pink, S., Lanzeni, D., & Horst, H. (2018). Data anxieties: Finding trust in everyday digital mess. *Big Data & Society, 5*(1), 1–14.

Pink, S., Ruckenstein, M., Willim, R., & Duque, M. (2018). Broken data: Conceptualising data in an emerging world. *Big Data & Society, 5*(1), 1–13.

Pink, S., Sumartojo, S., Lupton, D. & Heyes La Bond, C. (2017). Mundane data: The routines, contingencies and accomplishments of digital living. *Big Data & Society, 4*(1), 1–12.

Psathas, G. (1980). Approaches to the study of the world of everyday life. *Human Studies, 3*(1), 3–17.

Quinn, E.K., Fazel, S.S., & Peters, C.E. (2021). The Instagram infodemic: co-branding of conspiracy theories, coronavirus disease 2019 and authority-questioning beliefs. *Cyberpsychology, Behavior, and Social Networking, 24*(8), 573–577. https://www.liebertpub.com/doi/pdfplus/10.1089/cyber.2020.0663

Rader, E., & Gray, R. (2015). Understanding user beliefs about algorithmic curation in the Facebook news feed. *Proceedings of the 33rd Annual ACM Conference on Human Factors in Computing Systems, ACM*, 173–182.

Raffa, M., & Pronzato, R. (2021). The algorithmic imaginary of cultural producers. Towards platform-optimized music? H-ermes. *Journal of Communication, 2021*(19), 293–321.

Rocha, Y.M., de Moura, G.A., Desidério, G.A., de Oliveira, C.H., Lourenço, F.D. & de Figueiredo Nicolete, L.D. (2021). The impact of fake news on social media and its influence on health during the COVID-19 pandemic: a systematic review. *Journal of Public Health*, 1–10. Published: 09 October 2021 10.1007/s10389-021-01658-z

Rosenbaum, H. (2020). Algorithmic neutrality, algorithmic assemblages, and the lifeworld. *Proceedings of the Americas Conference on Information Systems, 6*, 1–10. https://aisel.aisnet.org/amcis2020/philosophical_is/philosophical_is/6

Rosenberger, R., & Verbeek, P.P. (Eds.) (2015). *Postphenomenological investigations: Essays on human–technology relations.* Lanham: Lexington Books.

Sawyer, S., Crowston, K., & Wigand, R. (2014). Digital assemblages: Evidence and theorizing from the computerization of the US residential real estate industry. *New Technology, Work, and Employment, 29*(1), 40–57.

Schutz, A. (1945). On multiple realities. *Philosophy and Phenomenological Research, 5*(4), 533–576.

Schutz, A. (1970). *Alfred Schutz on phenomenology and social relations* (Vol. 360). H. Wagner, (Ed.). Chicago: University of Chicago Press.

Schutz, A. (1967). *The Phenomenology of the Social World.* Chicago: Northwestern University Press.

Schwennesen, N. (2019). Algorithmic assemblages of care: Imaginaries, epistemologies, and repair work. *Sociology of Health & Illness, 41*, 176–192.

Seamon, D. (2015). Situated cognition and the phenomenology of place: Lifeworld, environmental embodiment, and immersion-in-world. *Cognitive Processing, 16*(1), 389–392.

Segre, S. (2016). Social constructionism as a sociological approach. *Human Studies, 39*(1), 93–99.

Spieth, P., Röth, T., Clauss, T., & Klos, C. (2021). Technological frames in the digital age: Theory, measurement instrument, and future research areas. *Journal of Management Studies, 58*(7), 1962–1993.

Spinicci P. (2000), Il mondo della vita e il problema della certezza, CUEM, Milano.

Stecula, D.A., & Pickup, M. (2021). Social media, cognitive reflection, and conspiracy beliefs. *Frontiers in Political Science, 3*, 62. https://www.frontiersin.org/articles/10.3389/fpos.2021.647957/full

Stein, R.A., Ometa, O., Shetty, S.P., Katz, A., Popitiu, M.I., & Brotherton, R. (2021). Conspiracy theories in the era of COVID-19: A tale of two pandemics. *International Journal of Clinical Practice, 75*(2). Published online 2021 Jan 21. doi: 10.1111/ijcp.13778. https://www.ncbi.nlm.nih.gov/pmc/articles/PMC7995222/

Striphas, T. (2015). Algorithmic culture. *European Journal of Cultural Studies, 18*(4–5), 395–412.

Sun, Y., Li, Y., Bao, Y., Meng, S., Sun, Y., Schumann, G., Kosten, T., Strang, J., Luy, L., & Shi, J. (2020). Brief report: Increased addictive internet and substance use behavior during the COVID-19 pandemic in China. *The American Journal on Addictions, 29*(4), 268–270.

Sundin, O., Haider, J., Andersson, C., Carlsson, H., & Kjellberg, S. (2017). The search-ification of everyday life and the mundane-ification of search. *Journal of Documentation, 73*(2), 224–243.

Vaitkus, S. (2005). The "naturality" of Alfred Schutz's natural attitude of the lifeworld. In M. Endress, G. Psathas, & H. Nasu, (Eds.). *Explorations of the Life-World: Continuing Dialogues with Alfred Schutz* (pp. 97–121). Netherlands: Springer.

Verbeek, P.P. (2015). Toward a theory of technological mediation. *Technoscience and postphenomenology: The Manhattan papers, 189.*

Weiss, G. (2016). De-naturalizing the natural attitude: A Husserlian legacy to social phenomenology. *Journal of Phenomenological Psychology, 47*(1), 1–16.

Willson, M. (2016). Algorithms (and the) everyday. *Information, Communication & Society, 20*(1), 137–150.

Yeung, K. (2017). 'Hypernudge': Big data as a mode of regulation by design. *Information, Communication & Society, 20*(1), 118–136. 10.1080/1369118X.2016.1186713

Zaner, R.M. (1970). Introduction. In R.M. Zaner, (Ed.). *Reflections on the Problem of Relevance* (pp. xi–xix). Yale University Press.

Zhao, S. (2007). Internet and the lifeworld: Updating Schutz's theory of mutual knowledge. *Information Technology & People, 20*(2), 140–160.

Index

Printed in the United States
by Baker & Taylor Publisher Services